CYBERSPACE & SOVEREIGNTY

CYBERSPACE & SOVEREIGNTY

HONGRUI ZHAO
Harbin Institute of Technology, China

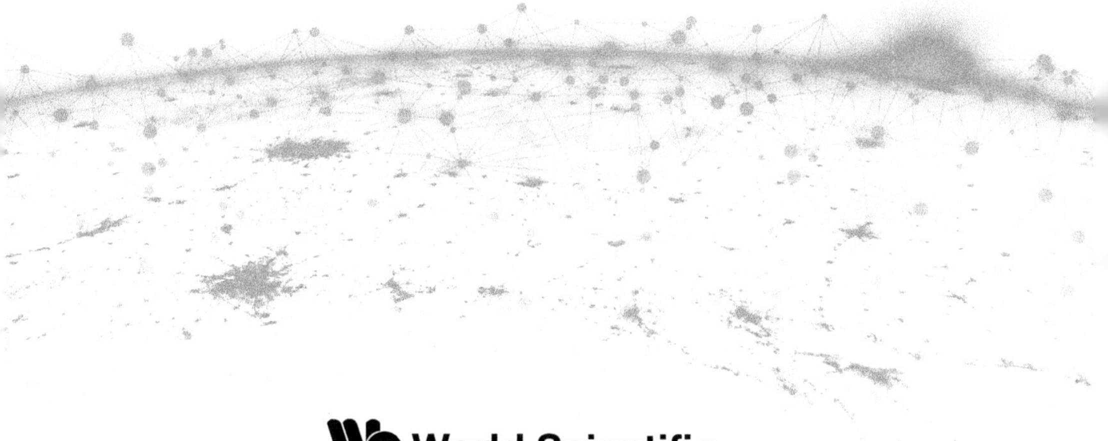

World Scientific
NEW JERSEY • LONDON • SINGAPORE • BEIJING • SHANGHAI • HONG KONG • TAIPEI • CHENNAI • TOKYO

Published by

World Scientific Publishing Co. Pte. Ltd.
5 Toh Tuck Link, Singapore 596224
USA office: 27 Warren Street, Suite 401-402, Hackensack, NJ 07601
UK office: 57 Shelton Street, Covent Garden, London WC2H 9HE

Library of Congress Cataloging-in-Publication Data
Names: Zhao, Hongrui, author.
Title: Cyberspace & sovereignty / Hongrui Zhao, Harbin Institute of Technology, China.
Other titles: Wang luo zhu quan lun. English. | Cyberspace and sovereignty
Description: Hackensack, New Jersey : World Scientific, [2022] |
Translation of: Wang luo zhu quan lun. | Includes bibliographical references and index.
Identifiers: LCCN 2020051834 | ISBN 9789811227783 (hardcover) |
ISBN 9789811227790 (ebook for institutions) | ISBN 9789811227806 (ebook for individuals)
Subjects: LCSH: Computer networks--Law and legislation. | Internet governance--
International cooperation. | Computer security--Law and legislation. | Sovereignty.
Classification: LCC K564.C6 Z49 2022 | DDC 343.09/99--dc23
LC record available at https://lccn.loc.gov/2020051834

British Library Cataloguing-in-Publication Data
A catalogue record for this book is available from the British Library.

《网络主权论》
Originally published in Chinese by Jiuzhou Press

For any available supplementary material, please visit
https://www.worldscientific.com/worldscibooks/10.1142/12027#t=suppl

Desk Editor: Lai Ann

Typeset by Stallion Press
Email: enquiries@stallionpress.com

Words of the Author

The computer was invented 70 years ago; computer networks came into being 50 years ago; and the Internet became popular 30 years ago. However, a consistent global public opinion on networks has still yet to form due to the rapid development of network information technology. People have high expectations of these networks as they can speed up the process of human civilisation, yet people are also wary of them because they intensify the hegemonic situation.

A network can be used for both legitimate and malicious purposes. Surfing the Internet to view the world brings a thrill of transcending time and space; on the contrary, cyber espionage and transnational cyberattacks in the form of invisible crimes or terrorist wars challenge national security. Then how do traditional sovereignty and rules of law protect beneficial cyberspace behaviours and punish crimes to safeguard national sovereignty in the age of the Internet?

Some think tanks in the United States have taken the lead in researching on the relationship between the Internet and sovereignty for over 20 years. Lawrence Lessig,[1] a professor of law at Harvard University, has written about the relationship between the Internet and sovereignty, including theories such as

[1] Lawrence Lessig, born on 3 June 1961, was the third-ranked candidate of the Democratic Party in the presidential election in 2016 after Hillary Clinton and Bernie Sanders.

"cyberspace-over-sovereignty", "cyberspace in global sovereignty", and "cyberspace's precondition of democracy". However, over the past 20 years, international debates about cyberspace sovereignty have not ceased. At present, the 196 member states and regions of the United Nations are still far from reaching a consensus on a rule of law for the Internet.

We study cyberspace sovereignty with a view to prevent the possible harm caused by losing control of network technology. However, this book focuses on cyberspace justice and sovereign justice. If the civilised tradition of sovereign justice were cut off, then the con side of the network "coin" would cast evil shadows over the world. In the modern era, when cyberspace hegemony undermines the survival of national sovereignty, this is a very dangerous moment for national sovereignty. At present, China is the world leader in its vow to "safeguard cyberspace sovereignty" via the National Security Law of the People's Republic of China.

Cognising networks is the first problem faced by the research. To cognise a network, it is necessary to cross the thresholds of different disciplines, including computer science, telecommunications, physics, and mathematics, because different disciplines have disparate perceptions of a network. I had to assume that I had returned to the age of 18 and entered the School of Computer Science, the School of Telecommunications, the School of Physics, and the School of Mathematics to resume my studies, in an attempt to address the weak links by reading many popular science books from around the world, and studying various terms, technical standards, institutional abbreviations, and other previously unfamiliar knowledge of global network governance institutions and a variety of disciplines.

Sovereignty evolution is the second problem encountered by this book. In the beginning, there was no such thing as sovereignty in this world. For 500 years, traditional theories of sovereignty originated from the West, such as "sovereignty lies with the monarch", "sovereignty lies with people", and "sovereignty lies with the nation". These theories constructed the modern theory of the state, which is not fully compatible with the world view formed in China during its 5000-year history. The law is a scale for order. I have categorised 249 Chinese domestic laws and almost 500 international laws, as of the end of 2017, in an attempt to clarify the legal boundary of cyberspace sovereignty.

Theoretical refinement is the third problem faced by this book. A good theory is the key to practice. Whether the key comes in handy or not depends on whether it can coordinate different possibilities and provide ground for policy practices. This book puts forward the theory of network coordination and the network entropy formula. Whether the key comes in handy as a "handle" and tool for network sovereignty has yet to be tested.

Like new-born babies, innovations are not always initially pleasing to the eye. There are many theoretical approaches to studying social innovation. However, "this is an era that requires theories and is sure to produce theories".[2] The author takes the liberty to propose a theory and earnestly urges you to point out any mistakes so that they can be corrected.

Zhao Hongrui
Harbin Institute of Technology

[2] Xi, J. P. (2016). *Remarks by H.E. Xi Jinping, President of the People's Republic of China at the Symposium of the Work of Philosophy and Social Sciences.* Retrieved from http://www.xinhuanet.eom//politics/2016-05/18/c_1118891128_2.htm.

Contents

Preface

A Study of Cyberspace Sovereignty and Plan for Fine Law and Good Governance

Information and communications technologies (ICTs) are dual-use technologies and can be used for both legitimate and malicious purposes. Any ICT device can be the source or the target of misuse. The malicious use of ICTs can be easily concealed and the attribution to a specific perpetrator can be difficult. The global connectivity of ICT networks exacerbates this problem.

— "Threats, Risks and Vulnerabilities"[3]

On 22 February 2016, the United States (US) *Time* magazine published an article entitled "The Internet is Undermining America's Power",[4] which suggested that America's cyber power is being diminished and the current situation may even be reversed. The article explains three reasons for this: first, China is developing new competing technologies; second, China, Russia, Iran, and

[3] The 68th United Nations General Assembly Document A/68/98, Article 5. (2016). Retrieved from https://documents-dds-y.un.org/doc/UNDOC/GEN/N13/371/67/PDF/N1337167.pdf?Open Element.

[4] Authored by Adam Segal, an expert on China-related issues and cyberspace policies of the United States Council on Foreign Relations. He is also the author of *The Hacked World Order*.

other countries have begun asserting cyberspace sovereignty; third, in creating the Internet and overseeing its global expansion, US history unwisely let down its guard, resulting in political neglect and short-sightedness in policy.

The international media immediately followed this view. Some believe that this was deliberate "whitewashing" for the whistle-blowing act of Edward Snowden and PRISM that took place in the US not long ago. Snowden's disclosure of the US' secret surveillance programme — code-named PRISM — caused an unprecedented panic among information security agencies of different countries, because it officially declared the advent of the "era of US cyber deterrence", even though the announcement was not from the White House or the US Department of State.

The invention of the Internet originated from the arms race during the period of the Cold War between the US and the Soviet Union. The Snowden incident exposed a "Hidden Web",[5] which exists outside the Internet, silently threatening the security of nations.

The US controls the "master switch" of the global network. The US National Telecommunications and Information Administration (NTIA) is responsible for managing the "phone directory" of the global network, including global domain names, root zone files, Internet Protocol (IP) addresses, and domain name server (DNS) resolutions. It is capable of thoroughly wiping off a country's DNS root zone from cyberspace. How the international community should coordinate the "administration of root zone files and systems" is high on the priority list of 14 public policy issues of the United Nations (UN) Working Group on Internet Governance. This has shown that cyberspace, as a non-traditional threat, is changing the existing world order.

I. Cyberspace Threats

The competition in cyberspace determines the future of humanity. This is how President Xi Jinping summed up his Wuzhen speech

[5] This refers to hidden websites that cannot be found using search engines.

delivered on 16 December 2015: "Respect for cyber sovereignty. The principle of sovereign equality enshrined in the Charter of the UN is one of the basic norms in contemporary international relations. It covers all aspects of state-to-state relations, which also includes cyberspace. We should respect the right of individual countries to independently choose their own path of cyber development, model of cyber regulation and internet public policies, and participate in international cyberspace governance on an equal footing. No country should pursue cyber hegemony, interfere in other countries' internal affairs, or engage in, connive at, or support cyber activities that undermine other countries' national security."[6] The promulgation and implementation of the *National Security Law of the People's Republic of China* in 2015 marked China, for the first time, advocating "safeguarding national cyberspace sovereignty" via legislation in the international community.

The future of our world rests on how cyber ontology is perceived and how cyber sovereignty is established. On 19 April 2016, President Xi Jinping pointed out at the symposium on cyberspace security and informatisation: "Looking at the history of social development, humankind has experienced the agricultural revolution and the industrial revolution, and is currently experiencing the information revolution." "The cyberspace security and informatisation undertaking represents new productive forces and a new development direction." "Core internet technology is the 'key' to China's internet development, and having other countries holding the key is our biggest threat." "We must strengthen our defence capabilities and deterrence capabilities concerning cyberspace security. The essence of cyberspace security lies in resistance, and the essence of resistance lies in the trial between the offensive and defensive capabilities of both sides."[7]

---

[6] Xi, J. P. (2015). *Remarks by H.E. Xi Jinping, President of the People's Republic of China at the Opening Ceremony of the Second World Internet Conference.* Retrieved from http://www.xinhuanet.comZ/politics/2015-12/16/c_1117481089.htm.

[7] Xi, J. P. (2016). *Remarks by H.E. Xi Jinping, President of the People's Republic of China, at Cyber Security and Informatization Work Conference.* Retrieved from http://www.cac.gov.cn/2016-04/25/c_1118731366.htm.

In the traditional transnational network of radios, telegraphs, telephones, and power grids, there are international laws in place to impose traditional international order. However, the Internet has blurred the sovereign boundaries of traditional telecommunication networks ever since its invention, popularisation, and transnational use. As of now, there exist pre-emptive technology monopolies in the development of the Internet. Countries around the world have a natural path dependence on these first-generation technology monopolies, therefore, the international community cannot agree on a fair and reasonable international network convention due to divided opinions.

The term "cyberspace" studied in this book refers to all electronic information communication networks that constitute the electromagnetic network space. At present, the functions of various electronic information communication networks include communication, storage, navigation, timing, and positioning. There is no consensus as yet on the scientific definition of the concept of "cyberspace" in the world, and the descriptions in textbooks of different countries are nothing but patchy technical definitions. Therefore, it is necessary for us to make logical generalisations and perceive cyberspace as an integrative whole or it will be difficult to make it the object of the rule of law.

The purpose of this book is to perceive cyberspace, the network world, and cyber sovereignty from a broader perspective, and to express its security level using minimalist mathematical formulas and providing a scientific legislative basis for cyber sovereignty. To perceive cyberspace, among others, from a broader perspective is to summarise the key elements of cyberspace while breaking free from technical definitions. To perceive the cyber world from a broader perspective is to include all the key elements of cyberspace and form ontological cognition. To perceive cyber sovereignty from a broader perspective is to inherit the traditional sovereignty theory and consider the reality game superimposed by overwhelming information technologies. To express the trend of overall security changes in cyber sovereign territory is to lay the theoretical foundation and serve cyberspace governance.

II. Counter-hegemony

Currently, the US controls core network technologies and the production of both key hardware and software. It produces 92% of the world's CPUs (Central Processing Units), 86% of operating system software, and 70% of large databases. Professor Lawrence Lessig of Harvard Law School put forward cyber sovereignty concepts of "cyberspace-over-sovereignty", "global citizen-sovereign", and "cyberspace's precondition of democracy" at the beginning of the 21st century, arguing that sovereign states have no sovereign jurisdiction over cyberspace. The essence of his theories is to oppose cyber sovereignty by means of cyber hegemony and his academic thoughts have laid the foundation for the present orientation of US cyber policies.

The popularity of the Internet poses new challenges to traditional national sovereignty. On 16 July 2014, President Xi Jinping mentioned, when addressing the National Congress of Brazil, "Although the Internet is highly globalised, the sovereignty of the information of all countries should be respected. No matter how developed a country's internet technology is, it must not violate the information sovereignty of others. No double standards should be allowed in upholding cyber security, and every country has the right to preserve its own information security. We cannot just have the security of one or some countries, leaving the rest insecure, and no country should seek the so-called absolute security of itself at the expense of the security of other countries."[8]

Countering cyber hegemony depends on the improvement of basic network theories and the innovation of a network discipline system to enhance the value judgment oriented into practice. If the network is a virtual technology, then technologies like radio, radar, and telegraphs, which date back over 100 years, have long been

[8] Xi, J. P. (2014). *Carry Forward Traditional Friendship and Jointly Open up New Chapter of Cooperation — Speech at the National Congress of Brazil.* Retrieved from http://www.xinhuanet.com/world/2014-07/17/c_1111665403.htm.

virtual technologies. The network, first of all, is the physical existence of the material carrier of information; the materiality of the carrier of cyber information determines the objectivity of cyber sovereignty.

To fight against cyber hegemony, it is necessary to clarify the legal principle of the fact that "cyberspace is within the scope of sovereign rights and sovereignty has jurisdiction over cyberspace". Unlike traditional sovereignty, cyber sovereignty is the result of rapid changes in contemporary technology. Breakthroughs in network technology may lead to a better future and may also have consequences that are contrary to the rule of law and our conscience. Promoting cyber sovereignty and co-governance on an equal footing in accordance with the spirit of the UN Charter is the only correct path of justice to counter cyber hegemony.

To counter cyber hegemony, it is also necessary to support cyber sovereignty research with multiple disciplines, such as international law, international politics, sovereignty theory, computer science, and telecommunications science, and widen the scope of cyber sovereign governance to include all network activities within the entire cyberspace such as electronic information systems, electromagnetic equipment, information data, the Internet, the telecommunications network, broadcasting network, internet of things, and industrial control network, to guard against the security risks caused by the abuse of network technology in an all-round way. In the recent 150 years, the development of international information and communication technologies has been based on information theory, cybernetics, and systems theory. This book, while based on the above-mentioned three theories, goes beyond them to develop a brand new coordination theory. It proposes the conceptual formula of "overall planning entropy" seeking to achieve a dynamic and quantitative representation of the overall picture of all elements of cyberspace, thus scientifically demonstrating the material properties and physical boundaries of cyber sovereignty.

III. Global Multi-Stakeholder Model of Internet Co-Governance

Cyberspace is an artificial space that stems from the universal connection of human beings. The universal connection between people constitutes a networked connection. The universal connection between people relies on communication, the platform of communication depends on the network, and all the activities of universal connection between people are based on information.

Hence, the historical evolution of universal connection and networked communication between people enables the evolution of human society and civilisation. In human society, equal sovereignty of different countries under the UN Charter is made possible on the premise of their respective territories, people, and regime. Countries have built traditional networks within the scope of their sovereignty and realised transnational connections, reaching a peaceful traditional world order.

The contemporary network originated from telecommunications, while the Internet originated from telecommunications networks. The US telecommunications legislation, which originated from the Radio Act of 1910, has a history spanning more than 100 years, showing that the US has long begun to plan for the rule of law regarding its own cyber sovereignty. The US is against the practice of the rule of law of other countries over cyber sovereignty only out of its consideration of technical hegemony, political hegemony, and military hegemony, which has deep and well-planned ideological foundation, theoretical support, strong backing, and strategic arrangements.

With the in-depth development of the Internet, no sovereign countries are willing to subject their own rights or interests to another country. Facing the call of countries for co-governance in terms of the Internet, the US has begun to adjust its network policy, transforming from advocating openness and freedom to seeking a multi-stakeholder model of co-governance of governments, enterprises, and civil societies around the globe.

The US National Telecommunications and Information Administration, which takes advantage of the reform of the Internet Corporation for Assigned Names and Numbers (ICANN), initiated the shift of US network policies in an attempt to establish a new model of internet co-governance using an open approach; this comprised of reshaping the shift with a multi-stakeholder process and a reached agreement based on consultation with non-governmental communities around the world. However, the so-called multi-stakeholder model of internet co-governance is still to the advantage of the strong.

Large-scale internet communities and large commercial enterprises in different countries generally support the multi-stakeholder model. However, outside of the US, the general public and the representative of their national sovereignty (i.e. the national government) have little or no opportunity to get involved.

Although the global multi-stakeholder model of internet co-governance has yet to gain the confidence of many governments, it is a step forward towards global internet co-governance. ICANN has decided to pursue a "bottom-up" principle of reform to optimise management of website domain names used by more than 4 billion netizens worldwide. This particular new model that features the participation of unofficial international organisations has some new characteristics of interdependence and co-governance based on the consultation between cyber sovereignties.

The cooperation and competition between cyber sovereignties determine the development orientation of the world. Although legislation over the cyberspace of most countries in the world still has room for improvement, this cannot change the justice consensus of "cyberspace naturally falls into the scope of sovereign rights and sovereignty, naturally, has jurisdiction over cyberspace". "Recognising the facts" and "applying the law" are the logic of the rule of law. "Be aware of danger to preserve safety at home and resist foreign invasion" are the responsibilities of a sovereignty. The coexistence and co-governance of cyberspace among sovereign states will inevitably return to the rational consensus among human civilisations.

China should, first of all, be clear about the right direction to take if it is to develop itself in respect of network technologies from being a country following behind, to one running alongside, and then to one taking the lead. Top-level design should not be "building a house on someone else's wall base", but be scientifically planning the future based on a blueprint that considers the history. To take an overwhelming leap forward in network technologies, there should be mature top-level design and theoretical foundation in place. This book, based on scientific and dialectical theory distillation and doctrine construction, reaches the prospective policy of "cyberspace justice = technological progress + sovereign equality + multi-stakeholder model of co-governance".

Looking into the future, a rough calculation of the development speed of the world's major economies leads us to realise that the international economic landscape is to undergo drastic changes. Based on the gross domestic product (GDP) of China, the US, Japan, and the 28 European Union (EU) countries during the past 17 years (as of the end of 2014), it can be calculated that China's GDP may surpass the US in 2022.

The 17-year curve shown in Figure 0-1 is based on an average economic growth rate, regardless of the variables such as the "new

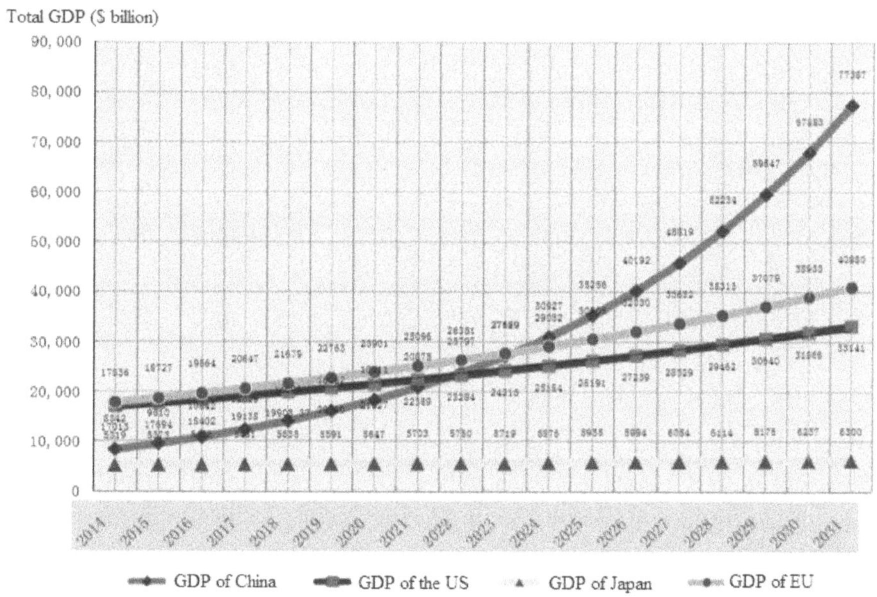

Figure 0-1: A 17-year curve — GDP projection for 2014–2031

normal" of the Chinese economy, the fact that the US Department of Commerce adjusted its domestic GDP calculation method upward, and that some geopolitical conflicts may impact global economic growth, as well as rapid technological changes and currency overshoots. It is just a simple estimate; during the course, variables such as cyberspace, currency, and military power are most likely to interrupt the inertia of world economic development and threaten world peace and stability. These variables deserve a heightened alertness. Preventing cyber threats and fighting against cyber hegemony through research on cyber sovereignty is the academic starting point for this book in the study of cyber sovereignty.

Part I
Ontology

Ontology is the questioning of the nature of all things. Cyber ontology is the summarisation and description of the nature and physical existence of cyberspace, i.e. by describing the general elements of cyberspace to comprehensively perceive its physical appearance and, in a general sense, answer questions such as "what is cyberspace?", "what kind of order exists in cyberspace?", "what is the relationship between cyberspace and traditional sovereignty?", and "what are the key elements of cyber sovereignty if it does exist and is tenable?"

Chapter One

Ontology of Cyberspace

A thorough study of questions concerning the ontology of cyberspace is the scientific premise of actively constructing fine law and good governance within cyberspace order. Cyber sovereignty is not a self-evident consensus; this is because the question of "what is cyberspace?" is perceived in different ways in various disciplines. Most people believe that cyberspace is equal to the Internet; however, for the disciplines of computer science, telecommunications science, management science, and sociology, cyberspace refers to the computer system, the telecommunication system, the big data system, and the space for public opinion, respectively.

Section One: Cyber and Information Space

In the history of science and technology, scientists explored electronic information before they created cyberspace (the net, the web, the network, the Internet). Even earlier than that, people saw spider webs before they could build a variety of artificial structures with circular layers. Scientists began to understand the circle-layered structure and created cyberspace, which greatly broadened the scope of human initiative.

I. *Cyberspace*

The network used by humans for information transmission was originally something made of natural materials and only became artificial later on using electronic carriers. Both natural information networks and artificial electronic networks carry the same functions of information inputting, identifying, transmitting, and interacting.

People began to store information, starting with keeping records by tying knots and inventing written words; they then used beacon fires and built post roads to send military messages. The history of human beings transmitting information via networks can be traced back to the ancient natural network era. The electromagnetic cyberspace that has been developed so far has the same information transmission function as the ancient communication network. Nowadays, information, people, goods, energy, and even currency are transmitted and exchanged through complex network systems.

People have been transmitting materials and information through networks since ancient times:

The beacon fire network: The beacon fire network, as an initial network structure, can be traced back to the pre-Qin period of China more than 2,000 years ago. The Great Wall was the first military security intelligence network that can be verified in history. Within the Great Wall network system, people built a large number of beacon towers used as a transmission node of information, and all the towers were connected so intelligence could be passed between them.

The road network: Due to transportation needs, the road system itself has also become a network for information transmission. Roads play an important role in promoting the integration, unity, and development of civilisations in both ancient China and Europe. In ancient times, devoid of electromagnetic transmission, the roads for passenger and freight transportation were, at the same time, the most important information channels. In the modern era, with the operation of road telephone systems, overspeed monitoring systems, electronic toll collection systems (ETCs), and driverless vehicles, the intelligent road system itself can readily be used as an infrastructure with electronic information interaction networks.

The shipping network: The world shipping network has a history spanning more than 5,000 years, from scattered trade routes to the development of trade networks all around the globe. Its development can be divided into four stages: the initial period (3000 BC–2000 BC), the balanced development period (2000 BC–1763 AD), the drastic change period (1763–the end of the 20th century), and the stable development period (from the end of the 20th century to present). The evolution of the world shipping network is not only related to the resource endowment of relevant regions and their market supply and demand situation, but is also closely related to their geographical location, geopolitics, and economic development.[1]

The trade network: Since ancient times, adventure, expansion, competition, tribute, and trade have always been the game played by the world's big powers. Only in a peaceful environment with geopolitical stability can a fair and reasonable trade order and network be established and developed. Around 1 AD, "the routes opened up by merchants extended rapidly",[2] which meant that networks of transnational trade and regional trade formed as early as 2,000 years ago. At present, led by the World Trade Organization (WTO), world trade has grown to a volume of 33 trillion US dollars (as of the end of 2016). Scholars including M. Ángeles Serrano have found that the world trade network against the background of globalisation today presents complex network features such as scale-free and small-world properties; other scholars believe that the scale-free property of today's world trade network is still closely related to the long-term economic cycle.[3]

[1] Li, Z. F. *et al.* (2014). A Study of the Evolution and Future Development Trends of World Maritime Networks. *Pacific Journal* (5), 104.

[2] Frankopan, P. (2016). *The Silk Roads: A New History of the World* (p. 14) (X. D. Shao, & F. Sun, Trans.). Hangzhou: Zhejiang University Press.

[3] Li, X., Jin, Y. Y., & Chen, G. R. (2003). Complexity and Synchronization of the World Trade Web, *Physica A* (328), 287–296.

The postal network: Even before the formation of networks of power, telecommunications, and energy, etc., a prototype network of ancient postal services had already been fledging. Modern postal services went ever further to cross national borders and connect together over 190 countries and regions around the world, taking the lead in forming the most extensive network for the transportation of material objects. Since the 1990s, research on the organisational structure of postal networks with internet properties has become popular, Since the 21st century, the study of the role and influence of postal networks on economic activities from an enterprise perspective has indicated the right direction for further development of the logistics industry.[4]

The telegraph network: In 1753, the British tried to transmit information via 26 wires representing 26 English letters; in 1804, the Spanish also tried to transmit a telegram using small bubbles from wires immersed in saltwater representing different letters and symbols. Communicating with electricity has experienced a long history of experimentation. In the 1830s, due to the rapid development of the railway, there was an urgent need for a communication tool that was weatherproof, had no time limit, and, at the same time, ran faster than the train. In 1836, Samuel Morse from the United States (US) invented a letter code, which transmitted text information as a series of on-off signals, This eventually resulted in the invention of the magnetic telegraph that later led to the formation of a telegraph network that transmits words “point-to-point”.

The telephone network: In 1860, the Italian-American Antonio Meucci invented the telephone, which he called a “speaking telegraph”. The earliest telephone communication was a wire-connected call between two telephones, and has since developed into a network enabling two-party or even multi-party calls of countless users at the same time. A telephone network, with a number of programme-controlled telephone exchanges working as its connection centre, connects the transmission circuit and user terminal. The current telephone network comprises of a service network and

---

[4] Lu, P. M. (2011). A Tentative Analysis of the Characteristics and Economic Effects of the Postal Network. *Studies and Posts* (2), 9.

support network. The support network further includes a clock frequency synchronisation network, a multi-level switching channel signalling network, a transmission monitoring network, and a management network. The telephone network has evolved from an analogue telephone network to an integrated digital telephone network, which is now compatible with numerous non-telephony services. The International Telecommunication Union (ITU), established in 1865, is responsible for imposing order for international telegraph, telephone, and telecommunications. As a specialised agency of the United Nations (UN), the ITU is in charge of international telecommunications standards, radio communications, and global telecommunications development.

The power network: In 1875, the world's first thermal power plant was built in Paris; in the 1880s, the world's first hydropower stations were built in the United Kingdom (UK) and the US; in the early 20th century, large-scale power systems emerged, transforming natural primary energy into secondary energy of electric power through mechanical energy devices. After the mechanical revolution, with electric power as the energy and an electric power network consisting of power generation, transmission, substation, distribution, electricity, and other links, an electric power revolution was initiated. With the interconnection of power grids, power plants, and users, smart power grids came into being at the end of the 20th century and the dispatch centres of the power grids realised a two-way intelligent information exchange concerning the generation, transmission, distribution, delivery, and use of electrical energy.

The aviation network: In 1890, the Frenchman Clement Ader invented the first non-steerable steam engine aircraft; in 1903, the Wright brothers made an aircraft powered by a piston engine that could be controlled by its wings. Since then, humanity has entered the aviation era. Aviation refers to the flight of an aircraft in the Earth's air space.[5] Since the establishment of the International Civil Aviation Organization in 1944, the global aviation network system

[5] The World Air Sports Federation defines the limit between Earth's atmosphere and outer space as an altitude of 100 kilometers.

has regulated this airspace through planning international route networks and developing rules of communication, navigation, and air traffic control for air transportation. If airports are regarded as nodes, the routes connecting airports as edges, the throughput of airports as the point weight, and the traffic (or voyage) on the routes as the edge weight, then the aviation network can be abstractly viewed as a complex weighted network.[6]

The radio network: In 1895, Guglielmo Marconi from Italy and Alexander Popov from Russia both invented a radio receiving device at the same time; in 1906, at an experimental radio station in Massachusetts, the US made the first radio voice broadcast.[7] A radio network is a communication network that transmits sound through radio waves or wires. It is called a wireless radio when the sound is transmitted by radio waves; it is called wired radio when the sound is transmitted through wires. A radio station converts the sound into audio electric signals through a microphone, which then forms radio waves via a high-frequency current and is transmitted. A radio antenna restores the sound after receiving the radio waves, and completes the acoustic-electrical conversion. Radio broadcasts, while being instant, fast, and serving a large audience, also have the disadvantages of being passive and fleeting.

The television network: In 1925, based on the telegraph, which was capable of electro-textual transformation and the telephone, which was capable of electro-acoustical transformation, many inventors began to conduct research on television, which was capable of electro-graphic transformation. Among them, the British scientist John Logie Baird invented the first mechanical television to transmit images; in 1928, he again invented the first colour television; in 1930, he started experimental television broadcasting. As early as 1883, a German inventor invented the Nipkow Disc, using the mechanical scanning method to transmit pictures of

[6]Yu, G. J. (2006). Complex Network Theory and its Application in Aviation Network. *Complex Systems and Complexity Science* (1), 81.

[7]Li, M. X. (1996). Live Broadcast and Recorded Broadcast. *Journalism Bimonthly* (2), 60.

24 lines per image for the first time; in 1908, Alan Archibald Campbell Swinton from the UK and Boris Rosing from Russia described an electronic basis for the production of television; in 1931, American Philo T. Farnsworth invented a camera and television with phototubes and cathode ray tubes and established a monopoly of the electronic television system, marking the birth of the modern television in its true sense. At present, cable television has developed into an efficient and cheap comprehensive visibility network with advantages including broader bandwidth, larger capacity, more functions, lower cost, anti-jamming, supporting multiple services, connecting thousands of households, and enabling video-on-demand and interaction. It represents the direction of future development of the "information highway".

The oil pipeline network: After World War I, Britain was granted the mandate of Iraq, and intervened in the political affairs of Persia (Iran), Egypt, and Afghanistan. In 1925, it built the world's first oil pipeline, transporting oil from the Persian Gulf to the Mediterranean Sea, which became the "carotid artery of the British Empire".[8] At present, there are about 3,800 oil and gas pipelines in service worldwide, with a total mileage of approximately 2 million kilometres, including around 1.27 million kilometres of natural gas pipelines, which accounts for 65% of the total. There are also about 360,000 kilometres of crude oil pipelines, approximately 250,000 kilometres of product oil pipelines, and around 80,000 kilometres of liquefied petroleum gas pipelines. The distribution of global pipelines is as follows: 43% in North America, 15% in Russia, 14% in Central Asia, 14% in Europe and the Asia-Pacific region, 10% in Middle East and Africa, and 4% in Latin America. The total mileage of oil and gas pipelines in China is around 130,000 kilometres.[9]

---

[8] Frankopan, P. (2016). *The Silk Roads: A New History of the World* (pp. 3–296) (X. D. Shao, & F. Sun, Trans.), Hangzhou: Zhejiang University Press.

[9] Zhu, Q. Z. *et al.* (2017). Development Status and Trend of Global Oil and Gas Pipelines. *Oil and Gas Storage and Transportation* (4).

The satellite navigation network: in 1958, the Defense Advanced Research Projects Agency of the US Department of Defense began the construction of the Transit Navigation Satellite System. In the 1970s, the US Army, Navy, and Air Force jointly developed a new generation of satellite positioning — Global Positioning System (GPS). Human beings have been using natural objects such as the Sun and the Moon for navigation for thousands of years. Satellite navigation using artificial celestial bodies is a geo-spatial information network system consisting of three parts: navigation satellite (space end), ground station (ground end), and user equipment (user end); it has three major functions, i.e. positioning, navigating, and timing.[10] At present, the BeiDou Navigation Satellite System (BDS) of China is the third mature satellite navigation system following the US GPS and the Russian GLONASS; the European Union's Galileo Satellite Navigation System (GSNS) is also capable of initial operations with 18 successfully launched satellites.

The international financial network: with the continuous advancement of international financial integration, the concentration of financial activities has led to the frequent flow of financial assets. Since major international financial centres control most of the financial resources, the global financial network presents rather distinct characteristics of community structure and assortativity in networks. It is a typical scale-free network. If the world's major international financial centres (mainly in terms of stock markets and bond markets) are regarded as network nodes, then cross-market financial activities between these nodes are "connected", and the complex network built, thereupon, around the world can be called the international financial network.[11]

The Internet: the Internet is academically regarded as a set of interconnected computer networks.[12] According to computer

[10] Zhao, H. R. (2017). China Strategy for Navigation Satellite Legislation. *Aerospace China* (10), 10–13.

[11] Ba, Sh. S. (2015). International Financial Network and Its Structural Characteristics. *Hainan Finance* (9), 4.

[12] Zhao, Y. (2015). *Generation and Evolution of Network Rules* (p. 43). (PhD dissertation). East China University of Political Science and Law, Shanghai, China.

science textbook definitions, the Internet is a huge network connected by a set of standard network TCP/IP (Transmission Control Protocol/Internet Protocol) protocols, which link billions of devices around the world to form an enormous and logically compatible international network. A computer network is a combination of computers and traditional communication technology, which makes a novel structured computer system. It relies on a large number of independent, but interconnected, computers working together to accomplish computing tasks. In other words, a computer network is a collection of autonomous computers that are connected to each other to exchange information through a single logical technology.[13]

The contemporary logistics network: this is a modern freight system that combines transportation infrastructure with information and communication infrastructure. From the perspective of the coverage of modern logistics, the logistics network can be classified as a global logistics network, regional logistics network, urban logistics network, or field logistics network. The logistics network includes comprehensive information, such as the sources of goods, transport capacity, and users, and adopts management methods such as electronic labelling and global positioning to find out the interaction of all logistics activities on lines and nodes.

The above networks contain natural objects or electronic devices and they all exist in a real physical space.

II. *Information Activities*

From the beacon tower to the Internet, the networks mentioned above all exist physically in real space. They are neither a virtual world fabricated out of thin air nor an artificially simulated non-material world. Cyberspace, including the Internet, is linked to the physical space of the real world and is an artificial component of that physical space.

---

[13] Tanenbaum, A. & Wetherall, D. (2012). *Computer Networks* (5th ed.) (W. Yan, & A.M. Pan, Trans.). Beijing: Tsinghua University Press.

1. *The Principle of Information Activities — the Communication Principle of Wave-particle Duality*

Information relies on matter as a carrier; it is transmitted in networks based on the theory of "wave-particle duality". Wave, particle, and wave-particle all exist in reality, and have been proven to be information-carrying substances in quantum mechanics.

Some substances only have wave properties such as electromagnetic waves, while other substances only have particle properties, such as an electrical current; other substances have the properties of both waves and particles, such as light. Elementary particles carry and transmit information in the form of "wave-particle duality", creating electronic signals. The three substances (waves, particles, and wave-particles) constitute the material carrier of electromagnetic information.

2. *Information Virtualisation Technology*

In the internet age, so-called "virtualisation" technology in computer operating systems actually refers to the "mirroring" process that turns a physical entity into its logical counterpart.

In Chinese, "虚拟" (xu'ni) does not refer to exactly the same thing as the word "virtual" does in English. The English word "virtual" has three basic meanings: "existing in essence or effect though not in actual fact"; "made to appear to exist by the use of computer software, for example on the Internet"; and "denoting particles (such as photons) or interactions with extremely short lifetimes and (owing to the uncertainty principle) indefinitely great energies, postulated as intermediates in some processes". The last meaning here maps to the concept of "virtual" in Chinese. Foreign engineers use "virtual" to name virtualisation technology, not only because of the communication theory of wave-particle duality that serves as the scientific basis, but also because the name is a vivid description of virtual mirror technology. However, the vivid description should not be understood as nothingness, void, nor fiction; neither should the Internet be described as some sort of mythical non-material world or an unreal world.

Virtualisation technology is not nothingness.[14] Virtualisation technology is used to create a kind of "redundancy" of information storage that is applied for creating copies and caches of information. To the user, it seems to be a physical entity that actually exists while "mirroring" with virtual backup, cache, copy, or redundancy. It is simply called virtual technology by engineers and is applied to virtual processing, virtual memory, virtual external devices, virtual channels, and so on in the computer operating system. In fact, virtualisation technology is still real technology that uses real equipment, transmits real information, and exists in the real world.

Virtual technology is designed for security. The history of the Internet shows that there are five types of network virtual technologies that deepen network activities: Network Functions Virtualisation (NFV), Overlay Network, Virtual Local Area Network (VLAN), Virtual Private Network (VPN), and Active and Programmable Network (APN). These technologies accomplish task migration, security isolation, content distribution, and distributed storage under the condition of "multi-network coexistence" and lay the foundation for, and orient the development of, next-generation network technologies.

Virtual technology is more flexible. It shares physical network resources and creates multiple virtual networks. Each virtual network can be independently deployed, independently managed, and independently customised[15] to solve the problem of rigidity existing in current network systems and to eradicate hardware resource capacity limitations and the cumbersome process of network configuration, providing a technical foundation for building the next-generation Internet.[16] Based on the basic virtual network "mapping" algorithm, network virtualisation technology studies the allocation mechanism, energy-saving mechanism, and dynamic mechanism

---

[14] Yu, H. F., Sun, G., Di, H., & Liao, D. (2014). *Technologies for Virtual Network Mapping*. Beijing: Science Press.

[15] Zugenmaier, K. A. *et al.* (2012) Network Virtualization: A Hypervisor for the Internet? *Communications Magazine* (50), 136–143.

[16] Chowdhury, N. M. & Boutaba, R. (2010). A Survey of Network Virtualization, *Computer Networks* (54), 862–876.

of cross-domain resources in a multi-domain network environment to meet individualised needs and provide personalised services for networks.

Virtual technology is facing an upgrade. The so-called Software Defined Networking (SDN) is a further upgraded network technology system derived from, and working in parallel with, network virtualisation technology. The characteristic of SDN technology is to "separate" logical control from the underlying data, while network virtualisation technology features a logical "abstraction" of the underlying network. In addition, wireless network virtualisation technology, optical network virtualisation technology, and big data and cloud computing technologies all come together to make the breakthrough frontier of the intergenerational upgrade of network technologies.

Virtual technology is not the "end". Virtual technology decouples logical and physical resources and is designed to provide greater efficiency in resource utilisation and better flexibility in goal realisation. Network virtualisation technology has promoted the arrival of the second-generation Internet and the network activities of people have been upgraded from browsing to community interaction. What is more, based on that, technologies such as mobile Internet, big data and cloud computing, and SDN have emerged. They are currently considered to be one of the development trends of the next-generation (third-generation) internet technology, and a hot research topic in the field of ICT (information and communications technology).

3. *World Information Order*

Global information networks truly constitute an objectively existing world. Traditional national sovereignty territories and global commons exist in this world. Unlike global commons such as outer space, polar regions, and high seas, interconnected global information networks mainly exist within the traditional sovereign territories in which the main bodies and platforms of the networks are located, spanning global common areas such as territorial space, outer space, and seabed space. The international space in which global information networks physically exist is the same as that of traditional global long-distance telephone networks. The difference between the two lies in that the telephone number is defined and issued by individual countries independently, while the power to define a "network number" (network address), and the monopoly on the manufacture of high-end network chips, are currently mainly held by the US.

In 1865, 20 European countries signed the Paris International Telegraph Convention and established the International Telegraph Union (ITU). In 1906, 27 countries signed the International Radiotelegraph Convention of Berlin. In 1932, the international community combined the International Telegraph Convention and the International Radiotelegraph Convention into the International Telecommunication Convention in Madrid, and, on 1 January 1934, decided to officially rename the International Telegraph Union as International Telecommunication Union (ITU).

In 1947, the UN decided to include the ITU as one of its 15 specialised agencies. The headquarters of the ITU is based in Geneva and reports to the UN every year. The ITU is responsible for global telecommunication standardisation, the development of radiocommunication and telecommunication, and organising meetings of the council, plenipotentiary conferences, World Telecommunication Standardisation Conferences, World Telecommunication Development Conferences, and World Radio-communication Conferences.

The ITU has added four study groups (SG) to its Telecommunication Standardisation Sector (ITU-T) to research information networks (SG13: future networks including mobile and next-generation networks (NGN); SG15: optical transport networks and access network infrastructures; SG16: multimedia coding, systems, and applications; SG17: security). Both of the SGs in its Telecommunication Development Sector (ITU-D) are researching and developing information network policies (SG1: telecommunications development policy and strategy research; SG2: development and management of telecommunications services, network, and ICT applications). The functions, sectors of the ITU, and conferences it organises are shown in Figure 1-1:

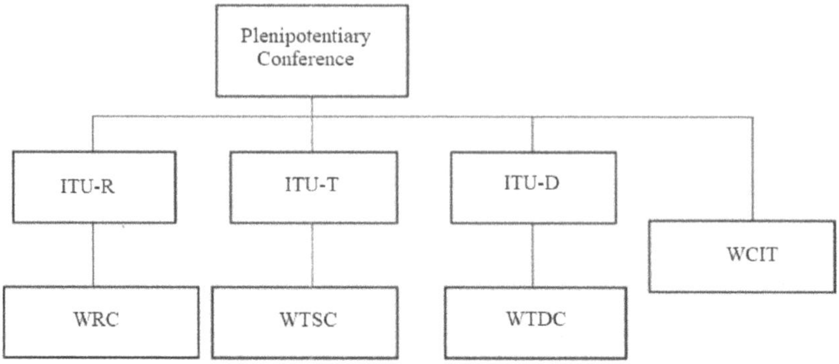

Figure 1-1: Functions, sectors, and conferences of the current ITU

Cyberspace, as defined by the ITU, is "the physical and non-physical terrain created by and/or composed of some or all of the following: computers, computer systems, networks, and their computer programs, computer data, content data, traffic data, and users".[17]

However, the ITU definition of cyberspace is merely an objective description that cannot solve the problem that individual countries have the right to define their own network address; nor can it break the global industrial monopoly of high-end network chip manufacturing. At present, there are approximately four billion internet users involved in global network activities in which information is transmitted, hence information security depends on cyber security, and cyber security depends on the establishment of cyber sovereignty. Therefore, it is of fundamental academic significance for the study of cyber sovereignty and cyber security to trace the essence of information and understand the ontology of cyberspace.

Section Two: Essential Elements of Cyberspace

Essential elements are a group or category of basic elements in a system that share common characteristics. The various elements in

[17] *ITU Toolkit for Cybercrime Legislation*.Retrieved from http://www.itu.int/cybersecurity.

the system jointly determine the basic attributes and its laws of motion.[18]

Cyber elements refer to various real elements that have common characteristics or attributes in an artificial information network system. These independent and interconnected elements, which never overlap with each other, constitute the macro structure of cyber systems. Cyber elements can not only form a hierarchical structure in the systems to make a difference in their authority, but can also form a network structure to realise node connection. The layer and node features of these cyber elements lead to power distribution and power control in the network.

This is a process that requires constant summarisation and evolution to understand the cyber elements. It is, first, an integration of interactive individuals, and then a combination of many forms of individual relationships. Here, the so-called individual refers to the subjects of cyberspace while interaction refers to information communication between the subjects through the objects; the so-called combination includes all the elements of cyber systems. From the perspective of security, cyber security must cover the four major elements of logic, physical parts, users, and information.[19] Graph theory and network theory emerged in the 1960s and once helped sociology to construct a model of social relations.[20] All the mathematical tools that appeared even earlier within the human knowledge base, such as number theory, Euclidean geometry, information theory, cybernetics, systems theory, and even game theory, can be applied to the study of cyber element interaction. However, in cyberspace, it is necessary to understand the real connection between cyber elements and to clarify the virtual presentation of cyber elements. People are prone to confusion and disagreement during the perception process.

---

[18] Zhao, H. R. (2013). *On RMB: Aggregate Money Approach* (p. 243). Beijing: China Economic Publishing House.

[19] Zhao, H. R. (2015). *World Civilizations Aggregate Approach: China's Civilized Rise and Rule of Law in National Security* (p. 218). Beijing: China Legal Publishing House.

[20] Liu, J. (2011). Network Structure and Power Distribution: Explanation from the Perspective of Elementary Theory. *Sociological Studies* (2), 134.

The network was invented as part of computer science, but it is a "virtual" technology based on telecommunications science. So, what are the essential elements of the ontology of cyberspace? The confusion about the concept lies in how we understand the relationship between the computer electronic information system and the corresponding physical space of the telecommunications discipline. The essential elements of the ontology of cyberspace can be understood through the differentiation and summarisation of the perspectives of the evolution of different disciplines and histories. Therefore, it is necessary to research the composition of cyber elements from the two aspects of system elements and the spatial elements of the ontology of cyberspace.

I. *The Ontology of Cyberspace*

Talking of the invention of the Internet, an operating system was developed prior to the interconnection protocol. The connection system, structural system, protocol system, and element system of the network not only feature the continuity of technological development, but also the progressiveness of cognition.

1. *Network Connection System*

In cyberspace, the Internet Protocol (IP) first defines the network layer, and is responsible for defining and locating addresses on the Internet. It provides an address for each networked device, so that all electronic devices can access the Internet in an orderly manner. The Transmission Control Protocol (TCP) defines the transport layer. It is responsible for the signal transmission in the network; it sends electronic signals as soon as the communication requirements on the Internet are discovered. In 1974, the US Department of Defense and three teams of scientists accepted and confirmed the TCP/IP protocol. The TCP/IP protocol finally adopted a four-layer structure — application, transport, internet, and network interface, connecting devices and data that were previously unconnected through new network protocols (rather than telecom signal protocols) and set standards.

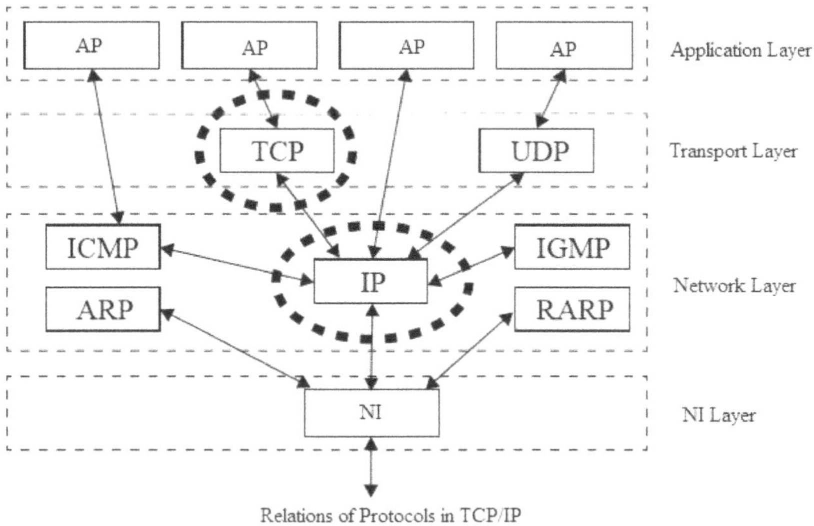

Figure 1-2: A connection system in cyberspace

2. *Network Structural System*

In 1981, the International Organisation for Standardisation (ISO) developed the Open System Interconnection Reference Model (OSI/RM). This model implements layered docking, peer-to-peer communication, and a two-way interoperability optimised system network. The network communication is divided into seven layers from low to high: the physical layer, the data link layer, the network layer, the transport layer, the session layer, the presentation layer, and the application layer. Each layer serves its upper layer and they also support each other, hence optimising the network structure for two-way communication from top to bottom (on the sending end) and bottom to top (on the receiving end).[21] Among them, the first, second, and third layers serve as the first doorway to cyberspace.

3. *Network Protocol System*

The deep integration of network data and telecommunication networks of traditional voice communication has resulted in an

[21] Baidupedia. Retrieved from http://baike.so.com/doc/5242527-5475561.html.

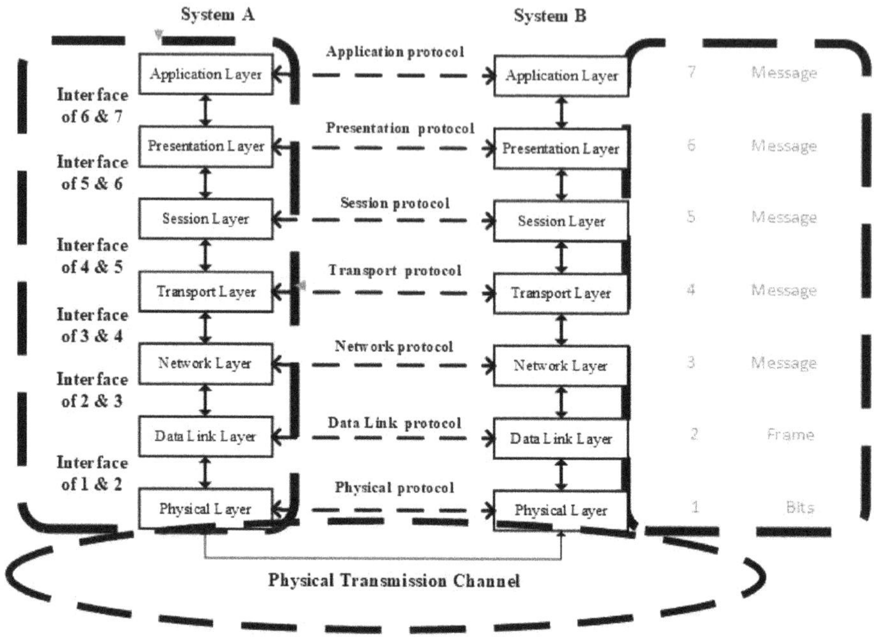

Figure 1-3: The structural system of cyberspace

interaction between the development of the entire telecommunication industry and that of the computer industry; great changes have also taken place. At present, the world's tens of billions of computers and internet equipment terminals produce billions of gigabytes of data every day. The activities of these network subjects are based on the continuous and synchronous development of various innovated network protocols and innovated communication protocols using traditional voice transmission (such as LAN/WAN (Local Area Network/Wide Area Network) protocol, TCP/IP protocol, SS7 (Signalling System number 7) protocol, narrowband and broadband ISDN (Integrated Services Digital Network) signalling protocol, mobile communication network protocol, fibre-optic backbone network protocol, ATM (Asynchronous Transfer Mode) protocol, etc.). There are already thousands of most basic protocols constructing logical links, such as the hierarchical functionality of the framework, and the Internet is the integrated electronic information system based on the combination of these networks and communication protocols.

4. *Cyber Elements System*

A cyber elements system not only includes the connection system, structural system, and protocol system of the network, but more importantly, it includes the subjects, objects, and activities that use the network. Cyber elements should not acknowledge technology platforms and ignore network subjects, objects, and activities. The technological changes brought about by connection technology, layered structure, and logical protocols of the network have changed the application and appearance of traditional networks. However, as an artificial cyberspace, its indispensable components should still contain human beings with subjective initiative. Although the interconnection, system composition, and logical methods within any network are technical issues, it is precisely the revolutionary changes brought about by technological progress that make it a labour tool that serves human subjects. On the contrary, if the user experience and convenience of the subject are neglected, then network development will lose its direction and momentum. Only by comprehensively summarising all the elements of cyberspace can we clearly understand all the cyber elements. We can then reveal the law of all the elements to improve their order.

II. *The Characteristics of Cyber Elements*

As a whole, regions of the world today are universally connected by information networks. The world can be seen as a large local area network, in which different regions are connected by cables/fibre-optic cables under the sea and on the shore. In 1850, Britain and France laid the world's first submarine cable through the English Channel; in 1863, the submarine cable connecting India with the Arabian Peninsula was built; in 1866, the UK and the US built a transatlantic submarine cable (The Atlantic Cable); in 1876, thanks to the invention of the telephone by Alexander Graham Bell, the submarine cable was given the new function of making phone calls in addition to sending telegraphs; in 1886, the government of the Qing Dynasty laid the first submarine cable connecting the Chinese mainland with Taiwan Island; in 1902, the global submarine communications cable was completed; in 1988, the transoceanic submarine fibre-optic cable was laid connecting the US, the UK, and France; in 1989, the submarine fibre-optic cable that spanned the Pacific Ocean was also successfully built. From then on, submarine fibre-optic cables have replaced coaxial cables. Submarine fibre-optic cables have been interconnected with the satellite communication system since the 1990s. In 1997, and with China's participation, the Fibre-optic Link Around the Globe (FLAG) was completed and put into operation. At a total length of 27,000 kilometres, it is an intercontinental fibre-optic cable system connecting 12 countries and regions including China, the UK, Egypt, India, Thailand, and Japan. In 2000, the Shanghai Landing Station of the Asia-Europe Fibre-optic Submarine Cable started service, connecting 33 countries and regions in Asia and Europe. At present, submarine fibre-optic cables adopt a management mode of cooperative construction, system integration, remote power supply, digital relay, and block maintenance.

1. *Reality of Cyberspace*

The flow of global electronic information clearly includes network subjects, information objects, network platforms, and network activities, and is increasingly becoming an indispensable tool for human work and life. From a micro perspective, the virtualisation technology widely used in networks is a real technical means for optimising services for the physical space. For example, the Online to Offline (O2O) technique, which appears to be a service mode or production mode, is also used to improve the efficiency of activities in the physical world. This also reflects the true nature of cyberspace, which is serving our work and lives from another perspective. Current digitisation technology and the activities of human beings have mapped the reality of physical space into cyberspace. Any behaviour in cyberspace is initiated, conducted, deployed, and benefited by subjects in physical space, meeting people's corresponding needs and achieving their corresponding goals. This serves well to reflect the realistic effect of the reality of cyberspace.

In science, the reality of cyberspace is embodied in the materiality of information and the virtuality of technology. It often explores and leads the simplification of communication and system optimisation through virtualisation. These virtualisation technologies essentially implement system optimisation and simplification through technologies of separation, abstraction, and mapping. The virtualisation-related name of internet mirroring technology must not be confused with virtuality, nor can the so-called virtualisation technology of the tip of internet technology be used to deny the reality and materiality of the overall elements of the Internet.

The reality of cyberspace creates the applicability and interactivity of the Internet in the physical world, reflecting the fact that cyberspace is truly usable, proving that the data generated by the networks is nothing but real. Of course, this also has a significant impact on user privacy. The risk of privacy leakage brought about by the reality of network data has also driven a new round of technological innovation, scientific invention, and other activities. To this end, virtual network technologies need to be protected, guided, and supervised, and this protection will be compulsory and aimed at network information protection with the criterion of law. It should be emphasised that only coercive sovereign power can exercise mandatory jurisdiction, and non-sovereign ordinary contractual behaviour cannot achieve universal order.

Cyberspace, which exists objectively under the jurisdictional framework of national sovereignty of all countries and international public spaces and constitutes the realistic basis and responsibility of the rule of law of cyberspace, is nothing but real. Only by recognising and agreeing with the reality of cyberspace can we play the role of the rule of law in punishing evil and promoting good in cyberspace; only by clarifying and mastering the reality of cyberspace can countries around the world, especially developing countries, meet the necessary requirements for achieving cyber security, building consensus about co-governance, promoting cyber justice, and sharing and enjoying network civilisation.

2. *Subjectivity of Cyberspace*

Cyberspace cognition is an ontological problem. The divergence of definitions in existing disciplines leads to one-sidedness in cyberspace cognition.

What is cyberspace from a legal perspective? The first item of Article 76 of the Cybersecurity Law of the People's Republic of China states: "Network refers to a system consisting of computers or other information terminals and related equipment that collects, stores, transmits, exchanges, and processes information according to certain rules and procedures." However, the legal definition requires explanation and should be supplemented with scientific understanding. Here, the logic underlying the legal definition of network is like a "computer system (or other information terminal and related equipment) processing (including collecting, storing, transmitting, exchanging) information (according to certain rules and procedures)"; does this mean that the ontology of network equals "computer system + processing + information"?

The ontology of the network cannot perform without the subjects. The problem lies in that there is no "person" in the network as defined by the abovementioned law. Then, does this Cybersecurity Law of the People's Republic of China not regulate the order of people in cyberspace? To understand the ontology of cyberspace, first and foremost, it is necessary to recognise the "person" in cyberspace. This is the logical starting point for studying the theory of cyber sovereignty.

Since the establishment of the UN, self-government within sovereignty has become the consensus of the international rule of law. Regarding the network era, when the Internet connects every corner of the world, where is the border of cyber sovereignty? This has become a problem that requires clarification. To answer this question, we need to examine what new things cyberspace has brought to humanity, and to think about how cyberspace has brought universal connections to human beings.

Some American scholars believe that the essence of cyberspace is code-law, which represents human cooperation and brings social paragenesis. However, this does not answer the question about the subjectivity of cyberspace and avoids the question of "whether cyberspace is within the scope of sovereign rights". If there is sovereignty over cyberspace, does it belong to independent states on an equal footing? Or does it belong to network users who transcend boundaries of states and sovereignty?

Since the invention and global popularisation of the Internet, the answers to these questions have never been clarified or agreed on in the country that invented the Internet among other things. Therefore, to study the ontology of cyberspace as a material existence, it is necessary to study the essential properties of cyber information.

Section Three: The Essence of Cyber Information

Cyberspace originates from the need for communication, to satisfy what human beings, based on ICT, have renamed user nodes, innovated code, and communication protocols; have given microscopic particles new data attributes to facilitate instant communication with each other; and, further, have created a new community of communication subjects, information objects, technology platforms and terminals, and instant messaging activities. Cyberspace exists as an artificial structure and relative space.

Cyberspace refers to physical space carrying digitalised information instead of the physical space that is utilised to carry macroscopic objects (such as transportation networks). Physical space contains cyberspace, which carries information. In cyberspace, human beings are subjects that communicate with each other; information is the object of communication and cyberspace is the physical platform, including the infrastructure of communication

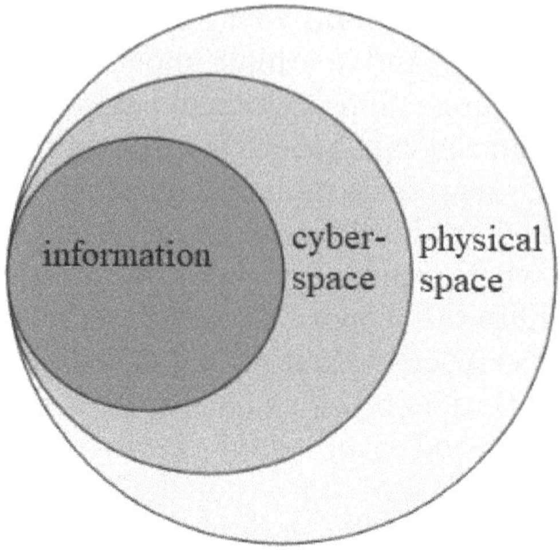

Figure 1-4: Relationship between information, cyberspace, and physical space

technology on which the communication activities between the subjects depend on. This platform includes all the terminals of telecommunications and networking, such as computers, mobile phones, network cables, routers, and other access devices. Information, cyberspace, and physical space are inclusively logic-relative from small to large.

Communication (or correspondence) is a platform and system on which human society can connect, cooperate, and communicate through information. In the field of technology, people create sociality based on communicativeness.

Information (or intelligence/digital data) is essentially human-specific thought and language. It is the content and the tool for human society to communicate, connect, interact, and develop. Information belongs to the spiritual world instead of the physical world, but the existence of information, such as electronic data, must be carried by materials. Information itself has no energy, but the transmission of information, such as electronic signals, must be driven by energy.

Digital data is a new concept developed by ICT. In cyberspace, data is the "raw material" and information is the "finished product". The process that makes raw material a finished product is the result of the programming and moving of particles that "process information according to certain rules and procedures".

Microscopic particles carry network information and network information exists objectively in programmed microscopic particles. When digitalised electronic information is stored and transmitted, the material carrier on which it depends on is a microscopic particle. The microscopic particles that are redefined in cyberspace are called digital data and are different from signals in traditional communication. Scientific discoveries about microscopic particles in the development history of science and technology have confirmed the objective existence property and information-carrying function of microscopic particles: they carry electronic information and constitute cyberspace.

I. *Cyber Information Theory*

Humans give full play to their wisdom through their consciousness to create knowledge and produce information (intelligence). Although non-human organisms can also create networks (such as spider webs and ecosystems), they are not capable of creating information that consists of consciousness, wisdom, and knowledge.

The information that human beings send, transmit, communicate, and store exists and is carried in real physical spacetime. Electronic information carriers such as radio waves and submarine cables occupy only a small part of the entire physical spacetime.

Consciousness is the only tool that drives human beings forward. Human consciousness systems and social systems in different times, such as the agricultural, industrial, and electrical eras, are different. However, now that we have entered the internet age, the emergence of networks is eliminating the obstacles among the physical environments, biological environments, and data environments faced by humans. The foundation of life is integrating with silica-based material and information that starts from carbohydrates.[22]

---

[22] Harari, Y. N. (2014). *Sapiens: A Brief History of Humankind.* Beijing: China CITIC Press.

Information only exists in artificial information cyberspace. In the general physical space, there are artificial information cyberspace and non-artificial biological networks. The "father of anthropology" Edward Burnett Tylor, proposed in his book *Primitive Culture* that "animism" was the earliest form of religion; however, only homo sapiens had the desire (consciousness) to unite and give full play to the role of unity (network), which serves as the driving force and root cause of the human beings that created the networks.

Electromagnetism is an information carrier. Entering the electrical age, human beings have extensively utilised electric power systems and functions; they have also developed great electromagnetic communication technology. The emergence of electromagnetic technology is the premise of human beings entering the era of digital data. Data is one of the information carriers, while information is the content of data; information is processed data. It is precisely the physical existence of electromagnetic information that makes information material and deterministic; this is a new feature of electromagnetic information, which is recognised by Claude Elwood Shannon, the founder of information theory: "Information is that which reduces uncertainty." The physical basis of this "thing" is the "data" and microscopic particles behind the information.

Cyberspace is a real physical space. It is an artificial physical space created by humans, which is embedded in the natural world to present and exchange consciousness, knowledge, and wisdom, using electromagnetic microscopic particles to create electronic information. From biological people to social people, people have created cyberspace by inventing information and building networks. People have invented and used telegraph networks, radio networks, telephone networks, and television networks one after another; during the past 50 years, the Internet has become the newest member of the artificial networks. People do not usually see microscopic particles; what they can see is network platforms and electronic terminals that are used daily.

Human understanding of information was initially unconscious; it has only been 130 years since people began to define information. Humans, in the beginning, communicated in a spontaneous way before they gave "information" a scientific definition. Looking back on the evolution of the cognition of information, for more than 100 years, scientists have experienced various stages of cognition accompanied by corresponding information theories.

1. *Electromagnetic Wave Propagation*

In 1873, the British physicist James Clerk Maxwell first developed a theory that explained the relationship between electricity and magnetism. He proposed the theory of electromagnetic wave propagation (*A Treatise on Electricity and Magnetism*), pointing out that electromagnetic waves propagate through space at the speed of light.

Figure 1-5: James Clerk Maxwell

2. *Electromagnetic Spectrum*

In 1887, the German physicist Heinrich Rudolf Hertz experimentally confirmed that the frequency of electromagnetic waves multiplied by wavelength equals propagation velocity ($f\lambda = v$). He discovered more forms of electromagnetic waves of the same nature, but with different wavelengths and frequencies. He found that partial differential equations can be used to express electromagnetic fields, and called them wave equations. He also discovered the photoelectric effect (the emission of electrons when light hits a material).

Figure 1-6: Heinrich Rudolf Hertz

3. *Physics and Information*

In 1889, American physicist Josiah Willard Gibbs founded statistical mechanics and proposed the definition of "entropy" by linking thermodynamics with electromagnetism. He defined "entropy" as a measurement of insufficient information of physical systems. He also created the theory of vector analysis (*Elementary Principles in Statistical Mechanics*). Since then, physicists have begun to believe that "information is the signal transmitted in electronic circuits".[23]

Figure 1-7: Josiah Willard Gibbs

4. *Radio Application*

In 1893, the American-born Serbian scientist Nikola Tesla publicly demonstrated radio communications for the first time; in 1894, Guglielmo Marconi of Italy experimented with radio technology and patented it at a later time; in 1895, the Russian inventor

[23] Yan, Y. M. (1994). *Information Science*. Wuhan: Wuhan University Press.

Figure 1-8: Nikola Tesla

Alexander Popov invented the radio receiving device. The utilisation of radio has evolved from vacuum tubes, to transistors, to integrated circuits, from shortwaves to ultrashort waves to microwaves, from an analogue signal to a digital signal, from a fixed application to a mobile application, and has now become an important pillar of the modern information society.

5. *Oscillation-based Transmission*

In 1928, American communications scientist Ralph Hartley proposed the modern information theory: electronic oscillation and electron transmission.

Figure 1-9: Ralph Hartley

6. *Information Entropy*

In 1948, the American mathematician Claude Elwood Shannon proposed in the article *A Mathematical Theory of Communication*

Figure 1-10: Claude Elwood Shannon

that "information is that which reduces uncertainty",[24] establishing the information theory. He also proposed "information entropy" by referring to "thermodynamic entropy" to determine the amount of information contained in a general message and the required channel capacity.

7. *Cybernetics*

In 1948, the American mathematician Norbert Wiener believed that information is neither material nor energy: "Information is a name for the content of what is exchanged with the outer world as we adjust to it, and make our adjustment felt upon it." Based on this, he developed cybernetics.[25]

Figure 1-11: Norbert Wiener

[24] Shannon, C. (1948). A Mathematical Theory of Communication. *Bell System Technical Journal* (27).

[25] Wiener, N. (2009). *Cybernetics (Or Control and Communication in the Animal and the Machine)* (2nd Ed.) (J. R. Hao, Trans.). Beijing: Science Press.

8. *Data Processing*

In 1985, American management scholar F. W. Horton defined information as "data that is processed to meet the user's needs for making decisions". Simply put, information is processed data, or information is the result of data processing.[26]

9. *Transmission Application*

Information defined in Chinese textbooks often refers to news, messages, objects of transmission, and processing of communication systems, or everything that is spread around in human society. In the field of philosophy, information is defined as a form of universal connection. Through information, human beings distinguish between different things and understand and transform the world.

10. *Particles Carrying Information*

In 2015, a team led by Fabrizio Carbone, a scientist at the EPFL (Swiss Federal Institute of Technology) in Lausanne, Switzerland, successfully took the first ever snapshot of light behaving both as a wave and as a particle, which truly reproduced the simultaneous existence of "wave", "particle", and "wave-particle", confirming that the microscopic particles used for telecommunication have the basic properties of information carrying.

As early as 1905, Einstein proposed that light behaves as both waves and particles, that is, "wave-particle duality". At that time, the cognitive problem about "waves" and "particles" was just as Einstein said, "It seems as though we must use sometimes the one theory and sometimes the other, while at times we may use either. We are faced with a new kind of difficulty. We have two contradictory pictures of reality; separately neither of them fully explains the phenomena of light, but together they do."[27]

---

[26] Zhang, K. *et al.* (1985). *Information Resource Management.* Beijing: Tsinghua University Press.

[27] *Internet Literature on Quantum Physics.* Retrieved from https://faraday.physics.utoronto.ca/GeneralInterest/Harrison/Complementarity/CompCopen.html.

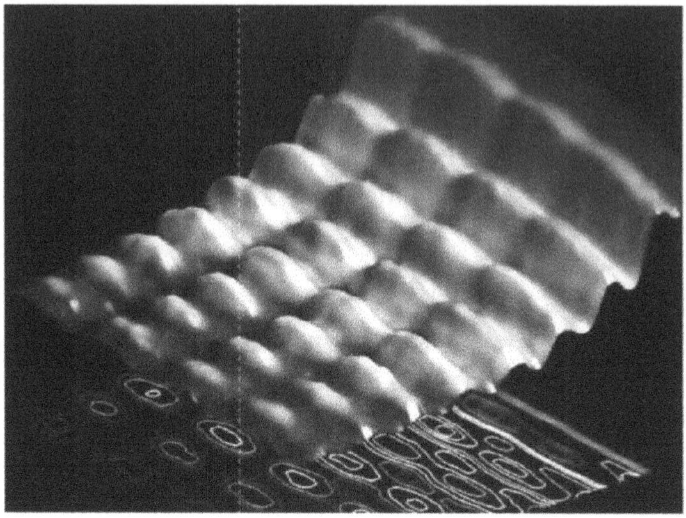

Figure 1-12: Photograph of light behaving "both as a particle and a wave" at the same time[28]

In 1924, the French physicist Louis Victor Pierre Raymond de Broglie postulated the wave nature of electrons and suggested that wave-particle duality is a feature common to light and all matter. However, the fact that a "wave", a "particle", and a "wave-particle" can all carry information was not scientifically proved until 2015, after Swiss scientists took snapshots of light as both a particle and a wave. This breakthrough was published in the journal *Nature Communications* and was evaluated as "a new approach on a classic effect".[29] At this point, the material properties of "wave", "particle", and "wave-particle", as information carrying electrons, were presented scientifically and clearly and were soon widely recognised.

II. *The Nature of Information*

The changes in information carriers reflect the development of technology. The development of information carriers also marks

[28] Ministry of Education, Science and Technology Development Centre (2015). Retrieved from http://www.cutech.edu.cn/cn/gwkj/2015/03/1425494187685818.htm
[29] (2015). *Science and Technology Daily*. A1.

the improvement of human civilisation. Historically, from knot notes to the Caesar cipher, movable type printing, scale calculation, punching statistics,[30] electromagnetic waves, and quantum communication, the scientific and technological progress of information carriers during different stages represent the corresponding improvement of the information utilisation of human beings.

1. *Information Has Scientific Attributes*

Nowadays, in an electronic information age when "wave-particle duality" has become a consensus, information is considered to have the following eight attributes:

(1) Interaction with consciousness

The value of information comes from the exchange between "source" and "sink". From a broad perspective, even if the content received is not explicitly expressed and responded to by "sink", but only exists in consciousness, it is still a type of stored stock information. Without the cognition and interaction of the subjective and objective world of human beings, the existence of information loses its meaning to humanity.

(2) Material carrying capacity

The existence of information depends on the carrying of the material carrier. According to wave-particle duality, information storage, processing, transmission, and feedback all rely on material carriers. Information cannot independently exist nor be generated or changed without these media. By extension, this means that the protection of cyber information cannot be limited to the protection of information itself. The comprehensive protection of cyber information necessarily involves the protection and maintenance of electronic information generation, transmission, bearing, storage, and presentation.

---

[30] Russell, T. (2003). *Telecommunications Protocols* (pp. 1–3) (Zh. Wang *et al.*, Trans.). Beijing: Tsinghua University Press.

(3) Objective measurement

The measurement of information has entered the era of aggregate storage and aggregate interactive communication. Binary digitised electronic data is in "bits", but there are other metrics. In theory, there is aggregate information, which is convenient for searching and duplicate checking. Electronic information has precise measurability and reproducibility due to its total amount.

(4) Storage handling

The storage of information has developed from human-brain storage and paper storage into "silica-based" storage. The information carried and stored by electronic materials can be accessed by human beings using different methods. This feature allows information to exist for a long time and can be processed at any time. The time limit of existence of information can be broken by people's storage behaviour, and its security properties can be altered by people's processing behaviour.

(5) Sharing and spreading

Information is different from general tangible goods in that it can be repeatedly shared. During the course of unlimited spreading and exchanging, the value of information will continue to be derived, which will produce a value growth trend. Therefore, this feature of information, which is different from that of material things and energy, often makes a value driver unique to information sharing activities.

(6) Cognitive relativity

Electronic information is not only a reflection of the objective world; it is also mixed with the subjective understanding of the information subject. In view of the difference in the cognition level of the subjects, the change of things in different development stages and the decline of quality and even human manipulation of information during transmission, information is always "absolutely inaccurate" and "relatively accurate", and "absolutely insecure", as well as "relatively secure".

(7) Virtual mapping and real mapping

Whether in the paper-and-pencil era or in the electromagnetic world, the information presented on the material carrier always maps, copies, reproduces, and reflects the real world. It is one of the essential characteristics of human initiative to use material carriers for information activities and then use information activities to reflect the real world. When information carries wealth and credit in human economic activities, the high-speed circulation of the modern credit economy often makes information flow replace the exchange of physical wealth. The reality-replacement capability of information greatly improves human productivity and life efficiency.

(8) Disciplinary integration

The definition of information calls for the revival of philosophy. While defining information from the perspective of traditional disciplines, we should not categorise information into just one of the respective disciplinary ranges of cognition, knowledge, science, technology, or intellectual property rights. Even in a legal context, information cannot be simply confused with concepts such as data, materials, intelligence, patents, or trademarks. Information cannot be defined by any one single existing discipline, and the philosophical new meaning of information must be framed from general human cognitive activities using the method of disciplinary integration.

2. *Information has Humanistic Functions*

The information phenomenon has humanistic features. Martin Heidegger, the German philosopher most known for his contributions to existentialism, believed that phenomena are a way of showing existence. However, phenomena may also exist in layers in an invisible way. Temporality can help prove phenomena and being. If "the meaning of being is not fully clarified", ontology is rootless.[31]

[31] Heidegger, M. (2014). *Being and Time* (p. 13, 36) (J. Y. Chen, & Q. J. Wang, Trans.). Beijing: SDX Joint Publishing Company.

Information is an undoubtable phenomenon; information is also undoubtedly being. The existence of an information phenomenon (i.e. the certainty of information and the fact that it can be stored) is not fleeting. Therefore, information exists for real. The existence of information phenomenon covers all kinds of cognitive activities during the entire human labour process. As a material structure, information carriers will change with the development of science and technology. However, information in itself remains the same as the phenomenon it represents.

The being of information has social network features. Information exists both in space and time. Information is not an isolated phenomenon; on the contrary, its interactive nature determines that it must exist in the network. Where information exists, time and space constitute the information cyberspace. In the view of Jean-Paul Sartre, the French philosopher of existentialism, the opposite of being is nothingness and nothingness originates from negation.[32] Both Sartre and Heidegger emphasised the cognitive starting point of human perception of various phenomena. The physical beingness of information networks embodies historical materialism, false and real knowledge, the cognitive rationality of humanity, and the cognitive path of human conscious logic.

The function of information has not only been recognised by phenomenology, but is also affirmed by philosophy; it has been empirically proven and applied by science and technology. The progress of our ICTs represents the maturity and development of human civilisation. In essence, information is created and presented in human intellectual labour. It is the subjective mapping and reflection of various objective existence during the course of human labour activities; it is the tool and result of human intellectual labour. It, essentially, features the role of "cognition" (mapping), "certainty" (storage), "interactivity" (network), and "decision-making" (basis) in human labour activities.

[32] Satre, J.-P. (2014). *Being and Nothingness* (pp. 23–44, 296) (X. L. Chen *et al.*, Trans.). Beijing: SDX Joint Publishing Company.

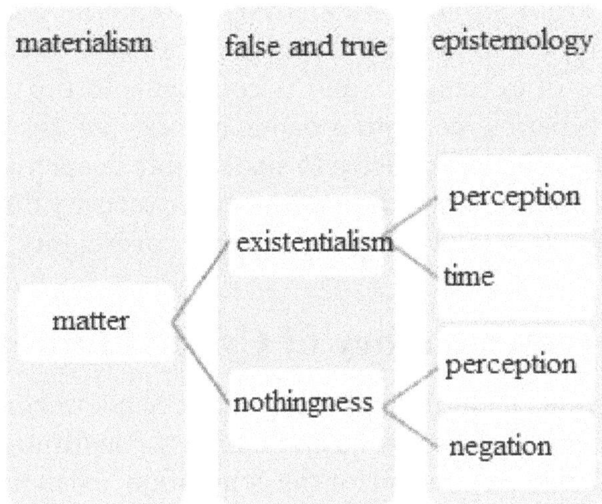

Figure 1-13: Cognitive path of human conscious logic

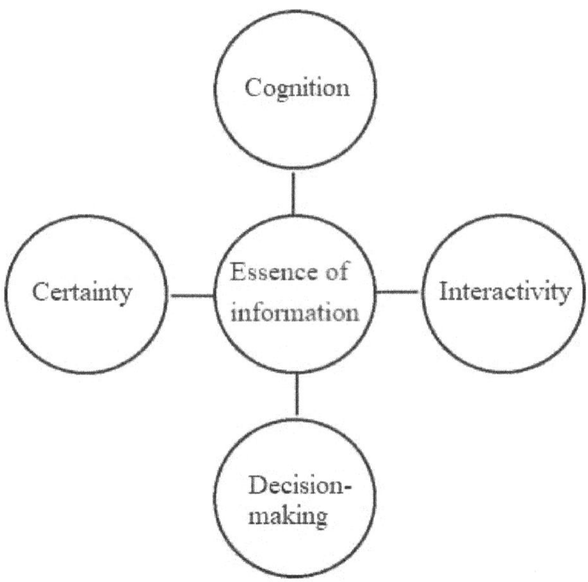

Figure 1-14: The essence of information: functions of cognition, certainty, interactivity, and decision-making

Starting from an accurate analysis of material attributes and humanistic functions of information is conducive to clarifying the true meaning of cyberspace, and is conducive to the macroscopic grasping of cyber elements to broaden and deepen the research on cyberspace. It is also conducive to sustainably deepen and consolidate the development direction of the cyber security discipline and comprehensively safeguard national cyber sovereignty.

Section Four: Theory of Cyber Elements

Cyber elements, including subjects, objects, platforms, and network activities are the most basic units that constitute cyberspace and the exclusive motivation for the generation, existence, development, and change of the ontology of cyberspace.

I. *The Four Cyber Elements: Subject, Object, Platform, Activity*

If cyberspace centred on electronic communication is defined in an exhaustive way, the cyber elements can be listed as network subject, network object, network platform, and network activity. These four basic elements constitute everything about cyberspace.

1. *Network Subject*

Network subjects refer to natural people and entities that are real subjects and actually use the network and their mirrored subjects in the real world. From the perspective of network information communication, a network subject plays an active role as an initiator, receiver, demander, consumer, operator, and user, who actively participates in information communication. They create and utilise their specific information and promote the realisation and application of the value of information. Cyberspace is a physical space for communication activities between human subjects through physical platforms and logical connections. A network subject is the first and foremost element of network composition.

2. *Network Object*

Network objects refer to the information and data carried by physical carriers that people create and use in cyberspace. They are the ontology of knowledge that human beings remember, contact, and communicate with each other about. Through interaction, human beings have created human society; through network objects, human beings create and inherit human civilisation. The development of the civilisation of human society is spread and deepened through the recording, storage, coordination, and creation of information. Currently, objects of the Internet are electronic information and data defined by various basic protocols. Network objects are the second element of network composition. A network without an object cannot exist and is meaningless.

3. *Network Platform*

Network platforms refer to the total of various network hardware, software, terminals, connected devices, and infrastructure that were invented, created, produced, and used by human beings. Network platforms are a visible and physical part of cyberspace, and include all software and hardware facilities that network subjects use to access the network, such as computers, smartphones, communication devices, routing devices, sensing devices, storage devices, and network cables. As a physical carrier of cyberspace that exists in reality, it enables people to see, perceive, and use the network. The various devices in the network platform category are also interconnected by "logical connections". The technological inventions that create these "logical connections" constitute the primary premise for human beings to create cyberspace and the fundamental power to harness the distribution of network resources. It is these "logical connections" that establish the network's connection system, structural system, protocol system, domain name system, address parameters, and activity rules.

4. *Network Activity*

Network activity refers to the various actions carried out by human beings using ICT to construct artificial cyberspace, which establishes the connection between each other; that is, all the activities that network subjects engage in that are specific to network objects. Overall, current network activities have brought together and instilled an increasing amount of human labour. The networking of human labour not only enhances labour efficiency, but may also facilitate a more accurate differentiation of the value of human labour in the future.

On the whole, for networks it is “the elements that determine everything”. Taijitu (or the Taiji Diagram) of ancient China actually contains four numbers: one, two, three, and four in the real phase, namely the yin and yang, the S-shaped dividing line, and the circle.[33] In the relationship of cyber elements, the ancient Chinese Taijitu can be used to illustrate the information network

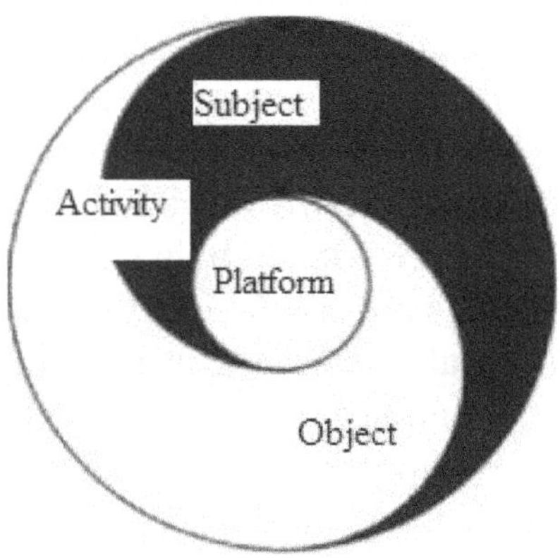

Figure 1-15: Taijitu of the four elements of cyberspace

[33] Zhong, Zh. Ch. (2015). *Internet Philosophy* (III, pp. 14–19). Beijing: Publishing House of Electronics Industry.

phenomenon. The four elements of cyberspace can be marked like this: yin and yang represent the subject and object of the network separately, while the S-shaped dividing line represents the interface and platform of the network; everything inside the circle are network activities.

II. *Boundaries of the Four Elements: Cyber Elements Coupled to Sovereign Territory*

Logical connections link the four elements (subject, object, platform, and activity) of the global network. However, the objective location of each network subject, object, platform, and activity clearly (and truly) fall into the jurisdiction of different sovereign states. Nevertheless, it is the boundaries between a global network connection and cyber sovereign jurisdiction that constitute the confusion of people in terms of cyberspace order. The boundary issue of cyber sovereignty refers to the problem of how sovereign states "see, connect, manage, and use" the four elements of the network.

So far, the international community has not yet reached an agreement in the form of an international convention on the issue of cyberspace in sovereign jurisdiction. The complex structure and rich connotation of cyberspace determine that countries would face various difficulties in safeguarding cyber sovereignty, including how to ensure its access to the Internet is not "denied", how to actively maintain cyber security, how to independently safeguard the security of network subjects, objects, platforms, and activities, and how to build a new cyberspace order that truly reflects sovereign equality and meets the endogenous needs of the development of ICT.

Regarding the sovereignty of cyberspace, the real question is not only whether cyberspace exists or whether cyberspace applies sovereignty principles, but it investigates the need to explore specific ways to implement the legislative procedure and information order governed by cyber sovereignty.

First, one of the difficulties is the achievement of an international consensus on cyber sovereignty. Some countries have claimed cyber sovereignty, but they have difficulty in technical management and cognitive understanding. Therefore, they are mostly a kind of political declaration that fails to clearly define cyberspace sovereignty from a legal perspective.

The second problem is the determination of the technical scope of cyber sovereignty. If a country has no sufficient capability in terms of network technology, it is difficult for it to determine the jurisdictional boundaries of its cyber sovereignty. When a country is claiming traditional territorial sovereignty, it can claim jurisdiction through land borders, territorial sea width, airspace altitude, etc. However, the jurisdiction of cyberspace must rely on demarcation criteria that are technically feasible, clear in rights and interests, autonomous in terms of nodes, and clarified legally.

The third problem is the identification of violations of cyber sovereignty. On the one hand, cyberspace violations are often transnational and invisible. Due to anonymity and information openness in cyberspace, it is rather difficult to confirm network identification and to trace network behaviour in cross-country scenarios. On the other hand, the results of cyberspace violations could be systematic and fatal. Some major damage may not be identified for a long time, and the ability of sovereign states to maintain the grading, early warning, prevention, and resilience of their network's critical infrastructure needs to be strengthened.

Finally, the open technical framework, the virtualised presentation of technology, and the diversified behavioural subjects of cyberspace constitute the complex objects and multi-dimensional connotation that cyber sovereignty governs. Sovereign states mostly use political, economic, diplomatic, military, and other resources to safeguard their traditional national sovereignty. In addition, they resort to international laws, international organisations, and other international mechanisms to resolve international disputes in a fair and reasonable manner. In contrast, cyber sovereignty is a non-traditional sovereignty and only when a country owns independent network technologies to a large extent can it effectively administrate network subjects, objects, platforms, and activities within its sovereignty.

Global cyber elements, except for those in international commons, are located in the territories of different sovereign states and the cyber elements within the sovereignty of each country naturally constitute the cyber sovereignty of the corresponding country. Although the scope of cyber elements and that of traditional sovereignty overlap, the technical level of countries to master the "logical connection" of the network is widely varied. When cyber sovereignty is compromised, such as when the network infrastructure is attacked, a network application system is invaded, or the network data is stolen, the technical resources and countermeasures are limited for those sovereign states with a low level of network technology. Therefore, it is imperative for technically underdeveloped countries to understand networks as a whole, via cyber elements, and defend cyber sovereignty by improving network technology.

In short, the ontology of cyberspace comprises four elements: subject, object, platform, and activity. The ontology of cyberspace contains all of the elements in the whole network. It is the combination of all subjects (individuals), objects (information), platforms (equipment), and activities (labour) in various electromagnetic spaces represented by the Internet. The ontology of cyberspace exists in traditional sovereign territory. The ontology of cyberspace contains both the network and sovereignty. Sovereignty governs the cyber elements, and the elements are subject to the sovereignty of different countries. Since the popularity of network activities originates from scientific revolution rather than the mobilisation of sovereignty, and because the traditional sovereign theory has never encountered the revolutionary challenge of ICT, research on the topic of how traditional sovereignty could govern cyberspace is absent. To better cope with this situation, we need to explore the innovation of ideas, focusing on the history of ICT from a social science perspective.

Chapter Two
Cyber Evolution

"Information is a name for the content of what is exchanged with the outer world as we adjust to it, and make our adjustment felt upon it."

— Norbert Wiener (1948),[1] founder of cybernetics

Section One: Invention of the Internet

Both "cyber" and "cybernetics" are derived from the Greek, originally meaning "steersman". A network inherently applies the logic of "control" through the movement of information. Its logic needs to be analysed from four perspectives: the origin, connection, utilisation, and security of the network.

For academic purposes, textbooks often define the network, especially the Internet, from the perspective of technical cognition rather than order governance. Although such a definition serves to describe the technical route of the Internet to a certain extent, it tends to ignore the most fundamental and essential philosophical perceptions such as "what role does the Internet

---

[1] Norbert Wiener, American mathematician of applied mathematics, the founding father of cybernetics. G. Klaus, a former East German philosopher, praised his theory: "As for its revolutionary impact, it can be compared with the discoveries of Copernicus, Darwin and Marx."

play in society?"[2] What it ignores is an integrative view of the system of elements of the Internet, which will result in mistakes in internet governance, such as taking stopgap measures to deal with problems, or even to deal with the wrong parts of the problems.

In 1946, the United States (US) announced the birth of the world's first general-purpose computer ENIAC (Electronic Numerical Integrator and Computer). When the Soviet Union launched the first man-made satellite in 1957, the US military began to worry about whether US military communications would be interrupted if it were hit from space by the Soviet Union. In 1958, the Advanced Research Projects Agency (ARPA), under the US Department of Defense, proposed such countermeasures: first, to reinforce space development; second, to seek improvements in communications. In terms of improvements in communications, ARPA initiated research and development (R&D) of the network, which represented significant achievements, greatly promoting the pioneering development of network technology in the US.

I. *Initial Stage as a Military Network*

In the 1960s, the world was experiencing the sharpening confrontation of the Cold War. In order to win the arms race in the Cold War and ensure their traditional telecommunications network would remain functional, with communication enabled by part of the network even if the rest of it were to be destroyed under attack, the ARPA of the US Department of Defense built an experimental military network — the Advanced Research Projects Agency Network (ARPANET).[3] In the 1980s, ARPANET was split into the

---

[2] Zhong, Zh. Ch. (2015) *Internet Philosophy*. Publishing House of Electronics Industry.

[3] Wang, D. Q. (1998). On the Jurisdiction of Cases Involving the Internet. *Peking University Law Journal* (2), 25.

US military network (MILNET) and a civil network, and this civil network was, namely, the newly born "Internet".

1. *ARPANET's First Steps*

The research programme set up by ARPA in 1958 produced fruitful results in 1969, and ARPANET was officially created. At that time, ARPANET was merely experimentally connected to four mainframes (four computer network nodes) at the University of California, Los Angeles; the Stanford University Institute; the University of California, Santa Barbara; and the Department of Computer Science at the University of Utah. Besides, ARPANET was then only connected by telephone lines, allowing scientists to conduct computer networking experiments, transfer information to each other, and build a database.[4]

In 1970, ARPANET attempted to make itself technically accessible to non-military users. Many American universities and enterprises were connected to it. Moreover, a lot of universities and institutions had created their own networks, meaning that dozens of computer networks were emerging in the US. However, communication was only supported internally in these networks instead of externally between different computer networks. The emergence of separate and independent local area networks (LANs) resulted in a technical need to achieve interconnection between computer networks using different "languages".

In 1974, to solve the problem of LAN interconnection, Robert Kahn from ARPA and Vinton Cerf from Stanford University invented the Transmission Control Protocol/Internet Protocol (TCP/IP), which was a new method of connecting different computer LANs. Thereafter, ARPA set up another follow-up research project to support the research on network interconnection that was being carried by academic and industrial circles, enabling ARPANET to expand rapidly and grow.

---

[4] Lv, J. H. (2014) *A Study of U.S. Thought on Cyber Warfare*. Military Science Publishing House.

2. *Separation of the Internet*

In 1983, ARPANET was split into two parts: the military network and the civilian network. The former was known as MILNET for short while the latter was still called ARPANET. The US Department of Defense subsequently decided to use TCP/IP as the foundation of the civilian network (ARPANET), while the foundation of the military network (MILNET) was not made public.

In the same year, the US Department of Defense decided to rename ARPANET, calling it "the Internet", a term that remains in use today.[5]

In 1986, the US National Science Foundation (NSF) created a backbone network, the National Science Foundation Network (NSFNET). This was based on the TCP/IP, which replaced the original ARPANET core architecture as the backbone network of the Internet in 1990. At first, this network was responsible for connecting a number of supercomputers and research institutions, such as major US universities. It expanded rapidly, however, ultimately connecting universities and research institutions around the world, thereby becoming a global education and research network.

In 1983, only 562 computers were connected to the Internet; by 1989, the number exceeded 100,000. Between 1986 and 1991, the number of LANs integrated into the Internet increased from 100 to more than 3,000 worldwide.[6] Indeed, by the 1990s, the Internet had become a globally interconnected network.

II. *Internet Corporation for Assigned Names and Numbers*

1. *The Addresses of the Internet*

The new network-interconnection method developed by ARPA compiled multi-level and unified network addresses for each

---

[5] *Internet Society of China.* Retrieved from http://www.isc.org.cn/ihf/info.php?cid=215.

[6] Qi, J. G. *et al.* (2000) *Cyber Warfare: The Life Line of Information Warfare* (p. 20). Military Publishing House of Friendship and Literature.

network and generated an integrated "network-address book" via 13 geographically distributed root servers. In other words, under the ARPA method, each computer needs to be addressed by the nearest root server before confirming and sending information to another computer.

The institutions that were responsible for running these root servers and "network-address books" evolved into the Internet Corporation for Assigned Names and Numbers (ICANN). ICANN assigns geographically defined and clearly categorised network addresses to different regions and different types of organisations around the world by managing top-level domains, such as ".jp" for Japan, ".de" for Germany, ".cn" for China, ".uk" for the UK, ".com" for global business organisations, ".edu" for global educational institutions, and ".org" for global government agencies.[7]

The predecessor of ICANN is the Internet Assigned Numbers Authority (IANA). Directly funded by the US government, IANA has always been a subsidiary of the US Department of Defense. In 1998, with the development of the Internet, ICANN was established to replace IANA through a contract with the National Telecommunications and Information Administration (NTIA) under the US Department of Commerce, adopting the so-called "bottom-up, consensus-driven, multi-stakeholder mode" in the process. The reasoning behind this replacement was that IANA was controlled by one country, i.e. the US. Moreover, the global Internet domain-name distribution structure set up by NTIA in 20 years was also inherited and managed by ICANN, excluding military networks, the dark web, and a large number of LANs not connected to the Internet.

2. *Host of the Internet*

ICANN's role is to allocate, manage, and coordinate the Internet's web address (unique identifier) system, ensuring safe and stable operations worldwide. This includes the allocation of internet

[7] Shi, Y. (2002). Background Information and Latest News about ICANN. *News University* (4), 64.

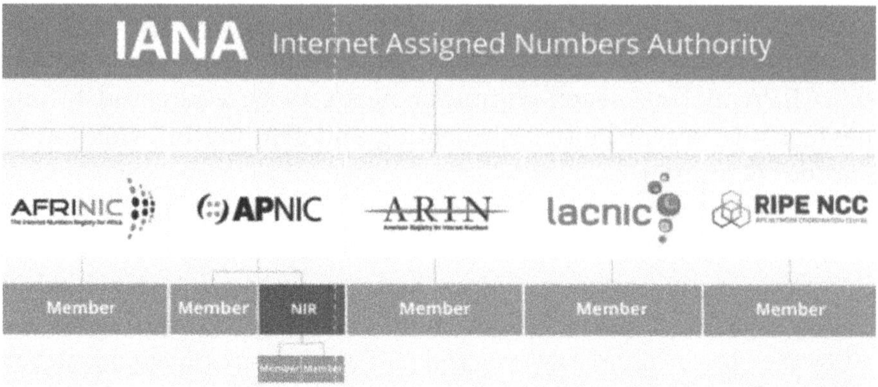

Figure 2-1: Internet-address allocation system of the "five regions" of the world

Protocol (IP) addresses, the assignment of protocol identifiers, the management of generic top-level domains (gTLDs) and country code top-level domains (ccTLDs), as well as the management of the root-server system. Global web addresses can be divided into five major regions: North America, Europe, Asia Pacific, Latin America, and Africa. Regional Internet Registries (RIRs) then allocate Internet addresses to members and users in different countries and regions. However, ICANN is still responsible for global domain-name management.

The Internet-address allocation systems of the aforementioned five regions are outlined below.

The Réseaux IP Européens Network Coordination Centre (RIPE NCC) was established in 1992, serving 15,000 local internet registries (LIRs) in 75 countries and regions in Europe, including the Asian part of Russia.

The Asia-Pacific Network Information Centre (APNIC) was established in 1993, serving 56 countries and regions in Asia and Oceania. It is divided into four sub-regions: South Asia, Southeast Asia, East Asia, and Oceania. In these regions, seven Asia-Pacific economies have established their respective National Internet Registries (NIRs).

The American Registry of Internet Numbers (ARIN) was established in 1997 and is responsible for IP-address allocation in North America, South America, the Caribbean, and the North Atlantic islands.

The Latin America and Caribbean Network Information Centre (LACNIC) was established in 2002 to serve approximately 7,000 network providers in 33 countries and regions in Latin America and the Caribbean.

The African Network Information Centre (AFRINIC) was established in 2005, consisting of six RIRs: Northern, Western, Central, Eastern, and Southern Africa, and the Indian Ocean.

Through the aforementioned five regions of the world administering their respective countries and sub-regions, ICANN is able to create address-allocation orders.

ICANN is positioned to be a non-profit organisation and a non-government agency independent of the US government. Currently, ICANN is not controlled by the US Department of Defense. However, it has long maintained "a contractual relationship of administrative subordination" with the US Department of Commerce and its National Telecommunications and Information Administration. Even if it is no longer managed by the US Department of Commerce, ICANN remains subject to US law because it is located in the US.

3. *Expansion of the Internet*

At present, the number of global Internet users is more than 50% of the total global population.[8] Moreover, the number of Internet-connecting terminals has exceeded hundreds of billions; these include electronic computers, smartphones, network cables, power cables, optical cables, routers, and other electronic devices with embedded communication chips.

[8] Meeker, M. *Annual Internet Report*. Retrieved from http://news.xinhuanet.com/newmedia/2015-06/04/c_134297239.htm.

Section Two: Connection of Chinese Networks with the Internet

Since the Internet was created by the US, other countries need to obtain approval from the US before being connected, which means that it can also deny or interrupt the internet access of any country at any time. This is the so-called first-mover advantage of the US for inventing the Internet, and it also lays a historical foundation for US Internet hegemony in technology. For instance, China originally connected to the Internet indirectly by taking a detour through Europe.[9]

I. *Difficult Connection*

1. *China's First Email to "Reach Every Corner in the World"*

In Beijing on 14 September 1987, Chinese and German scholars jointly drafted China's first email — the text of which was "Across the Great Wall we can reach every corner in the world", which was successfully received in Germany on the 20th of the same month. This was the first email sent to a foreign country, becoming a symbol of China's entry into the Internet era.[10]

In fact, the network that China was originally connected to was not the Internet backbone. Instead, the email was sent through two networks: CSNET and BITNET. At the time, these two networks were autonomous despite the fact that they were both an integral part of the Internet. The Chinese emails were first sent to Germany, where they were then forwarded through the German server. Indeed, receiving emails was just as troublesome as sending them. Moreover, the cost of renting channels was high, with one kilobyte

---

[9] Li, N. J., & Werner, Z. (2007). A Review of Early Efforts to Connect China to the Internet. *Chinese Journal of Computer-Mediated Communication*, 239.

[10] Editorial Office of the Journal of Innovation Science and Technology. (2009). China Linked to the Internet for the First Time in 1994. *Innovation Science and Technology* (10), 54.

of traffic costing more than six yuan. For the purposes of comparison, countries that were connected to the Internet backbone network only had to pay a few li (1 li = 0.001 yuan) per one kilobyte of traffic.[11]

2. *Hesitation of the US in Connecting China to the Internet*

At the time, stewardship of the Internet had been transferred from the US military to the National Science Foundation (NSF). In order to be connected to the Internet, China required the approval of the NSF, which initially assisted the country; on 8 November 1987, Stephen Wolff, the director of the Foundation, sent an approval letter with respect to connecting China to the Internet, opening a door for China to have full access to the Internet.

However, when China finally got ready to be connected to the Internet, the Foundation began to hesitate because the Internet backbone was originally a combination of networks, specifically the US Department of Defense and the NSF, which is to say that the Internet had not completely broken away from its US-military background. Indeed, many US government departments were also involved in the Internet backbone, including some military organisations. Accordingly, due to concerns, the US-Internet policy did not allow China to connect to the Internet.[12]

3. *The Initial Establishment of Chinese LANs and their Connection to the Internet*

In 1988, the network of the Institute of High Energy Physics (IHEP) of the Chinese Academy of Sciences (CAS) was created, which was the first LAN with modern high-performance computers built in China. It was directly connected to the International

---

[11] Tang, Zh. (2014). Chinese Internet Comes out from a Meandering Path. *International Talent* (10), 24.

[12] Ibid., p. 25.

Computer Network of the European Organization for Nuclear Research upon completion.

In May 1990, the network began to provide non-commercial network services to other users. In addition, the network was connected to the computer network of the Stanford Linear Accelerator Center (SLAC) in March 1991. The network was continuously developed and improved with respect to technical equipment before adopting a high-speed communication channel. In March 1993, the network was connected to the US Energy Sciences Network.[13]

4. *Domestic Routers and the Completion of the Zhongguancun Triangulated Network*

In April 1990, after being funded by a loan from the World Bank and domestic funds, the Chinese State Science and Technology Commission began to build China's largest all-optical cable computer network in Zhongguancun, Beijing. It was named the Demonstration Network for Education and Research of the Zhongguancun District. The first of China's large-scale LANs, it was jointly created by the Chinese Academy of Sciences, Tsinghua University, and Peking University.[14]

The network was an internally operating LAN. It was connected by fibre-optic cables and the routers were independently developed by China; they supported the RIP (Routing Information Protocol) protocol of a 10-megabit ethernet. The LAN, which was supported by more than 30 routers, was completed in 1992. In 1993, its backbone network was opened, enabling interconnection between the three institutions involved in the design, which is why it was called the Zhongguancun Triangulated Network.

---

[13] *Chinese Internet is Unprecedented.* Retrieved from http://media.people.com.cn/GB/nZ2014/0415/c40606- 24898154.html.

[14] Tang, Zh. (2014). Chinese Internet Comes out from a Meandering Path. *International Talent* (10), 24.

Indeed, this network laid the foundation for China's connection to the Internet.

II. *Domain-Name Allocation*

1. *International Registration of China's National Top-Level Domain ".cn"*

On 28 November 1990, China registered the international top-level domain name "CN" for the China Academic Network (CANET) at the Internet Network Information Center (InterNIC) with the support of the Chinese State Science and Technology Commission. Since then, an international e-mail service using the Chinese top-level domain name "CN" has been accessible worldwide.

InterNIC's records of CANET are as follows: "CANET is the Chinese state research and development network, begun in 1988. It currently includes approximately 35 institutions. The gateway is through XLINK at the University of Karlsruhe in Germany. CANET uses dial-up nodes as well as X.25 protocol in the major cities of China. Currently, 1,200 bits per second is the typical transmission speed. CANET plans to move completely to X.25 and PAD connections. They expect to install Telebit Trailblazer modems for the dial-up lines."[15]

In 1990, four countries and organisations had their applications for top-level domains approved, including ".cn" for China, ".eg" for Egypt, ".hu" for the Hungarian Academy of Sciences, and ".za" for the UNINET project team.[16]

Since January 1991, Karlsruhe University in Germany has been running a primary server for the ".cn" domain name. It was not until May 1995, when a direct internet connection between China

---

[15] Li, N. J., & Werner, Z. (2007). A Review of Early Efforts to Connect China to Internet. *Chinese Journal of Computer-Mediated Communication*, 244.

[16] Ibid., p. 245.

and the US was established, that China's ".cn" domain-name server was officially settled in China.[17]

2. *China-US Agreement: China will have Full Access to the Internet*

As early as July 1992, China realised its national e-mail system nationwide and named it the China Public Email System. In early April 1994, Song Jian, the then director of the Chinese State Science and Technology Commission, went to the US to participate in the China-US Joint Commission Meeting on Science and Technology Cooperation. The NSF directors, Ryan and Stephen Wolf, were present at the meeting, and the two sides formally decided on China's internet access.

On 20 April 1994, China opened a dedicated 64K international line through the US Sprint Corporation, achieving connection to the Internet with fully functional access and becoming the 77th country in the world to do so. Accordingly, China officially joined the international family of the Internet.[18]

3. *The International Interconnection of China's "Digital Data Network"*

In May 1994, IHEP set up the first web server with the first set of web pages in China, which was named the Window of China. This provided a wide range of graphic-information services, including news, economy, culture, and commerce. In the same month, the National Research Center for Intelligent Computing Systems (NCIC) launched the Dawning BBS website, which was the first online forum in the Chinese mainland.

---

[17] Li, N. J., & Werner, Z. (2007). A Review of Early Efforts to Connect China to Internet. *Chinese Journal of Computer-Mediated Communication*, 245.

[18] *Internet Society of China, A History of China's Link to the Internet.* Retrieved from http://www.isc.org.cn/ihf/info.php?cid=217.

In August 1994, China's Ministry of Posts and Telecommunications signed an agreement with Sprint Corporation, prescribing that Sprint Corporation would assist China in establishing the ChinaNet. International nodes were set up in Beijing and Shanghai, completing the interconnection of the China digital data network (China DDN) with the Internet.

In June 1997, the China Internet Network Information Center (CNNIC) was set up. Currently, CNNIC is a directly affiliated institution of the Office of the Central Cyberspace Affairs Commission and Cyberspace Administration of China, and undertakes the responsibilities as the national internet network information centre. CNNIC is responsible for providing services associated with domain-name registration and resolution, as well as domain-name root-server operations within China. In essence, it serves as China's network root-server.

CNNIC is a member of its "logic superior", the Asia–Pacific Network Information Centre (APNIC), as a national internet registry (NIR), undertaking the responsibilities of providing multi-level IP addresses and AS (Autonomous System)-number allocation services to both Chinese internet service providers (ISPs) and network users. Moreover, it is also responsible for ensuring the reliability, security, and stability of China's system of fundamental network resources, as well as for collecting development statistics and externally cooperating with China's networks.

Section Three: Globalisation of the Internet

At present, almost all countries and regions in the world have access to the Internet. Even flights and cruise ships on the global commons are able to provide internet-access services. The surge in the number of internet users around the world has rapidly expanded the production, sales, and service of "Internet Plus", as well as the R&D and production of internet-related electronic devices, telecommunication equipment, and smart devices, which are responsible for promoting the globalisation of both the industrial economy and the technological economy.

The popularity of the Internet is reflected in the fact that it has not only entered people's lives, but also quickly embedded itself in their production. Indeed, the cyber economy is responsible for driving forward the production and life of human beings; its economic and social forms are known as the media economy, the digital economy, the sharing economy, and the information economy. The application of the Internet from the technical level to the economic level represents the popularity of the Internet in the broadest sense, marking the beginning of the cyber era.

I. *Marketisation of the Internet*

Internet operators created a new market based on the concept of "mass media". At present, traditional media is declining all around the world while online media is developing rapidly.

In China, the market share of television (TV) and newspaper advertising demonstrates a significant decline since 2009. In 2011, China's online advertising revenue exceeded newspaper advertising revenue. Moreover, in 2013, Chinese online advertising revenue surpassed TV advertising revenue. Indeed, network media has become the largest media in terms of advertising revenue. In 2014,

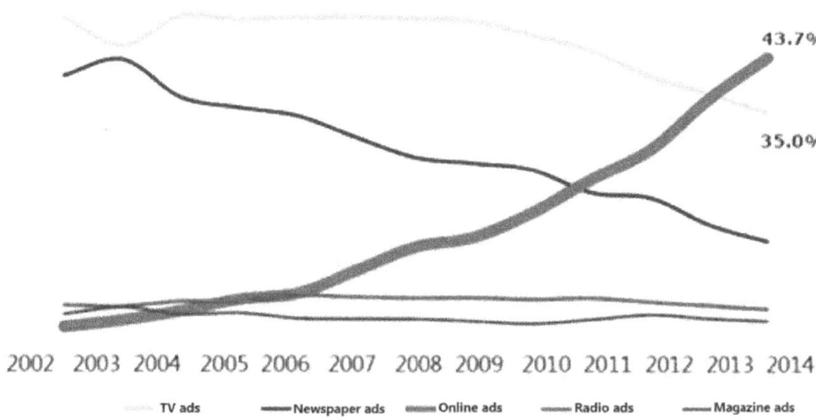

Figure 2-2: Advertising revenue share of different types of media in China, 2002–2014

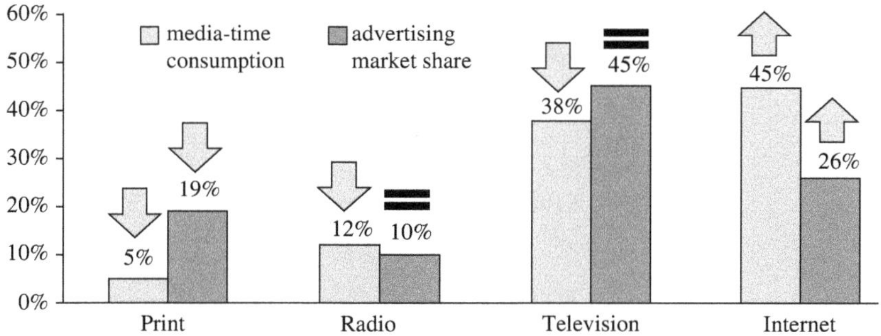

Figure 2-3: Comparison of media-time consumption and advertising market share of different types of media in the US in 2013

the share of online advertising revenue continued to grow, while the revenue share of newspaper and TV advertisements continued to decline.

In the US, the share of internet advertising is also on the rise, while the share of traditional print, radio, and TV are all in decline. In 2013, although internet advertising in the US had not yet overtaken TV advertising, the gap was narrowing. For instance, media-time consumption with respect to the Internet has significantly exceeded that of TV, which led to further prosperity of the US internet advertising market. During the same period, print media and radio were both in decline with respect to media-time consumption and market share.

A number of precision online marketing methods currently exist: cost per mille (CPM), which is charged per thousand impressions of an advertisement; cost per click (CPC), which is charged for each click; cost per time (CPT), which is charged according to the duration of the advertisement; and cost per action/cost per sale (CPA/CPS), which is charged according to successful transaction volume.

Precision advertising, a technique that accurately selects specific target users and regions via the Internet and precisely delivers advertisements to users in a comprehensive form of text, images, or video, will become the most important driving force for the online advertising market. Indeed, big data-based precision-advertising

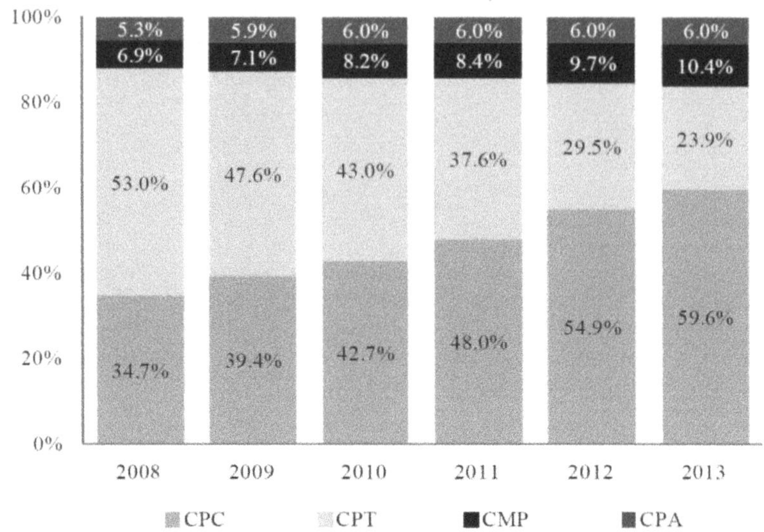

Figure 2-4: Share of different charging methods adopted in China's online advertising market

providers have risen rapidly — e.g. Qihoo 360's online-marketing platform "Touching System" (点睛系统) and Tencent's "Tencent Open Platform" (广点通) — and their market position is already comparable to traditional portal websites. Indeed, online games and online e-commerce are the main customer groups of these precision advertisements. With the further expansion of these customer groups and the optimisation of precision advertising in terms of big data, precision advertising has become vital in the online advertising market.

II. *Consumerisation of the Internet*

The new e-commerce format, which develops online and offline businesses in an integrative way, has rapidly expanded market consumption. As of June 2017, the number of online shoppers in China reached 514 million, an increase of 10.2% compared with the end of 2016. Among these shoppers, the number of mobile

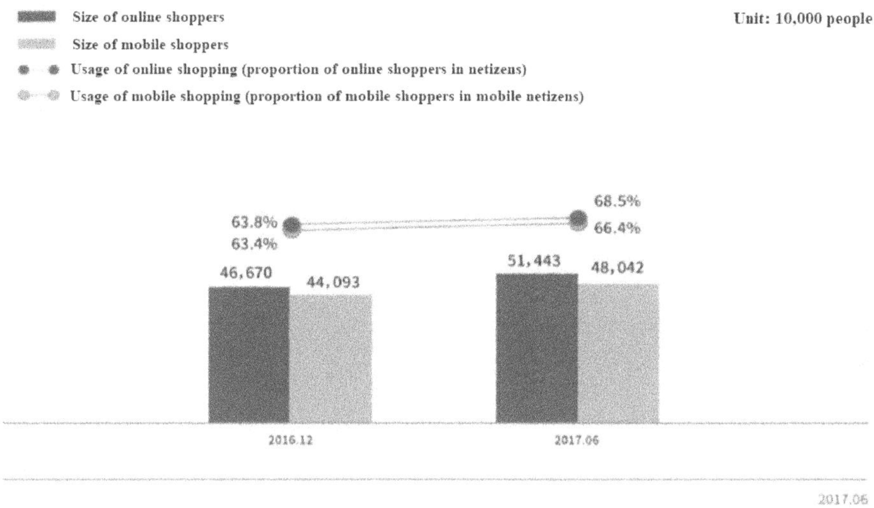

Figure 2-5: Online/mobile shopper size and usage, December 2016–June 2017
Source: CNNIC Statistical Survey on Internet Development in China

shoppers reached 480 million, with a half-year growth rate of 9%; the usage increased from 63.4% to 66.4%.[19]

Indeed, young people have become the main driving force behind online consumption. The strategies of "channel sinking" and overseas expansion of e-commerce enterprises have worked together to stimulate the consumption potential of online shopping, resulting in consumption upgrading.

III. *Financialisaton of the Internet*

With the improvement of cyber security, financial activities (e.g. online payment, settlement, credit and wealth management) have become more and more popular. Internet-based consumer finance

[19] CNNIC. *Statistical Report on Internet Development in China*. Retrieved from http://cnnic.cn/hlwfzyj/hlwxzbg/hlwtjbg/201708/P020170807351923262153.pdf.

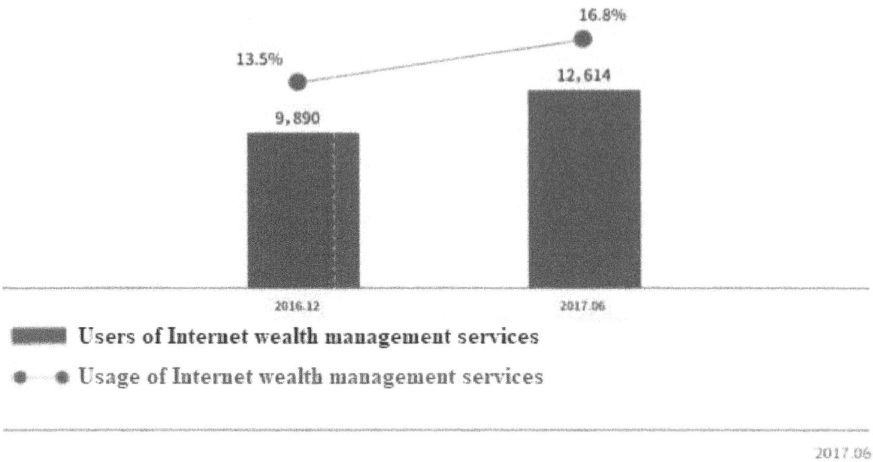

Figure 2-6: Size of users of internet wealth-management services and utilisation rate, December 2016–June 2017

Source: CNNIC Statistical Survey on Internet Development in China

refers to modern financial services that offer loans for consumers who shop online, including housing loans, auto loans, travel loans, and student loans. In 2013, the transaction volume of China's internet consumer finance market reached six billion yuan, most of which consisted of P2P consumer credit. In 2014, e-commerce giants entered the field for the first time. JD.com took the lead in launching its "IOU service" at the beginning of the year, while Tmall followed this with its "instalment payment service" later the same year.

At present, China's internet consumer finance market is undergoing a transition from the initial stage of development to the outbreak period. Moreover, online wealth-management currently has the mainstream position in the market. As of the end of June 2017, the number of Chinese internet users purchasing online wealth-management products reached 126 million, an increase of 27.24 million compared to the end of 2016. Accordingly, the internet wealth-management utilisation rate rose from 13.5% to 16.8%.

In 2016, the State Council officially issued the *Plan to Implement Special Rectification Work on Internet Finance Risks*, after which certain high-yield, high-risk, and inferior wealth management

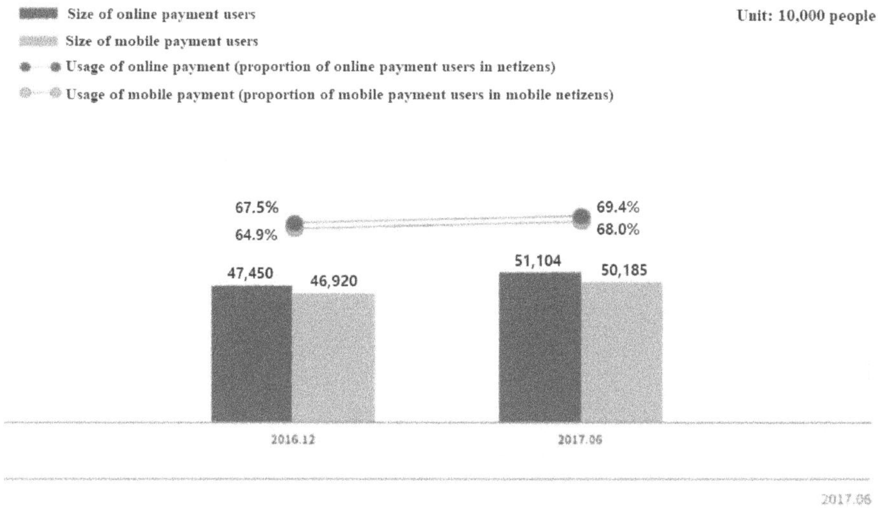

Figure 2-7: Online payment/mobile online payment user size and usage, December 2016–June 2017

Source: CNNIC Statistical Survey on Internet Development in China

products provided by some online platforms were gradually withdrawn from the market. Accordingly, the return rate of the internet wealth-management industry fell back to a reasonable level. In June 2017, the rectification work was extended for a year, while the transformation and standardisation of the internet-financing industry continued to increase.

As of June 2017, the number of people using online payment methods in China reached 511 million, an increase of 36.54 million compared to the end of December 2016. Indeed, the proportion of internet users in China making payments online increased from 64.9% to 68.0%, of which the number of mobile-payment users reached 502 million, with the proportion of users increasing from 67.5% to 69.4%.

In terms of consumer credit, the forceful entry of e-commerce giants into the market has resulted in significant changes to the market landscape. With the market entry of JD.com and Tmall, the scale of consumer credit transactions in 2014 exceeded 16 billion yuan, a growth rate of more than 170%. Indeed, more and more platform-based internet companies are joining the market, resulting in the rapid growth of consumer finance transactions.

Section Four: Evolution of Cyber Security

While the Internet provides reliable and transparent information, it also hides the darkness. With its evolution, people are faced with associated security problems and threats while enjoying the convenience it brings.

I. *Cyber Security Awareness*

Article 76, paragraph 2 of the 2016 *Cyber Security Law of the People's Republic of China* suggests that "cyber security refers to preventing attacks, intrusions, interference, destruction, and illegal use of the Internet and accidents by taking necessary measures to make the Internet stable and reliable, and to ensure the integrity, confidentiality, and availability of online data". This is the first legal definition of "cyber security" in the world.

On the one hand, research on cyber security must start from practice; on the other hand, it must also take into consideration network theory, information theory, and sovereignty theory. In the modern era, cyber security is the premise and guarantee of national security. Therefore, national security in all aspects can only be guaranteed by studying the security norms of the four fundamental elements of a network and by comprehensively improving the Internet's security capabilities, especially by scientifically assessing both the state and capacity of cyber security through regulating the generation, acquisition, processing, disposition, dissemination, and storage of cyber information.

1. *Understanding the New Features of Cyber Security*

In order to understand cyber security from the perspective of national security, it is necessary to recognise the technical features outlined below.

(1) Immediacy. Different from the traditional information-exchange mode, the sender and receiver of cyber information communicate synchronously at the speed of light, with virtually zero lag. This means that, while safeguarding cyber security, it is necessary to adopt the same review method used for the traditional information-transfer process and media release, as well as to carry out top-level security design to safeguard the national cyber "frontier", focusing on the four elements of the Internet in the process.
(2) Boundary. Cyber information not only features a temporal state in time, but it also represents a so-called virtual state of discrete, random distribution, and multi-terminal interconnections in terms of space. Due to the global interconnection of the Internet, it is difficult for a single country to draw a clear sovereign border in safeguarding its cyber security. Indeed, only by fully grasping the four fundamental elements of a network and by having the corresponding technical capabilities to establish the rule of law in cyberspace from said four aspects — i.e. independent logical connection in network, independent network chip technology, independent network system development, and independent jurisdiction of network users — can cyberspace be expected to be in a secure state. If the above four capabilities are not available, then the boundaries of cyber security will not be clarified, nor will they be safeguarded.

2. *Guarding Against New Threats to Cyber Security*

To understand cyber threats from the perspective of national security, it is necessary to first recognise the practical risks outlined below.

(1) Technical Differences. Obviously, there are risks that the hardware part of cyberspace may be destroyed. In order to occupy the commanding heights of the information era, countries all over the world have issued national cyber security plans, procedures, or strategies on different levels in order to

actively promote infrastructure construction within their national cyber sovereignty. However, in underdeveloped countries and regions, roughly two–thirds of the world's population are removed from the "information society" due to an insufficiency of the hardware components required to organise the Internet. Some countries try to maintain their own cyberspace sovereignty through substantial control over both hardware components and information software, since they cannot have access to the authority over the logical connection part. At the same time, said countries propose international network co-governance to force the international community to reshare or redistribute administration authority over the logical connection part of the Internet.

(2) Monopoly Game. Only through the rules and standards established by the data exchange between operational computers running in different geographic coordinates to enable interconnection between different systems and subjects in the network can we finally achieve the purpose of data-information sharing. Indeed, the management of these protocols, standards, and IP addresses belongs to different agencies, which are controlled by different international organisations and even sovereign states. The US has control of the basic logical connection system of the Internet through ICANN. International organisations, such as the International Telecommunication Union (ITU), the United Nations (UN) Internet Engineering Task Force (IETF), the World Wide Web Consortium (W3C), and the Internet Society (ISOC), compete with each other with respect to the governance of the Internet, constantly putting forward the idea of global cyberspace co-governance in the sense of a monopoly.

(3) Chaotic Surveillance. Information in cyberspace is in a highly open state, in which it can be easily transcribed, disseminated, tampered with, and monitored. Obviously, once destroyed, information loses its value. Cyberspace information is on a networked virtual platform. Different from information stored in other forms, it has a large number of potential infringers and its damage tends to expand rapidly.

Hence, it is difficult to identify the subject of rights and the person responsible for the infringement of information; moreover, it is even more difficult to carry out legal protection and accountability.

(4) The Freedom of Anonymity. Agencies and natural persons as users (along with their mirroring devices and agent software and hardware) fall within the jurisdiction of national laws of different countries because of the territorial principle. As a result, this kind of legal conflict between countries (caused by the sharing and dissemination of information resources) is unavoidable. Accordingly, it is important to identify how to effectively regulate users' anonymous online activities, as well as to promote global governance of cyber security and establish the jurisdiction of every country in terms of cyberspace information-protection issues, so as to resolve the problems associated with conflicting international laws. In reality, cyberspace users, operators, and sovereigns often transcend their respective national boundaries, so it is necessary to clarify their cyberspace rights under different circumstances and the corresponding rights of remedy for illegal activities.[20]

3. *New Practices for Exercising Cyberspace Sovereignty*

Generally speaking, the five major security threats to contemporary sovereign states come from the sea, land, air, space, and cyberspace, while traditional international laws corresponding to sovereign security correspond to the five traditional security aspects of nuclear weapons, chemical weapons, regular weapons, humanity, and international peacekeeping. The five frontier areas of non-traditional security threats to traditional sovereignty are outer space, cyberspace, counter-terrorism, finance and new energy. Therefore, cyberspace sovereignty is a new kind of sovereignty, which is

[20] Zhao, H. R., Yang, Y. Z., & Zhang, Sh. Sh. (2016). Basic Theoretical Construct for China's "Cybersecurity Law". *Cognition and Practice* (1), 43.

derived from the emerging non-traditional security category. In the absence of an international cyberspace convention, countries carry out corresponding legislation and policy declarations based on cyberspace sovereignty.

(1) At the level of multilateral non-governmental international organisations and the UN, the International Cyber Security Protection Alliance (ICSPA), a global non-profit organisation founded in July 2011, is a good attempt at transnational cooperation in cyber security.

In 2002, the UN General Assembly also mentioned "building the awareness and culture of cyber security" in its discussions. In May 2006, UN Secretary-General Kofi Annan reiterated the importance of "building a global culture of cyber security" in his speech. In 2007, the International Telecommunication Union launched the Global Cybersecurity Agenda. In 2012, the UN's group of governmental experts submitted the report *Developments in the Field of Information and Telecommunications in the Context of International Security*, emphasising that information security is one of the most serious challenges in the 21st century.[21]

(2) At the level of regional rule of law, on 27 April 2016, the European Parliament released *On the Protection of Natural Persons with Regard to the Processing of Personal Data and on the Free Movement of Such Data*; i.e. the *General Data Protection Regulation* (GDPR). Within the following two years, 28 member states of the European Union (EU) converted the GDPR clauses into domestic laws and established unified rules for data-information storage, identification, classification, and transmission. In 2018, the regulation took effect in the EU.

(3) At the level of rule of law in different countries, apart from the US effort to strengthen domestic legislation in cyberspace, Britain promulgated the *Terrorism Act 2000* in February 2000, which

[21] Zhao, H. R. (2015). A Brief Analysis of "Four-Dimensional Overall View of the Rule of Law in Cyberspace". *w* (7), 43.

explicitly put forward the concept of combating "cyberterrorism" and regarded hacking activities affecting the interests of the government or society as cyberterrorism. Germany formulated the *National Plan for Information Infrastructure Protection* in 2005 and Sweden published the *Strategy to Improve Internet Security in Sweden* in 2006. Europol released the *Organized Crime Threat Assessment* in May 2011, which regulated issues related to cybercrimes, including credit-card fraud, audio and video piracy, illicit-drug synthesis and circulation, endangered-species smuggling, human trafficking, and money laundering.

Obviously, the technological capability of a country determines its cyberspace sovereignty capability. The law, which is a balance of the game of interests of all parties, will regulate the existing order for a long period of time. However, the rapid development of information technology, especially under the guidance of specific needs, is similar to a wild horse, with the reins of law lagging behind.

II. *Recognising Cyber Threats*

In the face of international cyber conflicts, only with the strength of the government can a fair and reasonable world order in cyberspace be built. For example, the Computer Emergency Response Team (CERT), an international organisation responsible for handling computer and network security incidents, has founded the Forum of Incident Response and Security Teams (FISRT) in order to promote cooperation among CERT organisations in all countries with respect to addressing transnational attacks on networks. As these CERT organisations are non-governmental organisations (NGOs), which belong to "stakeholders" in the eye of ICANN in the US, they can only play the role of helping attacked enterprises carry out emergency response. In other words, they do not have the technology nor credibility to undertake tasks such as tracing domain names and verifying evidence. Therefore, transnational cybercrimes have become normalised due to the lack of appropriate law and regulation.

Regional military alliances have torn apart mutual trust in the global cyberspace. The US transferred the "EINSTEIN system" over to NATO (North Atlantic Treaty Organization) countries in order to build a cyber defence system in said countries. On the surface, this is a simple kind of cyber technology export. In fact, behind such exports, the information sharing of defence systems and security interests takes place, by virtue of which defence systems can become interoperable in cyberspace. This is equivalent to building a military alliance in cyberspace. Indeed, the networks of a military alliance in cyberspace must be linked with non-allied countries. For example, information sent from China to Brazil must be addressed through root servers in the US, which means that, during wartime, a military alliance in cyberspace can attack other countries' networks and can even turn other countries into "isolated islands in cyberspace".

Because cyberspace can be used for both military and civilian purposes, normal civilian activities and social life can face sudden military threats. The US has set up the PRISM System and Upstream System to monitor data on the Internet. Obviously, these surveillance systems are set up in the same networks built by telecom and network operators. Without exerting coercive forces by the sovereignty, relevant operators would never cooperate with it. Similarly, in the PRISM programme, the nine major US internet enterprises must provide internet information to the National Security Agency in accordance with the *Patriot Act*. This means that, domestically speaking, cyberspace hegemony also relies on the sovereign coercive force in order to fulfil its role.

As a new space of shared interests, global cyberspace requires the co-governance of the international community. Before the 21st century, internet users were small in number, with the majority of them accessing the Internet with a private identity. Originally, the Internet was an experimental virtual-communication cyberspace, and the governments of all countries did not properly understand it. However, with the continuous development of cyber-information technology, the corresponding interests of all countries were attracted to the Internet, and their political, economic, cultural, social, national defence, and other affairs were gradually brought into cyberspace. Therefore, the relevant countries have begun to exercise their sovereign jurisdiction over the Internet. As cyberspace is naturally interconnected, it objectively requires sovereign states to negotiate and coordinate with each other, which will inevitably lead to the formation of a global cyber system that is co-governed by the international community.

There are two prerequisites for the theoretical identification and rule of law behind the formation of a cyber system that is co-governed by the international community: (i) strengthening the states' international legal status in the cyber era and (ii) establishing the states' cyber sovereignty. The US emphasises the concept of "stakeholders", promoting the reform of ICANN in accordance with the plan of global stakeholders. On the surface, it advocates the idea that non-state actors should dominate the management of cyberspace. However, in reality, the US still adopts the hegemony model "dominated by information powers". This is because the majority of powerful stakeholders in the world are found in information powers.

The US is the hegemonic leader of information powers. Indeed, under its policy orientation, the strong will get stronger and the weak will get weaker. In other words, weak-information countries will gradually lose the opportunity to independently safeguard cyber sovereignty and security. Accordingly, only by addressing the security of national sovereignty, equally respecting cyber sovereignty, and allowing countries (regardless of their strength in terms of information technology) to have a voice and enjoy the technological dividends of the cyber era can a fair and reasonable world order in cyberspace be established.

To understand the threat to cyber security in an all-encompassing manner, and to strive to build a fair and reasonable world order in cyberspace, it is necessary to understand the connection, structure, protocol, and element systems of cyberspace on the basis of traditional information and cyber technologies. In other words, grasping the four elements of a network is required to safeguard the overall security of cyberspace sovereignty.

First, with regard to its subject element, through the redistribution of the domain name system (DNS), the Internet has changed the traditional identity of people accessing the network. With regard to the logical connection security of the subjects in cyberspace, countries need to build cyber sovereignty that is both "interconnected" and "autonomous", reconsider the security of the compatible logical connections of domain names in the top-level architecture, fully participate in the innovation of connection protocols at all levels (including TCP/IP), cooperate to build network-connection infrastructure over traditional geography, and embrace the scientific and technological opportunities brought about by the expansion of domain names by IPv6+ and even IPv9.

Second, with regard to its platform element, by constantly updating various interconnection protocols, the Internet has extended the maximum compatibility of various platform devices that can access it. With regard to the security of the hardware terminals of network platforms, especially the design of chips, all countries are actively developing advanced chips and routing terminals and other advanced equipment in an independent manner. Moreover, they are also attempting to innovate new standards of peripheral equipment, with some beginning to develop new functions of space-based routers and seeking new breakthroughs in quantum computing.

Third, with regard to its activity element, through asymmetric technologies, such as address tracing, identity recognition, and the "backdoor" of chips, the Internet has expanded the gap of people's ability to control information. Indeed, powerful cyber actors can easily steal the cyber information of others and infringe personal privacy. With regard to the security of user behaviour, all governments should promote access identity dynamic registration and identification technology, as well as popularise real-name technology on demand and strive to improve the rule of law in terms of the order of network activities.

Finally, with regard to its object element, the Internet once caused imbalances in the distribution of global data storage due to the differences between the first and the second in information coding and storage technology. With regard to the data security management of cyber objects, all countries are increasingly

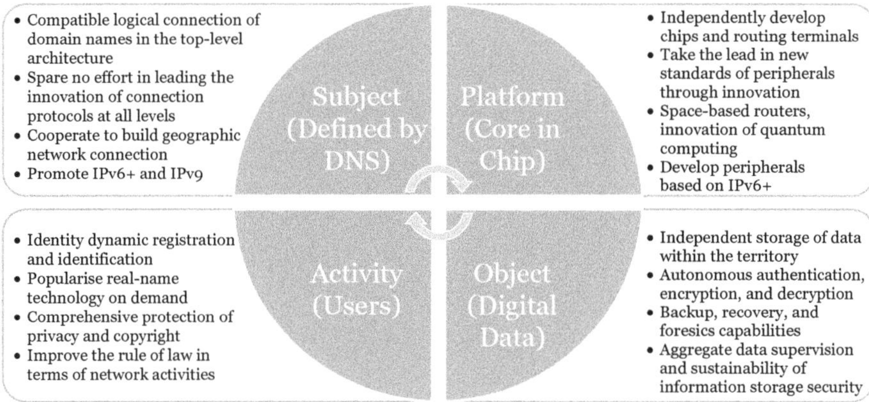

Figure 2-8: The typology of monitoring threats to cyber security through the four elements of a network

emphasising its various capabilities, such as self-storage, self-authentication, encryption, and decryption. Moreover, they are also increasingly emphasising the trusted computing of domestic data and improving the ability of backup, recovery, and forensics with respect to information data, as well as pursuing aggregate data supervision and exploring the sustainability of information-storage security.

In other words, the four elements of a network are responsible for controlling the overall security of cyber sovereignty in a comprehensive and exhaustive way. At present, in order to cope with the potential threats to information security brought about by the Internet, countries across the world are striving to enhance their overall understanding of cyberspace, promoting their own cyber security legislation, and enacting laws with their own respective emphasis to maintain logical-connection security, hardware-terminal security, user-behaviour security, and data-management security of the four elements of a network. In other words, the maintenance of cyber security shall be achieved through the four elements of a network in a comprehensive way, otherwise the overall security of cyber sovereignty cannot be realised.

Chapter Three
Cyber Security

Different countries have different perceptions and demands for cyber security. In order to recognise, express, and exchange their respective views toward cyber risks and defend cyber threats across the world, relevant organisations and member states of the United Nations (UN) have summarised their own cyber security interests and policy stances.

Section One: The View of the UN

Since the Information Society and Development Conference in South Africa and the Ministerial Conference on Terrorism in Paris in 1996, the UN has started to pay attention to the impact of transnational cyber incidents on national security, connecting national security to the development of information society.

I. *The Interests of World Peace*

Both domestic and foreign threats to cyber security would have an impact on the stability of international order and thus pose a threat to world peace. In 1999, the 53rd UN General Assembly adopted the *Developments in the Field of Information and Telecommunications in the Context of International Security* (A/

RES/53/70), which advocated the positions outlined below from the perspective of the UN.

1. *Involving International Interests*

The UN noticed that "the dissemination and use of information technologies and means affect the interests of the entire international community".

2. *Maintaining International Security*

The UN expressed the concern that "informational technologies and means can potentially be used for purposes that are inconsistent with the objectives of maintaining international stability and security and may adversely affect the security of states".

3. *Communicating the Positions of All Countries*

The UN called on all member states to inform the secretary-general of their "definition of basic notions related to information security", "general appreciation of the issues of information security", "advisability of developing international principles that would enhance the security of global information and telecommunications systems", and to submit reports to the UN General Assembly.

4. *Establishing the Agenda of the General Assembly*

The UN decided to include the item entitled "Developments in the field of information and telecommunications in the context of international security" into the UN General Assembly agenda.

II. *Cyberspace Sovereignty*

On 12 December 2003, the *Declaration of Principles* adopted by the UN World Summit on the Information Society in Geneva clearly stated that "policy authority for Internet-related public-policy issues is the sovereign right of states. They have rights and responsibilities for international Internet-related public-policy issues." It placed emphasis on "preventing the potential use of ICTs (information and communications technology) for purposes that are inconsistent with the objectives of maintaining international stability and security".

After 20 years of reflection, expression, mediation, and games, the 70th UN General Assembly formulated the *Report of the Group of Governmental Experts on Developments in the Field of Information and Telecommunications in the Context of International Security* (hereinafter referred to as the *Report of the Group of Experts*) (A/70/174). The *Report of the Group of Experts* emphasised the importance of applying the UN Charter and the principle of sovereignty to cyberspace.

1. *The Principle of Sovereignty*

In the *Report of the Group of Experts*, the UN General Assembly confirmed the basic principle of applying national sovereignty and international law to information and activities related to communications technologies (ICTs) and ICT infrastructure: the UN Charter and principle of sovereignty are the basis for increased security in the use of ICTs by states.

2. *The Principle of Security*

When refining the overall view of cyberspace, the *Report of the Group of Experts* came up with five principles of international ICT environment in the name of the UN General Assembly: an open, secure, stable, accessible, and peaceful ICT environment is essential for all and requires effective cooperation among states to reduce risks to international peace and security.

3. *Consensus on Cyberspace and Information*

In terms of the definition of cyberspace, the *Report of the Group of Experts* reached some consensus in the name of the UN General

Assembly. More specifically, they reached consensus on ICT-related activities and on ICT infrastructure within their territory (abbreviated as activity consensus and platform consensus), linking these two elements with state sovereignty and international law.

4. *Sovereign Jurisdiction*

In terms of the application and jurisdiction of cyberspace sovereignty, the *Report of the Group of Experts* reached some consensus on cyberspace sovereign jurisdiction in the name of the UN General Assembly: "27. State sovereignty and international norms and principles that flow from sovereignty apply to the conduct by states of ICT-related activities and to their jurisdiction over ICT infrastructure within their territory."

5. *Maintaining Security*

The *Report of the Group of Experts* also pointed out that the cooperation among sovereign states is vital in maintaining global cyber security: 17. States should consider additional confidence-building measures that would strengthen cooperation on a bilateral, subregional, regional, and multilateral basis. These could include voluntary agreements by states to:

"a. Strengthen cooperative mechanisms between relevant agencies to address ICT security incidents and develop additional technical, legal and diplomatic mechanisms to address ICT infrastructure-related requests, including the consideration of exchanges of personnel in areas such as incident response and law enforcement, as appropriate, and encouraging exchanges between research and academic institutions.

"b. Enhance cooperation, including the development of focal points for the exchange of information on malicious ICT use and the provision of assistance in investigations.

"c. Establish a national computer emergency-response team and/or cybersecurity incident-response team, or officially designate an organisation to fulfil this role. States may wish to consider such bodies within their definition of critical infrastructure. States should support and facilitate the functioning of, and cooperation among, such national response teams and other authorised bodies.

"d. Expand and support practices in computer emergency-response team and cybersecurity incident-response team cooperation, as appropriate, such as information exchange about vulnerabilities, attack patterns and best practices for mitigating attacks, including coordinating responses, organising exercises, supporting the handling of ICT-related incidents and enhancing regional and sector-based cooperation.

"e. Cooperate, in a manner consistent with national and international law, with requests from other states in investigating ICT-related crime or the use of ICTs for terrorist purposes, or to mitigate malicious ICT activity emanating from their territory."

The UN document demonstrates that only through the action of the governments of sovereign states, instead of the action of enterprises alone, can the world cooperate with respect to addressing transnational cyber risks as well as establish a co-governance system for cyberspace and information security. Unfortunately, the *Report of the Group of Experts* was just an appeal and it did not win US support, which originally invented the network. As a result, the report cannot effectively produce valid international laws.

Some subordinate UN organisations have been always discussing cyber security issues. From 21 to 26 April 2016, the UN Commission on International Trade Law (UNCITRAL) held the first Colloquium on Identity Management and Trust Services at the Vienna International Conference Centre in Austria. The conference aimed to achieve a consensus and feasible solution for establishing unified laws and regulations for future transnational identity management brought about by global trade. Its importance can be compared with the establishment of global rules for the mutual recognition of electronic passports.

Generally speaking, starting from the activity consensus and platform consensus, the UN will embark on a journey seeking the international co-governance of cyberspace. To be sure, these two elements are still conservatively limited to a few elements of cyberspace, such as "activities" and "platforms", which shows that the UN has yet to fully reach a general consensus on cyberspace. The activity and platform consensuses in cyberspace are rooted in the territorial sovereignty of all states, despite the fact that said states still hold different opinions about the "subject" and "object" of cyberspace with respect to their own territories.

Section Two: The Positions of All States

In 1999, the 53rd UN General Assembly adopted the *Developments in the Field of Information and Telecommunications in the Context of International Security* (A/RES/53/70), and, in 2015, the 70th UN General Assembly formulated the *Report of the Group of Governmental Experts on Developments in the Field of Information and Telecommunications in the Context of International Security* (A/70/174). During these 16 years, the UN received reports on information security and cyberspace sovereignty from its member states, among which the official positions of Western countries and non-Western countries are quite different.

I. *The Positions of Western Countries*[1]

1. *Canada*

Cyberspace has enhanced social interaction and transformed industries and governments, and continues to be an engine of economic growth, innovation, and social development. It has also introduced new threats and challenges to our society.

[1] In this book, "Western countries" refers to the United States (US) and countries with a military alliance with the US, e.g. NATO (North Atlantic Treaty Organization) countries, Japan, and South Korea.

Canada reiterates the clear affirmation of the applicability of international law in cyberspace as the cornerstone of norms and principles of responsible behaviour of states. Addressing the security of information and communications technology must go hand-in-hand with respect for human rights and fundamental freedoms.

Canada is committed to a secure Internet by means of implementing the national cyber security strategy and action plan. It has developed a cyber-incident management framework to provide a consolidated national approach to the management and coordination of potential or existing cyber threats or incidents; it has released new anti-spam law; it supports cyber security capacity-building projects, including establishing computer security incident-response teams; and it has also joined the Global Forum on Cyber Expertise as a founding member.

Canada supports the efforts of NATO (North Atlantic Treaty Organization) to strengthen the alliance on cyber security and that of individual allies. It works within the Regional Forum of the Association of Southeast Asian Nations (ASEAN) to build capacity; it partners with the United States to implement a cyber security action plan; and it also participates in initiatives to combat cyber-crime in the Group of Seven, the United Nations Office on Drugs and Crime, the Organization of American States (OAS), and ASEAN. Canada is a member of the Global Alliance against Child Sexual Abuse Online and suggests that all member states shall refer to the Council of Europe Convention on Cybercrime. (Position as of 4 June 2015)

2. *Germany*

An open, free, secure, and reliable Internet offers great opportunities for economic growth, social development, and scientific progress, as well as for the promotion of democracy, good governance, and the rule of law. At the same time, concerns are growing about international security risks emanating from cyberspace. Recent months have seen an increase in malicious software activities. Attacks against critical infrastructures, in particular, could have severe consequences. An all-out "cyber war" seems unlikely at present. However, the limited use of cyber capabilities as part of a larger war-fighting effort, including in the context of hybrid conflicts, has become a reality. In addition, incidents in cyberspace may escalate into real-world conflict.

Germany advocates a three-pronged approach to manoeuvre in that environment. First, the UN is the crucial forum for establishing the rules of responsible state behaviour in cyberspace. Second, international law, particularly the Charter of the United Nations and the "Law of Armed Conflict", is applicable in cyberspace. Third, Germany attaches the utmost importance to regional organisations. In 2013, the Organization for Security and Cooperation in Europe agreed on an initial set of cyber confidence-building measures. As part of its chairmanship of the organisation in 2016, Germany planned to prioritise cyber security and was working on an "information technology security" act to increase cyber resilience at the national level. The draft text of said act defines minimum requirements for the information-technology security of critical infrastructure. Moreover, it establishes an obligation to report significant incidents with a view of improving the overall security of systems and public protection in general. (Position as of 27 May 2015)

3. *The Netherlands*

In the view of the Netherlands, security would be served by the broad acceptance of and adherence to a set of norms of responsible behaviour of states. However, it is still necessary to enhance states' understanding of how existing international law and norms for the rules of conduct for states apply to cyberspace, and to define norms or additional measures of self-restraint or mutual assistance, particularly the idea to establish special normative protection for certain systems and networks, including critical infrastructure providing essential civilian services, civilian incident response structures, and certain critical components of the global Internet. As the Internet has become a strategic asset for all of us, broad international discussion on those topics is needed. (Position as of 29 May 2015)

4. *Portugal*

While progress in the fields of information and telecommunications means more opportunities for the development of civilisation, cooperation among states, the enhancement of the creative potential of humankind, and the circulation of information in the global community, on the other hand, Portugal finds that those technologies and means can potentially be used for purposes inconsistent with international stability and security, and may adversely affect the national integrity of states. Portugal considers that security in network information is important and has been increasing. It is necessary to highlight the increasing efforts to implement legislation in network security and integrity through the adoption of risk-assessment methods, which require the introduction of adequate cooperative security measures at the technical and organisational levels.

At the conceptual level, it is important to reinforce the idea that regulation should stem primarily from international rules. At the international level, it is important to increase information-sharing and the conduct of training exercises in the field in border areas. It is crucial to promote information-sharing among all interested parties (both public and private), taking into account the wider context of globalisation.

At the national level, Portugal's efforts have been focused on the conduct of joint exercises in which public and private entities have participated in the promotion of technical standardisation. Nevertheless, there are difficulties relating to the training and maintenance of human resources connected to those activities. There is a need to facilitate the access to knowledge and to promote collective training in several areas, including security among all the major interested parties. (Position as of 24 April 2015)

5. *Republic of Korea*

Cyberspace is a new horizon with endless possibilities, offering unprecedented economic and social benefits. However, on account of its open, anonymous, and borderless nature, cyber threats are emerging as a serious challenge to international security.

The Republic of Korea has been experiencing a series of cyber-attacks, including the recent attacks on its nuclear power plant operator in 2014. To respond more effectively to cyber threats, the Republic of Korea introduced comprehensive plans to enhance its cyber security posture in March 2015 and created the post of presidential secretary for cyber security affairs. The Republic of Korea firmly believes that it is important to agree on a set of international norms applied to cyberspace and implement confidence- and cyber capacity-building measures. In that respect, the Republic of Korea welcomes the results submitted in the 2013 report by the Group of Governmental Experts on Developments in the Field of Information and Telecommunications in the Context of International Security, which recognised the possibility of applying international law to state behaviour in cyberspace, and it expects further discussions on how the agreed principles can be applied to state behaviour in cyberspace. The Republic of Korea hosted the Asia-Pacific Regional Seminar on International Law and State Behaviour in Cyberspace in 2014, together with the UN Institute for Disarmament Research, providing an opportunity for countries in the region to discuss cyber security-related matters. The government of the Republic of Korea has also worked to strengthen bilateral and trilateral cooperation with key countries and is actively participating in regional and international forums on cyber issues, such as the ASEAN Regional Forum and the Group of Governmental Experts of the UN. As the host of the Seoul Conference on Cyberspace held in 2013, the Republic of Korea closely cooperated with the Netherlands in preparation for the Global Conference on Cyberspace held in the

Hague in 2015, and it will continue its contribution to the London Process Conferences. (Position as of 11 June 2015)

6. *Spain*

Spain considers that information and communication technologies provide essential support for all societies worldwide but that globalisation entails serious risks and threats such as cyberespionage, cyberterrorism, "hacktivism", and cyberwarfare. Following the establishment of the National Cybersecurity Council, Spain has continued to make progress in the development of plans derived from the National Cybersecurity Strategy to increase prevention, protection, detection, analysis, response, recovery, and coordination capacities in the face of cyber threats. Spain continues to participate actively in the promotion of international cooperation and is closely monitoring all strategic initiatives that affect cyber security, both in the European Union and in major international forums such as the Organization for Security and Cooperation in Europe, NATO, and the Council of Europe. Spain continues to uphold the importance of the UN in the process of achieving international consensus on cyber security issues and supports the holding of institutionalised dialogue, which should include other international forums, to promote regional cooperation and the establishment of global standards, best practices, rules of conduct among states, and confidence-building measures, with the ultimate goal of guaranteeing the peaceful and secure use of information technologies.

Spain considers that states should achieve consensus in four areas. First, they should develop confidence-building measures of a cooperative nature with the ultimate goal of promoting transparency among states in the area of cyber security and strengthening their capacity to neutralise any possible attacks identified as coming from third countries. Second, Spain considers that states should continue reflecting on how the principles and norms of international law should be interpreted and applied in cyberspace, especially those relating to the threat or use of force, humanitarian law, and the protection of the fundamental rights and freedoms of the individual. Third, Spain considers that international cooperation should be strengthened by improving channels of communication, establishing mechanisms for the coordination of Computer Emergency Response Teams, carrying out joint exercises and other similar operations, and promoting judicial and police cooperation mechanisms. Finally, capacity-building in countries where it is needed should continue to be encouraged and assistance should be provided to recipient states for the development of national laws establishing cyber security standards. (Position as of 26 May 2015)

7. *United Kingdom of Great Britain and Northern Ireland*

The United Kingdom (UK) uses its preferred terminology of "cyber security" and related concepts throughout its response, to avoid confusion given the different interpretations of the term "information security" in this context. The UK recognises that cyberspace is a fundamental element of critical national and international infrastructure and an essential foundation for economic and social activity online. Actual and potential threats posed by activities in cyberspace are of great concern.

The UK published its national cyber security strategy in November 2011: the UK continues to take a leading role in the international debate on cyber security. The UK has provided experts for all four Groups of Governmental Experts on Developments in the Field of Information and Telecommunications in the Context of International Security and consider that the consensus report of the previous Group showed valuable progress in reaching common understandings on norms of state behaviour in cyberspace and in affirming the applicability of international law in cyberspace. The UK also welcomes continued discussion of potential future confidence-building measures in cyberspace at the Organization for Security and Cooperation in Europe to build on those successfully negotiated in 2013, and similar work in other regional organisations. The UK looks forward to further participation in strengthening capability and international cooperation on cyber security. (Position as of 29 May 2015)

II. *The Positions of Non-Western Countries*

1. *Cuba*

Information technologies and means can potentially be used for purposes that are inconsistent with the objectives of maintaining international stability and security and may adversely affect the integrity of the infrastructure of states to the detriment of their security in both civil and military fields. It is necessary to prevent the use of information resources or technologies for criminal or terrorist purposes.

Cuba expresses its great concern over the covert and illegal use, by individuals, organisations, and states, of the computer systems of other nations for the purpose of attacking third countries, because of its potential for triggering international conflicts. Joint cooperation between all states is the only way to prevent and tackle these novel threats and to avoid cyberspace from turning into a theatre of military operations. The use of telecommunications with the declared or hidden intent of undermining the legal and political order of states is a violation of internationally recognised norms in this area and can give rise to tensions and situations that are not conducive to international peace and security. The peaceful use of information and communication technologies in compliance with the Charter of the United Nations and international law was also reaffirmed and it was stressed that these technologies should never be used with the purpose of subverting societies or creating situations that could promote conflicts between states. Nevertheless, those efforts are threatened by the constant radio and television broadcasts transmitted by the government of the United States against Cuba, in contravention of the purposes and principles of the Charter of the United Nations and various regulations of the International Telecommunication Union. Furthermore, and of no less significance, these broadcasts violate the sovereignty of Cuba.

Cuba reiterates that the use of information as propaganda or for the purposes of destabilisation, with the aim of subverting the internal order of other states, violating their sovereignty, and meddling and interfering in their internal affairs, constitutes an illegal act and must cease. They reiterate their strongest rejection of the use of information and communication technologies in a manner contrary to international law, and all actions of that nature. They stress the importance of guaranteeing that the use of these technologies is fully consistent with the purposes and principles of the Charter of the United Nations and international law, in particular sovereignty, non-interference in internal affairs, and internationally recognised standards of coexistence between States. Cuba reiterates that international cooperation is essential for confronting the dangers associated with the misuse of information and communication technologies. Cuba also highlights the importance of the International Telecommunication Union in the intergovernmental debate on cyber security issues.

Cuba has established the Council of Computerization and Cybersecurity, directed by the highest state body: the government and the Communist Party of Cuba. (Position as of 26 May 2015)

2. *El Salvador*

The armed forces of El Salvador, within the context of information and telecommunications security, have a centralised independent management on voice, video, and data telecommunications in the public network. A perimeter information security team has been acquired and configured. In addition, there is an encryption system for handling official information in order to protect all information from any external agent that may attempt to infiltrate the system, as well as from cyberattacks. (Position as of 21 April 2015)

3. *Georgia*

Georgia puts information and cyber security high on its political agenda and considers addressing cyber threats an integral part of the national security policy, especially in view of widespread e-government reforms throughout the country and the increased dependence of its critical infrastructure on information and communications technology tools. Voicing those concerns, and in order to strengthen information security, the government of Georgia has introduced several strategic, legal, organisational, and institutional measures.

Cyber security is one of the main priorities of the state's security policy, and the protection of cyberspace is considered as important for national security as the protection of land, water, and airspace. A further step in institutionalising information security was the establishment of the Data Exchange Agency of the Ministry of Justice of Georgia, in 2010, as a central government entity responsible for the development and implementation of information and cybersecurity policies and standards. The national governmental computer emergency response teams were also established.

The legal and regulatory framework of Georgia on information security is composed of the Information Security Act and its supplementary sub-normative acts adopted between 2011 and 2012. A number of bilateral cooperation agreements and memorandums of understanding between the Data Exchange Agency and European Union Military Staff (from Austria, Estonia, Poland, etc.) as well as neighbouring countries (Azerbaijan, Armenia, the Republic of Moldova, Turkey, etc.) had been signed.

Georgia acknowledges the increased importance of regional and international cooperation mechanisms in order to address information security challenges. In that perspective, much effort should be directed to extend the number of international events dedicated to those topics of high importance, increase the level of trust with major interested parties, and continue to work on strategic doctrines and legal concepts with the engagement of the international community. (Position as of 26 May 2015)

4. *Panama*

Information and communications technologies today are expanding rapidly. As a result, technology and communications are gradually becoming a more accessible part of daily life. It is a fact that our lives are now linked to these developments in how communications are sent and how information is processed. The government of Panama has acted in accordance with this trend, adapting it to the specific needs of this security agency. For that reason, it has been carrying out technological improvements to establish more efficient and secure connectivity.

As part of these improvements, the government of Panama has gradually been developing a communications implementation plan, which includes network, security, and telephony elements. The government of Panama protects the integrity of its information in the area of the Internet, data, and telephony by means of infrastructure based on internal firewall platforms and through connection with the national multi-services network. The government of Panama uses secure firewall-mediated data sessions in order to ensure the confidentiality and protection of information.

Panama believes that as increasingly advanced telecommunications solutions are adapted to the security requirements of security agencies, those agencies will have access to tools that foster harmony in the field of information, based on both active and preventative measures. Security agencies should take advantage of this technological situation, given that they have the mission of protecting society at the local and international levels. (Position as of 3 June 2015)

5. *Peru*

The corporate data network of the Peruvian National Police maintains control over its different systems through various security policies at different levels of its organic and functional structure. With regard to information security, the corporate data network has been outsourced through the managed security service, which is run by a security operation centre. Role and identity engineering work is planned; this will allow unique access control for users, ensuring traceability and providing audit tools.

Efforts taken at the national level to strengthen information security include preventive measures such as designation of network administrators, staff training in information technology, software licensing for the servers of the National Police data centre, implementation of the "private cloud", information backup, implementation of redundant electrical system (uninterrupted power supply), upgrading of electrical distribution panels and electrical connections, and outsourcing of perimeter security (external) in the event of attacks or denial of service.

Upgrading of the National Police technological platform and the police information systems, which are aimed at consolidating information, means effectively helping to improve national public security, as well as contributing to international security through the availability of services that ensure interoperability between countries.

Possible measures that could be taken by the international community to strengthen information security at the global level include standardisation of communication media, including with regard to the type of equipment and communication protocols; standardisation of a technology platform guaranteeing high availability, dedicated to interoperability among countries involved in international security; standardisation of information security mechanisms; within the concept of "field of information", the definition of risk factors existing in each country involved in international security and the possibility of establishing common goals with regard to what should be combated and/or curbed, with the creation of automated information mechanisms. For example, in the case of the Peruvian State, issues such as drug trafficking, terrorism, organised crime, smuggling, money laundering, and trafficking would be included. (Position as of 30 June 2015)

6. *Qatar*

The State of Qatar continues to monitor existing and potential threats in the field of information security. It has set forth strategies to confront such threats in a manner consistent with the need to maintain the free flow of information. The State of Qatar believes that information security is crucial for national and global security. With a view to maintaining information security, the State of Qatar has taken a range of measures to update relevant technologies and improve legislation, regulation, and enforcement. It also works to coordinate and cooperate on relevant issues at the regional and international levels, provided that domestic laws allow this. The State of Qatar believes that the international community can contribute to information security by continuing to work towards a binding international instrument to safeguard information security. Such an instrument should provide for the development of hacker-proof programmes and maintain the coherence of information systems. (Position as of 24 June 2015)

Section Three: The Concealed Positions of the United States

For 20 years, the US, the inventor of the Internet, has shied away from expressing its official position on the overall definition of cyberspace at the UN, which could be attributed to its national security strategy or, perhaps, the common law tradition of its case law. The US lacks a legal definition of the Internet in the fields ranging from domestic laws to government policies. However, in the relevant dictionaries, policies, and national strategy documents of the US, some connotations and characteristics of the Internet have been highlighted in each fragmented definition.

I. *The Definition from an Academic Point of View*

The American *New World Encyclopedia* defines cyberspace as "a global domain within the information environment consisting of the interdependent network of information technology infrastructures, including the Internet, telecommunications networks, computer systems, and embedded processors and controllers". The term "cyberspace" was coined by a science-fiction writer, and it includes various virtual realities (i.e. simulated experiences that may be similar to or completely different from the real world), wherein the global domain of the cyberspace is highlighted.

On the IT (information technology) Law Wiki, it is stressed that the virtual nature of the cyberspace is derived from science fiction. The site notes the origin of the term cyberspace (also spelled cyber-space), which was coined by science fiction author William Gibson in the short story "Burning Chrome" and later used in his novel

Neuromancer (1984). It refers to "the virtual world created within a computer and the network to which it is attached" (also called a "computer-generated reality"). It includes the internal computer memory and wiring and the networks to which the computer is connected. He called cyberspace a "consensual hallucination".

II. *The Definition from the Official Point of View*

The National Security Presidential Directive 54/Homeland Security Presidential Directive 23 (NSPD-54/HSPD-23) defines cyberspace by placing emphasis on the inclusion of the Internet, telecommunication networks, computer systems, and critical industries, i.e. cyberspace is the interdependent network of information technology infrastructures and includes the Internet, telecommunications networks, computer systems, and embedded processors and controllers in critical industries. The word also usually refers to the virtual environment in which information interacts with people.[2]

The *National Strategy to Secure Cyberspace* (2003) released by the White House stresses that "cyberspace is the nervous system — the control system of our country. Cyberspace is composed of hundreds of thousands of interconnected computers, servers, routers, switches, and fibre optic cables that allow our critical infrastructures to work."

Section Four: The Viewpoints of the Shanghai Cooperation Organisation[3]

On 9 January 2015, UN permanent representatives from the six member states of the Shanghai Cooperation Organisation (SCO),

[2] *The National Security Presidential Directive 54/Homeland Security Presidential Directive 23 (NSPD-54/HSPD-23)*. Retrieved from http://itlaw.wikia.com/wiki/Cyber_Space; http://www.newworldencyclopedia.org/entry/Cyberspace, 23 April 2016.

[3] The SCO is a permanent intergovernmental international organisation, the creation of which was announced in 2001 by the Republic of Kazakhstan, People's

comprising China, Kazakhstan, Kyrgyzstan, Russia, Tajikistan, and Uzbekistan, sent a letter to the UN Secretary General to submit the upgraded version of the *International Code of Conduct for Information Security* (2015). The previous version had been jointly submitted by China, Russia, Tajikistan, and Uzbekistan to the 66th UN General Assembly in 2011; it had been highly valued and well received by the international community. Later, Kyrgyzstan and Kazakhstan joined the four countries to jointly submit the new Code.

The *International Code of Conduct for Information Security* (2015) comprehensively revises the 2011 version to fully take into account all views and suggestions of all parties. It underlines several international codes of conduct, including "progress in science and technology for civilian applications needs to be maintained and encouraged", "policy authority for internet-related public issues is the sovereign right of States", and "to assist developing countries in their efforts to enhance capacity-building on information security and to close the digital divide" for the purpose of building a peaceful, secure, open, and cooperative information space to ensure that information and networks can promote human development and people's wellbeing as well as maintain international peace and security. The Code specifies its proposition from eight aspects, as follows:

To encourage information science and technology for civilian application. The Code opines that "scientific and technological

---

Republic of China, Kyrgyz Republic, Russian Federation, Republic of Tajikistan, and Republic of Uzbekistan based on the SCO Charter. The organisation has two permanent bodies: the SCO Secretariat based in Beijing and the Executive Committee of the Regional Anti-Terrorist Structure based in Tashkent. As of 2019, the SCO comprises eight member states, namely the Republic of India, Republic of Kazakhstan, People's Republic of China, Kyrgyz Republic, Islamic Republic of Pakistan, Russian Federation, Republic of Tajikistan, and Republic of Uzbekistan; four observer states, namely the Islamic Republic of Afghanistan, Republic of Belarus, Islamic Republic of Iran, and Republic of Mongolia; and six dialogue partners, namely the Republic of Azerbaijan, Republic of Armenia, Kingdom of Cambodia, Federal Democratic Republic of Nepal, Republic of Turkey, and Democratic Socialist Republic of Sri Lanka. See http://chn.sectsco.org/.

developments could have both civilian and military applications and that progress in science and technology for civilian applications needs to be maintained and encouraged"; this is necessary "to prevent the potential use of information and communication technologies for purposes that are inconsistent with the objectives of maintaining international stability and security and may adversely affect the integrity of the infrastructure within States, to the detriment of their security". The Code also underlines "the need for enhanced coordination and cooperation among States in combating the criminal misuse of information technologies and, in that context, stressing the role that can be played by the United Nations and other international and regional organisations".

To comply with the principles of sovereignty and international law. The 2015 version of the Code reaffirms that "policy authority for internet-related public issues is the sovereign right of States, which have rights and responsibilities for international internet-related public policy issues". According to the Code, it is imperative to "develop a common understanding of how norms are derived from existing international law relevant to the use of information and communication technologies by States... Each State voluntarily subscribing to this Code of Conduct pledges to comply with the Charter of the UN and universally recognised norms governing international relations that enshrine, inter alia, respect for the sovereignty, territorial integrity and political independence of all States, respect for human rights and fundamental freedoms, and respect for the diversity of history, culture, and social systems of all countries".

To close the digital divide by facilitating the transfer of information technology. The 2015 Code recognises that "confidence and security in the use of information and communication technologies are among the main pillars of the information society, that a global culture of cyber security needs to be encouraged, promoted and developed and that given the unique attributes of information and communication technologies, additional norms could be developed over time". It also notes that it is necessary to "enhance efforts to close the digital divide by facilitating the transfer of information technology and capacity-building to developing countries in the areas of cyber security best practices and training".

Not to threaten peace or interfere in internal affairs of other states; cooperate in combating terrorism. Each State voluntarily subscribing to this Code of Conduct pledges not to use information and communications technologies and information and communications networks to carry out activities that run counter to the task of maintaining international peace and security; not to use information and communications technologies and information and communications networks to interfere in the internal affairs of other States or with the aim of undermining their political, economic, and social stability; to cooperate in combating criminal and terrorist activities that use information and communications technologies and information and communications networks as well as in curbing the dissemination of information that incites terrorism, separatism, or extremism or that inflames hatred on ethnic, racial, or religious grounds; to endeavour to ensure the supply chain security of information and communications technology goods and services in order to prevent other States from exploiting their dominant position in information and communications technologies, including dominance in resources, critical infrastructures, core technologies, information and communications technology goods and services, and information and communications networks to undermine States' rights to independent control of information and communications technology goods and services or to threaten their political, economic, and social security.

To ensure equal rights in both cyberspace and reality; to safeguard civil rights and morals. Each State voluntarily subscribing to this Code of Conduct pledges to recognise that the rights of an individual in the offline environment must also be protected in the online environment; to fully respect rights and freedoms in the information space, including the right and freedom to seek, receive, and impart information, considering the fact that the International Covenant on Civil and Political Rights (Article 19) attaches to that right special duties and responsibilities. It may, therefore, be subject to certain restrictions, but these shall only be such as are provided by law and are necessary: (a) for respecting the rights or reputations of others; (b) for the protection of national security, public order, public health, or morals.

To distribute resources fairly and play their role equally. All states must play the same role in, and carry equal responsibility for, international governance of the Internet, its security, continuity, and stability of operation as well as its development in a way that promotes the establishment of multilateral, transparent, and democratic international internet governance mechanisms that ensure an equitable distribution of resources, facilitate access for all, and ensure the stable and secure functioning of the Internet.

To achieve full cooperation between the government and interested parties. All states must cooperate fully with other interested parties in encouraging a deeper understanding by all elements in society, including the private sector and civil society institutions, of their responsibility to ensure information security, by means including the creation of a culture of information security and the provision of support for efforts to protect critical information infrastructure. States should develop confidence-building measures aimed at increasing predictability and reducing the likelihood of misunderstanding and the risk of conflict. Such measures will include, inter alia, the voluntary exchange of information regarding national strategies and organisational structures to ensure a state's information security, the publication of white papers, and the exchange of best practices, wherever practical and advisable.

To peacefully resolve disputes and promote the development of international law on information security by the UN. States should bolster bilateral, regional, and international cooperation, promoting a prominent role for the UN in areas such as encouraging the development of international legal norms for information security, peaceful settlement of international disputes, and qualitative improvements in international cooperation in the field of information security. States should also enhance coordination among relevant international organisations and settle any dispute resulting from the application of this Code of Conduct through peaceful means, refraining from the threat or use of force.

Chapter Four

Cyber Sovereignty

New advances in network technology have remoulded the modes of human activity and produced new forms of social order. Even the popularity of the Internet has brought about national security issues; cyber security issues have promoted the development of the traditional theory of sovereignty. Therefore, network popularisation, cyber security, and cyber sovereignty are closely linked to each other, impelling the continuous exploration of the sovereign theory.

Cyber sovereignty is a new product that has developed through traditional ideas of sovereignty under the drive of science and technology. In law, the terminal (platform) of the network corresponds to traditional property rights; network data (object) can be classified as traditional intellectual property to a certain extent. The actor of the network or its agent (the subject) will be the natural person, legal person, institution, or other entity, together with its software and hardware agent. The application of the network and all the actions (activities) in cyberspace can be attributed to usufruct, civil liberty, business behaviour, or government policy. However, the legitimacy of cyber sovereignty should be gauged from the perspective of national security since the network is a military-civilian dual-use technology.

Today, without cyber security, there would be no national security. In the early days of internet popularisation, the subject, object, platform, and activity of cyberspace should have been regulated by adequate rules in civil and commercial laws. Nevertheless, once an incident endangering public safety occurs in cyberspace, it must be categorised as a criminal offence and judged by criminal law. Providing that it further evolves to the extent that it could jeopardise national security (e.g. cyber warfare) and threaten national sovereignty, traditional departmental law is insufficient to cover and safeguard state sovereignty. Therefore, cyber sovereignty should be studied at a new historical level akin to the international rule of law and the rule of law on the basis of sovereignty proposed by Hugo Grotius in his book *On the Law of War and Peace*, which has become a brand-new topic in traditional national political philosophy and traditional international law.

There are two paths to study the theoretical basis of cyber sovereignty, which is considered a new form of sovereignty. One of the paths focuses on the scientific nature of cyberspace; the conclusion that cyberspace is within the scope of sovereign rights will be achieved after network subjects, objects, platforms, and activities are proven to be traceable within the territory of each state. The other path focuses on the sociality of cyberspace; to justify the theory that sovereignty has jurisdiction over cyberspace, the traditional national sovereignty theory is used to study how "new sovereignty" appears, links, overlaps, governs, and works in traditional society to clarify how new sovereignty has resulted from the progress of traditional sovereignty theory.

The first three chapters of this part examined the scientific nature of cyberspace via the first path, while this chapter explores the sociality of cyberspace by taking the second path. The two paths, which verify that cyberspace is within the scope of sovereign rights and that sovereignty has jurisdiction over cyberspace, confirm each other and lead to conclusions that are essentially consistent. Cyberspace sovereignty has become one of the most urgent issues for most countries in the modern world, as they have to manage non-traditional security threats and solve new cyber security challenges. This issue also forces states into studying and developing traditional sovereignty theories. Considering that national security threats in the real world that are attributed to cyberspace cannot be managed by the traditional sovereignty theory, it is necessary to conduct further research on cyber sovereignty proceeding from the traditional theory of state sovereignty, as cyber sovereignty is an innovative sovereign right driven by the development of cyberspace.

Section One: The Origin of Cyber Sovereignty

Cyber sovereignty differs from traditional sovereignty. Even so, the latter is also a newcomer in the prolonged history of human civilisation, and cyber sovereignty merely marks its recent development. The history of traditional sovereignty in the Western world is not over 500 years old, and its legal practice in nations can only be traced back 400 years at most.

I. *The Origin of Traditional Sovereignty*

Over the past 2,500 years, the Western world has undergone an evolution from patriarchy to theocracy, then to monarchy, democracy, and sovereignty. The traditional concept of sovereignty was established in 1945, after World War II, by the Charter of the United Nations (UN) (hereinafter the UN Charter), developed through practices in World War I under the influence of Hugo Grotius' *On the Law of War and Peace*, published in 1625. Now, it has become the basic theory of contemporary international law. In the Eastern world, the traditional concept of state sovereignty can be seen as a modern version of China's ancient thoughts on maintaining internal security and repelling foreign invasion, as well as a fruit of the realistic and rational choice in China's 5,000 years of pursuit of the ideal of Great Harmony.

1. *Western Sovereignty Theories*

Regarding the origin of the concept of sovereignty, Western scholars often consider Aristotle's *Politics* and classical Roman law as the start,[1] which theoretically entitles states to the "supreme governing power of sovereignty" within their boundaries but not to an equal position or dominating status in the world.

Around the 16th century, the discovery of America, the Renaissance, and the Reformation marked the advent of modern times, as defined by G. W. F. Hegel in the history of philosophy. Although these three events are seen as watershed moments in Europe's development that ended the Middle Ages, they are not the historical events that fully brought Europe to the concept of state sovereignty.

Jean Bodin,[2] a French ideologist, jurist, and political philosopher, first proposed the theory of state sovereignty in the 16th century. In his book, *On Sovereignty,*[3] published in 1576, he advanced the idea of statism and the concept that monarchical sovereignty is the "supreme legislative authority". However, this remained only a theory. At that time, state sovereignty had not yet been widely recognised by other countries, nor had it ever been practiced internationally.

The legal practice of state sovereignty in modern times has a history of only 400 years in Europe. It originated from the games of European political order that started with the Thirty Years' War in 1618. At that time, European countries generally reached a domestic constitutional consensus on territories, people, and regimes by means of enacting a constitution and basic law.

(1) The Practice of Westphalian Sovereignty. When the Thirty Years' War ended in 1648, the countries involved signed The Peace of Westphalia, based on Grotius' *On the Law of War and Peace.*[4] This initiated their awareness, commitment, and

---

[1] Merriam, Jr. (2006). *History of the Theory of Sovereignty Since Rousseau* (p. 1) (H. H. Bi, Trans.). Beijing: Law Press.

[2] He, Q. Sh. (2004). Grotius, His Ideas and Related Theories of International Law. *Wuhan University International Law Review*, 356.

[3] Hinsley, F. H. (1966). *Sovereignty* (p. 121). London: Cambridge University Press.

[4] Grotius, H. (2013). *The Rights of War and Peace* (Q. H. He *et al.*, Trans.). Shanghai: Shanghai People's Publishing House.

implementation of state sovereignty in the practice of national political order and international relations. Since then, the theory of state sovereignty has truly become a core element in the operation of the modern state system.

(2) The Sovereignty Theories Prior to the Establishment of the UN. Before the arrival of the three waves of independence[5] of the modern nation-states, the early theories of sovereignty focused on the attributes of state sovereignty to maintain internal security. In the era in which "state sovereignty 1.0" dominated, from Jean Bodin's theory of "monarchical sovereignty" to Niccolo Machiavelli's "state sovereignty",[6] then to Jean-Jacques Rousseau's "popular sovereignty",[7] Jeremy Bentham's "utilitarian sovereignty",[8] and Henry Maine's "historical sovereignty",[9] the traditional theories of sovereignty could be summarised into two points: the indivisibility of sovereignty and the supreme authority of sovereignty. These theories were limited to the absolute dominance of sovereignty in each state.

2. *The Three Waves of Sovereignty Development in the World*

Modern sovereignty is based on the independence of all nations. As the basis and primary element of national sovereignty, territory did not exist in the beginning, given that the borders of all countries

[5] Huntington, S. P. (2013). *The Third Wave: Democratization in the Late Twentieth Century* (J. G. Ouyang, Trans.). Beijing: China Renmin University Press.

[6] Machiavelli, N. (2009). *The Prince* (H.D. Pan, Trans.). Beijing: The Commercial Press.

[7] Locke, J. (1964). *Two Treatises of Government* (Part 2, p. 2) (J. N. Qu, & Q. F. Ye, Trans.). Beijing: The Commercial Press.

[8] Bentham, J. (1997). *A Fragment on Government* (p. 133) (Sh. P. Shen *et al.*, Trans.). Beijing: The Commercial Press; Bentham, J. (2000). *An Introduction to the Principles of Morals and Legislation* (p. 60). Beijing: The Commercial Press.

[9] Maine, H. J. S. (1959). *Ancient Law* (p. 7) (J. Y. Shen, Trans.). Beijing: The Commercial Press.

were delineated by humans, but was settled in the three waves of the sovereignty development of nation-states.

(1) The first wave of development started with the signing of the Peace of Westphalia in 1648. It established European international order by means of delineating the boundaries of countries in Europe, recognising the independence and sovereignty of each country, and clarifying that principles involving state sovereignty, territory, and independence were rules that could in no way be violated in international affairs. After this, countries dispatched diplomatic envoys to conduct foreign affairs.
(2) The second wave is represented by the American Revolutionary War, the French Revolution, the Vienna system established in 1814–1815 after the defeat of Napoleon, the Latin American War of Independence in the 19th century, the Versailles system established in 1919, and the Yalta system established in 1945, which further expanded and strengthened the "sovereignty ripples" worldwide.[10]
(3) The third wave, in general, refers to the global national independence movements triggered by the European colonial system after World War II and the Cold War in the 20th century, when a large number of emerging nation-states appeared in Asia, Africa, and Latin America. The world has not stopped its alteration and evolution of sovereignty, even after the collapse of the Soviet Union, the disintegration of Yugoslavia, the incorporation of Crimea into Russia, the Syrian civil war, and the chaos caused by the Islamic State of Iraq and Syria (ISIS).[11]

[10] Zhao, H. R. (2015). *World Civilizations Aggregate Approach: China's Civilized Rise and Rule of Law in National Security* (p. 29 & 133). Beijing: China Legal Publishing House.
[11] Huntington, S. P. (2013). *The Third Wave: Democratization in the Late Twentieth Century* (J. G. Ouyang, Trans.). Beijing: China Renmin University Press.

3. *The Practice of Sovereignty in China*

In 1912, Liang Qichao stated that "everyone in China longs for an integrated country as well as a new regime to run it" and proposed to "develop China into a real member in the international community".[12] In 1919, Liao Zhongkai mentioned, "The most important factors constituting a modern state are people, territory, and sovereignty, which has been widely agreed on by scholars studying nations recently".[13] In 1987, Wang Huning published *State Sovereignty*, in which he pointed out the supremacy of sovereignty; the etymology of the word "sovereignty" is derived from the Latin words "super" and "superanus", implying "the highest authority". Huning also systematically studied the theories and the internality and externality of sovereignty.[14]

The connotations of modern state sovereignty are interdependent, indivisible, and indispensable. Before the founding of the UN in 1945, the theories of state sovereignty mainly came from Europe, which had undergone a thousand years of war. Since the Westphalian System was first established by European countries in 1648,[15] theories were proposed, practiced, re-examined, revised, and finally developed into the internationally recognised UN Charter in 1945.

The Charter was produced when the world reached a historic consensus on national sovereignty. According to the Charter, the theory of modern state sovereignty advanced by Liang Qichao, the vital status of territory, people, and government (or political system) opined by Liao Zhongkai, and the supremacy, internality, and externality of

[12] Liang, Q. Ch. (1989). *Principles for the Founding of the Republic of China, The Collected Works of Liang Qichao — Article 28* (p. 39). Beijing: Zhonghua Book Company.

[13] Liao, Zh. K. (1999). The Relations Between the Chinese People and Territories in the Construction of the New Country. *Construction Magazine.*

[14] Wang, H. N. (1987). *National Sovereignty* (p. 2 & 6). Beijing: People's Publishing House.

[15] Zhao, H. R. (2015). *World Civilizations Aggregate Approach: China's Civilized Rise and Rule of Law in National Security* (p. 29 & 133). Beijing: China Legal Publishing House.

state sovereignty proposed by Wang Huning constitute the essential features of the elements of modern state sovereignty. The territory, people, and government (and its governance) within any country are the three basic connotations of its state sovereignty.

II. *Introduction of the Concept of Cyber Sovereignty*

The connotations of modern state sovereignty are legally derived from the UN Charter and generally incorporated in the constitutions of states. For 20 years, the UN has discussed cyber sovereignty and the international consensus on cyberspace as well as states' opinions on and cooperation in internet regulation.

Although the history of the legal practice of traditional sovereignty is not long, contemporary international law holds that the state sovereignty is permanent. The effectiveness of national sovereignty is marked internally by the implementation of the constitutions of states and externally by their equal status recognised by the UN Charter. For a country, sovereignty is an inherent right endowed by its history. It naturally meets the requirements of any constitution and may remain untouched despite changes to the constitution, government, and head of state.

Extending the concept of modern sovereignty into cyberspace grants national cyber sovereignty the properties of territory, people, and political power in its basic connotations, together with the basic characteristics that conform to the UN Charter and the norms of international law in its fundamental extension. These are also the features of territorial sovereignty, popular sovereignty, political sovereignty, monetary sovereignty, and genetic sovereignty. In other words, both the internal and external characteristics of cyber sovereignty are natural extensions of the same factors as well as derivatives of the authority of state sovereignty.

The properties of territory, people, and political power are the fundamental preconditions for the existence of a state. As Liang Qichao, Liao Zhongkai, Wang Huning, and other scholars have summarised, state sovereignty has three basic elements: territory (including territorial waters, territorial airspace, and other resources), people (including foreigners living in or associated with the territory), and political power (including a regime that has not achieved full autonomy). The basic principle of national sovereignty conforms to the spirit of the state's constitution and features the unity of territory, people, and political power, which constitute an inseparable, sustainable, and complete sovereignty.

Generally speaking, the concept of modern sovereignty has naturally extended to the thinking, legislation, and practice of cyberspace governance not only at the UN level but also at the level of each country's law. Although its theory and practice are in the process of reaching a consensus, especially when considering the gap between the US and other countries, as well as between the West and the world, cyber sovereignty has become an international hotspot that is receiving increasing attention.

Section Two: The Connotation of Cyber Sovereignty

The connotation of cyber sovereignty features the properties of territory, people, and political power; even information communication technologies (ICTs) are the objective basis of network globalisation. In terms of network construction, connectivity, usage, governance, and jurisdictional disputes, cyber sovereignty still inherently covers the aforementioned three attributes.

I. *Domestic Cyber Sovereignty*

1. *The "Territorial Cyberspace" Sovereignty of States*

Article 78 of the UN Charter stipulates that "the trusteeship system shall not apply to territories which have become Members of the United Nations, relationship among which shall be based on respect for the principle of sovereign equality". From a theoretical perspective, territory is explained in *Oppenheim's International Law* as "a determined part on earth governed by the sovereignty of the country".[16] Wang Tieya, a famous jurist of Peking University, also notes in his book *International Law* that "in international law, territory mainly refers to the land owned by the state, i.e., the defined part of the earth subject to state sovereignty".[17]

The territory defined in international law extends to territorial lands, waters, and airspace but not to public areas such as outer space, polar regions, and the high seas. Out of respect for territorial sovereignty, a country can in no way occupy, divide, or annex the territory of another country, nor may its troops, warships, police, or aircraft enter or pass through the territory of others without their permission. It is also prohibited to embark on administration or jurisdiction, conduct official investigations, or direct citizens to engage in secret activities in the territory of other countries. Otherwise, there will be a violation of international law.[18] If a country starts different types of cyber warfare to infringe on the sovereignty of other countries, e.g. by using cyber weapons, electronic pulse weapons, or bio-electronic weapons to strike a precise attack on other countries' networks, it will cause damage to the civilian network or entities during the military attack.[19] Therefore, it can be concluded that cyber sovereignty and territorial sovereignty are unified. Whether as a national resource or a domestic asset, the data sovereignty included in cyberspace is also inherently unified with the territorial sovereignty of the state.

2. *The Netizen Sovereignty of States*

The first sentence of the preamble of the UN Charter reads, "We the people of the United Nations determined to save succeeding generations from the scourge of war, which twice in our lifetime has

---

[16] Jennings, R., & Watts, A. (1992). *Oppenheim's International Law* (9th ed., Vol. 1, Part 2, p. 563). London: Oxford University Press.

[17] Wang, T. Y. (1993). *International Law* (p. 229). Beijing: Law Press.

[18] Liang, Sh. Y. (1997). On the National Territorial Sovereignty. *Journal of Law Application* (5), 32.

[19] Song, L. (2014). *A Study on National Self-Defense Right in Cyber War* (Master's thesis). Jilin University, Changchun, China.

brought untold sorrow to mankind, and to reaffirm faith in fundamental human rights, in the dignity and worth of the human person, in the equal rights of men and women and of nations large and small, and to establish conditions under which justice and respect for the obligations arising from treaties and other sources of international law can be maintained, and to promote social progress and better standards of life in larger freedom, and for these ends to practice tolerance and live together in peace with one another as good neighbours, and to unite our strength to maintain international peace and security, and to ensure, by the acceptance of principles and the institution of methods, that armed force shall not be used, save in the common interest, and to employ international machinery for the promotion of the economic and social advancement of all peoples, have resolved to combine our efforts to accomplish these aims."

"The peoples", as defined in this sentence, refer to the totality of the people in each country. There are no people beyond sovereignty; otherwise, the singular word "people" would be used. The concept of popular sovereignty has been clarified as early as the days of Aristotle and Jean Bodin, but its core status in national security was not established until the creation of the UN Charter. Accordingly, since all activities of the people are protected by sovereignty, their activities in cyberspace are also protected by the cyber sovereignty of their country. By this connection, the cyber sovereignty and popular sovereignty in a country exist as a unit.

3. *Sovereign Rights of Governing Cyberspace*

Political sovereignty represents the sum of a country's regime and government. The government is the exerciser, governor, defender, and representative of state sovereignty. The first sentence of the second paragraph of the UN Charter's preamble states, "Accordingly, our respective Governments, through representatives assembled in the city of San Francisco, who have exhibited their full powers found to be in good and due form, have agreed to the present Charter of the United Nations and do hereby establish an international organization to be known as the United Nations." Article 57, paragraph 1 of the UN Charter stipulates, "The various specialized agencies, established by intergovernmental agreement and having wide international responsibilities, as defined in their basic instruments, in economic, social, cultural, educational, health, and related fields, shall be brought into relationship with the United Nations in accordance with the provisions of Article 63." Both manifest that the government is the representative of national sovereignty in each country in the eyes of the UN.

II. *Sovereignty in Non-Self-Governing Territories*

Sovereignty in non-self-governing territories is internationally recognised as "under-developed sovereignty". In the UN Charter, Article 73 of Chapter XI, titled "Declaration Regarding Non-self-governing Territories", stipulates that "Members of the United Nations which have or assume responsibilities for the administration of territories whose peoples have not yet attained a full measure of self-government recognize the principle that the interests of the inhabitants of these territories are paramount, and accept as a sacred trust the obligation to promote to the utmost, within the system of international peace and security established by the present Charter, the well-being of the inhabitants of these territories, and, to this end: a. to ensure their just treatment; b. to develop self-government, to take due account of the political aspirations of the peoples, and to assist them in the progressive development of their free political institutions, according to the particular circumstances of each territory and its peoples and their varying stages of advancement". The above provisions show that the UN fully respects the sovereignty of non-self-governing territories and supports the modernisation of the territories' self-governments instead of discriminating against them and condoning hegemony.

The UN has reached the preliminary consensus on cyber sovereignty that sovereign jurisdiction should cover information activities and communication platforms. However, apropos of the four elements of cyberspace, namely its subject, object, platform, and activity, a consensus on comprehensive governance has not yet been reached because the speed of the development of ICTs has exceeded that of an agreement among all members of the UN. This lag in speed is the reason it is widely agreed that cyber sovereignty is an "under-developed sovereignty" that remains to be observed by countries. To advance the common views of states, the varied recognitions of cyber sovereignty must be unified through in-depth study and clarification in theory.

Section Three: The Extension of Cyber Sovereignty

Just like traditional national sovereignty, the extension of cyber sovereignty covers international self-defence, autonomy, and equality. Each sovereign state has the right to claim and exercise these three sovereign rights within its border. At the land or sea boundaries of sovereign states, the networks between countries are connected physically and materially. In the international community, cyber sovereignty still has the natural attributes of international self-defence, autonomy, and equality.

I. *International Rule of Law*

In the UN Charter, every equal sovereign state is endowed with the rights of international self-defence, autonomy, and equality. Just like territorial sovereignty, popular sovereignty, and political sovereignty, the cyber sovereignty of sovereign states also comprises these external attributes.

1. *International Right of Self-Defence of Cyber Sovereignty*

The right of self-defence stems from international law and is explicitly recognised and supported by Article 51 of the UN Charter. The legal concept of defence originated from domestic law and was later incorporated into international law; it was employed by countries as grounds for the legitimacy of warfare at the outset. The right of self-defence in international law refers to the inherent or natural rights of a state to protect itself by means of force to fight against foreign armed attacks. Article 51 of the UN Charter specifies that "nothing in the present Charter shall impair the inherent right of individual or collective self-defence if an armed attack occurs against a Member of the United Nations, until the Security Council has taken measures necessary to maintain international peace and security. Measures taken by Members in the exercise of this right of self-defence shall be immediately reported to the Security Council and shall not in any way affect the authority and responsibility of the Security Council under the present Charter to take at any time such action as it deems necessary in order to maintain or restore international peace and security". In accordance with this, the right of self-defence of state sovereignty is exercised to repel external armed attacks by force or eliminate imminent threats to legally recover or maintain the status quo ante.[20]

Although the right of self-defence is inherent in sovereign states, its exercise is subject to strict restrictions. For example, in cyber warfare, for the confirmation of an armed attack, technical measures and proof are required, and the methods the UN uses to judge and take the necessary measures also need to be clarified. Network warfare can be subdivided into network information theft, system breakdown, remote control, pre-war strike, and compound strike.[21] Therefore, whether the right of self-defence of a sovereign state can be claimed and exercised in cyberspace depends, to a large extent, on the technical capability and judgment of the state in cyberspace. There is no doubt that a country's ability to resist

---

[20] Yu, M. C. (2003). Legal Issues in the Application of Self-Defense Right. *Jurists Review* (3), 154.

[21] This was taken from the speech "On Cyber Law and Rule of Law in Non-traditional Security" by Professor Hashimoto Yasuaki from the National Institute for Defense Studies of the Japan Ministry of Defense during his visit to Harbin Institute of Technology from 12–14 October 2014.

foreign aggression via exercising the right of self-defence in cyberspace will be impaired once it cannot safeguard its internal stability and loses the ability to maintain complete territorial, popular, and political sovereignty.

2. *International Autonomy of Cyber Sovereignty*

Article 2, paragraph 4 of the UN Charter stipulates that "all Members shall refrain in their international relations from the threat or use of force against the territorial integrity or political independence of any state, or in any other manner inconsistent with the Purposes of the United Nations". Political independence in the international community and autonomy within the country are two fundamental aspects of national sovereignty. However, in reality, many countries are nominally politically autonomous, i.e. they have willingly abandoned their autonomy in national security by resorting to military alliances.

In accordance with the objective criteria,[22] the 196 countries in the world can be divided into three categories in terms of national security: fully autonomous, semi-autonomous, and non-autonomous. According to this, one can re-categorise the Three Worlds theory from the perspective of security: only 3 countries in the

[22] The six criteria of "national security independence" are: complete political independence (without internal disorder), overall planning in military and politics (unity between the government and the armed forces), national defence independence (anti-aggression capabilities), strategic independence (nuclear weapons), a complete industrial system (production and research and development (R&D) capabilities in each major industry), and international recognition (standing as a permanent member of the UN Security Council). The countries with the above-mentioned six characteristics can be viewed as independent in their national security, as they do not rely on the forces of other countries. The three criteria of "national security semi-independence" are: a country that does not fully possess the six characteristics of "national security independence" and only owns partial national security independence, e.g. a country that owns nuclear weapons but is affiliated with a military group; one that owns nuclear weapons but is in hostile relations with certain military groups; or one that owns nuclear weapons but chooses to be neutral or not to ally with any sides.

world — China, the US, and Russia — are fully autonomous, accounting for 1.5% of all 196 countries. In addition, there are 14 semi-autonomous countries, accounting for 5.6%, and 159 non-autonomous countries, accounting for 92.9%.[23] Under the circumstances wherein all countries are divided into three categories in accordance with autonomy in security, the real world order proves the existence of Three Worlds with differentiated autonomy, although the principle of sovereign equality is clearly defined in the UN Charter. Even though all 196 UN members are generally equal in legal status, there are wide discrepancies in the proportions of the countries of the Three Worlds, as shown in Figure 4-1.

Without territorial sovereignty, popular sovereignty, and political sovereignty, an independent country can by no means have equal status with other countries in the world. In the field of non-traditional security, the networks of states are essentially interconnected and autonomous. However, autonomy in cyber security is not assigned equally in compliance with the positions of the five permanent members of the UN Security Council, among which only the United States (US) has achieved this. China is generally

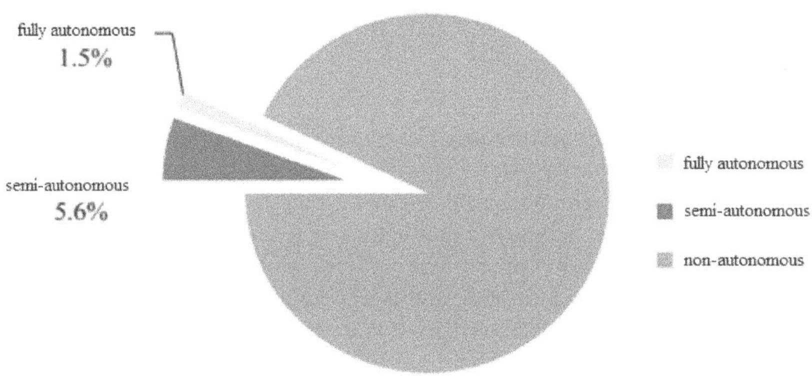

Figure 4-1: Three Worlds — The Proportions of Countries Divided Based on Autonomy in National Security

[23] Zhao, H. R. (2015). *World Civilizations Aggregate Approach: China's Civilized Rise and Rule of Law in National Security* (p. 443). Beijing: China Legal Publishing House.

autonomous in national security but semi-autonomous in cyber security in the field of non-traditional security.[24] In addition, China is relatively semi-autonomous in terms of security in currency, space, energy, and anti-terrorism, but the conditions in these fields are slightly better than those in cyberspace. Therefore, it is necessary to advance a feasible top-level design to maintain national cyber sovereignty to achieve autonomy in cyber security.

3. *International Right to Cyber Sovereignty Equality*

The right to equality is one of the basic rights of a state and a manifestation of its sovereignty. The term first appeared in the Moscow Declarations issued on 13 October 1943. The UN Charter clearly defines the principle of sovereign equality among its members at the outset because state sovereignty and equality are the basic constitutional principles[25] of public international law. It stipulates that "each member of the General Assembly shall have one vote"[26] and that "decisions of the General Assembly on important questions shall be made by a two-thirds majority of the members present and voting".[27] However, sovereign equality is essentially hierarchical. According to the UN Charter, national sovereignty can be divided into three levels of equality.

The first level is the "universal sovereign equality in principle". Article 1, paragraph 2 of the Charter stipulates this is "to develop friendly relations among nations based on respect for the principle of equal rights and self-determination of peoples, and to take other appropriate measures to strengthen universal peace". Additionally, Article 2, paragraph 1 of the Charter states, "The Organization is based on the principle of the sovereign equality of all its Members."

---

[24] The non-traditional security areas discussed here include currency, space, energy, counterterrorism, and cyberspace. Zhao, H. R. (2015). *World Civilizations Aggregate Approach: China's Civilized Rise and Rule of Law in National Security* (p. 205 & 262). Beijing: China Legal Publishing House.

[25] Brownlie, I. (2003). *Principles of Public International Law* (6th ed) (p. 287).

[26] See Article 2 of the UN Charter.

[27] See Article 18 of the UN Charter.

Universal sovereign equality in principle guarantees the two universal principles of each UN member having one vote and the minority being subordinate to the majority, which have also been specified in specific regulations, such as the Declaration on Principles of International Law Concerning Friendly Relations and Cooperation among States in Accordance with the Charter of the UN. The principles involve connotations of sovereign equality comprising the equality of legal status, the entitlement to full sovereignty, the obligation to respect the individuality, territorial integrity, and political independence of other countries, the free choice to develop political, economic, or cultural systems, and peaceful coexistence.

The second level regards the "vote of the 15 members of the UN Security Council for world peace", which means that 15 of the 193 member states of the UN have more voting rights than the other 178. As the only organ of the UN with the right to conduct military operations, the Security Council was established under the UN Charter to maintain international peace and security. A Member of the UN against which preventive or enforcement action has been taken by the Security Council may be suspended from exercising the rights and privileges of membership upon the recommendation of the 15 members of the Security Council. The exercise of these rights and privileges may be restored by the Security Council. Each member of the Security Council has one vote on security issues. In addition, while the Security Council is exercising the functions assigned to it in the UN Charter in respect to any dispute or situation, the General Assembly shall not make any recommendation with regard to that dispute or situation unless the Security Council requests so.[28] This manifests that the members of the Security Council have greater responsibilities and obligations in international security and more voting rights for maintaining international peace than the other 178 members.

The third level concerns "the veto by any of the five permanent members of the Security Council". The veto is the right of any

[28] See Article 12 of the UN Charter.

permanent member of the Security Council to prevent the Council from adopting recommendations on non-procedural matters it dissents. The UN Charter stipulates that China, the United States, the Russian Federation, the United Kingdom, and France are permanent members with a special voting power known as the "right to veto".[29] The equal voting power of these five major countries on non-procedural matters is more effective than the other countries.[30] They even have the power of veto over entry into force as well as amendments to the UN Charter, a significant origin of international law.[31] In addition to the general exercise of the veto, the permanent members of the Security Council can also make full use of the veto in two ways. The first way is the "Double Veto". Before the 1950s, the permanent members of the Security Council could extend their power by first making a matter non-procedural and then vetoing the resolution on this matter; however, later attempts were made to constrain this privilege. The president of the Security Council would rule that a matter was procedural in accordance with Article 30 of the Provisional Rules of Procedure of the Security Council, which could only be overruled by nine or more Security Council members. The second way is the "invisible veto", which means that major countries can always threaten to use their veto for the purpose of making recommendations conform to their will.

In summary, at the level of the international rule of law, there are few precedents in the international community, represented by the UN, to safeguard the cyber sovereignty of a state and stop cyber warfare.

II. *International Cooperation*

International cooperation in cyber sovereignty is conducted in the global commons, which refer to the internationally shared outer space, polar regions, and high seas that are not under the

[29] See Article 23 of the UN Charter.
[30] See Article 27 of the UN Charter.
[31] See Articles 108–110 of the UN Charter.

ownership or control of any state. After the consultation on the basis of equality, sovereign states have achieved a certain degree of international consensus and co-governance of the global commons under the framework of the UN.

Generally speaking, the ships, aircraft, and spacecraft of a sovereign country are regarded as natural extensions of its sovereignty when they sail in or fly over the high seas, polar regions, and space. Even so, such extensions must follow the principle of international co-governance and cannot go against the purpose of peaceful use. In other words, as an extension of its sovereignty, any subject, object, platform, and activity of a sovereign state in the global commons cannot violate or threaten to violate the sovereignty of other states.

On a global scale, the basic principle of state sovereignty should conform internally to the spirit of the constitution of each state and externally to the global order under the UN Charter. The connotation and extension of sovereignty and the co-governance of the global commons constitute the entire global order of mankind in all spaces.

With the development of ICTs, the global commons in cyber sovereignty have reached the fibre-optic cables in the high seas, communication in the polar regions, and spacecraft in outer space. Given that there is no global order to regulate fibre-optic cables in the high seas, polar codes, and outer space treaties, cyber sovereignty is in no way interconnected in the global commons and could give rise to chaos in international cooperation.

Article 32 of the National Security Law of the People's Republic of China, which came into effect on 1 July 2015, stipulates that "China insists on the exploration and peaceful use of the outer space, the international seabed area, and the polar regions, the strengthening of the safe access, scientific investigation, development, and utilisation of these commons, as well as the enhancement of international cooperation so as to guarantee the security of China's activities, assets, and other interests in outer space, the international seabed region, and the polar regions". It manifests that China's national law has connected with international law in terms of the order in global commons, which ensures that its national sovereignty can connect with the legal rights stipulated by international conventions in scientific investigation, development and utilisation, international cooperation, and asset security.

In general, the connotation and extension of cyber sovereignty and the co-governance of the commons in cyberspace constitute the entire civilised order of cyberspace. Without them, a brutal order violating the UN Charter would emerge in cyberspace.

Section Four: The Role of Cyber Sovereignty

Is sovereignty ruling cyberspace or being ruled by cyberspace? This is not only a constitutional issue in law but also a question prompting thoughts on justice. Originating from historical judgments in human systems, modern justice has been modified by both positive and negative practices in the development of human civilisation in various countries. Investigating justice via historical differences in this evolution is a research approach used to clarify the relationship between cyberspace and sovereignty and confirm the justice of cyber sovereignty.

I. *Spatial Game*

Any conception of the world system is based on its spatial design. Global order cannot exist without geographic space.

1. *Unbalanced Historical Rights*

In traditional state sovereignty, international equality is unbalanced and refers to equality involving geographical differences rather than absolute and actual equality. The exercise of this kind of sovereignty in reality is determined by the geographical and historical endowment of sovereign states.

(1) The "equilibrium" endowment of the circum-Alpine European countries. The historical endowment of the European order

originated from the military parity of the circum-Alpine European countries. This balance was largely determined by the geographical features of Europe, which is a part of Eurasia. With the Arctic Ocean, Atlantic Ocean, Mediterranean Sea, and Black Sea to its north, west, and south, respectively, and Asia adjacent to its east and southeast, it boasts a zigzag coastline and numerous mountains and forests separating the population centres in each area. The land in Europe, a continent with an average height of 340 meters, is mostly plains, except for the mountain ranges in the middle known as the Alps. Countries such as Greece, Italy, France, Spain, Portugal, Britain, and Germany are at the foot of the mountains circuiting the Alps, which led to incessant war for 2,500 years as well as the birth of sovereignty. Paul Kennedy believed that the diversity in European politics is mainly due to the geographical situation.[32] Even though the US embarked on a global war on terror and implemented the "pivot to Asia" after the September 11 attacks in 2001, the overall international security pattern since World War II has been caught up in the "intercontinental balance of power" and "intercontinental containment". In the next 30 years, the world security pattern may still be beset by the legacy of the equilibrium in Europe,[33] which will be the fate of sovereignty under European geopolitical order.

(2) The endowment of "Tianxia" ("all under heaven") in East Asia. Comprising China, Japan, South Korea, North Korea, and Mongolia, and facing the Pacific, East Asia features higher elevations in the northwest and lower elevations in the southeast, like a three-step ladder. The first step is formed by the Qinghai-Tibet Plateau with an average height of over 4,000 metres, the second by basins and plateaus, and the third by plains, foothills,

[32] Kennedy, P. (2006). *The Rise and Fall of the Great Powers* (p. 16). Beijing: China International Culture Press Limited.

[33] Zhao, H. R. (2015). *World Civilizations Aggregate Approach: China's Civilized Rise and Rule of Law in National Security*. Beijing: China Legal Publishing House.

and a few islands. East Asia's geographical features can be represented by those of China, which owns the largest amount of land in this region. Approximately 4,000 years ago, the country was established on the basis of Chinese civilisation, originating from the Yellow River Basin (Central Plains), and has since become the most important civilisation in East Asia. In ancient China, "Tianxia" usually referred to nine regions and four seas, i.e. the territory and domain centred on the Zhou dynasty. Tianxia is a view of the global order that was created in ancient Chinese thought based on the concept of space. It influenced each dynasty's policies in dealing with relations with the outside world and became the foundation for the Tianxia system.[34] The concept of Tianxia constructed by Chinese philosophers constitutes the largest unit of space as a result of its inclusion of outside space. In ancient China, spaces outside China were within the limits of Tianxia, namely the marginal part opposite to the centre. Specifically, "between the heaven above and the earth below is the country known as 'the middle kingdom' (China); those on the borders are known as the 'four barbarian tribes'; in accordance with their locations, the boundary between China and other nations was created to separate the inner area from the outer". The "Liyun" section of the *Book of Rites* also put forth the view of "taking all land under heaven as a family". This concept led to an overall pattern of China and its neighbouring ethnic groups of Yi in the east, Man in the south, Rong in the west, and Di in the north coexisting in the Four Seas and constituting Tianxia.[35] Under its influence, the ancient dynasties in the Central Plains could not legally recognise the regimes of the surrounding nations, and the boundary between them was more a line of actual control between different regimes than a boundary at the country level. The concept of Tianxia

[34] He, X. H. (2006). An Analysis of the View of the World in Ancient China. *Southeast Asian Studies* (1), 50.

[35] He, X. H. (2006). An Analysis of the View of the World in Ancient China. *Southeast Asian Studies* (1), 52.

aimed to achieve "great unity", not the coexistence of various sovereign states as in Europe.[36] Throughout the history of East Asia, unity could always be achieved due to the geographical advantage of high altitude in the northwest and low altitude in the southeast. The fate of East Asia under the concept of Tianxia was different from that of Europe under the concept of sovereignty. In Europe, national borders and sovereignty were finally established by virtue of signing peace treaties as a result of the parity in military force. However, in East Asia, the endowment of Tianxia in the geopolitical order did not lead to the establishment of sovereignty, as the people in this region reached a consensus that national security could be attained only after the realisation of national unification.

(3) Known for isolationism, the Cold War, and global dominance, North America owns the endowment of hegemony. Since the Roman Empire, no other country has been as dominant as the US.[37] Its primary goal is to safeguard the peace and interests under its rule through the construction of geopolitical order. The geographical characteristics of North America fit its three historical stages of isolation, the Cold War, and its hegemony in the development of state sovereignty. The region enjoys a great location. With the Atlantic Ocean to the east, the Pacific Ocean to the west, and the Arctic Ocean to the north, it is separated from South America by the Panama Canal in the south and faces Europe in the east, across the Atlantic Ocean. The US is the most developed country, not just in North America but also in the world, and a typical country with the endowment of sovereignty featuring isolation, Cold War, and hegemony. Its power is based on its unique natural conditions: it has the fourth largest land space in the world, of which two-thirds of the territory is habitable, and it boasts a long coastline and many natural harbours on the East and West Coasts, accessing the world's largest fishery areas. The climate in the territory is

---

[36] He, X. H. (2006). An Analysis of the View of the World in Ancient China. *Southeast Asian Studies* (1), 51.

[37] Nye, J. S. (2003). U.S. Power and Strategy after Iraq. *Foreign Affairs* (82), 73.

diverse, the resources abundant, and the raw materials and agricultural products various.[38] Its superior geography bordering two oceans in the east and west and neighbouring powers in the north and south have played an important role in the formation of its national sovereignty featuring isolationism and hegemonism since the country's founding. At the end of the 18th century, the US concluded various treaties with other countries while pursuing isolationism. As it was too weak to possess defensive power on its own at that time, the US government intended to make full use of the country's geographical superiority to maintain a casual relationship with Europe, wherein the US neither entangled in nor isolated itself from world affairs while maintaining liberty of action.[39] After World War II, the US shifted its foreign policy from isolationism to global interventionism. There was no reason to follow isolationism any longer because the comprehensive strength of the US had reached its peak, and President Franklin Roosevelt, an extraordinary genius, led the country to hegemony.[40] As an open country with a short history and thinly populated land, the US required a large number of immigrants and introduced unique modes of economic development and immigration policy, which have since played a decisive role in the development of its cutting-edge high technology and advanced weapons.[41] Since the Cold War and the second half of the 20th century, the US has established its supremacy in the international system, and one of its strategic goals is to prevent the decline of its dominance.[42] Hans Morgenthau, a well-known American

---

[38] Gao, Z. G. (2004). An Analysis of the Roots of American Hegemony. *Peace and Development* (4), 16.

[39] Yuan, Zh. G. (2007). *The Formation of Early American Isolationism* (Master's thesis). Sichuan University, Chengdu, China.

[40] Men, H. H. (2006). America's Hegemony and International Order. *International Review* (1), 19.

[41] *America's Democracy on Its Way Towards Hegemony* (Reposted). Retrieved from https://bbs.tianya.cn/post-worldlook-269122-1.shtml.

[42] Yuan, J. J. (2016). Hegemony, System and America's Global Strategic Choice after the Cold War. *Forum of World Economics & Politics* (1), 8.

scholar in international relations, declared that "international politics, like all politics, is a struggle for power. Whatever the ultimate aims of international politics, power is always the immediate aim".[43] Nicholas Spykman also said that the competition for rights is the fundamental essence of human relations, which is especially true in the field of international affairs; "all else is secondary, because in the last instance only power can achieve the objectives of foreign policy".[44] Under the guidance of these ideas, the sovereign acts of the US after the Cold War demonstrated its unique endowment of hegemony.[45]

2. *Worldview of "Over-Sovereignty"*

The geographical endowments of different countries always determine their worldview and perceptions of sovereignty. Geopolitics is a combination of geography and politics, especially international relations. Hegemonic powers, in most cases, study and design various theories beyond their territory and sovereignty. Friedrich Ratzel's *Political Geography*, published in 1897, marked the formation of geopolitical theories. For the first time in history, the book systematically combined the two major factors of politics and geography and specified the relationship between the space occupied by a country and its geographical position. Although the term geopolitics had not been introduced at that time, the main ideas and contents of geopolitical theory had been fully expressed.[46] In the later development of geopolitics, several important theories such as the sea power theory, land

---

[43] Huntington, S. P. (2010). *The Clash of Civilizations and the Remaking of World Order* (Q. Zhou *et al.*, Trans.). Beijing: Xinhua Publishing House.

[44] Daugherty, J. (1987). *Contending Theories of International Relations: A Comprehensive Survey*. Beijing: Knowledge Press.

[45] Wang, Y. X. (2004). *A Brief Analysis of America's New Hegemony After the Cold War* (Master's thesis). Shandong Normal University, Qingdao, China.

[46] Zhang, H. M., & Hao, Ch. Y. (2013). An Analysis of the Development Trend of Geopolitical Theory from the Perspective of Its History and Status Quo. *Contemporary International Relations* (2), 53.

power theory, rimland theory, and airpower theory were formed, which influenced state sovereignty and security strategies. These theories displayed the attributes of "over-sovereignty".

(1) Mahan's Sea Power Theory. In 1890, Alfred Thayer Mahan, a US navy general and the creator of the sea power theory, published *The Influence of Sea Power Upon History, 1660–1783*. In the book, he proposed that sea power is vital to the development, prosperity, and security of a country. For any country or alliance, control of the high seas means control of the world's trade and wealth. There are six fundamental elements of sea power: a country's geographical position, physical conformation, extent of territory, population size, character of people, and character of government. To become a world power, a country must have the ability to navigate freely on the ocean and be able to monopolise maritime trade if necessary.[47] Mahan also proposed paying attention to Eurasia and believed that different strategies and ideas should be employed to control different parts of the region. According to him, the US should work with powers in the margins of Eurasia, such as the UK and Japan, to oppose those in its core region. This way, major powers in important positions in Eurasia would not be able to control its marginal areas through controlling Eurasia, which would prevent a strategic posture wherein the US would be attacked by Eurasia from both sides.
(2) Mackinder's Land Power Theory. British geographer Halford John Mackinder analysed world political power from the perspective of a global strategist. According to Mackinder, the history of the world is full of conflicts between land powers and sea powers. He asserted that land powers, by virtue of their rich human and material resources and increasingly improved transportation, will suppress sea powers. He believed that "the

[47] Kong, X. H. (2010). An Analysis of the Connotation and Main Theories of Geopolitics and its Approaches to Influence National Security Strategies. *World Regional Studies* (2), 34.

relationship between human and most of the world's reality" had been changed by the development of land transportation technology, which strengthened the superiority of the countries in Eurasia. In his 1904 book *The Geographical Pivot of History*, Mackinder put forth the Heartland theory (also known as the "Pivot Area" theory). He described the central inland of Eurasia as the Heartland and the peripheral ring surrounding the Heartland as the Inner Crescent (including most of continental Europe west of Russia, the Middle East, India, and China) and the Outer Crescent (including Britain, Japan, and other islands on the margin of Eurasia, sub-Saharan Africa, Oceania, and the Americas).

Mackinder also asserted that the key to ruling the Heartland is control over Eastern Europe. From his global strategic views, he concluded that whoever rules East Europe commands the Heartland, whoever rules the Heartland commands the world-island, and whoever rules the world-island commands the world. He warned the West to prevent Russian expansion and a Russian-German alliance, for Russia and Germany, as he pointed out, were most likely to control the Heartland.

(3) Douhet's Airpower Theory. In 1921, Italian General Giulio Douhet proposed the airpower theory in his book *The Command of the Air*. He thought that "aeronautics opened up to men a new field of action, the field of the air. In so doing it of necessity created a new battlefield."[48] In the air domain, aircrafts have become a new and unique means of human warfare. Command of the air is the key to victory: "having command of the air means to have the ability to fly against an enemy so as to injure him, while he has been deprived of the power to do likewise... an adequate national defense cannot be assured except by an aerial force capable in case of war of conquering the command of the air". Therefore, Douhet thought the following modest programme should be adopted: "a progressive decrease of land

[48] Douhet, G. (1986). *The Command of the Air* (p. 19). (Y.F. Cao *et al.*, Trans.). Beijing: PLA Press.

and sea forces, accompanied by a corresponding increase of aerial forces until they are strong enough to conquer the command of the air". Additionally, he stated it was necessary to destroy all the sites where the enemy's aircraft were stationed and produced. The principles outlined in Douhet's book exerted great influence on Italy and Germany's air warfare strategies during World War II. Moreover, the influence of the airpower theory on the US "was affirmed by General Mitchell during World War II".[49]

In sum, the traditional spaces of sea, land, and air have evolved into traditional sovereign territory. Since human civilisation has entered the era of cyberspace, which includes space facilities, the formulation of the concept of cyber sovereignty will play a progressive role in eradicating hegemony and advocating equality.

II. *Equal Right to Development*

The rule of law offers an objective perspective to reflect on historical justification, and the consensus on the rule of law originates from the historical judgments of human systems. As the constitutions of all nations and the UN Charter constitute the main body of the modern rule of law, it is necessary to analyse and study the non-traditional characteristics of new concepts when legally reflecting on them. Regarding the relationship between the rule of law and cyberspace, there is the proposition of "ruling the cyberspace or being ruled by cyberspace".

1. *Cyber Sovereignty Endows All Countries with the Equal Right to Development*

In the international political system, cyberspace power determines the strength of a country in international society. In a cyber war,

[49] Liu, C. D. (1998). *Geopolitics: History, Approach, and World Pattern*. Wuhan: Central China Normal University Press.

countries with stronger cyberspace power are more likely to gain the upper hand. For example, Russia took the lead in launching a fierce cyberattack on Georgia in the Russo-Georgian War in August 2008, while Georgia was at a disadvantage because it could not use the Internet to release accurate information about the war. Therefore, exploring and demonstrating the natural extension of traditional state sovereignty in a non-traditional security field such as cyberspace is a critical issue that deserves attention from the contemporary international political community, international law community, network technology community, and citizens of all countries.

The traditional theories of state sovereignty and the rule of law are applicable to the domain of traditional national security. However, in the non-traditional field of national cyberspace security, cyber sovereignty must be supported by technology and consolidated by consensus before it can effectively prevent threats.

In 1999, British political scientist Tim Jordan systematically expounded the concept of "cyberpower" from the perspective of politics and sociology for the first time: cyberpower is a form of power that organises culture and politics in cyberspace or on the Internet.[50]

Joseph Nye, a US scholar, also stated that "cyber power behaviour rests upon a set of resources that relate to the creation, control and communication of electronic and computer-based information — infrastructure, networks, software, human skills. Defined behaviourally, cyber power is the ability to obtain preferred outcomes through use of the electronically interconnected information resources of the cyber domain. Cyber power can be used to produce preferred outcomes within cyberspace or it can use cyber instruments to produce preferred outcomes in other domains outside cyberspace."[51]

The definitions of cyber power demonstrate the fierce competition for cyberspace between Western powers to obtain cyberspace

---

[50] Yu, L. A (2012). Study on the Role of the Internet in International Politics. *CASS Journal of Political Science* (4), 23.

[51] Nye, J. S. (2004). *Power in the Global Information Age: From Realism to Globalization*. New York: Routledge.

dominance. This new type of state power affects not only the Internet but also state sovereignty and the international community. Thus, only with sovereign equality can we handle the abuse of cyber power and ensure that all countries share equal development rights.

2. *Cyber Sovereignty Establishes the Right to Maintain Security of All States*

At the National Cybersecurity and Informatization Work Conference held on 19 April 2016, Xi Jinping reiterated that "cyber security is holistic rather than fragmented, dynamic rather than static, open rather than closed, relative rather than absolute, common rather than isolated".[52] His speech further clarified China's overall recognition of the five characteristics of the current cyber security situation, namely integrity, dynamics, openness, relativity, and commonality, and embodied the national security work principles of "basing the overall situation, national conditions, the people, relativity and overall planning" on the National Security Law of the People's Republic of China.

The concept of overall planning determines the actions of sovereignty; the enhancement of understanding spurs the progress of methodology. We should not only avoid pursuing absolute safety regardless of cost but also abandon the idea that safety can be maintained forever by installing safety devices and software. The deepening of China's understanding of the connotation of cyber sovereignty further verifies the concept of cyber sovereignty equality put forth by China and the Shanghai Cooperation Organisation (SCO) in the UN.

Pacifying the interior and resisting foreign aggression are obligatory missions of state sovereignty. All types of sovereignty, whether traditional or cyber, including the "Tianxia" concept of East Asia, the "equilibrium" of Europe, and the "hegemonic

---

[52] Xi, J. P. (2016). *Speech at the National Conference on the Work of Cyber Security and Informatization.* Retrieved from https://www.cac.gov.cn/2016-04/25/c_1118731366.htm.

endowment" of the US, should be integrated into the rule of law under the two frameworks of the UN Charter and their own constitutions to maintain national and international security.

The differences inside and outside national territory comprise the changes of *yin* and *yang*. Zhang Zhongjing, a Chinese medical scientist during the Han Dynasty, recorded that "glycyrrhiza is sweet and natured, with the ability to keep the body stable and fight the external disadvantages" in "Taiyang Disease (1)" of *Treatise on Febrile Diseases*. Since then, "pacifying the interior and resisting foreign aggression" has been adopted in China's national strategy. In *Reporting Six Things to Emperor,* published in the Ming Dynasty, Zhang Juzheng stated, "As far as I know, an emperor must pacify the interior before resisting foreign aggression." That is, to solve foreign troubles, a country must first preserve peace at home.[53] At present, the overall planning of both domestic and foreign situations embodies the rule of law principle that China exercises sovereignty in accordance with its constitution and the UN Charter. As the international community is undergoing dramatic changes, China has "kept in mind both its internal and international imperatives" and truly achieved the goal of "pacifying the interior and resisting foreign aggression", which is in line with the relevant provisions of its constitution internally and simultaneously exercises and maintains China's sovereignty externally under the UN Charter.

National sovereignty consists of two aspects: internal security and external resistance. For example, the *Britannica Concise Encyclopedia* divides sovereignty into "internal sovereignty" (the ultimate responsibility or authority in the process of national decision-making) and "external sovereignty" (a nation's freedom from foreign control, which represents the autonomy or independence of the country). The internal and external sovereignty of a country, including the sovereignty partially transferred to other

---

[53] Gong, L. Zh. (2006). Pacifying the Interior Before Resisting the Foreign Aggression: From the "Art of War of Sun Zi" to "Wei Liao Zi". *Journal of Binzhou University* (4), 36.

organisations, are regarded as integral parts of state sovereignty. Together, they constitute unified and indivisible state sovereignty. All activities related to extraterritoriality or a "state within a state" are an infringement upon this sovereignty. All countries have the right to exercise their own sovereignty independently, free from arbitrary interference by other countries. All countries are equal, regardless of their size or strength.

The internal-external characteristics of state sovereignty have been recognised by domestic and foreign legal scholars. Lassa Oppenheim believed that "sovereignty is supreme authority, which on the international plane means legal authority, which is not in law dependent on any other earthly authority. Sovereignty in the strict sense and narrowest sense of the term implies, therefore, independence all round within and without the borders of the country."[54] Zhou Gengsheng noted that "sovereignty is the supreme authority of a state to deal with internal and external affairs independently. State sovereignty has two characteristics: supreme authority at home and independent action in foreign affairs."[55]

More justified global governance hinges on more effective use of cyber sovereignty; a stronger governance capacity is the key to creating a stronger development momentum and pursuing a more peaceful world order.

III. *Conclusion: Cyberspace is Within the Scope of Sovereign Rights*

The world has no borders in nature. However, due to the establishment of countries, the distinction of nations, and the need for international and domestic governing, human beings have had to divide land, water, and airspace with national borders to form the traditional domains of sovereignty. As a new domain, cyberspace can be neither seen nor touched, but it objectively exists in real life. Cyberspace contains four elements: subject, object, platform, and

[54] Oppenheim. (1971). *International Law* (p. 97). Beijing: The Commercial Press.
[55] Zhou, G. Sh. (1981). *International Law* (p. 75). Beijing: The Commercial Press.

activity. It is a self-existing and self-made new domain, new boundary, and new space driven by technological progress.

Cyberspace has no borders in nature either, but for the sake of maintaining international cyberspace order as well as the cyber and national security of all nations, cyberspace cannot remain independent of countries. Therefore, it should also have borders and sovereignty. The four elements of cyberspace integrate the scientificity and sociality of cyberspace, show cyberspace's connection with materials, territory, sovereignty, people, and society, and constitute the legal basis for the objective existence and justified governance of cyber sovereignty. The proposition of cyber sovereignty in traditional sovereignty and domains will be helpful in formulating a more secure and reasonable new paradigm for cyberspace governance.

Since cyberspace contains subjects, objects, platforms, and activities, only when cyber security issues endanger national sovereignty will the relative border of cyber sovereignty arise.

The new theory of cyber sovereignty put forth in this book is completely based on the actual needs of the development of science, technology, and social change, which have given rise to a concept of cyber sovereignty that is distinct from but still related to the traditional concept of sovereignty. There are three differences between cyber sovereignty and traditional sovereignty. First, cyber sovereignty is based on territorial land, water, and airspace within the scope of traditional sovereignty and is used to govern the completely new territory of cyberspace. Second, cyber sovereignty is not superior to traditional sovereignty but is derived from traditional sovereignty theories and international principles of rule of law. Third, cyber sovereignty is essentially born out of the need to oppose cyber hegemony and cope with non-traditional security threats in cyberspace. Thus, it is a "new weapon" that traditional sovereignty has to devise. However, there are natural commonalities and interrelations between cyber sovereignty and traditional sovereignty: both fall under the category of safeguarding popular sovereignty, undertake the mission of safeguarding national security, and naturally feature inalienability.

In short, the overall definition of cyber sovereignty is a new theory of sovereignty originating from the development of ICTs and the popularisation of networks based on and derived from the traditional theories of state sovereignty and basic principles of international law after the rise of new issues endangering national security. The theory, built on new perceptions of the four elements of cyberspace and the new trend of equal state sovereignty in the cyberspace era, is used to safeguard the territorial land, water, airspace, cyberspace, and citizen security of sovereign states as well as construct new legal mechanisms for international and domestic use in cyberspace in a peaceful manner. Moreover, it is used to establish new concepts for a series of basic theories, such as "cyberspace is within the scope of sovereign rights", "sovereignty has jurisdiction over cyberspace", "the governance of cyberspace should be coordinated", "cyber sovereignty is equal", and "opposing cyberspace hegemony" to propel new justifiable developments of traditional scientific, political, and legal philosophy in cyber society and construct a new order of rule of law in relation to cyber sovereignty at both the international and domestic levels.

Part II
Epistemology

Although the Internet is highly globalised, the sovereignty of the information of all countries should be respected. No matter how developed a country's internet technology is, it must not violate the information sovereignty of others. No double standards should be allowed in upholding cyber security, and every country has the right to preserve its own information security. We cannot just have the security of one or some countries, leaving the rest insecure. And no country should seek the so-called absolute security of itself at the expense of the security of other countries.

— Excerpt from the speech delivered by
Chinese President Xi Jinping at the
Brazilian National Congress
16 July 2014[1]

---

[1]Xi, J. P. (2014). *Carry Forward Traditional Friendship and Jointly Open up New Chapter of Cooperation — Speech at the National Congress of Brazil.* Retrieved from http://www.xinhuanet.com/world/2014-07/17/c_1111665403.htm.

Chapter Five

The Consideration of Cyberspace Order

The concept of cyberspace order embodies changes in the disciplines of the superstructure, such as politics, philosophy, economics, law, and society, as a result of the transformation of the basis of the cyber economy, which is driven by the improvement of scientific and technological productivity.

Cyberspace is a great invention of mankind to improve macro efficiency by remoulding micrologic. Cyberspace has strengthened the real-time connections between subjects. However, to what extent have connections in cyberspace gone beyond the boundaries of traditional sovereignty? To what extent have they not gone beyond them? If the boundaries of cyberspace order are not clear, their consideration has to be improved.

The practice of sovereignty is often based on power and tradition; it also leads to new policies and development. The traditional concept of sovereignty, especially in the sense of rule of law, has a practical history of less than 400 years. The core of traditional sovereignty concerns dealing with internal and external relations based on the physical boundaries of countries, which is, to some extent, contrary to the idea of the Internet.

Technology changes life, and innovation drives the evolution of rules. From the beginning, the technological revolution of the Internet has brought about great changes to people's lives. However, the current system of textbooks related to network technology under the engineering disciplines is restricted to finding technological solutions while ignoring research on the order of cyber society.

Technological innovation reshapes the elements of cyberspace. In the early stage, technological progress surely disrupted the existing social order of cyberspace subjects. However, along with the initiation and mutation of network technologies, especially with the repeated occurrence and escalation of cyber security incidents, optimistic and pessimistic discussions on cyberspace order have emerged in academic circles. Following the appearance of so many views on cyberspace order, the governments of all countries, out of technological impulse rather than deliberation, tend to formulate policies and strategies different from those of other countries.

As the most obvious corresponding adjustment in the superstructure is legislative change and the sovereignty law in domestic legislation and sovereignty principles in international law are the first to undergo realistic challenges from cyber sovereignty, the change brought about by cyberspace order has most notably manifested in domestic and international law. Through scientific and technological analyses and human social practices, the concept of cyber sovereignty will naturally develop from the concept of cyberspace order. Cyber sovereignty is a concept of the rule of law that comprises the entire process of "the invention of cyberspace, the practice of sovereignty, the popularisation of network, and the legal guarantee". Initially, especially at present, disciplines are divided, theories are fragmented, arts and sciences are separated, double or even multiple standards are adopted, and viewpoints contradict each other. These ubiquitous problems have limited the macro vision and overall application of cyber sovereignty, which must be changed and regulated through the wide implementation of the rule of law in cyberspace.

Section One: Problems in United States Textbooks

Along with scientific and technological progress, human activities are constantly reshaping the social order. In the “natural” order of cyberspace, there are a series of network behaviours that need to be regulated by justice and order, such as anonymity, reputation stealing, hacking, secrets divulging, attacks, and even warfare. From the perspective of the rule of law, we can observe that technological rules in network science and technology textbook systems are not equal to the justified order of cyberspace activities. In other words, these textbook systems do not completely cover, emphasis, and solve the problem of ordered justice between the elements of cyberspace.

I. *Domain Name Security Issues of Ignoring Cyberspace Subjects*

From the perspective of cyberspace subjects, all networks are networks of people.[2] However, the system of internet textbooks does not clearly state how to tell true from false, real from virtual, good from evil, or strong from weak in cyberspace. If these problems are not identified, it will be difficult to create a mature system of internet education. This is similar to the early stage of the invention of automobiles, when there were no highway and traffic regulations. However, after these regulations were improved and good order was established, technological standards, such as those for the design and manufacturing of automobiles, were placed under rule of law, and the technology and rule of law formed a benign symbiosis. Only in this way could they work together to build an overall safe and good order. In terms of today’s Internet, a large problem with internet textbooks is the lack of a rule of law despite advancing technologies.

---

[2] Zhong, Zh. Ch. (2016). *Internet Game Theory*. Beijing: Publishing House of Electronics Industry.

Generally, US computer textbooks focus on layered communication while ignoring the security of elements. Popular textbooks, such as Andrew S. Tanenbaum and David J. Wetherall's *Computer Networks (5th Edition)* published in 2011, Umakishore Ramachandran and William D. Leahy Jr.'s *Computer Systems: An Integrated Approach to Architecture and Operating Systems* published in 2011, David A. Patterson and John L. Hennessy's *Computer Organization and Design: The Hardware/Software Interface* published in 2014, and William Stallings' *Cryptography and Network Security* published in 2015, primarily focus on communication technologies related to layered connections in networks and connections between hardware and software rather than the security of cyber elements. Certain issues that require attention have been ignored in American textbooks. In terms of the overall security of cyberspace, how can "layered connections" be transferred into "cyber elements" in reality?

1. *The Security of Subject Domain Names: The "Address Directory" for the Access of Cyberspace Subjects*

American textbooks do not discuss cyberspace subjects as the primary element of security, similar to those who must take care of the security of coins in circulation instead of those kept in their own safe. From the beginning, the US has maintained control of internet domain names and root servers. ICANN (Internet Corporation for Assigned Names and Numbers), which takes full charge of the DNS (domain name system), has taken control of the root servers and manages the 13 top-level domain root servers. One of these is the primary root server located in Dulles, Virginia, while the other 12 are secondary root servers, 9 of which are in the US, 2 in Europe (Britain and Sweden), and 1 in Asia (Japan). On 1 July 2005, the US Department of Commerce announced that it would retain the right to monitor the 13 root name servers indefinitely.

If the US took control of the root servers for domain name resolution, it would control all corresponding domain names. If the US does not want people to access certain domain names, it is able to block these domain names by making their IP (Internet Protocol) addresses unresolvable so that the websites to which these domain names point to seem to have disappeared from the Internet. For example, in April 2004, Libya disappeared from the Internet for three days due to paralysis of its top-level domain name ".ly". Moreover, the US can also monitor other countries' cyberspace activities by manipulating its privilege in domain name management. For example, the US can view the statistics of the network flow of certain websites in a certain country, from which it can roughly analyse the distribution of popular websites in the country and the preferences of its netizens.[3] However, none of these facts are displayed in US textbooks, which promote the Internet as an open, free, and transparent world. In fact, they purposefully conceal the threat of cyberspace hegemony.

Disputes over domain name management and "being removed" cannot be resolved fairly. The US National Telecommunication Industry Administration has authorised ICANN to take charge of the "root files and system management" of global cyberspace, making ICANN one of the agencies that has the power or mandate to "remove" a country from cyberspace at will. If the country or agency "removed" is unsatisfied, it can only file lawsuits under US jurisdiction in California, where ICANN is located.

2. *Network Technological Standards Highlighting Layered Interconnections Cannot Ensure Cyber Security*

The book *Computer Networks* by Andrew S. Tanenbaum and David J. Wetherall was the first textbook in the field of cyberspace.[4] In the first chapter, it introduces the Open System Interconnection reference model, which, according to technological systems, divides the Internet into seven layers, including the physical layer, data

[3] Cheng, Q. (2015). An Analysis of Internet Corporation for Assigned Names and Numbers (ICANN) and the Future Trend of International Internet Governance. *International Forum* (1), 8.

[4] Tanenbaum, A. S. & Wetherall, D. J. (2012). *Computer Networks* (5th ed.) (p. 24) (W. Yan, & A.M. Pan, Trans.). Beijing: Tsinghua University Press.

link layer, network layer, transport layer, session layer, presentation layer, and application layer. The concept was formulated by the International Organization for Standardization in 1984. It has become a basic model for computer network communications and is regarded as the "law" for network technologies. Similarly, the TCP/IP (Transmission Control Protocol/Internet Protocol) model in the early stages of the Internet was generally regarded by the technology community as the technological standard or "de facto standard" of the Internet.[5] Although the elaboration of these technological standards ensures the interconnection of networks, it is unable to ensure the security, stability, autonomy, or controllability of the order and rule of law in cyberspace.

3. *The Definition of the "CIA (Central Intelligence Agency) Triad of Cyber Security" is a Double Standard and Differential Treatment Aimed at Serving Itself*

In the field of computer science in the US, *Network Security Essentials: Applications and Standards (5th Edition)*[6] is a textbook devoted to cyber security. Its definition of cyber security is cited from *An Introduction to Computer Security: the NIST Handbook*, published in 1995: computer security refers to the protection afforded to an automated information system in order to attain the applicable objectives of preserving the integrity, availability, and confidentiality of information system resources (includes hardware, software, firmware, information/data, and telecommunications). It emphasises the confidentiality, integrity, and availability of cyber security, which are enshrined in the textbook as the standard principles of "the CIA triad of cyber security".

The abovementioned triad represents cryptography, layered network application, and computer system security, respectively. Within the textbook's structure, a description of the security of the

---

[5] Yu, X. Q. (2007). Similarities, Differences and Correlation Between OSI Reference Model and TCP/IP Model. *Science and Technology of West China* (27), 50.

[6] Stallings, W. (2014). *Network Security Essentials: Applications and Standards* (5th ed.) (G.Q. Bai, Trans.). Beijing: Tsinghua University Press.

address directory of cyberspace subjects, the most critical element, is also omitted. This is possibly out of a similar consideration that so long as the address directory is placed in the keeper's own safety box, it is safe for the keeper. Omitting a description of the security of the addresses of other cyberspace subjects is probably normal on the author's part but could give rise to readers' concern.

About confidentiality. Upon comparing a topological graph of the core security elements of the Internet, we can see that the US' bases of architecture, chip technology, intelligence surveillance, and data capabilities are superior to those of other countries. Even allies' secrets are usually not secrets to the US, while highly classified US information is primarily used to defend from outside attacks and theft.

About integrity. As the US has taken absolute control of the allocation of all internet domain name addresses, the largest security threat to its integrity is local resilience. However, the integrity of the internet security of countries and regions whose domain name addresses are assigned by the US faces a risk of life and death, e.g. being paralysed or "removed".

About availability. To other countries, availability originates from access to the Internet and the internal interconnection of local routers; to the US, availability implies the power to control the information in the entire Internet and to access the Internet or "remove" domain names, which it considers the top level of overall control.

In a word, "the CIA triad of cyber security" defined by the US is the academic reflection of its hegemonic view of security, featuring "double standards" and differential treatment. As Xi Jinping noted in his speech in Wuzhen on 16 December 2015, "No double standards should be allowed in upholding cyber security... We cannot just have the security of one or some countries, leaving the rest insecure. And no country should seek the so-called absolute security of itself at the expense of the security of other countries."[7]

---

[7] Xi, J. P. (2015). *Remarks by H.E. Xi Jinping, President of the People's Republic of China, at the Opening Ceremony of the Second World Internet Conference.* Retrieved from http://www.xinhuanet.com/politics/2015-12/16/c_1117481089.htm.

II. *The Ideological Trend of Information Freedom with an Emphasis on Cyberspace Objects*

Since the 20th century, a group of US scientific elites has emerged in the field of the Internet, such as Alan Turing, the father of artificial intelligence; Grace Murray Hopper, the mother of computer programming; Jay W. Forrester, the inventor of magnetic-core memory; John von Neumann and John Vincent Atanasoff, the fathers of electronic computers; Douglas Engelbart, the father of the computer mouse; and Ted Nelson, the father of hypertext transfer protocol (HTTP).[8] In the field of internet theory, there is also a group of famous US scholars, some of whom are still active in the world academic arena.

1. *Advocating Cyber Innovation and Internet Media Communication*

(1) Stanford: Top Scholars + Technology Companies + Defence Appropriations + Silicon Valley Rent = A World-Class University

Frederick Terman received his bachelor's degree in chemistry and master's degree in electronic engineering at Stanford University in 1920 and his doctor's degree in computer science at MIT (Massachusetts Institute of Technology) in 1924. He was a US expert on air-defence radars during World War II and became a founding member of the US National Academy of Engineering in 1964. In the 1940s, he returned to Stanford University and solved the critical problem facing the university in its endeavour to build a world-class university: how to make a profit from the university's land to bring in first-class professors. In 1951, he encouraged Stanford University to establish the world's first university industrial park on 2.65 square kilometres of Stanford's land and transferred technologies from the university to companies in the park. In

[8] Fang, X. D. (2004). *IT History Part 4 (Chapters of Heroes in Thought and Science Elites)* (p. 3). Beijing: CITIC Press.

1955, the park hosted 90 companies and 250,000 employees; in 1971, the site was named "Silicon Valley" and became the holy land of the IT (Information Technology) industry, hatching leading companies in the information, electronics, and internet industries such as Intel, HP, Cisco, 3Com, Sun, Netscape, Oracle, Silicon Graphics, Apple, Adobe, and Yahoo. Terman is known as the "father of Silicon Valley" for his "Silicon Valley concept" (university research and development + enterprise innovation).

In Terman's view, a world-class university needs to rely on top-notch talents rather than those merely above the average. During his tenure as vice-president of Stanford University from 1955 to 1965, he increased the funds acquired from the US Department of Defense by a large margin for the university's schools and departments in the fields of science, statistics, and engineering. Along with the income from the leased land of Silicon Valley, he implemented a "top-notch talent" strategy by spending a large amount of money on bringing in famous scholars to strengthen the teaching staff. Terman also became known as the "father of the electronic revolution" by uniting companies in Silicon Valley and Stanford University to train the employees of these companies as graduate students. In 1991, when Stanford University celebrated its centennial anniversary, the former "countryside university" had surpassed Harvard, Yale, and Princeton University to become the top US university in terms of academic reputation and ranking.

(2) Patrick J. McGovern: Promoting the Dissemination of Thought in the Computer and Cyber World Through Physical Investment

Patrick J. McGovern, named by Forbes as one of the world's richest people in 2013, graduated from MIT and received a master's degree in biological sciences in 1959. He established the American International Data Group (IDG)[9] in 1964, founded the American weekly *Computerworld* in 1967, and co-founded the Chinese

[9] American International Data Group (IDG) is the world's largest company involving information technology publishing, research, exhibition, and venture investment. According to an estimation by Bloomberg, IDG has more than 280 million readers worldwide and an annual revenue of more than US$3.6 billion. McGovern,

version of *Computerworld* in China in 1980.[10] In early February 1991, he acquired China's magazine *Network World*. In 1993, he invested US$20 million in cooperation with the Shanghai Municipal Committee of Science and Technology to establish the first venture investment company in China. At present, through building joint ventures and cooperating with other ventures in China, IDG has published over 40 newspapers and magazines related to computers, electronics, communication, and consumption and managed over US$4 billion in venture funds. In 2000, McGovern promised to donate US$350 million within 20 years to build the McGovern Institute for Brain Research in MIT, from which some researchers have already won several prizes, including the Nobel Prize. In 2011, he decided to donate three IDG/McGovern institutes for brain research to Tsinghua University, Peking University, and Beijing Normal University. The institutes are now functioning properly.[11]

2. *The Ideological Trend Advocating Cyberspace Freedom and the Abolition of Copyrights*

(1) Richard Matthew Stallman: The Pioneer of Free Software, Open-Source Code, and the Abolition of Restrictions on Copyright Resources

Richard Matthew Stallman is the pioneer of free software, open-source code, and the abolition of copyright resource restrictions, the spiritual leader of the free software movement, the founder of the GNU Project and the Free Software Foundation, and a famous hacker. His major accomplishments include Emacs, GNU Emacs, GNU C compiler, and GNU debugger. His GNU General Public

---

the founder of IDG, was named one of the 400 richest people in the world by Forbes in 2013.

[10] McGovern, P. Retrieved from https://en.wikipedia.org/wiki/Patrick_Joseph_McGovern.

[11] Xiong, X. G. *A Memorial Essay by Xiong Xiaoge to McGovern, the Founder of IDG*. Retrieved from https://www.aliyun.com/zixun/content/2_6_626100.html?spm=5176.100033.400001.9.u41Fts.

License (GNUGPL), the most widely used free software license in the world, has blazed a completely new path for the "copyleft" concept. His greatest influence is the moral, political, and legal framework that has been created for the free software movement. He is known by many people as an advocate for free software and a great idealist.

Stallman is a staunch advocate of the free software movement. Unlike those advocating open-source codes, he views free software from the perspective of morality rather than software quality. He believes that using patented software is immoral and that only programmes with source codes are ethical. Many people disagree with this, leading to the "free software movement" and the "open-source software movement" factions. Stallman hopes that one day, software developers will receive the rewards they deserve by providing services (such as technical support and training) instead of forcing customers to spend a large amount of money to buy their software by means of copyright laws. In a word, the basic principle for the future of the software industry is "free resources, charged service".

(2) Lawrence Lessig: A Harvard Cyberspace Jurist Who Regards Code as Law and Advocates the Abolition of Limitations on Copyrights

Lawrence Lessig is an American scholar, professor at Harvard Law School, and academic and political activist. He advocates reducing legal restrictions on copyrights and trademarks, especially those on the application of RF (radio frequency) spectrum technology. Lessig believes that cyberspace is a type of public resource, which, in essence, implies freedom, and that code is the law in cyberspace. He also thinks that cyberspace is independent of physical space and that conflicts in cyber sovereignty can be resolved through the coordination of international cyberspace treaties.

Lessig is a founder and sponsoring member of Creative Commons and the director of the Edmond J. Safra Center for Ethics at Harvard University. He is also a member of the Software Freedom Law Center, the Advisory Committee of Sunlight Foundation, and former member of Electronic Frontier Foundation.

He raised US$1 million to take part in the 2016 Democratic presidential primary but withdrew on 2 November. He has been hailed as "the most important thinker on intellectual property in the internet era" by the *New Yorker* and as "the guardian of the internet age" by *Businessweek*.

(3) Yochai Benkler: A Harvard Cyberspace Jurist Who Regards Cooperation as Human Nature and Advocates Information Sharing

Yochai Benkler, a professor of law at Harvard University, is currently leading the Berkman Center for Internet & Society at Harvard University, one of the top internet research institutions in the world. Benkler is a practitioner of the Creative Commons concept and the initiator of the Creative Commons movement. Lawrence Lessig has praised him as the greatest genius of the information age.

Benkler thinks that human nature has the gene of cooperation and that human beings can work together to create enormous value for themselves. He believes that the Internet, which has abandoned the old systems of the Industrial Age, such as monitoring, salaries, rewards, and punishments, represents a new culture, mechanism, and platform that drives humans to create great value through "cooperation". The Internet will create a new pattern of social innovation, within which technological progress will form a collaboration platform that transcends traditional organisations and regions. Professor Benkler believes that openness, sharing, cooperation, and win-win outcomes will become the world's value proposition and that new business ethics, social relations, and human knowledge systems will also be constructed. On this basis, the culture of cooperation will create a new era of "emotion, consensus, joy and order".

Section Two: Problems in Chinese Textbooks

Followers can rarely surpass leaders, but subverting them is even better than overtaking them. Since China gained access to the

Internet in 1994, its textbooks have experienced three stages of development: following others' technologies, trying to surpass them, and trying to subvert them. However, its views on cyber security and the rule of law in cyberspace once seriously lagged behind western countries; this was reflected as a limited research horizon in the field of law.

I. *Copied Textbooks*

The internet architecture in Chinese textbooks is copied from US textbooks, lacking a keen understanding of the design of US internet architecture as well as independent innovation in terms of the architecture of knowledge and overall concept of cyber security. In the textbooks of Chinese colleges and universities, most of the information about cyberspace theories does not go beyond the scope of that in US textbooks. Therefore, it is urgent to reflect on the formulation of China's own cyberspace views and academic theories.

China's computer science textbooks also follow US textbooks and focus on layered communication. The Chinese versions of previously mentioned US textbooks such as *Computer Networks (5th Edition),*[12] *Computer Systems: An Integrated Approach to Architecture and Operating Systems,*[13] *Computer Organization and Design: The Hardware/Software Interface,*[14] and *Cryptography and Network Security,*[15] which are currently the mainstream textbooks in China, also focus on layered connections in networks, connections between hardware and software, and communication technologies.

---

[12] Tanenbaum, A. S. & Wetherall, D. J. (2012). *Computer Networks* (5th ed.) (W. Yan, & A.M. Pan, Trans.). Beijing: Tsinghua University Press.

[13] Ramachandran, U., & Leahy, W. P. (2015). *Computer Systems: An Integrated Approach to Architecture and Operating Systems* (W.Y. Chen *et al.*, Trans.). Beijing: China Machine Press.

[14] Patterson, D. A., & Hennessy, J. L. (2015). *Computer Organization and Design: The Hardware/Software Interface* (D.H. Wang *et al.*, Trans.). Beijing: China Machine Press.

[15] Stallings, W. (2015). *Cryptography and Network Security* (M. Tang *et al.*, Trans.). Beijing: Publishing House of Electronics Industry.

However, apart from these "copied textbooks", Chinese colleges and universities have particularly highlighted the research on and practice of the following issues with regard to national cyber security.

1. *The Development and Practice of the Independence and Security of the Four Elements of Cyberspace: The Security of Cyberspace Elements such as the IPv6 Outside the "Address Directory"*

Since 2014, China has made strong moves across the board in the independent research and development of IPv6 capacity expansion,[16] security chips (integrated circuits), operating systems, security databases (information centres), middleware, disaster backup (data centres), cryptography technologies, firewall/VPN (virtual private network) technologies, electronic authentication, and quantum communication technologies.[17] It has made gratifying progress in each aspect of the four cyberspace elements, namely the security of cyberspace platforms, subjects, objects, and activities. However, due to its late start, there is still much room for improvement in the fields of key equipment, key technology, and core logic.

2. *The Governance Practice of Independence and Security of Cyber Sovereignty: Increasing the Practice of the Rule of Law in Fields such as Cyber Security Review and the Right to Privacy*

Article 59 of the National Security Law of the People's Republic of China stipulates, "The state shall establish a system and mechanism for national security review and supervision, conduct a

---

[16] Chen, Y. Q. *et al.* (2012). *Constructing Carrier-Grade IPv6 Network* (p. 269). Beijing: Publishing House of Electronics Industry; Davies, J. (2014). *Understanding IPv6* (3rd ed.) (p. 1) (H. L. Wang, Trans.). Beijing: Posts and Telecom Press.

[17] China Electronic Information Industry Development Institute. (2015). *Blue Book of the Cyber Security Development in China (2014–2015)* (p. 81). Beijing: People's Publishing House.

national security review on foreign investments, specific items, key technologies, and network information technology products and services, construct projects involving national security matters and other major matters and activities that affect or may affect national security, and effectively prevent and mitigate national security risks." Within less than a year, relevant authorities in China have conducted national security reviews on cyber products and services such as Windows 10, Apple Pay, and "cloud computing", during which relevant foreign and domestic companies have been very cooperative. This mechanism is a good example of exercising sovereignty in cyberspace.

Despite the rapid development of China's practices in cyber sovereignty and cyber security legislation, compared with the US (which has over 100 years of history in terms of the rule of law in the fields of information and cyberspace), it still has a long way to go in improving its legal system of cyber sovereignty.

II. *Segmented Departmental Laws*

For a long time, due to a lack of comprehensive ideas about cyberspace, few Chinese experts have taken an approach contrasting international cyber theory and studied the cyber world from the perspective of departmental laws. The existing problems are as follows:

1. *Research is Confined to the Legal Protection of Local Information from the Perspective of Departmental Laws*

In the field of civil law, jurists have undertaken detailed problem-oriented research on the rule of law in cyberspace from the perspective of private law theories,[18] such as the protection of personal information rights and interests and information flow from the perspective of contract law, the infringement of cyberspace

[18] Yang, Y. J. (2013). *A Study of Private Law Protection of Personal Information* (pp. 31–36) (PhD dissertation). Jilin University, Changchun, China.

information from the perspective of tort law, and the protection of cyberspace copyrights from the perspective of intellectual property law.[19] Moreover, there are many legal research works on specific cyberspace services, such as studies on legal mechanisms to safeguard the security of internet-based banking business. Research from the perspective of departmental law has covered most specific issues in cyberspace in relation to the operation of micro businesses and macro supervision. However, they are limited due to excessive emphasis on the part while barely seeing the whole as well as the lack of an overall approach to the entirety of cyber security.[20]

In the field of criminal law, some scholars analyse information security at three levels, i.e. state, society, and individual, and elaborate on legal issues endangering information security. Some researchers focus on the protection of personal information from the perspective of criminal law alone, summarise the mode of protection through criminal law, and compare content about the protection of personal information outlined in foreign criminal laws.[21] China's national conditions are different. It has the most netizens, which has given birth to the world's largest network operator, network service market, and network user group. Thus, China's cyberspace subject behaviour features a large user base socially. As network activities in China are far more complex than those in other countries, surveys on national conditions and theoretical improvement with Chinese characteristics based on cyber sovereignty theories are needed during the legislation of anti-crime and anti-terrorism, social stability, cyberspace public opinion monitoring, and cyberspace infrastructure protection.

---

[19] Zhang, T. (2012). *Defining the Right of Personal Information and its Civil Law Protection — Based on Benefit Balancing* (pp. 74–80) (PhD dissertation). Jilin University, Changchun, China.

[20] Li, Y. L. (2014). *Criminal Law Protection of Information Security in the Big Data Era* (pp. 32–42) (Master's thesis). China University of Political Science and Law.

[21] Duan, X. N. (2011). *A Study on Criminal Law Protection of Personal Information* (pp. 13–15) (Master's thesis). Jilin University, Changchun, China.

In the fields of administrative law, economic law, social law, and sovereignty law, cyber security falls within the social practice category, whose basic theory should be constructed as a whole. There are many prospective studies on legal protection through telecommunication law, mass communication law, communication technology standards, and computer protection in China's legal circle. Particularly in some discussions about future policies and regulation in low-ranking departments, people have expressed concern about the pluralism of agencies and overlapping of mechanisms for the management of cyber security, which is a call for the restructuring of the governance in cyberspace as a whole. The legislation on cyberspace order needs to consider the integration of departmental laws based on an overall recognition of network technologies, break down barriers among various subjects, reduce the overlap of powers in multi-agency management settings, and fully consider the entirety, boundary, technicality, and systematicness of cyber sovereignty to resolve the theoretical discrepancies and backward cognition resulting from one-sided viewpoints.

2. *Being Confined to Discussing the Legitimacy and Jurisprudential Analysis of Cyberspace Rights in an Abstract Way*

Some Chinese scholars use the theory of rights to analyse the legitimacy of cyberspace activities and the value of information protection from a jurisprudential perspective.[22] However, they often ignore the social and technical characteristics of cyberspace itself. Research from the perspective of rights and values often lags behind cyberspace phenomena, which emerge in an endless stream, while research on cyberspace from a jurisprudential perspective often concludes with far-fetched interpretations of these phenomena. From where do rights in cyberspace originate? This is a technical question that cannot be avoided. If this question cannot be

[22] Li, X. H. (2004). *A Study on the Reasoning of Information Right* (pp. 45–78). (PhD dissertation). Jilin University, Changchun, China.

solved, subsequent inferences will be a castle in the air, and people will be unable to conduct solid research or will have to set too many premises and assumptions. Due to the rapid development of technology, it is impossible to undertake enough legal research on recently emerged problems. For example, existing legal theories can barely manage new situations and problems in the era of big data, and it is difficult to rigorously explore the technical source, hardware support, information essence, and subject activities of cyberspace rights under the framework of network technology.

3. *Being Confined to Research on Private Rights While Ignoring Overall Research on the Ontology of Cyberspace*

In 1995, the European Union (EU) issued many instructions demanding its member states to establish personal information protection mechanisms that can be incorporated into domestic laws.[23] The relevant member states also established a series of relevant legislation. For example, Germany enacted the unified Federal Personal Data Protection Act. The protection of personal information in the US has mainly been placed under the restrictive regulations of the Privacy Act of 1974 and is accompanied by many other separate legislations. Aside from privacy, other information is protected by the regulations of the National Security Department.

Information in cyberspace cannot be equated with the right of privacy defined by traditional law. Some scholars study information or cyberspace as their research subject and study information law or cyberspace law as a separate departmental law,[24] which is often reflected in practice as the improper separation of virtual networks from entity information. Cyber security is not merely about information security or privacy security. Information security

[23] Ma, M. H. (2009). *EU Legal Framework of Information Security — Regulations, Directives, Resolutions and Conventions* (p. 2). Beijing: Law Press.

[24] Qi, A. M. (2010). *The Authentic Thesis on Information Law* (p. 60). Wuhan: Wuhan University Press.

only refers to the security of the "object", which is only one of the four elements of cyberspace. The interaction of network operation behaviour and personal network information behaviour has mixed the traditional creditor, copyright, privacy, and other civil and commercial rights in cyberspace. In other words, the traditional division of the science of law hardly covers all aspects of cyber sovereignty and security.[25]

Section Three: The New Cyber Security Discipline

I. *New Discipline in Cyber Security in China*

In 2015, when Professor Wu Jianping of Tsinghua University proposed to establish China's cyber security discipline, he advocated a five-section model composed of application security, system security, cyber security, foundations of cyberspace security, and cryptography and its application (Figure 5-1).

As a newly established discipline system, the four elements of cyberspace need to be clarified. Thus, it needs improvement with the theory of cyber sovereignty. For example, the system in the draft lacks the consideration of logical security between modules. Logical security, an important component in addition to network hardware, specifically refers to the logical structures, key parameters, domain name addresses, and link premises in cyberspace. Consisting of root name servers, domain names, IP addresses, and a series of public and hidden "data protocols", it is the fundamental power for the allocation of cyberspace resources. The logic of root domains is fundamental to the establishment of the cyber security discipline. Only by independently controlling the DNS can we secure the logical security of all network IDs. Questions will naturally arise during the follow-up development of the discipline, such as how to organically link international

[25] Zhao, H. R., Yang, Y. Z., & Zhang, Sh. Sh. (2016). Basic Theory Construction for China's "Cybersecurity Law". *Cognition and Practice* (1), 39.

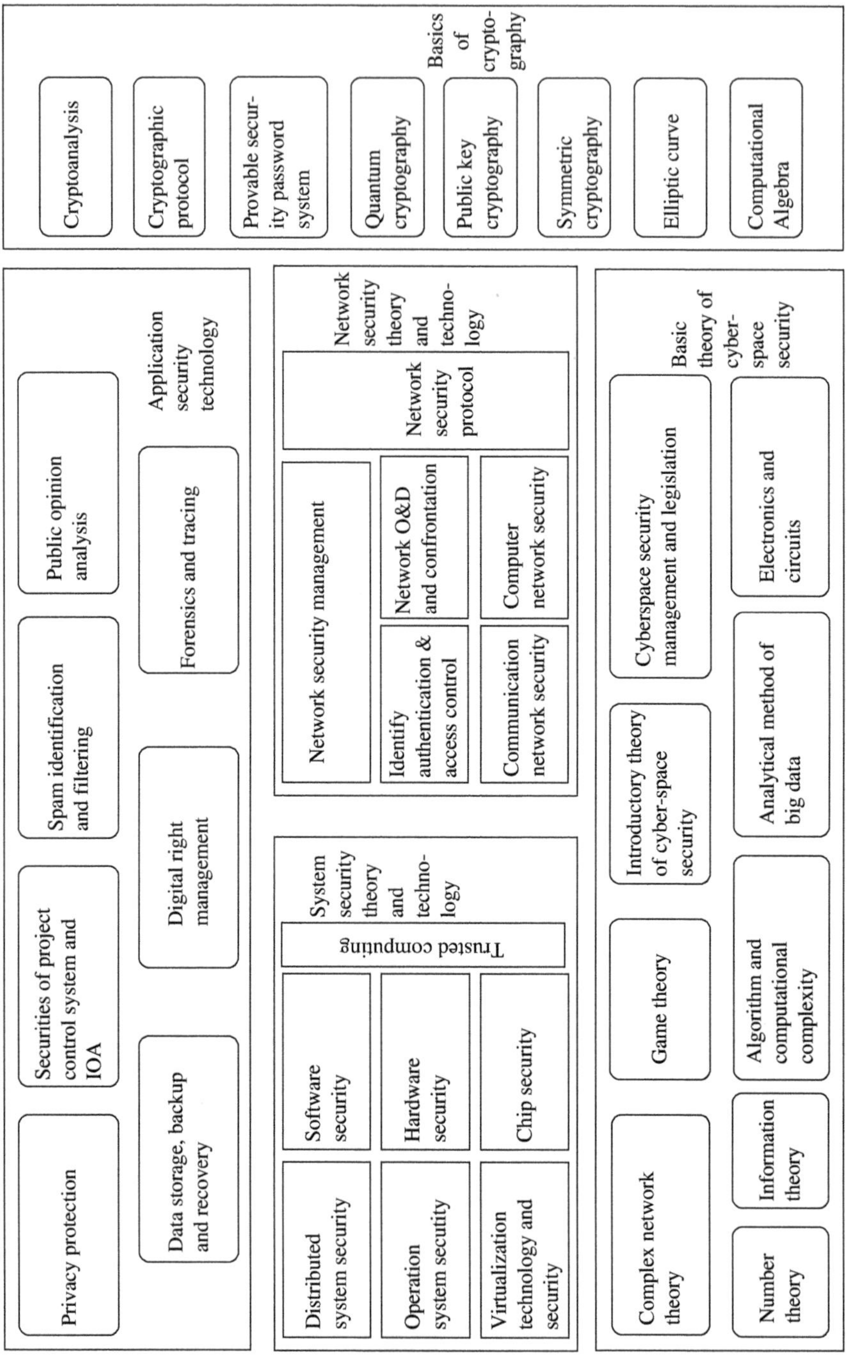

Figure 5-1: A draft of the knowledge system of the early-stage cyberspace security discipline in China

co-governance and sovereign autonomy, how to establish cyber sovereignty independently, how to achieve the relative security of autonomous networks, and how to safely manage and control cyberspace infrastructures.

The US purposefully ignores the logic of root domains in its computer theories because it has taken full control of this logic. However, as China cannot control its own root domains independently, it is presently unable to ensure the absolute security of its own root domain systems. Without consideration of the security of root domain systems, the development of other superstructures in this field cannot be ensured. Therefore, in the development of the cyber security discipline, China must constantly improve deficiencies such as copying US textbooks, lacking due consideration of the logic of root domains, and ignoring the importance of root domain security.

As the top-level architecture of the four elements of national cyber security, the security of network connections is about ensuring the permanent and independent existence of networks. As for the protection of the logical system, safeguarding the effective use of the country's top-level network logical connection system and top-level domain name is the most fundamental research mission in the field of cyber security. As such, China should regard it as the core of the cyber security discipline.

In today's ICT (information and communications technology) world, where strength is more dominant than rules, we should correspondingly adhere to the "four-dimensional legislation" of cyber security proceeding from the four elements of cyberspace. The aim of studying cyberspace ontology from the perspective of subjects, objects, platforms, and activities is to clarify the entirety of the rule of law in cyberspace, oppose one-sidedness of the rule of law in cyberspace, uphold the justice of the rule of law in cyberspace, and oppose the unfair multiple standards adopted by the countries monopolising network technologies. The development of the cyber security discipline in China should also follow this pattern.

Generally speaking, China has some advantages in terms of platforms (routers and terminals). However, it is still behind in terms of root domain logic, chip technology, software technology, and data storage. Therefore, the most urgent question facing the development of this discipline is whether China should turn the tide in the field of root domain logic and chip technology to establish the rule of law in cyberspace as well as a discipline system that could promote its national security. It can be seen that the root of the problem lies in the autonomy of cyber security. The most basic goal of the construction of this discipline is the autonomy of cyber security, while the difficulties faced by the rule of law in cyberspace concern how to promote the development of network technology and safeguard cyber sovereignty at the domestic level as well as how to advocate equal cooperation in terms of cyber sovereignty while attaching as much importance to non-traditional "cyber warfare" as to the traditional "nuclear balance" at the international level.

II. *The Restructured Discipline of Cyber Security in the US*

CloudPassage hired an independent consultant to analyse undergraduate courses on computer science, computer engineering, and computer information systems in degree programmes in 121 US universities and published a research report about the status quo of cyber security education in the computer science major of American universities.

The report suggests that none of the top 10 US universities with the best computer-related undergraduate majors require the students to take cyber security courses. Three of them do not offer an elective course in cyber security. In fact, only 1 of the top 36 US computer science programmes requires a security course for graduation: the computer science programme at the University of Michigan.

Robert Thomas, the CEO of CloudPassage, said that the US had over 200,000 job vacancies in the field of security in 2015, but the capability and level of expertise of the applicants were far from satisfying. When examining these applicants, who had computer science degrees from top universities, CloudPassage found that few universities regard cyber security credits as an essential condition for the undergraduate degree. Thus, it was hard for these undergraduates to meet the requirements of cyber security jobs.

Of the 121 universities studied, the following offer the highest number of elective courses on cyber security: Rochester Institute of Technology (ten electives), Tuskegee University (ten electives), Depaul University (nine electives), University of Maryland (eight electives), University of Houston (seven electives), Pace University (six electives), California Polytechnic State University (five electives), Cornell University (five electives), Harvard University (five electives), and Johns Hopkins University (five electives).

The American education system is failing computer science students by deprioritising cyber security training. Universities are inadvertently contributing to the lack of cyber security readiness in the US by failing to teach students how to implement security thinking and awareness into new code design, development, and testing. The study also found that the major root cause of the lack of security education and training is that cyber security issues are not widely recognised in universities. Cloud Passage is prepared to donate technology to universities committed to tackling this important issue.

At present, US colleges and universities are restructuring the cyber security discipline. For example, in Stanford University, many cyber security courses have been added to the computer science programme. However, cyber security is a new comprehensive discipline that covers computer, telecommunication, management, law, and sociology sciences. The situation in China is generally similar to that of the US. Four to five independent disciplines and colleges are "tied" together mechanically; therefore, it is difficult for them to form a completely integrated discipline in colleges and universities and rapidly enhance the maturity of the cyber security discipline.

Section Four: The New Ideas on Cyber Sovereignty

I. *The US: From Lawrence to Hillary*

Lawrence Lessig, a professor at Harvard Law School, was born in 1961. He signed up for the democratic presidential race in 2015 but subsequently quit, as Hillary Clinton was more popular. Hillary Clinton, born in 1947, won the democratic presidential primary in February 2016 but lost the election in the end. We cannot rule out the possibility that Lessig will continue to run for US president on behalf of the Democrats in the future. Notably, Lessig's three books laid the foundation for US cyber sovereignty theory, which became the theoretical cornerstone for the US foreign policy of "cyberspace-over-freedom" introduced by then-Secretary of State Hillary Clinton.

1. *Lessig's Perspective on Cyber Sovereignty is that Communication, Control, Code, and Architecture Constitute Hierarchical Cyberspace*

Deconstructing cyberspace from the perspective of law, Lessig thought that cyberspace consists of four progressive hierarchies:

(1) The "End-to-End" Principle
First described by network architects Jerome Saltzer, David Clark, and David P. Reed in 1981, this principle — called the "end-to-end (e2e) argument" — guides network designers in developing protocols and applications for networks. The computers at the end of a network are the machines used to access the network. The computers "within" the network are the machines that establish the links to other computers and, thereby, form the network itself. Computers within the network should perform only very simple functions that are needed by many different applications, while functions that are needed by only some applications should be performed at the edge. Thus, complexity and intelligence in a network are pushed away from the network itself.[26] Aimed at simplicity and flexibility, the e2e argument says that a network should provide a very basic level of service (data transport) and that the intelligence (the information processing needed to provide

[26] Lessig, L. (2004). *The Future of Ideas* (p. 35) (X. Li, Trans.). Beijing: CITIC Press.

applications) should be located in or close to the devices attached to the edge (or ends) of the network.[27] The result is that the "ends" push forward the unlimited development of the network, which is the core of the e2e principle. He quoted Tim Berners-Lee, the inventor of the World Wide Web, as saying, "Technically, if there was any centralized point of control, it would rapidly become a bottleneck that restricted the Web's growth, and the Web would never scale up. It being 'out of control' was very important."[28] The consequences of this commitment to e2e are many; the birth of the World Wide Web is just one. The World Wide Web is a set of protocols for displaying hyperlinked documents linked across the Internet. These protocols specify how "browsers" retrieve content on the World Wide Web, but they simply run on top of the protocols that define the Internet. These internet protocols, referred to as TCP/IP, are the foundation upon which the protocols that make the World Wide Web function run.[29] The e2e principle renders the Internet an innovation commons.[30]

(2) "Control" Makes Freedom in Cyberspace

Lessig claimed that the word "cyberspace" suggests not freedom but control. Its etymology reaches the world of "cybernetics", i.e. the study of control at a distance through devices.[31] Liberty in cyberspace will not come from the absence of the state. Liberty, as anywhere, will come from a state of a certain kind. We build a world where freedom can flourish not by removing any self-conscious control from society but by setting it in a place wherein a particular kind of self-conscious control survives.[32] However, such

---

[27] Ibid., p. 35.

[28] Ibid., p. 41.

[29] Lessig, L. (2004). *The Future of Ideas* (p. 42) (X. Li, Trans.). Beijing: CITIC Press.

[30] Lessig, L. (2004). *The Future of Ideas* (p. 49) (X. Li, Trans.). Beijing: CITIC Press.

[31] Lessig, L. (2009). *Code: And Other Laws of Cyberspace, Version 2.0* (p. 4) (X. Li *et al.*, Trans.). Beijing: Tsinghua University Press.

[32] Lessig, L. (2004). *Code: And Other Laws of Cyberspace* (p. 5) (X. Li *et al.*, Trans.). Beijing: CITIC Press.

self-conscious control does not come from regulations by the government, which can deter but not control cyberspace activities. The regulation of cyberspace by the law often serves no practical purpose. Since the network follows the e2e principle, it is born free. Freedom is its technical nature.[33]

(3) Code is the Nature of Cyberspace and the "Law" of the Community

Code refers to the instructions embedded in the software or hardware that makes cyberspace what it is. These software/hardware and instructions constitute the code, which regulates activities such as identity recognition, digital signatures, information encryption, screening, and filtering in cyberspace. Code can be divided into source code (human-written, made up of logic and language) and object code (machine-readable, an undifferentiated string of 0s and 1s). Code is the link between humans and computers.[34] The Internet is a network of networks. In the main, these networks connect over wires. All of these wires and the machines linked by them are controlled by code.[35] Networks are real-time communication systems that connect standalone "ends" through codes and physical links and share information through data links. In a network, the code dominates connection and communication as well as information and exchange. Lessig also explained the differences between the Internet and cyberspace: compared with the Internet, cyberspace has changed our way of life and created unprecedented modes of interaction.[36] Cyberspace is not one place; it is many places. The characters of these many places differ in fundamental ways. These differences come in part from the differences in the people who populate these

[33] Lessig, L. (2009). *Code: And Other Laws of Cyberspace, Version 2.0* (p. 3) (X. Li *et al.*, Trans.). Beijing: Tsinghua University Press.

[34] Lessig, L. (2009). *Code: And Other Laws of Cyberspace, Version 2.0* (p. 52) (X. Li *et al.*, Trans.). Beijing: Tsinghua University Press.

[35] Lessig, L. (2004). *The Future of Ideas* (p. 27) (X. Li *et al.*, Trans.). Beijing: CITIC Press.

[36] Lessig, L. (2009). *Code: And Other Laws of Cyberspace, Version 2.0* (p. 83) (X. Li *et al.*, Trans.). Beijing: Tsinghua University Press.

places.[37] Different sites also form different communities. For example, American Online (AOL) describes itself as a "community" (this community has a constitution, not in the sense of a written document but in the sense of a way of life for those who live there).[38] Moreover, the Counsel Connect (CC) community, an online lawyers' cooperative, allows its users to engage in conversations with each other; through this access and these conversations, value can be created.[39] There are many other communities, such as LambdaMOO, IBEX, Second Life, Tape, TV, and Radio Tags.[40] Network codes "construct" the layered, open, controlled, and regulated cyberspace.

Architecture 1: Layers

Lessig explained the concept of "layers" within cyberspace with the definition formulated by Yochai Benkler, a law professor at New York University, who suggested that we understand a communications system by dividing it into three distinct layers. At the bottom is a "physical" layer, across which communication travels. This is the computer or wires that link computers on the Internet. In the middle is a "logical" or "code" layer, i.e. the code that makes the hardware run. Here, we might include the protocols that define the Internet and the software upon which those protocols run. At the top is a "content" layer, i.e. the actual things that are said or transmitted across these wires. Here, we include digital images, texts, online movies, and the like.[41] The Internet mixes freedom with control at different layers. The physical layer of the Internet is fundamentally controlled. Similarly, at the content layer, much of

---

[37] Lessig, L. (2009). *Code: And Other Laws of Cyberspace, Version 2.0* (p. 84) (X. Li *et al.*, Trans.). Beijing: Tsinghua University Press.

[38] Lessig, L. (2004). *Code: And Other Laws of Cyberspace* (p. 83) (X. Li *et al.*, Trans.). Beijing: CITIC Press.

[39] Lessig, L. (2009). *Code: And Other Laws of Cyberspace, Version 2.0* (p. 95) (X. Li *et al.*, Trans.). Beijing: Tsinghua University Press.

[40] Lessig, L. (2009). *Code: And Other Laws of Cyberspace, Version 2.0* (p. 118) (X. Li *et al.*, Trans.). Beijing: Tsinghua University Press.

[41] Lessig, L. (2004). *The Future of Ideas* (p. 23) (X. Li *et al.*, Trans.). Beijing: CITIC Press.

Table 5.1: The "freedom and control" in cyberspace

	Speakers' Corner	Madison Square Garden	Telephone System	Cable TV
Content	Free	Free	Free	Controlled
Code	Free	Free	Controlled	Controlled
Physical	Free	Controlled	Controlled	Controlled

the existing Internet is controlled (e.g. cable television (TV)). Not everything served across the Internet is free for the taking; much is properly and importantly protected by property law.[42] In comparison with the traditional modes of communication, the "freedom and control" in cyberspace are shown in Table 5.1.

Architecture 2: Open

Public resources in cyberspace can be divided into three parts: the first is the public resources of code, which refer to the public resources comprising the software and many applications based on basic network protocols; the second is the public resources of knowledge, which refer to the free exchange and sharing of all ideas and information related to cyberspace and the working mechanism of its codes; and the third is the public resources of innovation, which means that everybody has the opportunity to undertake construction and innovation on cyberspace platforms. Therefore, open public resources are critical. Less control over the code at the content layer will create more innovation and improvement of this code, and keeping this resource in the public domain will increase its value.[43] Another problem related to public resources is open and

[42] Lessig, L. (2004). *The Future of Ideas* (p. 25) (X. Li *et al.*, Trans.). Beijing: CITIC Press.

[43] Lessig, L. (2004). *The Future of Ideas* (p. 75) (X. Li *et al.*, Trans.). Beijing: CITIC Press.

closed code.[44] Architecture with open-source code implies a constraint on state power and means lifting the "control".[45]

Architecture 3: Public Key

Lessig cited Stewart A. Baker and Paul R. Hurst as saying, "Cryptography surely is the best of technologies and the worst of technologies. It will stop crimes and it will create new crimes. It will undermine dictatorships, and it will drive them to new excesses. It will make us all anonymous, and it will track our every transaction."[46] Thus, the technological basis for building cyberspace order is encryption with a "public key" and the construction of a perfect "public key" infrastructure to facilitate online authentication and website access.[47] Joel Reidenberg was the first to claim that "code is law".[48] Philip Rosedale also noted, "What is God in a virtual world? Your only God is the code."[49] Cyberspace contains structural values and substantial values. The man-made "architecture" built by code reflects structural values. Cyberspace is being "constructed" into another kind of control tool by business activities.[50]

---

[44] Lessig, L. (2004). *Code: And Other Laws of Cyberspace* (p. 132) (X. Li *et al.*, Trans.). Beijing: CITIC Press.
[45] Lessig, L. (2004). *Code: And Other Laws of Cyberspace* (p. 133) (X. Li *et al.*, Trans.). Beijing: CITIC Press.
[46] Lessig, L. (2004). *Code: And Other Laws of Cyberspace* (p. 46) (X. Li *et al.*, Trans.). Beijing: CITIC Press.
[47] Lessig, L. (2004). *Code: And Other Laws of Cyberspace* (p. 48) (X. Li *et al.*, Trans.). Beijing: CITIC Press.
[48] Lessig, L. (2009). *Code: And Other Laws of Cyberspace, Version 2.0* (p. 6) (X. Li *et al.*, Trans.). Beijing: Tsinghua University Press.
[49] Lessig, L. (2009). *Code: And Other Laws of Cyberspace, Version 2.0* (p. 304) (X. Li *et al.*, Trans.). Beijing: Tsinghua University Press.
[50] Lessig, L. (2004). *Code: And Other Laws of Cyberspace* (p. 8) (X. Li *et al.*, Trans.). Beijing: CITIC Press.

Lawrence described how these modalities — law, the market, norms, and architecture — interact as they regulate.[51]

Law: Law is a command backed by the threat of a sanction and is obviously much more than a set of commands and threats. It not only commands certain behaviours but also expresses the values of a community.

Social norms: Social norms constrain differently. Via social norms, normative constraints are imposed not through the organised or centralised actions of a state but through the many slight and sometimes forceful sanctions that members of a community impose on each other. A norm governs the socially salient behaviour from which deviation makes you socially abnormal.

The market: The market constrains through price. A price signals the point at which a resource can be transferred from one person to another. The constraints of the market exist because of an elaborate background of law and norms defining what is buyable and sellable as well as rules of property and contract for how things may be bought and sold. However, given these laws and norms, the market still constrains in a distinct way.

Architecture: Plainly, some of the constraints of architecture are constraints we have made, and some are not. The constraints of architecture are neither contingent nor, in their full range, dependent. Architects call this the built environment. Architectural constraints can be both absolute and relative; the constraints of man-made architecture are both self-implemented and self-executed.

Architecture 4: Governance by the "Invisible Hands" Jointly Constructed by the Government and Commerce

Lessig thought that the early Internet was open and designed to hide nothing. However, changes occurred when merchants tried to expand their business to cyberspace. Security changed first. Under the Secure Socket Layer (SSL) protocol and Secure Electronic

[51] Lessig, L. (2009). *Code: And Other Laws of Cyberspace, Version 2.0* (p. 340) (X. Li *et al.*, Trans.). Beijing: Tsinghua University Press.

Transaction (SET) protocol, the security on which commercial exchanges rely on successfully constructed the first step towards secure electronic commerce, thus opening up cyberspace governance. The architecture of secure electronic commerce is governed by authentication, authorisation, privacy, completeness, and non-repudiation.[52] The invisible hand of cyberspace, pushed by government and commerce, is building an architecture that is quite the opposite to its architecture at birth.[53] Overall, the first generation of cyberspace architecture was created by scientific researchers in the non-commerce field, the second generation was created by the commerce community, and the third generation should be created by the government to put an end to spam mail, computer viruses, identity theft, and other such phenomena. The government has the right to adjust the architecture of cyberspace.[54] It should practice fairness and justice in cyberspace.[55] However, it should not impose absolute regulation in cyberspace to avoid stifling innovation.[56]

(4) Architecture is sovereignty.

The sovereignty of the user community and cyber sovereignty that transcends national borders are different from state sovereignty. Lessig thought that the cyberspace architecture created by code is a type of cyber sovereignty. The architecture determines the degree of control and the dominion to control or regulate behaviours. Lessig claimed that the concept of sovereignty makes sense only when it is placed on a particular basic architecture of control. The state's power may be "absolute", but if the architecture does not

[52] Lessig, L. (2004). *Code: And Other Laws of Cyberspace* (p. 51) (X. Li *et al.*, Trans.). Beijing: CITIC Press.

[53] Lessig, L. (2009). *Code: And Other Laws of Cyberspace, Version 2.0* (p. 5) (X. Li *et al.*, Trans.). Beijing: Tsinghua University Press.

[54] Lessig, L. (2009). *Code: And Other Laws of Cyberspace, Version 2.0* (p. 5) (X. Li *et al.*, Trans.). Beijing: Tsinghua University Press.

[55] Lessig, L. (2004). *Code: And Other Laws of Cyberspace* (p. 73) (X. Li *et al.*, Trans.). Beijing: CITIC Press.

[56] Lessig, L. (2004). *Code: And Other Laws of Cyberspace* (p. 3) (X. Li *et al.*, Trans.). Beijing: CITIC Press.

support regulation, the state's effective power is quite slight.[57] Architecture is a kind of sovereignty that governs community life in the space. People have to consider the politics represented by that architecture.[58] Based on the regulation of this architecture, David Post elaborated on this viewpoint in his paper "Anarchy, State, and the Internet". He argued that communities in cyberspace are governed by "rule-sets". We can understand these rule-sets to be the requirements, whether embedded in the architecture or promulgated in a set of rules, that constrain behaviour in a particular place. The world of cyberspace, he argued, is comprised by these rulesets. As rulesets compete for our attention, the world of cyberspace will come to be defined by this competition of merchant-sovereigns for customers.[59]

Users' community sovereignty: As life moves online and increasing amounts of citizens from states X, Y, and Z come to interact in cyberspaces A, B, and C, these cyberspaces may need to develop the kind of responsibility and attention that develops (ideally) within a democracy. That is, if cyberspace wants to be considered its own legitimate sovereign and, thus, deserving of some measure of independence and respect, it must more clearly become a citizen-sovereignty. Only governance under citizen-sovereignty is legitimate, while non-democratic governance cannot be tolerated. Lessig argued that all present regulations in cyberspace are democracy-like but not democracy. Democracy is the practice of people choosing the rules that will govern a particular place. Citizen-sovereignty specifically refers to the right of political and social management.[60] Thus, the link between entitlement and geography makes sense. Lessig thought that the relationship

---

[57] Lessig, L. (2009). *Code: And Other Laws of Cyberspace, Version 2.0* (p. 303) (X. Li *et al.*, Trans.). Beijing: Tsinghua University Press.

[58] Lessig, L. (2004). *Code: And Other Laws of Cyberspace* (p. 26) (X. Li *et al.*, Trans.). Beijing: CITIC Press.

[59] Lessig, L. (2009). *Code: And Other Laws of Cyberspace, Version 2.0* (p. 309) (X. Li *et al.*, Trans.). Beijing: Tsinghua University Press.

[60] Lessig, L. (2009). *Code: And Other Laws of Cyberspace, Version 2.0* (p. 306) (X. Li *et al.*, Trans.). Beijing: Tsinghua University Press.

between the users and cyber community is like that between the citizens and government. The users, playing a role similar to that of shareholders who have a say, surely have the right to take part in management. The right to participate originates from users' participation in the community, which cannot be limited by actual locality. Communities in cyberspace will earn a similar immunity more quickly if they reflect citizen-sovereign values rather than merchant-sovereign values. The more responsible the communities become, the more likely real-space governments will defer to their norms through doctrines like immunity. The citizen-sovereignty in cyberspace is indeed the driving force to maintain and promote the realisation of the value of freedom in cyberspace. Lessig argued that at present, cyberspace is not yet dominated (or even broadly populated) by citizen-sovereignties and that the sovereignties people see so far are mostly merchant-sovereignties. However, the merchants' control in cyberspace lacks rationality,[61] while the users' right to participation is rational.

Cyber sovereignty that transcends national borders: Lessig tried to persuade sovereign states in the real world to acknowledge the cyber sovereignty he advocated and said that cyberspace rules are everywhere and netizens come from every corner of the world. He cited David Johnson and David Post's argument on the vulnerability of locality in relation to cyberspace: "The rise of an electronic medium that disregards geographical boundaries throws the law into disarray by creating entirely new phenomena that need to become the subject of clear legal rules but that cannot be governed, satisfactorily, by any current territorially based sovereign." We should endow cyberspace with independence so that it will not be limited by "actual locality". Lessig called for insights into the independence of cyberspace and the independence of "cyber communities that transcend national borders". He cited Dan Hunter and Greg Lastowska's viewpoint in *Laws of Virtual Worlds*: "Courts will need to recognize that virtual worlds are jurisdictions

[61] Lessig, L. (2009). *Code: And Other Laws of Cyberspace, Version 2.0* (p. 309) (X. Li *et al.*, Trans.). Beijing: Tsinghua University Press.

separate from our own, with their own distinctive community norms, laws, and rights. While cyborg inhabitants will demand that these rights be recognized by real-world courts and virtual-world wizards, they will need to arrive at these rights themselves within the context of the virtual worlds." Lessig thought that the independence of cyberspace is a result of the practical development of the economy and society. Ordinary citizens are connected internationally and can make international transactions as never before. The presence of a community that is beyond any individual state is increasingly undeniable. Cyberspace is an international community; there are constitutional questions for it to answer, and people cannot simply step back from this international space and say that these questions are local issues.[62]

The necessity of sovereign states to reach agreements among global cyberspace communities: Lessig thought international conventions are the product of extended negotiations in regulating international relations. Countries must come to an agreement about how laws will regulate and any norms that they will impose on private ordering. As their work relates to cyberspace in particular, this agreement is quite significant. It will require the nations of the world to come to a common understanding about this space and develop a common strategy to handle its regulation. Lessig thought that sovereign states have blind zones wherein one can identify others' mistakes but not its own. For example, "governments are unwilling to concede that national laws are limited to national borders, and are increasingly turning to explicitly extraterritorial legislation".[63] Lawrence argued that cyberspace is not a network without national borders but the source of three conflicts: local conflict under the rules within a country, transnational conflict under the rules among different countries, and a third stage of debate. In cyberspace, behaviour is systematically

---

[62] Lessig, L. (2009). *Code: And Other Laws of Cyberspace, Version 2.0* (p. 313) (X. Li *et al.*, Trans.). Beijing: Tsinghua University Press.

[63] Lessig, L. (2009). *Code: And Other Laws of Cyberspace, Version 2.0* (p. 319) (X. Li *et al.*, Trans.). Beijing: Tsinghua University Press.

governed within multiple non-coordinating jurisdictions.[64] Therefore, it is especially necessary to build an international consensus on code architecture to resolve cyber sovereignty conflicts. The basic architecture decided by code is the foundation for resolving sovereignty conflicts in cyberspace. For example, in terms of cyber games, governance comes from code. The rules of cyber games are implemented through neither social sanctions nor state sanctions but through this special space architecture. The rules are clarified here, not by law but by the codes of controls. Lessig mapped three separate strategies for the recognition of cyber sovereignty conflicts. The first is a cyber world without laws, which was the dream of the early Internet. The second is the present domestic rule of law governing cyberspace, which is the reality that many nations increasingly see today. The third is future cyberspace order, which is a world balanced by the laws of many countries. On the whole, the legislative process of cyberspace governance in all countries was relatively slow in the early stage but soon picked up speed. Subsequently, it directly aimed at the basic architecture of cyberspace and ultimately directly focused on information control. However, cyberspace has no political preparation.[65] Lessig was sceptical about the everlasting dominance of US laws over cyberspace governance. No one will assert that the US has stopped crime or even behaviour inconsistent with US law on the network. There is a growing desire among many governments around the world to check the power of the US. In 2005, some of these governments tried to wrest control of ICANN from US influence. This resistance, as well as a healthy dose of sovereign self-respect, is increasingly pushing for a regime that better balances the interests of the whole world.[66]

---

[64] Lessig, L. (2009). *Code: And Other Laws of Cyberspace, Version 2.0* (p. 323) (X. Li *et al.*, Trans.). Beijing: Tsinghua University Press.

[65] Lessig, L. (2009). *Code: And Other Laws of Cyberspace, Version 2.0* (p. 328) (X. Li *et al.*, Trans.). Beijing: Tsinghua University Press.

[66] Lessig, L. (2009). *Code: And Other Laws of Cyberspace, Version 2.0* (p. 329) (X. Li *et al.*, Trans.). Beijing: Tsinghua University Press.

The necessity of regulating freedom of speech, authenticating citizenship, and establishing international conventions: Lessig agreed that "national restrictions of freedom of speech are commonplace not only in the United States, but also around the globe. Individual nations, each intent upon preserving what they perceive to be within the perimeters of their national interests, seek to regulate certain forms of speech because of content that is considered reprehensible or offensive to national well-being or civic virtue".[67] He also proposed to establish an identity layer that can certify citizenship. Thus, as people pass across the Web, attached to their presence is a cryptographic object that reveals which government claims them. Lessig also introduced the concept of an international convention that populates a table with any rules that a government wants to apply to its own citizens when those citizens are elsewhere in the world. The table would be public and available to any server on the network.[68] Governments may require servers within their jurisdiction to respect the rules expressed in the table. Thus, if someone offered materials that are not allowed by the laws of a country, the access of citizens in that country to the materials would be blocked. That is, the laws of all countries would be implanted in cyberspace.[69] International coordination in cyberspace is acceptable, and the benefits it brings are reciprocal. Each state has its own stake in controlling certain behaviours, which can initiate a type of quid pro quo between jurisdictions.[70] The result of concession is a cyberspace that can be accepted by all states. It cannot remove the influence of the real world, nor can it be controlled by a country or a small number of major powers. This

[67] Lessig, L. (2009). *Code: And Other Laws of Cyberspace, Version 2.0* (p. 329) (X. Li *et al.*, Trans.). Beijing: Tsinghua University Press.

[68] Lessig, L. (2009). *Code: And Other Laws of Cyberspace, Version 2.0* (p. 309) (X. Li *et al.*, Trans.). Beijing: Tsinghua University Press.

[69] Lessig, L. (2009). *Code: And Other Laws of Cyberspace, Version 2.0* (p. 331) (X. Li *et al.*, Trans.). Beijing: Tsinghua University Press.

[70] Lessig, L. (2009). *Code: And Other Laws of Cyberspace, Version 2.0* (p. 331) (X. Li *et al.*, Trans.). Beijing: Tsinghua University Press.

regime endows all governments with the power to govern their citizens and prevents great-power chauvinism. Such a regime would return geographical zoning to the Internet. It would reimpose borders on a network built without those borders.[71]

2. *Hillary Clinton on Internet Freedom*

After Lessig elaborated on his view of freedom in cyberspace[72] in 2009, US Secretary of State Hillary Clinton immediately delivered a speech on internet freedom in Washington on 21 January 2010. She reaffirmed the freedom of thought, speech, religion, and property on the Internet, particularly adding freedom of access to the Internet and freedom of information flow. Clinton's view on the six freedoms of cyberspace constitute the core of US foreign policy in cyberspace. We can see from the US domestic cyber security strategy that the overall cyberspace strategy of the US combines the emphasis on freedom externally and on security internally. From Lessig to Clinton, we can see the connection between the US' cyber thinking and cyber policy.

II. *China: Safeguard Cyber Sovereignty through Legislation*

Advocating and promoting cyber sovereignty are at the core of China's policy, legislation, and diplomacy regarding cyberspace. Only by taking solid steps to establish the rule of law with regard to cyber sovereignty can we reduce, prevent, and defeat crimes, conflicts, and wars in cyberspace.

China, which used to be an underachiever in terms of cyber technology, now stands as a prominent country in cyberspace and is currently proactively building itself into a power in this respect.

---

[71] Lessig, L. (2009). *Code: And Other Laws of Cyberspace, Version 2.0* (p. 332) (X. Li *et al.*, Trans.). Beijing: Tsinghua University Press.

[72] Lessig, L. (2009). *Code: And Other Laws of Cyberspace, Version 2.0* (p. 332) (X. Li *et al.*, Trans.). Beijing: Tsinghua University Press.

Since the 18th CPC (Communist Party of China) National Congress, in the fields of law, policy, and diplomacy, with the establishment of the Central Leading Group for Cybersecurity and Informatization in February 2014, the enshrinement of cyberspace sovereignty in the National Security Law of the People's Republic of China in July 2015, and the release of the Cybersecurity Law of the People's Republic of China in November 2016, the rule of law in cyberspace has significantly picked up speed in China and played a significant role in governing the four elements of cyberspace. China's legislation aims to maintain cyber sovereignty and safeguard cyber security, which are consistent positions of the country.

On 1 March 2017, the Ministry of Foreign Affairs presented the International Strategy of Cooperation on Cyberspace,[73] which aims to "encourage the international community to come together to enhance dialogue and cooperation and build a peaceful, secure, open, cooperative and orderly cyberspace".

On 27 December 2016, the Office of the Central Leading Group for Cybersecurity and Informatization released the National Cyberspace Security Strategy,[74] which calls for "respecting and safeguarding cyberspace sovereignty. Cyberspace sovereignty cannot be violated. We should respect the right of individual countries to independently choose their own path of cyber development and model of cyber regulation and participate in international cyberspace governance on an equal footing. Cyber affairs within the sovereignty of each country shall be decided by its own people. Each country has the right to, based on its national conditions and international experience, formulate laws and regulations related to cyberspace and take necessary measures in accordance with the law to manage its own information systems and cyber activities within its territory, protect its own information systems and

[73] *International Strategy of Cooperation on Cyberspace*. (2017). Retrieved from http://news.xinhuanet.com/2017-03/01/c_1120552767.htm.

[74] *National Cyberspace Security Strategy*. (2016). Retrieved from http://www.cac.gov.cn/2016-12/27/c_1120195926.htm.

information resources from invasion, interference, attack, and destruction, protect its citizens' legitimate rights and interests in cyberspace, prevent, stop, and punish the dissemination of harmful information in its network that could endanger national security and interests, and maintain the order in cyberspace. No double standards should be allowed in upholding cyber security. No country should pursue cyber hegemony, interfere in other countries' internal affairs or engage in, connive at or support cyber activities that undermine other countries' national security."

On 27 July 2016, the General Office of the CPC Central Committee and the General Office of the State Council published the "Outline of National IT Development Strategy", which proposes "jointly building a new international network order to persist in the principles of respect for cyber sovereignty, maintain peace and security, stimulate openness and collaboration, build a desirable order, and promote the establishment of a multilateral, democratic, and transparent international internet governance system. Vigorously participate in moving forward the internationalisation and reform of the Internet Corporation for Assigned Names and Numbers (ICANN). Strengthen international law enforcement cooperation in cyberspace and promote the formulation of international anti-terrorism pacts in cyberspace. Complete mechanisms for judicial assistance in attacking online crime, and jointly ensure peace and security in cyberspace."

On 25 June 2016, China and Russia released the "Joint Statement between the Presidents of the People's Republic of China and the Russian Federation on Cooperation in Information Space Development", stating, "We uphold as always the principle of respecting national sovereignty in information space... We advocate for equal rights of all countries to participate in internet governance and acknowledge the right to ensure national security in information space based on our own laws and state system. We support the initiative of building a multilateral, democratic and transparent global internet governance system and maintain the UN's important role in setting up global internet governance mechanisms... We jointly advocate respect to and oppose infringements on every country's sovereignty in information space."[75]

On 29 April 2016, according to *People's Daily*, the first China-Russia Cyberspace Development and Security Forum was held in Moscow. The leaders of the Cyberspace Administration of China and the Assistant to the President of the Russian Federation attended the forum. The forum, co-sponsored by the Cybersecurity Association of China and Safe Internet League of Russia, was themed "prospects of ICTs cooperation between China and Russia".

On 22 December 2015, the Russian media reported that Russia had already signed a cooperation agreement with the Cybersecurity Association of China, indicating that the cooperation between the two countries might involve exchanges of experience in the information security field, exercises in the national information security field, and coordinated information defence.

On 18 December 2015, the Second World Internet Conference released the Wuzhen Initiative, which proposes a series of policy principles, such as "maintaining peace and security in cyberspace". It states that "we should respect national sovereignty in cyberspace and protect cyberspace and the critical information infrastructure from threats, interference, attacks, and destruction, protect personal privacy and intellectual property, fight against crime and terrorism in cyberspace ... and encourage the international governance of cyberspace. We call for the international community to cooperate in good faith, seek solutions that accommodate each other's legitimate concerns, stick together in trying times on the basis of mutual trust and shared interest, make joint efforts to develop international norms and rules in cyberspace, respect human's basic rights and fundamental interests on the Internet, maintain the order in cyberspace for the purpose of building a peaceful, secure, open, and

---

[75] *Joint Statement between the Presidents of the People's Republic of China and the Russian Federation on Cooperation in Information Space Development.* (2016). Retrieved from http://news.xinhuanet.com/politics/2016-06/26/c_1119111901.htm.

cooperative cyberspace and a multilateral, democratic, and transparent global internet governance system, with more significant functions played by governments, enterprises, civil organisations, communities, academia, international organisations, and other interested parties in accordance with their respective roles and responsibilities, thus ultimately creating a community with a shared future in cyberspace".[76]

On 17 July 2014, the "Joint Statement Between the People's Republic of China and the Federative Republic of Brazil on Further Deepening China-Brazil Comprehensive Strategic Partnership" proposed to "support all countries' efforts in managing their own Internet and their sovereignty in safeguarding its security". It states that "both sides express concern about present behaviours that apply information and communication technologies for purposes contradicting maintaining international stability and security and for infringement on personal privacy. We hold that the international community should jointly uphold cyber security through cooperation on the basis of mutual respect, equality, and mutual benefit ... We call for joint efforts by the international community to formulate a code of conduct that can be generally accepted by all sides; continue to stick to the principles of multilateralism, democracy, transparency, and full participation by all interested parties; improve the multilateral governance system of the Internet; and strive to achieve co-governance and fair distribution of basic resources on the Internet. At present, both sides are committed to pushing ICANN to achieve globalisation and accept supervision by the international community as well as enhancing the role of the UN Internet Governance Forum in the internet governance system."[77]

---

[76] *The Second World Internet Conference (Wuzhen Initiative).* (2016). Retrieved from http://news.xinhuanet.com/world/2015-12/18/c_128546176.htm.

[77] *The Joint Statement Between China and Brazil on Further Deepening Sino-Brazil Comprehensive Strategic Partnership.* (2016). Retrieved from http://news.xinhuanet.com/politics/2014-07/18/c_1111685756.htm.

As early as 8 June 2010, the State Council Information Office of China noted in the white paper titled "The Internet in China" that "the Internet is an important infrastructure facility for the nation. Within Chinese territory the Internet is under the jurisdiction of Chinese sovereignty. The internet sovereignty of China should be respected and protected."[78]

As can be seen, since 2010, China has been aware of the problem of cyber security and has proposed the notion of cyber sovereignty, which has been recognised by the international community. In the US, some scholars acknowledge that sovereign jurisdiction under international law is insufficient to meet the challenge of modern cyber terrorism. In light of the shortcomings of the existing international rule of law in the governance of cyberspace, some jurists have to compromise on their views. Cyber security must focus on reducing the degree of infringement, otherwise, it will not prevent wars or conflicts in cyberspace. However, subject to the political position of their own country, US scholars have proposed theoretical explanations to disprove China's proposition that only by advocating cyber sovereignty and realising global co-governance in cyberspace can we solve cyber disorder and mitigate cyber threats.

[78] Information Office of the State Council of the People's Republic of China. (2016). *The Internet in China.* Retrieved from http://www.scio.gov.cn/zxbd/tt/Document/1011194/1011194.htm.

Chapter Six

The History of Cyberspace Legislation

The relationship between cyber sovereignty and the rule of law in cyberspace is the relationship between theory and practice under actual cyberspace order. The rule of law in cyberspace is the practice of cyber sovereignty theories and the real reflection of the application of cyber sovereignty. As a "new sovereignty" theory, the theory of cyber sovereignty was developed at the beginning of the 21st century, but its mission to safeguard national security has been reflected in telecommunication laws over the past century. However, since virtual technology, wireless connections, and other communication protocol modes have not been substantially upgraded in the field of telecommunications and as traditional telecommunication security alone hardly posed a direct threat to the security of national sovereignty within the last century, there is no urgent need or objective basis for cyberspace legislation.

As the telephone network was established nearly 100 years ahead of the Internet, telecommunication legislation was created ahead of cyberspace legislation. Cyber technologies are being recoded, defined, and upgraded on the basis of telecommunication technologies. Nowadays, telecommunication and networks have been integrated into what is known as "cyber information". Networks and telecommunication together constitute the "platform", one of the four elements of cyberspace. Legislation on cyber information has a century-long history in international and domestic law.

Under the United Nations' (UN) official context, cyber-information technologies are collectively called ICTs (information and communications technology). The history of cyber-information legislation, including the International Telecommunication Union's 100-year history of international rule of law, can be collectively called the legislation history of ICTs. In retrospect of the history of legislation on cyber information in different countries, we can find that the United States (US) created legislation on information communication prior to the invention of computers and the Internet, and its cyber-information legislation has a history of over 100 years. At present, the US' achievements in the field of cyber-information legislation are presented as a comprehensive legal system for cyber information with a global cyber deterrence capability (including "long-arm jurisdiction"), which has always been established, developed, and improved out of long-term consideration for the US' national security.

Until now, every country's actual need for national cyber security has grown to such an extent that the rule of law in cyberspace should be realised via coordination by cyber sovereignty. The traditional departmental law of telecommunication is already unable to independently fulfil the major mission of safeguarding national cyber security, thus, it is necessary to update it from departmental law to sovereign law to comprehensively prevent new challenges of sovereignty security. Therefore, it is academically significant to review the 100-year history of cyber-information legislation, which can provide historical insights to improve the present legislation on cyber security.

Section One: The 100-Year Rule of Law in the Field of Cyber Information in the US

I. *From Self-Defence to Deterrence*

In 1901, the US established the National Institute of Standards and Technology (NIST) to promote the establishment of standards for new technologies in fields such as communication. For example, the federal Radio Act was enacted in 1912. With the evolution of the world situation during World War I, World War II, the Cold War, and the post-Cold War era, the US' information networks experienced five stages of development, from seeking the country's own national security to achieving global deterrence.

1. *The Embryonic Stage (1917–1966): Originating from Wars and Arms Races*

During World War I (1914–1918), the US enacted the Espionage Act in 1917 to safeguard US national security. As intelligence played an important role in World War II, the US invented the first general-purpose computer in 1946 and subsequently realised the electronisation of computers. The US Department of Defense (DoD) built the ARPANET (Advanced Research Projects Agency Network), which was designed to prevent an arms race in space. In 1966, the US passed the Freedom of Information Act, through which the confidentiality of national security information and citizens' rights to access public information were finally balanced.

2. *The Cold War Stage (1967–1991): Planning Information as a Whole and Winning the Cold War*

In 1978, the US enacted the Federal Computer Systems Protection Act, established the Information Security Oversight Office (ISOO) under Executive Order 12065, and formulated an independent national cyber security policy. In 1981, the US re-specified the functions and powers of its intelligence agencies. In 1984, the US established the cross-agency coordination mechanism for national security. In the same year, it also enacted the Counterfeit Access Device and Computer Fraud and Abuse Act. The implementation of the above-mentioned laws for the overall planning of information and intelligence helped the US win the Cold War in 1991.

3. *The Bubble Stage (1992–2000): The Boom of the Internet Economy*

After the Cold War, the US civilian internet entered a period of rapid development. The Clinton administration released the following policies, laws, and strategies in succession:

(1) The NII Programme in 1993

The National Information Infrastructure (NII): Agenda for Action of 1993, also called the Information Highway Programme, signified the beginning of the US' informatisation construction.

(2) The GII Programme in 1994

The Global Information Infrastructure (GII): Agenda for Cooperation of 1994 was committed to promoting the development of information infrastructure and cooperation among all countries and encouraging cooperation between governmental and non-governmental organisations to promote the development of global information.

(3) The NGI Programme in 1996

The Next Generation Internet (NGI) programme in 1996 aimed to promote the renewal of the old, backward, and overburdened network infrastructure to maintain the US' leading position in terms of ICTs and ensure that it continued to be an indisputable leader in the fields of world economy and politics. In the same year, the US issued the NII Protection Act.

(4) The Internet2 Programme in 1997

In 1997, the US unveiled the Internet2 programme to ensure that universities and research institutions could use advanced networks. It was also aimed at promoting high-level education and information services around the globe, facilitating the growth of the US economy, and maintaining the US' competitive edge in the world.[1]

---

[1]Wang, J. J. (2006). *An Analysis on the America's Reference to China from the US Government's Internet Management* (Master's thesis). Huazhong University of Science and Technology, Wuhan, China.

(5) The National Security Strategy in 2000

In the National Security Strategy Report in 2000, the US President Bill Clinton incorporated an information security strategy into the US' national security strategy.

During this stage, the US' cyberspace policies placed equal emphasis on both military and civilian purposes. The US economy experienced a surge in the field of civilian internet, but this was called the "internet bubble" due to the subsequent steep fall in the stock prices of internet companies. However, the US government had always played a positive role in either network construction or management and wished to control the new world in the post-Cold War era by virtue of its advantages in internet development.

4. *The Anti-Terrorist Stage (2001–2011): From Anti-Terrorism to Internet Freedom*

After the 9/11 incident in 2001, the US immediately passed the Patriot Act of 2001 and the Homeland Security Act of 2002, created the post of Advisor to the President for cyberspace security (also called the "cyber tsar"), and established the President's Critical Infrastructure Protection Board under the US National Security Council. In 2007, the Protect America Act was enacted to fully protect the US' cyber security through strategies, policies, and laws. However, after strengthening its cyber infrastructure and defence capabilities through anti-terrorist policies, the US started to focus on internet freedom with regard to foreign policy.

On 21 January 2010, then-US Secretary of State Hillary Clinton delivered a speech entitled "Internet Freedom" at the Newseum in Washington, DC., during which she proposed six assertions about internet freedom. Apart from Franklin Roosevelt's 1941 "Four Freedoms" speech (which included the freedom of speech and expression, freedom to worship God in one's own way, freedom from want, and freedom from fear), Clinton added the freedom to access the global internet and the free flow of information.

The US has recognised that there are many other networks in the world. Some of them help the flow of people or resources, while some provide aid for interpersonal communication. However, the Internet is a network that improves the strength and potential of all other networks. Therefore, this calls for all sovereign states in the world to allow for the free expansion of networks on the theoretical basis of moral and industrial self-discipline.

The US government's policy orientation and theoretical arguments on internet freedom and the theory of the premise of democracy with regard to popular sovereignty have all played a role. Behind this policy shift, the administrative measures of the US government and the relevant theories of some scholars have "endorsed" such a change.

(1) The US Government's Policies Encouraging Internet Freedom

To begin with, the US government started from internet service providers, operators, and foreign and domestic users and called on them to obey the code of conduct on the Internet and maintain the internet order; then, it called on foreign governments to focus on internet users, cultivate their awareness of self-protection and security, and forbid misbehaviour on the Internet. By advocating the protection of people's legitimate rights from infringement and the maintenance of personal rights, as well as restricting citizens from infringing on others' interests and endangering the state and society, the US government has turned its internet freedom policy into a series of administrative measures and diplomatic guidelines that encourage free access to the Internet and free information flow.

(2) US Scholars' Arguments about Internet Freedom

Lawrence Lessig, a cyber jurist and professor at Harvard Law School, believes that as increasing amounts of citizens from states interact in cyberspaces, these cyberspaces may need to develop the kind of responsibility and attention that develops within a democracy. That is, if cyberspace is to be considered its own legitimate sovereign and, thus, deserving of some measure of independence and respect, it must more clearly become a citizen-sovereignty. Lessig argues that cyberspace, which the government is unwilling and unable to govern, was born free; therefore, the government can deter but not control behaviour in cyberspace. It can enact laws with regard to cyberspace, but these have no practical significance to cyberspace because no government can gain dominance. He claims that the word "cyberspace" suggests not freedom but control, i.e. the study of control at a distance through devices. He believes that to build a world where freedom can flourish, we cannot remove from society any self-conscious control but must set it in a place wherein a particular kind of self-conscious control survives.[2]

(3) Global Citizen-Sovereignty and Cyber Democracy

In his book *Public Domain: Enclosing the Commons of the Mind*, Professor James Boyle of Duke University School of Law proposes the view of "libertarian gotcha". He holds that no government can control anything happening on the Internet and that governments in real space are as pathetic as the Soviet system in its last moments. Cyberspace can only be free, as freedom is its nature. Lessig agrees with the argument that extends from cyberspace freedom to citizen-sovereignty. He states that this kind of freedom in cyberspace is similar to people's freedom in real space, which is set upon a certain constitution. Only governance under citizen-sovereignty is legitimate, while non-democratic governance cannot be tolerated. Lessig believes that all present regulations in cyberspace are democracy-like but not democratic. Democracy is the practice of the people choosing the rules that will govern a particular place. However, what does this kind of citizen-sovereignty specifically refer to? Lessig thinks it refers to the right of political and social management.[3]

---

[2] Lessig, L. (2009). *Code: And Other Laws of Cyberspace, Version 2.0* (p. 306) (X. Li *et al.*, Trans.). Beijing: Tsinghua University Press.

[3] Lessig, L. (2009). *Code: And Other Laws of Cyberspace, Version 2.0* (p. 306) (X. Li *et al.*, Trans.). Beijing: Tsinghua University Press.

5. *The Deterrence Stage (2012–Present): From Snowden to the Reform of ICANN*

In June 2013, Edward Snowden, a 30-year-old former technical analyst for the US Central Intelligence Agency, disclosed secret documents of the US surveillance programme PRISM to Britain's *Guardian* and the US' *Washington Post* in Hong Kong, after which he was wanted by the US government. Subsequently, he flew to Russia and obtained a residence permit there. On 21 June 2013, Snowden exposed Britain's secret intelligence surveillance programme Tempora through the *Guardian*. In February 2015, Snowden was nominated for the Nobel Peace Prize. In September of the same year, he won the Norwegian Bjornson Prize for Freedom of Expression. From the ensuing panic regarding information security in all countries, we can see that the Snowden incident actually announced the incoming era of US cyber deterrence, even though this announcement was delivered by Snowden rather than the US Department of State.

With the in-depth development of the Internet, no sovereign country is willing to subject its own rights and interests to another country. Facing conflict with other sovereign countries in terms of internet security policies, the US has begun to adjust its official foreign policy in cyberspace, transforming from advocating openness and freedom to seeking for a multi-stakeholder model around the globe.

Taking advantage of the reform of ICANN (Internet Corporation for Assigned Names and Numbers), the US initiated a shift of its modern foreign network policies to try to promote the smooth operation of the global Internet by means of representing an organisational and open approach with a multi-stakeholder process and an agreement reached via consultation with non-governmental communities around the world. However, the implementation of this so-called multi-stakeholder model of foreign network policy is more conducive to the strong. Large internet business enterprises in all countries generally support this model, while the general public and their representatives for sovereignty (national governments) are unable to participate in it.[4] This global multi-stakeholder model is questioned by many countries, which argue that the proportion of representatives for special interest groups among ICANN decision-makers is too large. They hope it will be similar to traditional international organisations, which often stick to the UN's principle of sovereign equality that features "one vote for each country".

II. *The System of the Rule of Law in Cyberspace*

The US' information technologies, security standards, and legislation on the entire cyber system have a history of over 100 years. The US' cyber law system originates from the legislative power of the Congress, the president's executive power and power to formulate national security strategies and policies, and the legislative power of all states. These include four sources of legislation, namely federal laws, the president's orders, the policies of the National Security Council, and state acts, respectively, which jointly constitute the four dimensions of the US' rule of law in cyberspace.

1. *The 80 Federal Laws Related to Cyberspace*

Approximately 80 federal laws constitute the primary source for the US' rule of law in cyberspace, including the NIST Organic Act of 1901; the Radio Act of 1912; the Espionage Act of 1917; the Communications Act of 1934; the National Security Act of 1947; the Automatic Data Processing Act of 1965; the Freedom of Information Act of 1966; the Privacy Act of 1974; the Federal Computer Systems Protection Act of 1978; the Foreign Intelligence Surveillance Act of 1978; the Counterfeit Access Device and Computer Fraud and

---

[4] Singer, P. W., & Friedman, A. (2015). *Cybersecurity and Cyberwar: What Everyone Needs to Know* (p. 18) (China Academy of Information and Communications Technology, Trans.). Beijing: Publishing House of Electronics Industry.

Abuse Act of 1984; the Cable Communications Policy Act of 1984; the Computer Fraud and Abuse Act of 1986; the Electronic Communications Privacy Act of 1986; the Computer Security Act of 1987; the Video Privacy Protection Act of 1988; the Computer Matching and Privacy Protection Act of 1988; the High-Performance Computing Act of 1991; the Communications Assistance for Law Enforcement Act of 1994; the Prohibition of Child Pornographic Pictures Act of 1995; the Telecommunications Act of 1996; the Communications Decency Act of 1996; the Information Technology Management Reform Act of 1996; the Secure Public Networks Act of 1997; the Digital Millennium Copyright Act of 1997; the Computer Security Enhancement Act of 1998; the Children's Online Privacy Protection Act of 1998; the Identity Theft and Assumption Deterrence Act of 1998; the Cyberspace Electronic Security Act of 1999; the Government Information Security Reform Act of 2000; the Convention on Cybercrime of 2001 (which took effect in the US on 1 January 2007); the USA Patriot Act of 2001; the Federal Information Security Management Act of 2002; the Homeland Security Act of 2002; the Cyber Security Research and Development Act of 2002; the E-Government Act of 2002; the Fair and Accurate Credit Transactions Act of 2003; the Containment of Illegal Pornographic Information and Commercial Information Act of 2003; the Identity Theft Penalty Enhancement Act of 2004; the Intelligence Reform and Terrorism Prevention Act of 2004; the Protect America Act of 2007; the US Invention Program to Maintain Technology, Education, Scientific Advantage Act of 2007; the Energy Independence and Security Act of 2007; and the Health Information Technology for Economic and Clinical Health Act of 2009.

2. *The 30 Presidential Orders (Executive Orders) Related to Cyberspace*

The US presidential orders related to information and cyberspace security include the Prescribing Regulations Establishing Minimum Standards for the Classification, Transmission, and

Handling, by Department and Agencies of the Executive Branch, of Official Information Which Requires Safeguarding in the Interest of the Security of the United States of 1951; the Providing for the Physical Security of Facilities Important to the National Defense of 1953; the Classification and Declassification of National Security Information and Material of 1972; the National Security Information of 1978; the Assignment of National Security and Emergency Preparedness Telecommunications Functions of 1984; the Access to Classified Information of 1995; the Further Strengthening the Sharing of Terrorism Information to Protect Americans of 2005; and the Improving Critical Infrastructure Cybersecurity of 2013. These presidential orders, derived from US presidents' executive power to plan national security affairs as a whole, which originated from the federal National Security Act of 1947, have the effect of national administrative regulations. They constitute the second source of the US' rule of law in cyberspace.

3. *The 100 National Security Strategies and Policies Related to Cyberspace*

With the constant revision of the National Security Act of 1947, the power of the National Security Council (NSC), which is the US president's legitimate agency for the overall planning of national security affairs, is increasingly expanding in terms of formulating strategies and policies. Although policies related to information security, such as the National Policy on Use of Cryptomaterial by Activities Operating in High Risk Environments (NCSC-5) of 1981; the National Security Communications Instruction (NACSI-6002) of 1984; the Communications Security Monitoring (NSTISSD-600) of 1990; the Protective Distribution Systems (NSTISSI-7003) of 1996; the National Information Assurance Training Standard for Systems Administrators (CNSSI-4013) of 2004; the National Policy for Public Key Infrastructure in National Security Systems (CNSSP-25) of 2009; the National Policy Governing the Release and Transfer of US Government Cryptologic National Security Systems Technical Security Material, Information, and Techniques to Foreign

Governments and International Organizations (CNSSP-8) of 2012; and the National Secret Enclave Connection Policy (CNSSP-29) of 2014, are not laws, they have a binding force within the US government system.[5] In particular, after the 9/11 incident in 2001, the US established a special National Security Telecommunications and Information Systems Security Committee (NSTISSC) under the State Security Council that strengthened the formulation and release of cyber strategies and policies. Although the full texts of some policies have not been published, they have strong pertinence and executive power and jointly constitute the third source of the US' rule of law in cyberspace.

4. *The 10 State Acts (Local Regulations) Related to Cyberspace*

In 1978, Florida issued the world's first Computer Crime Act, which other states followed; these were the earliest written acts. Now, most of them have been replaced by federal laws and international laws, such as the Computer Fraud and Abuse Act of 1986, the Computer Security Act of 1987, and the Convention on Cybercrime, which took effect in the US in 2007.[6] However, at present, there are still state acts related to cybercrime, identity information, digital signature, telecommunications security, digital copyright, protection of privacy, and data protection in states such as Florida, Illinois, California, Massachusetts, Michigan, Nevada, and Utah. These state acts constitute the fourth source of the US' rule of law in cyberspace.

Among the over 220 laws, strategies, and policies in the four sources of the US' rule of law in cyberspace, the presidential orders and national security strategies are the most numerous and flexible. Over the past 100 years, these federal laws have established the world's most complicated and sound national rule

[5] Liu, F. *et al.* (2015). *Overview of the Cybersecurity System in USA* (p. 39). Beijing: Science Press.

[6] Lv, J. H. (2014). *A Study of U.S. Thought on Cyber Warfare* (p. 14). Beijing: Military Science Publishing House.

of law in cyberspace. State acts often take the lead in placing some concepts of the rule of law in cyberspace into practice and are then included into federal laws. However, until now, some state acts have still kept their local characteristics and their people's consensus. Generally speaking, federal laws are comprehensive and systematic, and policies and strategies are flexible and changeable. These are the advantages and characteristics of the US' rule of law in cyberspace.

Section Two: The Modern Western Cyber Strategies

Following the legislation on cyberspace by the US, which is the inventor of the Internet, other Western countries and some emerging economies have established cyber strategies, policies, and legislation with their own characteristics. In this section, we will discuss such rules of law in cyberspace to draw a global picture through comparison.

I. *The European Union's (EU) Cyber Strategies*

The history of the EU's cyber security strategies can be generally divided into three stages:

1. *The First Stage: New Establishment of Mechanisms (1993–2000)*

In 1993, the EU released the "Delors White Paper", which, for the first time, included promoting the development of the ICT industry into a development strategy towards the 21st century to build an information society. In support of this, the EU improved the rule of law and put forth policies and proposals such as "protecting data and privacy" and "solving the security problems of information and communications systems".

2. *The Second Stage: Upgrading Mechanisms (2001–2009)*

Since the 21st century, international non-traditional security threats have become increasingly serious. After the cyberattack in Estonia in 2007, the EU realised the reality of cyber threats. It started to place emphasis on cyber security and promoted the rule of law and internationalisation of its cyber security strategies. In its "Proposal for a Policy Towards Network and Information Security" of 2001, the European Commission emphasised the importance of cyber information security for the first time. Moreover, in 2004, the European Union Agency for Cybersecurity (ENISA) was created to enhance the EU's cyber security and promote the exchange of information and sharing of experience among its member states. In 2006, the EU adopted the Strategy for a Secure Information Society, which further proposed to cultivate a cyber security culture that could be shared by everyone in the entire union. In March 2009, the European Commission issued a policy on critical information infrastructure protection (CIIP) to increase the EU's shift from the previous goal of "emphasizing technological innovation while ignoring security control" to "placing equal emphasis on technology and security" in the face of major cyber security incidents. The EU's shift was no longer only focused on the protection of personal data and business privacy. To protect the EU from massive cyberattacks and network outages, the organisation started planning to enhance the overall risk resistance capacity of its networks at both the EU level and the member state level.

3. *The Third Stage: Deepening Mechanisms (2010–Present)*

In May 2010, the EU released the five-year plan for the Digital Agenda for Europe (DAE) as one of the "flagship programmes" implementing the EU 2020 strategy. In February 2013, the EU formally released the "Cyber Security Strategy of the European Union: An Open Safe and Secure Cyberspace", which was its first strategic document in the field of cyber security. The EU's main objectives were clearly identified as countering cybercrimes and maintaining the security of critical infrastructures. When formulating the mechanisms, it designed a joint cooperation network connecting the "member state/EU/international" levels. By then, the overall architecture of the EU's strategic system for cyber security had been established. On 27 April 2016, the European Parliament released the General Data Protection Regulation (GDPR), which created unified rules for the storage, identification, classification, and transmission of data and information. The hefty fines on illegal activities imposed by the regulation make the EU the strictest region in terms of information protection.

Generally speaking, the EU's cyber security strategies are centred around information security, particularly the protection of personal data and business privacy, and expand to the fields of information security, data security, and cyber security. Differing from the US with regard to the governance of cyber security, the EU is more inclined towards a broad and comprehensive model of social governance that, by placing emphasis on the protection of citizens' personal rights and interests, strives to view cyberspace as a place of democracy and rule of law rather than an arena for an arms race.[7]

II. *The Characteristics of Western Strategies*

By summarising Western countries' cyber policies, we can observe the following characteristics:

1. *Placing Equal Emphasis on Development and Security*

In its cyber security strategy, the UK put forth the idea of "seizing opportunities and facing challenges", which refers to enhancing its capability to maintain cyber security and protect national security and development on the one hand and creating a good cyber environment, attracting foreign investment, and seizing opportunities to expand the market for cyber security products and services on

---

[7]Zhou, Q. J. (2015). An Analysis of EU's Cyber Security Strategy. *European Integration Studies* (3), 63.

the other hand. Japan also endeavours to seize opportunities and increase the development of the cyber security industry to gain an advantage in the international market.

2. *Choosing Different Strategic Priorities*

The cyber security strategies of countries with strong comprehensive national strength, such as the US, Germany, and Russia (which does not belong to the group of Western countries), are not only aimed at safeguarding these countries' security but also place emphasis on striving for and maintaining their advantage and voice in cyberspace and struggling for the right to formulate cyber rules. The cyber security strategies of countries with weaker comprehensive national strength, such as India and South Korea, only focus on safeguarding the countries' own cyber interests and the healthy development of their economy and society.

3. *Increasing International Cooperation*

Due to the virtual and transnational nature of cyberspace and restraints in terms of funds and technologies, many countries tend to "huddle together for warmth" in the field of cyber security. The EU member states are the most typical of these. They not only work together to develop network security strategies but also establish relevant agencies to promote cooperation among themselves. In its cyber security strategy, Japan argues that it is important to strengthen cooperation with countries that share US values. The strategies of countries such as South Korea, Australia, and Canada also emphasise the importance of international cooperation, although they know that the US hopes to play a dominant role in terms of international cooperation in cyber security.

4. *Emphasising the Rule of Law in Cyberspace*

Starting from their own existing laws and regulations on cyber security, the major Western countries have established clear strategic goals and measures for their cyber security strategies. In the face of future cyber security issues, they have put forth legislative conceptions and made every effort to fill the legislative gap caused by the technology gap.

5. *Strengthening Cooperation with Private Sectors*

Privatisation is generally at a very high level in Western countries. Many critical information infrastructures are operated by private sectors. Therefore, these countries' cyber security strategies strive to join forces through cooperation between governments and private sectors, through which the governments' major responsibilities include urging private sectors to implement protection measures for cyber security and strengthening information sharing to prevent cyber threats.[8]

Section Three: The Dimensions of China's Cyber Risks

As root DNS (Domain Name System) servers are under the control of Western countries, represented by the US, these countries take control of the allocation of root domains and network addresses, through which they dominate the value tendency of the global information platform, the right to set agendas, and the political pertinence of mainstream public opinion, thus weakening the cyber sovereignty of other countries. Due to its lack of control of its root DNS servers, China's computer networks face severe security risks. In particular, the constant increase of netizens and weak core technologies have amplified the vulnerability and risk of China's networks.

I. *A Large Number of Cyber Citizens*

With the emergence of mobile networks and smartphones, China has experienced explosive growth in terms of network users, and

[8] Liu, X., & Hao, Y. J. (2015). Experience and Enlightenment of Foreign Cyber Security Legislation. *Secrecy Science and Technology* (7), 17.

the corresponding amount of cyber information has also shown a trend of explosive growth. According to the "37th Statistical Report on Internet Development in China" published by the China Internet Network Information Center (CNNIC) in 2016, by December 2015, China had 688 million internet users with an internet penetration rate of 50.3%; the number of mobile phone internet users had reached 620 million, its proportion up by 90.1%. Its wireless network coverage had undergone a remarkable improvement, with 91.8% of the internet users having access to wi-fi, up by 2.4% relative to 2014.

China's internet users account for more than half of its entire population. With the explosive growth of the internet population and the network information and terminals that go with it, China's demand for internet order and governance has notably risen. The idea of cyber sovereignty has been mentioned, and proactive attempts have been made to maintain China's own cyber sovereignty. Against the bigger picture of multi-polarisation of the global network, wherein China, Japan, and the EU act as the driving forces, the US, sensing the pressure, has adopted a global cyber policy based on "multi-stakeholder" governance.

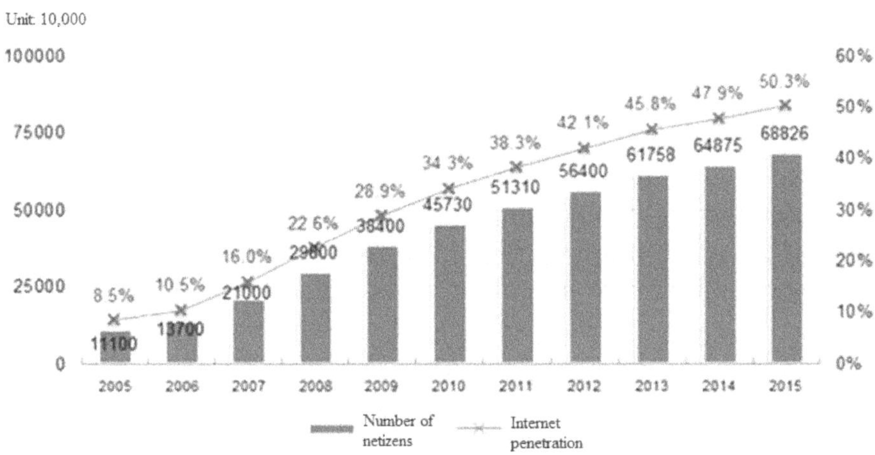

Figure 6-1: The scale of internet users and the internet penetration rate in China

II. *The Fragility of Cyber Platforms*

Although China took the lead in enacting the Cyber Security Law of the People's Republic of China, the law's implementation is subject to the availability of technology. Currently, the fragility of cyber technology impedes the implementation of the rule of law in cyberspace. This problem manifests itself as follows:

1. *At the Level of Computer Applications*

Users are prone to attack from a variety of viruses and hackers as they log onto the Internet through operating computer networks whose core technology is still controlled by others. This problem primarily takes the following two forms: first, computers are infected with Trojan horses or invaded by hackers, as computer users lack cyber security awareness and click on websites or links indiscriminately; second, network users know little about software and hardware configuration and other cyber technologies, which gives rise to cyber security vulnerabilities that can lead to cyber security issues.

2. *At the Level of Computer Physics*

Computer physics mainly refers to the hardware, including terminals, intermediate equipment, and network media, e.g. the mainframe, server, switch, router, and cyber security firewall. The setting and binding of the mainframe and server's IP (Internet Protocol) addresses have been proven effective to some extent; VLAN (Virtual Local Area Network) segmentation and security configuration via the switch can guarantee a certain extent of security protection. Configuration of the rule in the router can effectively limit abnormal accesses; firewalls can be either hardware or software, and high-quality firewall NAT (network address translation) technology can effectively ward off attacks from external networks. Overall, configuring network hardware is an indispensable protective measure. However, it can lead to security threats if used inappropriately.

3. *At the Level of the Operating System*

The computer operating system is the fundamental basis upon which the entire computer network maintains safe and smooth operation; however, it is usually where cyber security problems occur. Today, the most commonly used computer operating systems are of the Windows family. None of the operating systems are 100% bug-free upon release, and each have to be patched and upgraded as problems emerge during use. Some people use pirated operating systems, which greatly increases the chances of security breaches and instabilities among other risks. These security breaches and loopholes allow viruses and hackers to wage destructive attacks that put the security, completeness, and effectiveness of the network users' data information at risk and can trigger further cyber security problems.

4. *Application of the "Firewall"*

In the face of these dangers, China has begun to use "firewall" technology, which was initially invented by the US, announcing the dawning of the age of firewalls. It is also the major precautionary approach currently adopted by China to ensure cyber security. Installing a firewall in a computer network system basically involves configuring hardware equipment to connect the inside with the outside of the network. By using packet filtering and proxy server techniques, a firewall can effectively impede malicious interference of the external network to the internal network, thus ensuring the operation security of the computer network. At the same time, a firewall, when combined with various kinds of anti-virus software, effectively prevents attacks launched by the external network to the internal network. It conducts real-time monitoring of the computer network system to protect it from the intrusion of malicious information and handles malicious information and attacks to keep the information in the computer network system relatively safe.

Section Four: The Establishment of the Rule of Law in Cyberspace in China

Research on cyber security (including the birth of the cyber sovereignty principle and creation of the cyber security discipline) for anti-cyber-hegemony purposes has become a hot topic in China in recent years. On 5 July 2015, the Academic Degrees Committee of the State Council approved "Cyberspace Security" as a first-grade discipline and approved the creation of a PhD programme in the new discipline at 29 colleges and universities. From the protection of private rights to that of sovereign rights and from technological research and development to subject layout, progress has quickened in both the academic study and state legislation of cyber sovereignty and cyber security.

I. *Research and Legislation*

1. *Research on Cyber Sovereignty*

Pivoting on the basic theories of cyber sovereignty (including cyber security and the discipline paradigm), four major views on cyber legislation have been developed in the Chinese academic circle:

(1) The Theory of the Cyber Sovereignty Premise

Cyber security is based on the certainty of cyber sovereignty, which serves to consolidate the position of international law in the age of the Internet, maintain economic sovereignty, create a military presence in cyberspace, construct a frontier defence in the dissemination of information, and maintain cyber security.[9]

---

[9] Huang, H. F. (2016). A Dialogue with Academician Fang Binxing: Cyberspace Security is Not Only About the Security of Platforms. *Communication World Weekly* (9), 14.

(2) The Theory of the Four Elements of Cyber Sovereignty

Based on cyber security, cyber sovereignty comprises four major elements, i.e. the logical link, physical terminal, user management, and data information, which constitute the closed topology of the discipline system, research orientation, legislative style, and cyber sovereignty.[10]

(3) The Theory of Cyber Security Discipline Modules

The newly established cyber security discipline system should consist of five main modules: cyberspace security foundation, application security, system security, cyber security, and cryptology and its application.[11]

(4) The Theory of the Big Network and Cyber Sovereignty

Cyber security involves security issues that concern electromagnetic equipment, electronic information systems, data operations, and system applications in cyberspace. It entails data security in relation to the Internet, telecommunication network, radio and television network, the internet of things, industrial control network, online social network, computer system, communication system, and control system. Effort is required to prevent security breaches stemming from abuse of technology.[12]

2. *The Establishment of the Rule of Law in Cyberspace*

Developing countries like China should consider their realities carefully and independently produce their own cyber sovereignty-related theories and policies. As an internet giant, China aims to assign greater importance to policymaking, followed by the

---

[10] Zhao, H. R. (2015). A Brief Analysis of "Four-Dimensional Overall View of the Rule of Law in Cyberspace". *China Information Security* (7), 43.

[11] Wu, J. P. (2016). Look-Ahead Layout of the Next-Generation Internet. *People's Daily*.

[12] Fang, B. X. (2010). *Convergence and Harmony — Theory, Practice and Information Security of Triple Play*. Beijing: Beijing University of Posts and Telecommunications Press.

creation of the concept of cyber sovereignty and the formulation of cyber sovereignty legislation.

(1) The First Conference of the Central Leading Group for Cyberspace Affairs

On 27 February 2014, Xi Jinping, Head of the Office of the Central Leading Group for Cybersecurity and Informatization, chaired the first conference of the Leading Group and delivered an important speech wherein he noted that "cyber security and informatization are major strategic issues that are closely pertinent to national security, national development, and the lives and work of the people. We must follow the general domestic and international trend and design the overall layout to channel the forces of all parties involved into innovation and development with the aim of building our country into a cyberpower."[13]

(2) Xi Jinping's First Advocacy of Information Sovereignty During His Speech in Brazil

On 16 July 2014, President Xi Jinping mentioned in his speech addressing the National Congress of Brazil, "Although the Internet is highly globalized, the sovereignty of the information of all countries should be respected. No matter how developed a country's internet technology is, it must not violate the information sovereignty of others. No double standards should be allowed in upholding cyber security, and every country has the right to preserve its own information security. We cannot just have the security of one or some countries, leaving the rest insecure. And no country should seek the so-called absolute security of itself at the expense of the security of other countries."[14]

---

[13] Cyberspace Administration of China. *The First Meeting of the Central Leading Group for Cybersecurity and Informatization Convened.* Retrieved from http://www.cac.gov.cn/2014-02/27/c_133148354.htm?from=timelineo.

[14] Xi, J. P. (2014). *Carry Forward Traditional Friendship and Jointly Open up New Chapter of Cooperation — Speech at the National Congress of Brazil.* Retrieved from http://www.xinhuanet.com/world/2014-07/17/c_1111665403.htm.

(3) Xi Jinping's First Advocacy of Cyber Sovereignty During His Congratulation Speech in Wuzhen

On 19 November 2014, Chinese President Xi Jinping noted during his congratulation message at the opening ceremony of the first World Internet Conference that "the development of the Internet has posed new challenges to national sovereignty, security and development interests... Following the principle of mutual respect and mutual trust, China is ready to work with other countries to deepen international cooperation, respect sovereignty on the Internet, uphold cybersecurity, and jointly build a cyberspace of peace, security, openness and cooperation, and an international internet governance system of multilateralism, democracy and transparency."[15]

(4) Respecting Cyber Sovereignty and Never Seeking Cyber Hegemony

On 16 December 2015, Xi Jinping attended the opening ceremony of the second World Internet Conference in Wuzhen, Zhejiang Province, and delivered a keynote speech, wherein he further elaborated on the policy of respecting cyber sovereignty: "The principle of sovereign equality enshrined in the Charter of the United States is one of the basic norms in contemporary international relation. It covers all aspects of state-to-state relations, which also includes cyberspace. We should respect the right of individual countries to independently choose their own path of cyber development, model of cyber regulation and internet public policies, and participate in international cyberspace governance on an equal footing. No country should pursue cyber hegemony, interfere in other countries' internal affairs or engage in, connive at or support cyber activities that undermine other countries' national security."[16]

[15] Xi, J. P. (2016). *Message of Congratulations from Chinese President Xi Jinping to the First World Internet Conference (full text).* Retrieved from http://news.xinhuanet.com/zgjx/2014-11/19/c_133800180.htm.

[16] Xi, J. P. (2015). *Remarks by H.E. Xi Jinping, President of the People's Republic of China, at the Opening Ceremony of the Second World Internet Conference.* Retrieved from http://www.xinhuanet.com/politics/2015-12/16/c_1117481089.htm.

(5) The National Security Law of the People's Republic of China, Article 25

Article 25 of the National Security Law of the People's Republic of China, which took effect on 1 July 2015, stipulates, "The state shall build a network and information security guarantee system; improve the network and information security protection capability; strengthen the innovation research, development, and application of network and information technologies; realise the controllable security of the core technologies, crucial infrastructure, and information systems and data in important fields; strengthen network management; prevent, block, and legally punish network attack, network invasion, network information theft, dissemination of illegal and harmful information, and other network-related infractions of law and crimes; and maintain the state's sovereignty, security, and development interests in cyberspace."

(6) Introduction to the Cyber Security Law of the People's Republic of China

The Cyber Security Law of the People's Republic of China was deliberated and promulgated on 7 November 2016. It came into force on 1 June 2017. The first article provides a clear explanation of the objective of the law: "This Law is developed for the purposes of guaranteeing cybersecurity; safeguarding cyberspace sovereignty, national security and public interest; protecting the lawful rights and interests of citizens, legal persons and other organizations; and promoting the sound development of economic and social informatization." This was the first sovereign legislation in the world to systematically regulate cyber sovereignty and safeguard national cyberspace sovereignty.

II. *Directions and Challenges*

With regard to cyber sovereignty, there has already been a disagreement on its theoretical recognition among major powers such as China, the US, and Russia. With regard to creating cyber security discipline, China has already come abreast of the US. Although no international consensus has been reached on which direction cyber sovereignty and cyber security research should take, this issue will be at the core of global debate in the future.[17] Discovering ways to define cyber sovereignty in general terms and improve the effectiveness of the discipline paradigm of cyber security is academically significant and will increase its teaching efficiency. To deepen national strategic research on cyber security, help improve the construction of the subject of cyber security, and take the lead in the cry of justice for the collaborative governance of networks by global participants, further research on cyber sovereignty is important due to its cross-disciplinary and innovative nature. Specifically, research on cyber sovereignty should concern the following challenges:

1. *International Challenges Concerning the Application Limit of Cyber Sovereignty*

A global consensus was achieved long ago on the limit of traditional sovereignty in telecommunications networks. However, the transnational development of computer networks has caused widespread dispute over the clarity of the limit of traditional sovereignty. Is internet security non-traditional security? Does sovereignty apply to the Internet? Opinions on these issues are unclear and divided.

2. *Challenges Caused by the Transnational Flow of Information in Cyberspace*

On 27 February 2014, Xi Jinping, the General Secretary of the CPC (Communist Party of China) Central Committee, Chinese President, Chairman of the Central Military Commission, and Head of the Office of the Central Leading Group for Cybersecurity and Informatization, chaired the first conference of the Leading Group, during which he emphasised that information in cyberspace flows

[17] Kelly, K. (2016). *I'm Afraid China May Be Lost*. Retrieved from http://tech.sina.com.cn/i/2015-06-16/doc-ifxczyze9639354.shtml.

in a cross-border fashion. The information flow facilitates the flow of technology, capital, and talents. Information resources have become increasingly important as a factor of production and a form of social wealth, and the amount of information available at hand has become a major index of a country's soft power and competitiveness.[18]

3. *Challenges Posed to State Sovereignty by the Development of the Internet*

On 19 November 2014, Xi Jinping remarked in his congratulation message at the opening ceremony of the first World Internet Conference, "The Internet is increasingly becoming a pacesetter of innovation-driven development, profoundly changing people's way of production and life and powering social development... Meanwhile, the development of the Internet has posed new challenges to national sovereignty, security and development interests, which requires the international community to meet urgently and seriously and pursue common governance and win-win outcome."[19]

4. *The Challenge of Whether Cyberspace and Sovereignty Meet in Theoretical Terms*

Technological advances change people's lives, and, in turn, technological development brings about change. If cyber sovereignty for all countries existed as defined by the UN Charter, could countries govern their national and regional top-level domain names independently? If no such independent and equal cyber sovereignty exists for countries, what kind of theory is capable of offsetting and

[18] *Xi Vows to Build China into a Cyber Power*. Retrieved from http://politics.people.com.cn/n/2014/0227/c70731-24486582.html.

[19] Xi, J. P. (2016). *Message of Congratulations from Chinese President Xi Jinping to the First World Internet Conference (full text)*. Retrieved from http://news.xinhuanet.com/zgjx/2014-11/19/c_133800180.htm.

countering technological hegemony or cyber hegemony beyond the traditional boundaries of sovereignty?

In conclusion, China's overall cyber development is based on sovereignty and the rule of law. China's construction of cyberspace order is the legislative extension of its specific national security demands and reflects the theme of peace underlying the country's efforts to maintain its cyber sovereignty and defend its national security.

Chapter Seven

The Rule of Law in Cyber Sovereignty

The rule of law in cyber sovereignty represents a new practice in which "sovereignty has jurisdiction over cyberspace". Before the theory of cyber sovereignty took shape, the platform section of cyberspace was subject to the rule of law in telecommunication, the object section was grouped under the rule of law in intellectual property rights and information, and the subjects and activities were mainly governed by civil law and criminal law.

After people were alerted to the threats to national security posed by cyber security issues as well as the necessity of imposing the rule of law on the cyberspace order from a sovereignty perspective, the concept of the rule of law in cyber sovereignty was created and established by means of legislation. With cyber sovereignty as the definite starting point, the governments of all countries have begun to step up their efforts in formulating national-security-oriented blueprints in technological, economic, legal, and social areas that overlap with cyberspace to prepare themselves for threats to national sovereignty and security in the new age of networks.

At the level of international law, the difficulty in administering the rule of law in cyber governance in today's world has manifested itself in a hegemonistic situation wherein the "orientation of power" takes precedence over the "orientation of rules". The International Telecommunication Union (ITU), which consists of

200 member states and regions, convened the World Conference on International Telecommunications in Dubai on 3 December 2012, wherein it hoped to review and amend the 1988 International Telecommunication Regulations as well as draft a new treaty on global telecommunications with widespread recognition. The draft of the new treaty was greeted with backlash from 20 Western countries, including the United States (US), Canada, the United Kingdom (UK), and Australia because it contained provisions on the ITU's supervision of the Internet. The US IT (information technology) giants Google and Cisco, among others, even sent lobbyists, while *The New York Times* published a long commentary saying, "The decisions taken in Dubai in December have the potential to put government handcuffs on the Net." This shows that history often evolves quickly when recognition and consensus have yet to take shape. The formation of such recognition and consensus depends on foresight based on a sense of justice and will be achieved when the powers of states are balanced.

At the level of the history of science and technology, there is a marked difference between the evolution of the Internet and that of the telecommunication network. "The telecommunication network was constructed by each country within their own boundaries at the beginning. Then, the demand for connectivity required the countries to come to the negotiation table and discuss the standards for connectivity, wherein they made concessions on matters of interest in the environment of international collaborative governance. However, the internet first started operation in the US, which later invited other countries to access it. The latecomers have no choice but to follow the standards set by the inventor. From the beginning, the US has kept itself off the path in which it has to deal with the governments of other countries. Instead, it hands over the internet from its armed forces to its National Science Foundation (NSF), which in turn entrusts it to scientific research departments and enterprises for construction and operation. Meanwhile, the US invites all the countries in the world to access the internet as a nongovernmental force, thus presenting the US government as not having a hand in the internet and leaving the impression that everything is dominated by civil factors from beginning to end. The discourse power appears to be in the hands of the interested parties that make the greatest contributions to the development of the internet. However, as the creator of the internet, the US holds the true dominance over it."[1]

Section One: An Overview of Countries

Since the 1990s, the revolution in information technology represented by the Internet and the tide of globalisation that followed have been pushing human history into a brand-new phase: the Information Age.[2]

I. Overview of Understanding

Regarding the rule of law in cyberspace, the definitions of "cyberspace" vary among countries, as shown in Table 7-1:

The reference to "cyberspace sovereignty" in international law is in Article 20 of Document A/68/98 of the 68th session of the UN General Assembly Group of Governmental Experts on Developments in the Field of Information and Telecommunications in the Context of International Security (Document A/70/174 of the 70th session of the UN General Assembly, Article 27): "State sovereignty and international norms and principles that flow from sovereignty apply to the conduct by States of ICT-related activities and to their jurisdiction over ICT infrastructure within their territory." Different countries and international organisations have different interpretations of the above issue. For instance, the USA Patriot Act authorises law enforcement departments to request cooperation on the

---

[1] Fang, B. X. (2017). *On Cyberspace Sovereignty* (p. 127). Beijing: Science Press.
[2] Guo, Y. J. (2011). *Research on International Legal Issues in Cyberspace*. Wuhan University Press.

Table 7-1: Definitions of "cyberspace sovereignty" by different countries/organisations

Relevant Decrees and Strategies of Different Countries/Organisations	Definitions of Cyberspace Sovereignty
National Security Presidential Directive 54/ Homeland Security Presidential Directive 23 (NSPD 54/HSPD-23)	Cyberspace refers to the interdependent network of information technology infrastructures and includes the Internet, telecommunications networks, computer systems, and embedded processors and controllers in critical industries.
Cyber Security Strategy of the United Kingdom 2009	Cyberspace is all forms of networked, digital activities.
2008 French White Paper on Defence and National Security	Cyberspace, consisting of the networking of all networks, is radically different from physical space in that it has no frontiers, is constantly changing and anonymous, making it hard to identify an aggressor with certainty. Cyberspace has become a new area of action, in which military operations are already taking place.
The United Nations (UN) A/70/174 Group of Governmental Experts on Developments in the Field of Information and Telecommunications in the Context of International Security	State sovereignty and international norms and principles that flow from sovereignty apply to ICT (information and communications technology)-related activities by states and to their jurisdiction over ICT infrastructure within their territory.

part of US internet firms to provide intelligence; this is a demonstration of cyber sovereignty. The UN World Summit on the Information Society published a Declaration of Principles entitled "Building the Information Society: A Global Challenge in the New Millennium" (WSIS-03/GENEVA/DOC/4-C) on 12 December 2003, which stipulates, "Policy authority for Internet-related public policy issues is the sovereign right of States. They have rights and responsibilities for international Internet-related public policy issues." Moreover, it emphasises the need to "prevent the potential use of ICTs for purposes that are inconsistent with the objectives of maintaining international stability and security". The UN Document A/70/174 further clarifies the obligations of sovereign states as follows: "28 (e) States must not use proxies to commit internationally wrongful acts using ICTs; (f) States must meet their international obligations regarding internationally wrongful acts attributable to them under international law."

With respect to "collaborative internet governance", UN Document A/70/174 mentions, "States should consider additional confidence-building measures that would strengthen cooperation on a bilateral, sub-regional, regional and multilateral basis." On 19 November 2014, Xi Jinping noted in his congratulation messages at the first World Internet Conference that "the Internet has turned the world into a global village and made the international community a highly interdependent community of common destiny", and that "the development of the Internet has posed new challenges to national sovereignty, security and development interests, which requires the international community to meet urgently and seriously and pursue common governance and win-win outcome".[3]

II. *Overview of the Rule of Law*

The internet-related laws and regulations issued by various countries are shown in Table 7-2:

The above practices in the six aspects of the rule of law in cyberspace are all state actions to regulate the four elements of cyberspace. On the one hand, this is only a start, and all countries are working on their own legislation on cyberspace; on the other hand, each country has its own distinctive features in cyberspace legislation.

---

[3]Xi, J. P. (2016). *Message of Congratulations from Chinese President Xi Jinping to the First World Internet Conference (Full Text).* Retrieved from http://news.xinhuanet.com/zgjx/2014-11/19/c_133800180.htm.

Table 7-2: Internet-related laws and regulations issued by various countries

Category	Laws and Regulations Issued by Various Countries
Aspect One: Management of information endangering national security, disseminating terrorism, and promoting racism	USA Patriot Act of 2001 European Union (EU) Additional Protocol to the Convention on Cybercrime, Concerning the Criminalisation of Acts of a Racist and Xenophobic Nature Committed through Computer Systems of 2003 Law of the Russian Federation on Mass Media of 1991 French Anti-Terrorism Law of 2014 German Network Enforcement Act of 2017 Singaporean Internet Code of Practice of 1991
Aspect Two: Management of network behaviour	Russian Bloggers Law of 2014 Law of the Russian Federation on Wi-Fi of 2014 South Korean Act on Promotion of Information and Communication Network Utilization and Information Protection of 2001 Singaporean Network Behaviour Law of 1996 French Information Society Act of 2006
Aspect Three: Management of pornography, violence, intimidation, and other information endangering children's physical and mental health	US Children's Internet Protection Act of 2001 US Megan Meier Cyberbullying Prevention Act of 2009 French Children's Protection Act of 2000 German Website Login Hindering Act of 2009 Russian Law on Protection of Children from Information Harmful to Their Health and Development of 2010
Aspect Four: Cracking down on spam mail	Russian Amendment to the Law on Promoting Usage of Information Communication Networks and Data Protection of 2003 US CAN-SPAM Act of 2003 Singaporean Amendment to Spam Control Act of 2008 Japanese Law on Regulation of Transmission of Specified Electronic Mail of 2002
Aspect Five: Banning cyber gambling	Australian Interactive Gambling Act of 2001

Table 7-2: (*Continued*)

Category	Laws and Regulations Issued by Various Countries
Aspect Six: Privacy protection	US Electronic Communications Privacy Act (ECPA) of 1986 EU Directive Concerning the Processing of Personal Data and the Protection of Privacy in the Electronic Telecommunications Sector of 2002 German Federal Data Protection Act of 1995 UK Privacy and Electronic Communications Regulations of 2003 South Korean Personal Information Protection Act of 2011 Japanese Personal Information Protection Act of 2003

Section Two: The US' System

The US law system related to cyber sovereignty springs from the demands of national security. The first US National Security Act was introduced in 1947. In the wake of World War II, the US government reflected on its disordered command and misplaced security system during wartime as well as the post-war surge of foreign security affairs among other issues. Following this, US President Harry Truman formulated the law at a critical time, reorganising the three sectors of the armed forces, diplomacy, and intelligence and creating the so-called "Truman Doctrine". This, together with the Marshall Plan, marked the beginning of the Cold War and announced the dawn of the American-style age of "national security" aimed at promoting the US' world leadership.

I. *National Security Act and National Security Strategy*

The US National Security Act has been continuously developed over the past 60 years, during which the following amendments have been made: the National Security Act Amendments of 1949, Intelligence Identities Protection Act of 1982, CIA Information Act of 1984, Intelligence Organization Act of 1992, Counterintelligence and Security Enhancements Act of 1994, Intelligence Renewal and Reform Act of 1996, Counterintelligence Enhancement Act of 2002, and Intelligence Reform Act of 2004. This Act has been expanded from 6 to 11 chapters. Following the "as a whole" principle, the current US National Security Act integrates the US' three major resources, i.e. armed forces, diplomacy, and intelligence, in a comprehensive manner.

In the "Note" of the 2015 National Security Strategy, President Barack Obama wrote:

> "America's growing economic strength is the foundation of our national security.
>
> We are now the world leader in oil and gas production.
>
> We continue to set the pace for science, technology, and innovation in the global economy.
>
> We possess a military whose might, technology, and geostrategic reach is unrivalled in human history. We have renewed our alliances from Europe to Asia.
>
> Violent extremism and an evolving terrorist threat raise a persistent risk of attacks on America and our allies. Challenges to cybersecurity are escalating. We must be clear-eyed about these and other challenges and recognize the United States has a unique capability to mobilize and lead the international community to meet them.
>
> The question is never whether America should lead, but how we lead.
>
> To succeed, we must draw upon the power of our example — that means viewing our commitment to our values and the rule of law as a strength, and not an inconvenience.
>
> The United States will always defend our interests and uphold our commitments to allies and partners.
>
> ...What unites us is the national consensus that American global leadership remains indispensable."

II. *Cyber Security Strategy*

The US is the first country in the world to create a cyber security strategy. In February 2003, the US issued the National Strategy to

Secure Cyberspace, which integrates and calls upon the federal government, local governments, private sectors, and US citizens to handle cyberspace threats. In May 2011, the US announced the International Strategy for Cyberspace, which underscores the importance of cyber security in diplomacy, national defence, and economic affairs. In November 2011, the US National Defense Authorization Act established the domestic law principle that the US is entitled to militarily retaliate against major cyberattacks targeting its economic, governmental, or military sectors.

As the US surveillance programme PRISM, exposed in June 2013, incurred a lack of trust from various countries around the world regarding US cyber governance because of its severe infringement on netizens' privacy and other countries' sovereignty, the US was compelled by pressure from the international community to issue a statement through the National Telecommunications and Information Administration, wherein it created a plan to hand over its supervisory right of ICANN (Internet Corporation for Assigned Names and Numbers). It proposed a transfer of the technical management function to the so-called "global internet community" and suggested that ICANN convene a conference on "global stakeholders" to discuss and decide on the transfer plan. However, the US expressed its unequivocal rejection of any transfer plan led by other countries' governments.

An examination of the member composition of the internal working group of ICANN suggested that 75% of the "stakeholders" come from North American countries, while 15% come from Europe and 10% come from Asian, African, and Latin American countries. This means that the US possesses a majority of the stakeholders. Big IT names in the US, such as Apple, Microsoft, Google, Cisco, Intel, Amazon, Twitter, and Facebook, hold about 8 places among the top 10 of the world's IT industry, virtually cornering the entire "technical chain" ranging from internet hardware, operation systems, and security protection to core technology applications. They are subject to the jurisdiction of US law and incorporated into cyberspace strategic protection systems, such as the National Strategy to Secure Cyberspace and International Strategy for Cyberspace.

The US is impeding international collaborative governance in cyberspace, intentionally or not. However, it has been active in promoting the rule of law in cyberspace within the US and formulating cyber strategies, thus spearheading cyber security strategy in the world.

Section Three: The Russia-EU System

I. *The Overarching Position of Russia's General Law*

Russia's rule of law in cyber security can generally be attributed to its unique legislative mode wherein "national security is underscored by the Constitution". The "constitutional" mode of Russia's national security is as follows:

Entering the Constitution: On 24 May 1991, before the collapse of the Soviet Union, the Russian Federation passed the Amendment to the Constitution (Basic Law). In Chapter 9, it added: "The President of the Russian Soviet Federative Socialist Republic leads the security conference of the Russian Federation whose organisational structure, duties and rules for operation shall be decided by the law of the Russian Federation."

General Law: On 5 March 1992, the State Duma of Russia approved the Security Act of the Russian Federation, which was formulated in conjunction with President Yeltsin, stipulating the legal status, function, authority, and procedure of the Security Council of the Russian Federation (SCRF). On 3 June 1992, the SCRF was officially founded.

System: Russia has already established a national security legal system that includes the Constitution, the Security Act, the Regulations for Security Council, the Regulations for Security Council Authorities, and the National Security Strategy for the Period Up to 2020.

Externally, Russia has upheld its stance to reach an international agreement on cyber security. The ITU under the UN framework is dedicated to promoting an international treaty on the global governance of cyberspace. In July 2010, 15 UN member states, including the US, China, and Russia, signed a draft treaty aimed at mitigating computer network risks, in which it was suggested that the UN prepare a set of norms of state behaviour in cyberspace. However, due to disagreement among the powers on the nature and force of the treaty, the negotiation on the treaty has been exceptionally sluggish. For instance, Russia expects to prevent another round of arms race through the treaty by imposing the same restrictions and supervision applied to preventing the expansion of weapons of mass destruction. However, the US is opposed to the creation of a UN institution that curbs cyber warfare, hoping that no restrictions will be imposed on its own cyber technological advantage and shunning discussions on how to avoid cyberattacks.

II. *EU Law on the Right to Privacy*

The right to privacy was first proposed by Samuel Warren and Louis Brandeis in their article titled "The Right to Privacy" published in the *Harvard Law Review* in 1890. As an important human right, legal protection of the right to privacy soon gained international recognition, especially that of the European law community.

On 27 April 2016, the European Parliament released "On the Protection of Natural Persons with Regard to the Processing of Personal Data and on the Free Movement of Such Data". This replaced the former "Directive 95/46/EC" and was called the GDPR (General Data Protection Regulation).[4] The 28 EU member states will translate the provisions of the GDPR, which took effect on 25 May 2018, into domestic laws within two years.

The EU GDPR is generally directed at enhancing the protection of the individual right to data and giving EU citizens a larger

---

[4] *On the Protection of Natural Persons with Regard to the Processing of Personal Data and on the Free Movement of Such Data, and Repealing Directive 95/46/EC (General Data Protection Regulation).* Retrieved from http://ec.europa.eu/justice/data-protection/reform/files/regulation_oj_en.pdf.

say in how their own personal data are to be used. The GDPR even maintains operability in the internal control and compliance management of enterprises by stipulating detailed management norms and extends its applicability from EU enterprises to all enterprises that provide internet and business services to EU users.[5]

Some key provisions of the GDPR are as follows: the possible penalty for violating the data protection regulation can be as high as 4% of the company's global turnover, and for technological giants such as Google, fines can be billions of dollars. Parties accountable for data leaks are extended to include any data processor that is employed and used by data controllers, including any third party providing certain services related to data processing, which is common in the cloud business mode. The so-called "right to be forgotten" is enshrined by law; once you do not want your data to be dealt with by a certain company and as long as no legitimate reason exists to retain such data, the data have to be deleted, which has a major impact on digital marketing. If companies need to deal with sensitive data or collect information from a number of consumers, they are required to designate data protection officers, with the exception of small and medium-sized enterprises whose core businesses do not include data processing. In the case of severe data leakage, companies or institutions are required to immediately notify the relevant state supervisory authorities. Children are only allowed to use social media with parental consent, and each member state may set its own rules for a specific age range from 13 to 16 years. A one-stop supervisory authority for data protection and complaint has been created with the aim of streamlining the procedures for enterprises to follow; it guarantees the right to portability of personal data, which allows people to transfer their personal data between different services more conveniently.

The EU GDPR lists 40 network subjects, far more than the 28 listed in China's Cyber Security Law. With such a complex and

[5]Fang, B. X. (2017). *On Cyberspace Sovereignty* (p. 283). Beijing: Science Press.

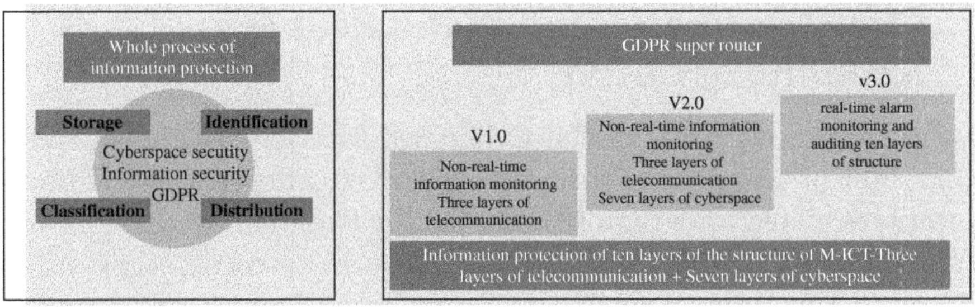

Figure 7-1: The legal approach of the "GDPR super router"

harsh data protection regulation in place, local telecommunication operators and network operators are vulnerable to huge fines.

Via studying the four elements of cyberspace, the author presents an M-ICT solution that "conforms to legal requirements" to protect information during the overall process of "storage, identification, distribution, and delivery" and create the legal approach of the "GDPR super router" for the reference of technical experts. It is expected to achieve a legitimate, reasonable, and better information data order as well as realise full-coverage data security step by step over the "three layers of telecommunication" (physical layer, data link layer, session layer) and "seven layers of cyberspace" (physical layer, data link layer, network layer, transport layer, session layer, presentation layer, application layer).

Section Four: The Chinese System

Compared to the US' practice of supporting the rule of law in cyberspace with numerous policy-oriented legal documents on cyber security, China has adopted the National Security Law of the People's Republic of China of 2015, the Counter-terrorism Law of the People's Republic of China of 2015, the Cyber Security Law of the People's Republic of China of 2016, and the E-Commerce Law of the People's Republic of China of 2018 in addition to a number of rules and regulations, all of which form the sovereignty-based rule of law in cyberspace with Chinese characteristics to promote China's cyber development and build China into a cyber power.

I. *Cyber Security Law of the People's Republic of China*

Before the 2016 draft of the Cyber Security Law of the People's Republic of China was formally approved after review, China's internet-related laws mainly included the National Security Law of the People's Republic of China, the Counter-terrorism Law of the People's Republic of China, the Copyright Law of the People's Republic of China, the Electronic Signature Law of the People's Republic of China, the Criminal Law of the People's Republic of China, Amendment IX to the Criminal Law of the People's Republic of China, the Decision of the Standing Committee of the National People's Congress Concerning Strengthening Network Information Protection, and provisions related to the information network in the Decision of the Standing Committee of the National People's Congress Concerning Cyber Security. Other relevant regulations include the Regulations on Computer Software Protection, Regulations for Security Protection of Computer Information Systems, Administrative Measures for the Security Protection of International Networking of Computer Information Networks, and Regulations on Protection of the Information Transmission Rights on Internet issued by the State Council. In addition, there are a number of regulations and related judicial interpretations. From these public instruments, we can see that although China has developed many laws and regulations regarding the Internet, there is still a lack of cyber security law to coordinate cyber sovereignty.

Article 4 of the National Security Law of the People's Republic of China stipulates, "All national security work shall adhere to the leadership of the Communist Party of China (CPC), and a centralized, unified, efficient, and authoritative national security leadership system shall be established." In observing this provision, cyber security legislation needs to define a functional structure with the CPC supervising cyberspace security, i.e. the central leadership of the CPC needs to administer China's cyber security affairs (such as the Central Leading Group for Cybersecurity and Informatization) while combining the four elements of cyber sovereignty to completely regulate network connection security, network terminal security, network user security, and network data security.

There are many legislations and theories on cyber sovereignty. Some scholars have proposed to improve the draft of the Cyber Security Law of the People's Republic of China promulgated in 2015, arguing that it should neither be a "network infrastructure protection law" nor a "network industry promotion law", which are far from the legislative needs concerning cyber security in China.

As China's cyber sovereignty once fell short in diplomacy, industry, and rule of law, changing the situation requires not only a general improvement at the technical level but also active promotion of an orientational consensus on policies and academic research to clarify a cyber sovereignty definition with Chinese characteristics. In addition, the Cyber Security Law of the People's Republic of China should be in line with the sovereignty laws, civil and commercial laws, criminal laws, economic laws, administrative laws, and social laws of the legislative system with Chinese characteristics.

Formally promulgated after review in 2016, the Cyber Security Law of the People's Republic of China follows up with the provisions of Article 25 of the National Security Law of the People's Republic of China on "maintaining national cyberspace sovereignty" and establishes the principles of overall planning, coordination, collaboration, and cooperation in the administration of cyberspace affairs while considering both security and development interests. Since the 18th CPC National Congress, the National Security Law of the People's Republic of China, the Counter-terrorism Law of the People's Republic of China, the National Intelligence Law of the People's Republic of China, the National Anthem Law of the People's Republic of China, the Law of the People's Republic of China on National Medals and National Honors, and the Law of the People's Republic of China on National Defense Transportation have constituted the "Seven Sovereignty Laws" promulgated within the sovereignty law category. Among these sovereignty laws, the Cyber Security Law of the People's Republic of China has established a cyber sovereignty legal system with Chinese characteristics by virtue of its own features of "overall planning and coordination".

The Cyber Security Law of the People's Republic of China stipulates the following in Article 76 of the "Supplementary Provisions": "'Network' refers to a system comprised of computers or other information terminals and related equipment that follows certain rules and procedures for information gathering, storage, transmission, exchange, and processing". It defines the network's object (information), platform (a system comprised of computers or other information terminals and related equipment that follows certain rules and procedures), and activities (information gathering, storage, transmission, exchange, and processing). For the network subject, Article 2 states that "this Law is applicable to the construction, operation, maintenance, and use of networks, as well as to cybersecurity supervision and management within the mainland territory of the People's Republic of China". Thus, the network subject is indirectly defined by way of clarifying "sovereign territory + network activities".

In addition to the indirect definition mentioned above, the Cyber Security Law of the People's Republic of China with Chinese characteristics also defines 28 types of network subjects by listing them in full detail. From an industrial perspective, the most important of the 28 types of regulated network subjects, including network equipment suppliers (e.g. Huawei, ZTE), telecommunications operators (e.g. China Mobile, China Telecom, and China Unicom), and network operators (e.g. Baidu, Alibaba, and Tencent), have been given corresponding rights and responsibilities in the sense of the rule of law in cyberspace, as shown in Figure 7-2.

With the implementation of the Cyber Security Law of the People's Republic of China, China's rule on cyberspace law has been quickly and widely applied to the nation's economic construction and various undertakings via the vigorous advocacy and active promotion of the country, bringing profound changes to the lifestyle and modes of production, working, and studying of its people. It plays an important role in accelerating China's "internet + development" strategy for the national economy as well as the strategy

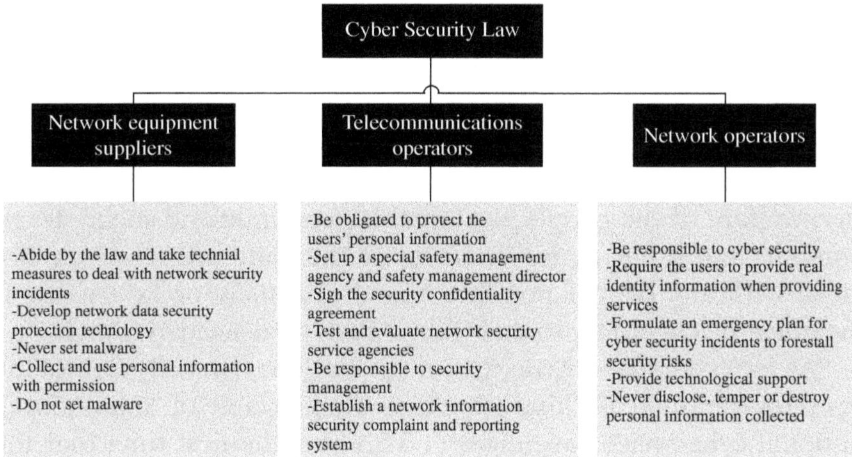

Figure 7-2: The Cyber Security Law of the People's Republic of China regulates subjects' rights and responsibilities

of pursuing cutting-edge developments in science and technology and the informatisation and orderly process of social services. In the meantime, the implementation of this law, which concerns the issue of how to ensure the security of network operations and information security for the general attention of society as a whole, plays a significant role in effectively safeguarding China's cyber sovereignty, national security, and economic and social development benefits.

II. *Cyber Security Examination*

On 23 May 2014, the Cyberspace Administration of China stated for the first time that a national cyber security examination system needs to be established to reinforce the examination of important information technology products and services related to national security and public interest. It is necessary to encourage frequent, focused, unannounced, and propositioned examinations. Additionally, it is necessary to pay special attention to cyber security examinations as the first line of defence for national information security.

1. *Superior Law*

Regarding security, the National Security Law of the People's Republic of China, promulgated on 1 July 2015 as the superior law of cyber security legislation, defines national security in Article 2 as a status in which the regime, sovereignty, unity, territorial integrity, welfare of the people, sustainable economic and social development, and other major interests of the state are relatively not faced with any danger nor threatened internally or externally. It includes the capability to maintain a sustained security status.

As for cyberspace, Article 25 of the National Security Law of the People's Republic of China stipulates the principle of "maintaining national cyberspace sovereignty". This was the first time that the concept of the rule of law of cyberspace sovereignty had been proposed in China's legal system and also the first time that China, of all the countries in the world, had cyber sovereignty written into its law. Article 59 of the National Security Law of the People's Republic of China stipulates that "the state shall establish the system and mechanism for national security review and supervision; conduct national security review on foreign investment, specific items and key technologies, network information technology products and services, construction projects involving national security matters, and other major matters and activities that affect or may affect national security; and effectively prevent and mitigate national security risks". The article also mentions that a cyber security examination system that is part of the overall national security plan should be established as soon as possible.

For overall planning, the National Security Law of the People's Republic of China is a major law with the distinctive feature of "conducting overall planning" of the legal system with Chinese characteristics. From the perspective of overall planning, the National Security Law of the People's Republic of China provides for the overall coordination of the five major aspects of national security affairs, i.e. coordinated leadership mechanism, coordinated scopes and ranges, coordinated central and local authorities, coordinated law enforcement systems, and coordinated statutory measures.

Article 19 of the Counter-Terrorism Law of the People's Republic of China, promulgated on 27 December 2015, stipulates that network operators and network service providers should see to the maintenance of cyber security and that the competent authority responsible for cyberspace affairs should promptly order the deletion of information containing terrorism content. This is also one of the superior laws of cyber security legislation.

2. *Institutional Origin*

The national security examination system originates from Article 21 "Security Exceptions" of the General Agreement on Tariffs and Trade signed in 1947.[6] The agreement regulates the circulation order of international goods and services, which now account for about 95% of world trade. The provisions of Article 21 refer to the legislative and jurisprudential exceptions of sovereign states on the issues of trade equality and investment pairing, i.e. exceptions related to essential national security interests. Correspondingly, there are also certain exceptions to a series of national security examination measures that show a certain degree of arbitrariness, such as the anti-dumping and countervailing measures adopted by

[6] It is stipulated in the General Agreement on Tariffs and Trade, "Nothing in this Agreement shall be construed (a) to require any contracting party to furnish any information the disclosure of which it considers contrary to its essential security interests; or (b) to prevent any contracting party from taking any action which it considers necessary for the protection of its essential security interests (i) relating to fissionable materials or the materials from which they are derived; (ii) relating to the traffic in arms, ammunition and implements of war and to such traffic in other goods and materials as is carried on directly or indirectly for the purpose of supplying a military establishment; (iii) taken in time of war or other emergency in international relations; or (c) to prevent any contracting party from taking any action in pursuance of its obligations under the UN Charter for the maintenance of international peace and security. In such cases, trade restrictions may be imposed, such as restrictions on imports and exports of certain members, and the termination of their relationship with other members in rights and obligations."

the US as well as the examinations of foreign investment carried out by the US National Security Council (NSC).

In practice, the Cyberspace Administration of China, as a competent authority, has organised a number of meetings calling for the cyber security examination system to be developed in the form of legislation and made effective as soon as possible. The theory and practice of the past 40 years of reform and opening-up have proven that China's rule of law is much more civilised than that of the US, whether in the examination of cyber security affairs or that of foreign investments. The rule of law in China's strategies necessitates the maintenance of cyber sovereignty in cyber security examinations.

3. *International Comparison*

Lawrence Lessig of the US was the first scholar to propose cyber sovereignty among the Western heavyweight thinkers. His in-depth interpretation of cyber sovereignty in his three books, namely *Code: Version 1.0*, *The Future of Ideas*, and *Code: Version 2.0*, serves as a valuable mirror for self-reflection in theoretical research in China. His works have become a must-read for law, business, public administration, communications, political science, and information science and technology majors in developed Western countries. Lessig only proposed cyber sovereignty in an attempt to deny it because the US advocates cyber hegemony and free use of the Internet instead of cyber sovereignty.

On 13 October 2014, Professor Hashimoto Yasuaki of the Japanese National Institute for Defense Studies of the Japan Ministry of Defense proposed in his speech on cyber legislation and the rule of law in non-traditional security issues that international governance programmes concerning cyberspace should emphasise "collective security" or "collective self-defence" in the UN Charter. When Hillary Clinton and certain US media opposed the definition of cyberspace by the UN ITU, the emphasis was on "internet freedom"; however, neither the old concepts of "collective security" or "collective self-defence" nor the new concept of "internet freedom" that they claimed explicitly reflects the subject and object required in the rule of law and rights protection in cyberspace.

China has proposed a "three-step" strategy for carrying out cyber security examinations, namely cyber sovereignty, interested parties, and international co-governance. Only by improving the regulatory framework of cyber sovereignty (including cyber security examinations) can countries maintain a just order to participate in international affairs on an equal basis as members of the UN and promote the establishment of the World Cyber Convention. Therefore, the international academic community needs to establish the theory on the rule of law regulating the legal rights of "network users and network information" as soon as possible. As one of the fastest-growing developing countries, China needs to adhere to its international stance of "safeguarding the rights of i nternet users and safeguarding the security of information" and should take advantage of its total number of internet users and total amount of information to speak for justice in the definition of rights in cyberspace by way of laws including the National Security Law of the People's Republic of China and Cyber Security Law of the People's Republic of China.

In sum, the national cyber legislation of individual nations originates from and is developed on the basis of considering national sovereign security and development interests as an integrated whole. Since networks are naturally interconnected, the national legislative trend of individual countries will be the basis for establishing a world cyberspace order in the future.

Part III
Methodology

According to Karl Marx, human activities, or human labour, are divided into four types: production activity for reproduction, labour and practice activity, social relation production activity, and reproduction activity performed to save for the future.[1]

The social relation production activity must be based on networks. Networks help human beings construct social relationships efficiently, which, in turn, helps humans improve their scientific and technological utility in terms of labour and practice, reproduction, and future-oriented activities. From the perspective of a sovereign state, territorial sovereignty, popular sovereignty, and political sovereignty depend on the overall planning of networks. Networks can naturally be coordinated. The overall coordinated governance of cyber sovereignty is conducive to modernising national governance and controlling the advanced direction of human civilisation brought about by the Fourth Technological Revolution.

---

[1] Lee, W. L. (2014). *On Marx* (p. 29) (W.Q. Chen, Trans.). Beijing: Zhonghua Book Company.

Chapter Eight

Cyberspace and Order Coordination

The law of nature is the supreme order of the world. Although humans have discovered laws such as thermal energy conversion and energy conservation, there are still a great number of unknown natural laws.

Civil order is the secondary order of the world. It is the public order and customs of work and life based on the understanding of natural laws and the progress of inventions and technologies. For example, the consensus of domestic laws (e.g. China's 242 laws as of the end of 2017) and the consensus of international laws (e.g. the over 20,000 bilateral treaties and over 3,000 plurilateral and multilateral international treaties currently involving China) are both civil orders, and the civil orders of modern countries are based on national sovereignty.

Should the methodology of cyberspace governance follow natural law or civil order? The unexpected development of ICTs (information and communications technology) somewhere between the laws of nature and civil order tends to result in misunderstandings and conflicts in people's views of order. Therefore, to recognise the ontology of cyberspace, cyber elements, cyberspace order, rule of law in cyberspace, and cyber sovereignty, we still need to carefully locate the origin of the cognitive conflicts regarding the two major orders from the rapid development of network technology.

Section One: Nodes and Natural Order

Natural order comprises the basic laws of the existence and movement of the Earth, such as the law of motion, the law of balance, and the law of attraction. Nature is moving and balanced. Individuals and groups in nature are attracted to each other and are generally connected. So, how do things connect? All connections rely on "nodes". The four network elements first follow the laws of science and then make a self-contained system that involves nodes.

I. *Nodes in a System*

The older the thought, the simpler and clearer it is.

An old Chinese saying states, "If there are tigers in the mountains, monkeys become the kings." Why do monkeys become the kings? Because monkeys and tigers are both "nodes" in the "mountain" system. In the natural world, where only the fittest survive, dominant nodes always eliminate those that are not dominant in the system, i.e. only the fittest nodes survive.

Nodes are the single objects in a system that can connect to each other to form advantages and avoid risks. To recognise nodes in nature more objectively and accurately, humans have invented methods such as numbers, abaci, geometric charts, mathematical models, and equation formulas to calculate the pros and cons and discover the laws.[2]

Through methods such as graph theory and drawing arrow graphs, it is easy to see that there are different connection methods between nodes. They can be connected in simple ways to form regular graphs such as stars, rings, trees, and other shapes with uniformly distributed nodes; they can also be connected in complicated ways, i.e. serially, randomly, or sparsely, or in imbalanced ways to form irregular graphs.

[2] Mackenzie, D. (2015). *The Universe in Zero Words: The Story of Mathematics as Told Through Equations* (Y. X. Li, Trans.). Beijing: Beijing United Publishing Company.

When nodes connect with one another, they usually choose those within the shortest distance, thereby forming a "clustering effect"; the centre of the cluster becomes the "central node".

The central node is attractive to the other nodes. One of the reasons for this is that it features "betweenness", which has the value of global variables and can give rise to the function and influence of the system as a whole. That is, it has the characteristic of being able to claim "king in the mountains".

The "non-central nodes" can always find the central node through multiple connections in the system, just as a letter or email that is sent and forwarded six times can always find its target receiver among strangers (the theory of six degrees of separation).[3] If regarded as a six-layer connection system, it is a system with a "gathering effect" and innate six-layer connection characteristics.

As new nodes continue to join or old nodes continue to leave, the original system shows continuous expansion or contraction dynamically. This dynamic process embodies the trends of randomness, imbalance, growth, and variability of the whole system's order.

II. *Trade-Offs in Order*

By dint of the law of nature, people developed early social thoughts on human society such as fairness, harmony, orderliness, and coordination, all of which are characterised by the integrity of the system and mark the evolution of the theory of balance. In the real world, the balance of the whole is incarnated in the history of the equilibrium in the entire system, covering the progression from collision to interdependence to orderliness, as well as the friction and accommodation among different kinds of equilibrium. People always need to conduct overall planning and trade-offs to cope with dilemmas, which is the inescapable tendency of such a system.

---

[3] Bao, J. G., Xia, Sh. T., & Liu, X. J. (2013). *Information, Entropy, and Economics: The Road to Human Development*. Beijing: Economic Science Press.

As the basis for the mainstream philosophical thought and social climate, the law of nature is often employed to prove that the development of the entire economy and society shows an objective trend just as the laws of nature, which can overcome human interference and automatically approach an ideal state. People often use the form of natural law to explore laws in economy and society, regarding it as a powerful rational support and philosophical foundation. In the past, physiocrats described the concept of balance as "the only simple law based on nature itself",[4] which was a plain historical judgment made after considering the natural order.

1. *The Trade-Offs in Systems*

The idea of weighing the overall order of the law of nature has long been ignored. Although the naturalistic equilibrium model has become a tool for constructing theories in contemporary economics (Wicksell's "natural interest rate" and Friedman's "natural unemployment rate"), it is still imperative to further explore the comprehensive theory of a system's order to try to determine what makes an ideal state of social order and how to achieve and maintain this state. This is more because of the necessity for macroscopic overall planning and trade-offs to count the system order as "an interdependent unity"[5] than the fact that "the complete body is easier to study than its cells".[6]

The comprehensive theory of system order mentioned before is a method for a system's overall planning rather than merely a reminder of its overall consideration. Requiring both a high level of understanding and broad horizon, it adheres to the priority of the whole over its parts as well as the universality of connection via the

---

[4] Spiegel, H. W. (1999). *The Growth of Economic Thought* (Vol. 1). Beijing: China Social Sciences Press.

[5] Marx, K. & Engels, F. (1972). *The Marx-Engels Collected Works* (Vol. 23). Beijing: People's Publishing House.

[6] Wicksell, K. (1983). *Lectures on Political Economy* (Foreword). Shanghai: Shanghai Translation Publishing House.

central node; it draws scientific conclusions from trade-off cases in reality. The thinking stemming from the law of nature has also been endowed with the connotations of fairness, harmony, orderliness, and coordination in diverse historical orientations under different historical and social backgrounds. After repeated trade-offs, these orientations constitute the knowledge reserve of human beings, which is the basis for civilisation ushering in a better order.

2. *The Law of the Jungle in Reality*

Originating from nature, the law of the jungle highlights the realistic truth that the weak will be the prey of the strong. The attributes of the law are reflected in both nature and human society. Due to the limited resources in nature, only the strong can obtain the most control over the resources.

The natural attributes of the law are limited by the objective boundaries of nature, which are not affected by human or social factors; the social attributes are generally manifested in a realistic social environment resembling the animal kingdom. The competitions among people, enterprises, countries, and regimes embodying the law of the jungle are historically destined. In most cases, the result of this kind of fatal competition depends on the comprehensive strength of each competitor's power, wisdom, and manoeuvres as well as its overall planning and trade-offs.

3. *The Game of Nodes*

Upon examining nodes in today's world order, one can see that they embody the realistic truth that the order is dominated by the law of the jungle. In recent years, the proportion of the peacekeeping military expenditures of the United Nations (UN) to the overseas military expenditures of various countries has presumably not been less than 1:50.[7] Through a comprehensive comparison of the

[7]The data on the total "overseas military expenditure" of all countries in the world in this book include that of the NATO (North Atlantic Treaty Organization)

number of troops, military expenditures, and equipment quality, it can be seen that the number of peacekeeping soldiers is only one-fifth of the number of various countries' troops stationed abroad; the peacekeeping military expenditures are only one-fifth of various countries' overseas military expenditures (US$7 billion: US$350 billion); and the investment in equipment used by peacekeeping soldiers is only one-tenth of that provided by various countries for their overseas troops'. Even with the public international law's maintenance of traditional security, at least 80% of overseas soldiers and 90% of the equipment of overseas troops are beyond the jurisdiction of the UN.

The number of UN peacekeepers is far lower than the constant 300,000 to 500,000 overseas troops dispatched by the US and its allies, indicating that, in the real world, the rule-oriented transnational peacekeeping military operations are nowhere near the power-oriented military interventions of hegemonic groups. The proportion of the quantity of UN peacekeepers to that of the overseas troops of hegemonic groups without the approval of the UN is roughly 1:5, mirroring the current situation in which the present international order is more a result of the dominance of the law of the jungle rather than the governance of public international law.

Cyberspace order falls under the category of non-traditional security in maintaining world peace; it always makes powerhouses with strong traditional security forces more powerful when intertwined with the field of traditional security. According to the "Global Firepower Index 2013"[8] report published by the Center for Strategic and International Studies (CSIS) in the United States (US), the United Kingdom (UK), the US, Russia, and France currently have the most overseas troops and bases in the world. Among the 23 overseas military bases with more than 1,000 troops, 10 were established by the UK, 8 by the US, 3 by Russia, and 2 by France. If the order of public international law is used as the

countries, America's allies in the Asia-Pacific region, and other major powers. In this paper, it is estimated that roughly 70% of the military expenditure budget of the United States in 2015 ($495.6 billion) could be included.

[8] CSIS. (2016). Retrieved from http://csis.org/.

independent variable in the construction of a consensus among all human beings, the space beyond the jurisdiction of the public international law constitutes the dependent variable of the law of the jungle in the world today. Are we in a safe world now? The disparity between the UN peacekeeping force and overseas troops of countries indicates that in building an order to maintain world peace in the field of traditional security, mankind still has a long way to go.[9]

Section Two: Structure and Social Order

The nodes connected and adjacent to each other form a structure. The structure presents the characteristics of a system and determines the function of the network. It is a key component in various social systems and social networks, wherein people are the subject. In human history, it can be observed that structure is a key component that plays an institutional role in the evolution of social order. The network structure contains systems and nodes. It should comply with the laws of society, keep pace with the times, and gain experience from the past.

I. *Structural Pattern*

In general, the pattern of structure refers to the state involving the movements and changes of various nodes and connections (including linkage and adjacency) in the system. It accords with the description of a system's state by the power-law distribution in another branch of theory in the history of human science and technology.

1. *The Power-Law Distribution*

The central node represents the features of power in the system, i.e. the characteristics of power laws. In accordance with its definition,

[9]Zhao, H. R. (2015). *World Civilizations Aggregate Approach: China's Civilized Rise and Rule of Law in National Security* (pp. 200–201). Beijing: China Legal Publishing House.

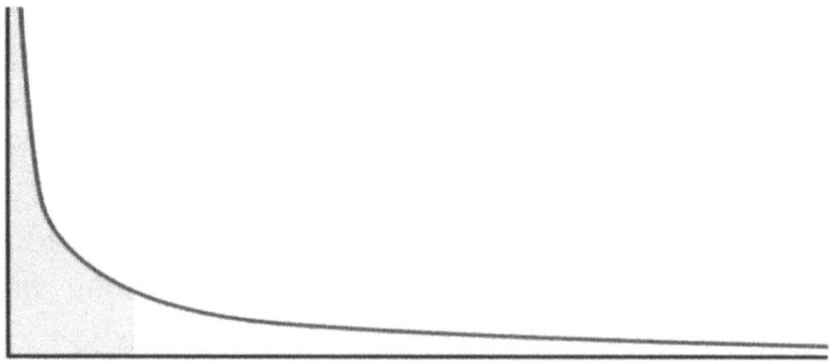

Figure 8-1: Power-law distribution in the system

the power law refers to the sum of the products of each node in the system and its connections. Therefore, the power law of the system is equivalent to the product of the total number of nodes and the total connections, which can be expressed as the following equation: the "power law of the system = the number of nodes × the number of connections". The definite product corresponds to the total geometric amount according to the power-law distribution of the system. In a system, if there are 10 large nodes with 10,000 connections, 100 medium nodes with 1,000 connections, and 1,000 small nodes with 100 connections, there will be a downward oblique line in the logarithmic coordinates, as shown in Figure 8-1.

The power-law distribution reveals the structure and functions of the system network.

It can always be reflected in economic and social activities. Vilfredo Pareto, an Italian economist in the 19th century, discovered that the income of "the vital few" is much higher than that of "the trivial many"; then, he proposed the 80-20 rule, asserting that 80% of the world's income is in the hands of only 20% of the population. This is called the Pareto law and describes the distribution of wealth among individuals in society.

The power-law distribution can also be observed in the field of language. In 1932, George Kingsley Zipf, a linguist at Harvard University, discovered Zipf's law (i.e. given a large sample of words used, the frequency of any word is inversely proportional to its rank in the frequency table) when studying the frequency of English words. Apart from a few frequently used words, the vast majority of words are rarely used.

Likewise, the structural pattern of the power-law distribution exists in cyberspace. The mathematical relationships among nodes, connections, probabilities, frequencies, scales, and heat constitute the structural characteristics of the network system. The laws of structure reflected in the Pareto law and Zipf's law also prevail in cyberspace; both reflect the structural pattern and characteristics of the power-law distribution centred on people.

The power-law distribution in cyberspace presents the features of "heat" and "density" in its structure. The slope on a power-law distribution graph is a line or curve with a negative exponential relationship. This slope shows the heat of nodes and the density of connections. In the network system, it can be subdivided into the slopes of four dimensions on the power-law distribution graph; these dimensions comprise the subject (the sum of people acting as nodes or the nodes they set using software or hardware), the object (all information required to complete information processing or write each file in the system), the platform (all the material connections of all network terminal devices), and the network activity (the sum of hours of online communication of people as nodes of the network). The overall slope of the four elements on the graph of the power-law distribution demonstrates the structural characteristics of the network system.

Scale-free phenomena are another explanation for the randomness that is in conformity with the power-law distribution provided by statistical physicists. The characteristics of nodes in systems or domains involving life, evolution, and competition are always different from each other. These nodes often form models that lack the optimal power-law distribution, assuming the randomness of this type of distribution. That is, all types of systems in the world exhibit scale-free phenomena to a certain extent.

The power of nodes, power-law distribution, and scale-free phenomena have always been the structural features of social order in its long history of development and are constantly being strengthened by the structural pattern of cyber society.

2. *Social Structure*

The network age has created stronger connections for the power-law distribution of nodes in the social structure. With the deepening of universal connections in this age, the development and integration of the main social models derived from different civilisations are being further expedited.

(1) Contractual Society

Contractual society is a political theory that emerged in the Middle Ages when the West toppled the feudal theocratic system and established modern capitalism. The theory specifies a social structure or revolution based on the idea of a social contract. It not only occupied a dominant position in the history of Western political thought in the 17th and 18th centuries but also provided a solid foundation for the establishment of modern Western countries, the implementation of the rule of law, the formation of government, and the division of social functions.[10]

The social contract theory has created an expression of "the state of nature" to describe the conditions under which a social contract comes into being; it regards individuals in this state as the source of the establishment of political order. Thomas Hobbes, the creator of the social contract theory, demonstrated the origin of a country and the legitimacy of political authority by starting with an analysis of individuals in the state of nature. He believed that although individuals in the natural state have equal status, this kind of equality has led to a state in which "every man [is] against every man", which is essentially a manifestation of the law of the jungle. As "the state of nature is the worst possible situation in which men can find themselves", people need to establish a state in accordance with a social contract, which would involve a sovereign with absolute authority. The primary task of the sovereign is to

[10] Hong, X. B. (2009). Marx's Critique of Social Contract Theory and its Practical Significance. *Wuhan University Journal (Humanity Sciences)* (1), 11–16.

defend the lives of the people and to pursue "peace at home and mutual aid against their enemies abroad".[11]

John Locke of Britain also believed that the authority of political order comes from the social contract. He noted that the establishment of a country must be agreed upon by all people and that the responsibility of the state or government is to protect the public interest, rights of individuals, and private property. He stated, "The great and chief end, therefore, of men uniting into commonwealths, and putting themselves under government, is the preservation of their property."[12] Nonetheless, he opined that individuals do not surrender all their natural rights to the state, for the lives, liberties, and estates of individuals are their inalienable natural rights and signify the limit of the government's power.

Jean-Jacques Rousseau of France noted that it is ridiculous and unreasonable for the social contract not to unite individuals' wills internally but to force individuals to unite by means of external material forces. Only when individuals are voluntarily obedient rather than submitting themselves to power under compulsion can power have a moral value and basis for legitimacy. He believed that the fundamental problem to be solved by the social contract is "to find a form of association that will bring the whole common force to bear on defending and protecting each associate's person and goods, doing this in such a way that each of them, while uniting himself with all, still obeys only himself and remains as free as before".[13]

Immanuel Kant of Germany stated that the social contract is an "idea of reason". The agreement in the original contract is based on certain legal attributes of the contracting parties. These attributes incorporate the freedom of every member of the state as a human

---

[11] Hobbes, T. (1985). *Leviathan* (p. 132) (S. F. Li, & T. B. Li, Trans.). Beijing: The Commercial Press.

[12] Locke, J. (1964). *Two Treatises of Government* (J. N. Qu, & Q. F. Ye, Trans.). Beijing: The Commercial Press.

[13] Rousseau. J.-J. (1982). *The Social Contract* (p. 19) (Z. W. He, Trans.). Beijing: The Commercial Press.

being, the equality of each with the others as a subject, and the independence of every member of a commonwealth as a citizen, all of which are prior principles that any moral agent should follow.[14]

In sum, the social contract theory is aimed at the proper organisation of the social structure proceeding from individuals as nodes in the network. As a basic theory of sovereignty with the characteristics of Western countries, it was developed for the resistance to theocracy, triumph of bourgeois revolution, and establishment and maintenance of the capitalist regimes of Western European countries.

(2) Democratic Republic

Aristotle said, "Democracy is when the indigent, and not the men of property, have the government in their hand."[15]

Montesquieu said, "A love of the republic in a democracy is a love of the democracy, as the latter is that of equality. A love of the democracy is likewise that of frugality."[16]

As early as the period of the Roman Empire, republicanism related to democracy has been an organisational democratic form of political power recognised by European politicians and jurists. They believe that it enables the full use of various social and political resources. Democracy ensures that the people are masters of their country, and republicanism is the organisational structure of sovereignty. The democratic republic is the mainstream political order advocated by modern scholars in Europe.

In contemporary Europe, the political order of the democratic republic has become "a religion, a form of government, a philosophy, and a way of life".[17] Even in the face of the economic stagflation of the current European debt crisis, there are still European

---

[14] Kant. I. (1990). *A Collection of the Critique of Historical Reason* (pp. 180–190) (Zh. W. He, Trans.). Beijing: The Commercial Press.

[15] Aristotle. (2008). *Politics a Treatise on Government* (p. 41). Book Jungle.

[16] Montesquieu. (1987). *The Spirit of the Laws* (Vol. 1) (p. 57) (Y. Sh. Zhang, Trans.). Beijing: The Commercial Press.

[17] Mastellone, S. (1988). *A History of Democracy in Europe* (Foreword) (H. G. Huang, Trans.). Beijing: Social Sciences Academic Press.

scholars proposing to adopt the method of initiating another wave of republicanism or renaissance to solve the dilemma.

(3) Consultation and Dictatorship

Apropos of consultation, the preamble of the Constitution of the People's Republic of China, adopted in 1982, states that the system of multi-party cooperation and political consultation led by the Communist Party of China (CPC) constitutes the political order of a dictatorship with consultation with Chinese characteristics that will exist and be developed for a long time to come. People of all nationalities, state organs, armed forces, political parties, public organisations, and enterprises and undertakings in the country must view the Constitution as the basic norm of conduct, and they have a duty to uphold the dignity of the Constitution and ensure its implementation.

Here, dictatorship refers to the theory of a People's Democratic Dictatorship. As an important part of Mao Zedong Thought, it is a combination of the Marxist-Leninist theory of the dictatorship of the proletariat and experiences from the Chinese revolution, construction, and development practices. Additionally, it is the creative application of the Marxist-Leninist theory of the state in China and the fundamental political order laid down by the first-generation central collective leadership of the CPC for contemporary China.[18]

According to Marx and Engels, the historical tasks of the dictatorship of the proletariat are as follows: to suppress the resistance of the exploiting classes and ensure that the broad masses of people involving the working class are the masters of the country; to abolish capitalist private ownership and establish public ownership of the means of production to eliminate exploitation and the exploiting classes; to liberate and promote productive forces; to form peasant cooperatives to attract peasants to the socialist side; to remould all economic and social relationships that are compatible with private ownership; and to change the traditional concepts

[18] Zhang, J. Ch. (2014). A Historical Verification of People's Democratic Dictatorship Theory and the Interpretation of its Contemporary Values. *Studies on Marxism* (9), 83.

of people. They also specified that whether it is a proletarian revolution or the establishment and implementation of a dictatorship of the proletariat, it must proceed under the correct leadership of a proletarian party.[19]

The preamble of the Constitution of the People's Republic of China declares that "the people's democratic dictatorship led by the working class and based on the alliance of workers and peasants is in essence the dictatorship of the proletariat". Article 1 reads that "the People's Republic of China is a socialist state under the people's democratic dictatorship led by the working class and based on the alliance of workers and peasants".

On 5 April 1956, *People's Daily* published "The Historical Experience of the Dictatorship of the Proletariat", stating for the first time that "the dictatorship of the proletariat is fundamentally different in its nature from any of the previous kinds of dictatorship, which were dictatorships by the exploiting classes. It is a dictatorship of the exploited classes, a dictatorship of the majority over the minority, a dictatorship for the purpose of creating a socialist society in which there is no exploitation and poverty, and it is the most progressive and the last dictatorship in the history of mankind".

The dictatorship of the proletariat and People's Democratic Dictatorship have the same political connotation. When Mao Zedong mentioned state power in his speech titled "On the Ten Major Relationships" on 25 April 1956, he used the term "dictatorship of the proletariat". This was also employed as the second principle in the speech titled "Upholding the Four Cardinal Principles" made by Deng Xiaoping in March 1979.[20] The term "people's democratic dictatorship" was used in the constitutions approved by the 12th, 13th, 14th, 15th, 16th, 17th, and 18th CPC National Congresses.[21]

---

[19] Zhao, Y., *et al.* (2001). *Basic Issues of Marxism-Leninism* (pp. 162–163). Beijing: Party School of the CPC Central Committee Press.

[20] Deng, X. P. (1994). *Selected Works of Deng Xiaoping* (Vol. 2) (p. 168). Beijing: People's Publishing House.

[21] Zhang, J. Ch. (2014). A Historical Verification of People's Democratic Dictatorship Theory and the Interpretation of Its Contemporary Values. *Studies on Marxism* (9), 88.

II. Equilibrium in Structure

From the perspective of the global political order, political structure is not a static process but one full of turns, games, confrontations, and balances. World peace is, in essence, the dynamic equilibrium of world politics.

Dr Henry Kissinger, the 56th Secretary of State of the United States, noted in his book *World Order* that although the world order was established by the West and "thought to be applicable to the entire world", it was "at a turning point", upon which he proposed that the trinity of equilibrium, power, and legitimacy could theoretically be the core of world order.[22]

At the end of September 2015, Chinese President Xi Jinping met Kissinger during his visit to Seattle. He also quoted Kissinger's *World Order* in a speech during a welcome banquet jointly hosted by the local government and communities in Seattle, stating that "each generation will be judged by whether the greatest, most consequential issues of the human condition have been faced".[23]

1. *War and Peace under the Equilibrium of Power in Europe*

Almost 400 years ago, Hugo Grotius, a Dutch jurist hailed as the "father of international law", pioneered the study of war and peace among nations and published *On the Law of War and Peace* in 1625. He noted in his book that before the advent of public international law, "if indeed both parties are upon an equal footing, it is the opinion of Caesar, that it is the most favourable moment for making peace, when each party has confidence in itself; even for the stronger party, when flushed with victory, peace is a safer expedient, than the

[22] Kissinger, H. (2015). *World Order* (p. 69). Beijing: CITIC Press.

[23] Xi, J. P. (2015). *Speech by Xi Jinping at the Welcome Banquet jointly hosted by local government and friendly communities in Washington, the United States.* Retrieved from http://www.xinhuanet.com//world/2015-09/23/c_1116656143.htm.

most extensive successes".[24] Grotius' idea of signing treaties for peace laid a solid foundation for the political order of an equilibrium with European characteristics, making it clear that only when Europe has achieved an equilibrium of power among large countries can it obtain a stable structure in international politics.

2. *The US' Strategy of "Leading the World"*

The political order of the US features the separation of powers. The Constitution of the United States, published in 1787, established the political order of the "balance and separation of power among the three branches of the Government" based on its conditions. However, until now, it has continued to be reconsidered and questioned by politicians and scholars in the US. For example, President Wilson and Professor Francis Fukuyama believed that the largest flaws in the political order under the balance and separation of power consisted of multiple authorities, confusion of responsibilities, veto supremacy, and low efficiency.[25]

More than 70 years ago, the formulation of the UN Charter and the establishment of the UN were major achievements in planning a system for world peace after World War II, where the UN Security Council and five permanent members were established, thus shaping a new world political order combining "equilibrium of power and balance". According to the Charter, the UN Security Council is

---

[24] Grotius, H. (2013). *Rights of War and Peace* (p. 358) (Q. H. He *et al.*, Trans.). Shanghai: Shanghai People's Publishing House.

[25] As Woodrow Wilson, the former President of the United States, noted in the *Congressional Government*, "As at present constituted, the federal government lacks strength because its powers are divided, lacks promptness because its authorities are multiplied, lacks wieldiness because its processes are roundabout, lacks efficiency because its responsibility is indistinct and its action without competent direction." In *America in Decay: The Sources of Political Dysfunction*, published in the US bimonthly *Foreign Affairs* (2014, September/October), the famous contemporary American political scientist Francis Fukuyama made an in-depth analysis on the contemporary political system of many abuses: "The U.S. political system has decayed over time because its traditional system of checks and balances has deepened and become increasingly rigid", and at the end of the article he lamented that the reform is impossible and the US has "no way out".

the only organ that can take decisions for the competency of military actions for the world peace, and the members of the Security Council have the right to vote, and the five permanent members are entitled to veto. As such, a global order featuring collective decision-making and the veto of powers was established.

For more than 70 years, the practice of constructing international political order by the international community and the 196 member states of the UN has proven that the UN Security Council veto mechanism was a historic innovation in world politics. The advent of World War II signified the collapse of the political order featuring unanimity among all members that the League of Nations had upheld after World War I. In the post-war period, the old order was supplanted by one featuring unanimity among the great powers, and the international community recognised the implementation of the morality and justice of these great powers as a guarantee of world peace. Proven to have played a significant role in the elimination of regional crises and the prevention of another world war, the new order is none other than the system of maintaining world peace that human beings have sought after for thousands of years.

For the nearly 30 years since the end of the Cold War, the US has boasted that the post-Cold War was an era of unipolar hegemony enabling it to "lead the world". It has proclaimed to have a responsibility and obligation to "lead the world", as manifested in its National Security Act of 1947 and reports titled "National Security Strategy of the United States of America" made by its presidents. The country has dominated global governance by virtue of the two-ocean strategy: it can be in an alliance with NATO (North Atlantic Treaty Organization) to contain Russia and control resources in the Middle East across the Atlantic as well as implement the so-called "rebalance towards Asia-Pacific" with its alliance across the Pacific to hinder the rise of China and tackle the threats from Russia's Far East.[26]

Since ancient times, the world order has seemed to be manoeuvred by an "invisible hand"; for a long time, its structure depended on geographical relationships.

---

[26] Subramanian, A. (2012). *Eclipse: Living in the Shadow of China's Economic Dominance* (p. 236) (Y. Ni, & B. Cao, Trans.). Beijing: CITIC Press.

The transformations of world politics over the last century, which include the order of the power equilibrium in Europe before World War II and the US' two-ocean strategy for the purpose of "leading the world" after the war, reveal that the world's political structure is in dynamic evolution. It covers not only the law-based order of the UN Charter but also the power-oriented order engendered by hegemony, both of which indicate that the world order has achieved an equilibrium featuring neither complete rule of law nor utter chaos.

In the future, the functions of the Internet, a new tool for humankind, will continue to be exploited, which will increasingly affect the new trend of world order.

Section Three: Network Functions and Order

Nodes and structures endow a system with an ontological function that pursues the objectives of optimisation and evolution. In the principle of the "survival of the fittest" and after trade-off analysis, security and order will be the top priorities of the objectives, followed by fairness and efficiency, enabling faster, better, and more economical results. The generalisation of network functions is increasingly focusing on security, efficiency, and justice, which go beyond its original intention.

I. *Security and Order*

The primary functional requirements of the ontology of any system with a power-law distribution are a high degree of stability and security. A stable system, enhanced efficiency, and cost-saving process mathematically constitute an ideal system with a power-law distribution.[27]

---

[27] Xia, Sh. T., Bao, J. G., & Liu, X. J. (2015). *Entropy-Controlled Network — Information Theoretic Economics* (p. 14). Beijing: Economic Science Press.

As such, how can a complete assessment be made to mathematically achieve the ideal system? This requires the separation and analysis of the quantitative indexes of the system ontology in the five dimensions of space, time, energy, matter, and information together with the historical quantitative indexes.

A powerful cyber army is required to create a peaceful cyberspace, prevent information technology from being used for purposes contrary to the maintenance of international security and stability, jointly resist a cyberspace arms race, prevent conflicts, and peacefully use cyberspace for the common interest of mankind to safeguard world peace and order as well as the principle of sovereign equality established by the UN Charter.

A cyberspace in peaceful development is of great significance to each country and the whole world. Cyberspace should by no means become a battleground, not to mention a hotbed of crime. All countries should work together in effectively preventing the use of cyberspace for crimes such as terrorist activity, pornography, drug trafficking, money laundering, and gambling. Bot commercial espionage and the hacking of government networks are crimes that must be handled in accordance with the law and relevant international treaties.

Frontier defence in cyberspace refers to the combination of cyber defence and counterattack on the borders of nations in cyber space to defend national interests in the political, military, economic, and cultural fields. Cyberspace is the new domain of national sovereignty. As the concept of cyber sovereignty is widely accepted by the international community, its guarantee has become the key to effective national sovereignty. Sovereignty involves borders, and borders must be fortified. The co-construction of frontier defence in cyberspace by the military and civilians is not only an urgent task for China to protect its cyber sovereignty but also a cornerstone to safeguard cyber sovereignty for a long time.

From the perspective of the global protection of cyber sovereignty, civil-military integration is the only way to develop safeguards in this field.[28] For example, the US established the US Cyber Command in June 2009[29] to direct its operations in cyber warfare and initiated the National Cyber Range project in June 2009. As of 2011, the US military had developed more than 2,000 kinds of weapons for cyberattacks,[30] enlisted nearly 100,000 people in its cyber forces,[31] and employed 3,000 to 5,000 experts.[32] After the exposure of PRISM, Martin Dempsey, who served as the 18th chairman of the Joint Chiefs of Staff, pledged to hire 4,000 cyber operators to join the ranks of the US Cyber Command over the next four years and to invest US$23 billion[33] in cyber security to strengthen the US' defences against cyberattacks. In the 2011 Department of Defense (DoD) Strategy for Operating in Cyberspace, the DoD specified that cyberspace is considered the fifth battlefield after land, sea, air, and space and that it would launch military operations against serious cyberattacks. The US has also conducted a series of cyber warfare exercises such as Cyber Storm,[34] organised by the Department of Homeland Security, and Silent Horizon,[35] organised by the Central Intelligence Agency (CIA).

---

[28] Fang, B. X. (2017). *On Cyberspace Sovereignty* (pp. 422–423). Beijing: Science Press.

[29] *United States Cyber Command.* Retrieved from https://en.wikipedia.org/wiki/United_States_Cyber_Command.

[30] *The U.S. Military has Developed More Than 2,000 Virus Weapons to Strengthen its Cyber Warfare Capabilities.* (2016). Retrieved from http://www.china.com.cn/military/txt/2009-06/03/content_17881319.htm.

[31] *Cyberspace has become a New Battlefield for the US Military, with the Strongest 100,000 Hackers in the World.* (2016). Retrieved from http://www.china.com.cn/military/2013-03/ 06/content_ 28150970.htm.

[32] *The U.S. Military Cyber Force — the Equivalent of Seven 101st Airborne Divisions.* (2016). Retrieved from http://news.xinhuanet.com/mil/2013-08/11/c_125148975.htm.

[33] *The Internet Should NOT Become a New Tool for the U.S. to Seek Hegemony.* (2016). Retrieved from http://www.qstheory.cn/zxdk/2013/201315/201307Zt20130729_253893.htm.

[34] *Cyber Storm: Securing Cyber Space.* Retrieved from https://www.dhs.gov/cyber-storm.

[35] *CIA's "Silent Horizon" Internet War Games.* Retrieved from http://usatoday30.usatoday.com/tech/news/techpolicy/2005-05-26-cia-wargames_x.htm.

II. *Large Quantity, Fast Speed, High Quality, and Low Cost*

Large quantity: In a network system, a large quantity of nodes, especially central and influential nodes, is the fundamental feature of the network's abundant subjects, well-rounded functions, rapid development, and orderly progress.

Fast speed: Fast connection speeds, short distances, fewer levels, and good connection stability among subjects also demonstrate the full development of a network system's functions.

High quality: A well-designed structure that is dense and efficient lays a scientific and technological foundation for the exploitation of the advantages of a network's functions. If the central node of the star network is too fragile, developing a distributed blockchain is a good direction for the optimisation of the network structure.

Low cost. The construction of a network system should not only achieve the optimal functions but also save a marginal cost of investment. High costs arising from overly fast connections, excessive subject identities, and overly intensive site construction for equipment may cause system failure.

The creation of a secure network requires the effective control of cyber security risks, a sound and complete national cyber security guarantee system, safe and controllable core technology and equipment, stable and reliable operation of information systems, and overall development enabling faster, better, and more economical results. However, China is currently a major importer of ICTs, which has resulted in technological asymmetry between the hegemonic powers in cyberspace and itself. The level of ICTs determines the ability to safeguard cyber sovereignty. Therefore, to change its current situation, China should continue its construction featuring large quantities, fast speeds, high quality, and low costs by strengthening the capacity building of independent technologies, actively developing fundamental, general, and disruptive technologies, and putting a premium on the independent and controllable development of core software and hardware together with the independent construction of a cyberspace defence system.

In terms of the independent research and development of core software and hardware, it is necessary to make consistent efforts and take the lead in studying and formulating a development strategy for core technology and equipment in the national information field. It is also important to take the initiative in competition and development for the purpose of making breakthroughs in core technology as soon as possible. The development of core software and hardware is vital to the capacity building of the research and development of key information infrastructure. The key information infrastructures, including CPUs (central processing units), operating systems, industrial control equipment, domain name systems, and large databases, are the cornerstone of defending national cyber sovereignty. Therefore, it is necessary to gradually improve China's independent research and development capabilities for key infrastructures to spur demand to invigorate the market and further drive independent innovation.

With regard to the construction of a network defence system, departments including the Office of the Central Cyberspace Affairs Commission, the Ministry of Industry and Information Technology, the Ministry of Public Security, and the Ministry of State Security should work together to arouse the enthusiasm of domestic companies in the fields of security and internet to achieve a shared defence with the armed forces and civilian sectors. It is necessary to formulate a development strategy for the national cyberspace defence system, make more use of standards to regulate behaviour in cyberspace, and improve the monitoring, early warning, and emergency response mechanisms for major incidents in cyber security by completing basic tasks such as hierarchical protection, risk assessment, and vulnerability detection. It is also imperative to create a strong network technical investigation capability by vigorously building technical platforms[36] in fields such as national intelligence analysis, big data analysis, and network address tracing, thus constantly improving the management and law-based governance of cyberspace in security.

---

[36] Fang, B. X. (2017). *On Cyberspace Sovereignty* (pp. 419–421). Beijing: Science Press.

Section Four: Coordination in Network and Order

When sovereignty is the research object, it is necessary to academically generate the perspective of the coordinator. To view cyber sovereignty from this perspective, one should view the central node, network structure, and ontological function of networks as a trinity and believe that information theory, cybernetics, and system theory also constitute a whole. The innate interconnectivity of network technologies determines the necessity of coordination in network governance. The coordination of cyberspace order must be based on historical wisdom and involve real choices to integrate the law of nature and civilised order.

I. *Wisdom of History*

The mechanisms of exchange, communication, and cooperation are the bases for the formation of social networks and the creation of value. Even for the greatest people, "as it is this disposition which forms that difference of talents, so remarkable among men of different professions, so it is this same disposition which renders that difference useful".[37] In the geopolitics of the East and West, the history of each country approximately manifests the idea and wisdom of coordination comprising alliances, cooperation, or co-movements.

1. *Vertical and Horizontal Alliances: The Rise of the Qin Dynasty in China and the Success in New Nation Building*

After the balance among the seven powers of the Warring States Period was broken, political strategists, a product of that period, played a significant role in military and diplomatic activities. They

[37] Smith, A. (2015). *An Inquiry into the Nature and Causes of the Wealth of Nations* (Vol. 1, p. 14). Beijing: The Commercial Press.

proposed many military strategies and contingencies that were profound, had an abundance of philosophy and practicability,[38] and embodied the unique historical wisdom on coordination of the Chinese nation.

To topple the Qin regime, the feudal princes "formed an alliance vertically and horizontally" that was facilitated by Wei Wuji, Zhao Sheng, Huang Xie, and Tian Wen. "The Faults of Qin" demonstrated the outstanding diplomatic and military strategy of the Warring States, namely the overall game strategy of the vertical and horizontal alliance.

A vertical alliance refers to the strategy of allying with weak states to resist a powerful country together and was advanced by Su Qin in his strategic idea of uniting six states to jointly resist Qin. A horizontal alliance refers to an alliance between powerful and backward countries to check and balance other countries, which was put forth by Zhang Yi, who suggested that Qin form an alliance with backward countries to capture other countries separately.

The adoption of the vertical and horizontal alliances was determined by the situation and the disparity in strength of the different states in the Warring States Period. This strategic thought is still valued and widely used in modern times in China. No longer employed to seek hegemony, it now plays a significant part in the fight against hegemony. For example, the strategy of "unifying the weak to resist against the strong" and the theory of "three worlds" are derivatives of the ancient Chinese wisdom.[39]

The establishment and prosperity of the Qin dynasty in Chinese history signified the victory of the horizontal alliance over the vertical alliance. The Qin dynasty achieved the Great Unity.

Vertical alliance or horizontal alliance? The right choice requires wisdom learned from history, namely scientific judgment of the

---

[38] Zhou, Sh. C. (2012). Vertical and Horizontal Alliances: A Brief Analysis of Military Diplomacy in the Middle Period of the Warring States Period. *Journal of Ningbo University (Liberal Arts Edition)* (6), 68.

[39] Liu, Y.Q. (2012). Vertical and Horizontal Alliances Against Hegemony in the Ancient Time. *Xinkecheng (Part I)* (8), 106.

situation and decision-making enabling the coordination of all resources.

2. *Allies and Axis: The Two World Wars and Veto Mechanism of the UN Security Council*

Henry Kissinger noted in *World Order* that "every international order must sooner or later face the impact of two tendencies challenging its cohesion: either a redefinition of legitimacy or a significant shift in the balance of power". From the Entente countries and Allied countries during World War I to the Axis powers and Allied powers during World War II, major countries like China, the US, and Russia or large economies such as Europe have become the pivot of the world's equilibrium. In addition, as the fruit of the World War II victory, the UN embodies the legitimacy of the world order.

With more than 70 years of history, the UN is currently the world's most important, universal, and intergovernmental organisation. As the supreme authority to safeguard world peace after the war, it makes decisions on issues affecting world peace through the veto mechanism of its Security Council in global governance.

The resolutions of the UN Security Council provide the only legal process in global governance for handling issues relating to war and peace. The UN Security Council consists of a total of 15 members, including 5 permanent members. These five countries maintaining the equilibrium of the world order have historically been entitled to show their strengths and express their opinions under the statutory protection of the UN Charter. In practice, they can use their veto power to prevent the final entry into force of Security Council resolutions that go against their national interests and ideals.

By no means an embodiment of hegemony and dictatorship, the veto mechanism of the Security Council falls under its collective voting mechanism. As the core of the Security Council's voting system, the veto mechanism has proven to be far more civilised than hegemony or dictatorship, apropos of the changes in the decision-making voting mechanism, which has undergone a transition from a democratic proposal to a decision under hegemony or dictatorship.[40] The Charter contains provisions on the veto: Article 23 stipulates that the five permanent members — comprising China, the US, Russia, the UK, and France — are entitled to the right to veto; Article 27 states that decisions of the Security Council on procedural matters shall be made by an affirmative vote of nine members. The decisions of the Security Council on all other matters shall be made by an affirmative vote of nine members, including the concurring votes of the permanent members. This suggests unanimity among the great powers, revealing that the five permanent members are endowed with the privilege of veto and that the voting power of the five largest permanent members has more legal effect than that of the other UN members. Articles 108–110 of the Charter stipulate that the five permanent members of the Security Council have the power of veto over the entry into force as well as the amendments to the Charter.

Decisions on world peace or conflict resolution always require prompt voting. Additionally, decisions on regional security across Asia, America, and Europe must also be unanimously approved by the five powers of the Security Council. Liang Xi, a famous Chinese international jurist, put forth the "tripod" principle when analysing the veto power of the five permanent members, stating that "the three sets of Articles are mutually beneficial and support the entire UN system like a tripod".[41] This not only reflects flexibility, efficiency, and compliance with the principles of the world peace system but also shows that the veto mechanism has laid a unique, historically formed, and indispensable basis for global consensus in the operation of the UN global governance system.

On 14 November 2015, terrorist attacks occurred in Paris, France[42]; on 18 November of the same year, French President

---

[40] Shi, Zh. (2002). The Security Council's Veto Power — Image of "Power Politics". *Europe* (6), 37.

[41] Liang, X. (2011). *The Law of International Organizations — Principles and Practice* (p. 147) (Z.W. Yang, Rev.). Wuhan: Wuhan University Press.

[42] Ma, Y. (2015). France's Another Lose: Anti-Terrorism War in Europe Is Far from Over. *World Vision* (23).

François Hollande called for a UN Security Council meeting to crack down on terrorist organisations as soon as possible. The proposal pushed the fight against extremist terrorism (which France called "war") high on the agenda of the Security Council for the first time, inaugurating the trend of using the UN Security Council veto mechanism to make decisions on global counter-terrorism and peacekeeping on a broader scale. Two days later, the 15 members of the UN Security Council approved the resolution unanimously. As of 3 December 2015, four of the five permanent members (Russia, the US, the UK, and France) were engaged in military operations against the Islamic State (IS) successively.

Official data show that by the end of 2012, the five permanent members had invoked the veto more than 270 times. Russia (together with the Soviet Union) invoked it 129 times, of which six were backed by China, which was proof of the efforts of China and Russia (two countries driven by national interests) in forestalling the adoption of irresponsible international policies to jointly maintain international peace and security. The US invoked it 78 times and the UK 32 times, of which 22 were backed by the other; France invoked it 18 times, of which 13 were backed by the US and the UK.

The People's Republic of China has invoked the veto nine times since it resumed its legitimate seat in the UN in 1971. However, China, the largest contributor of peacekeepers, has invoked the veto the least among the permanent members.

Although the veto of the five permanent members is designed to maintain world peace, the UN, as a multilateral platform, has become a tool for countries to contain each other and seek their

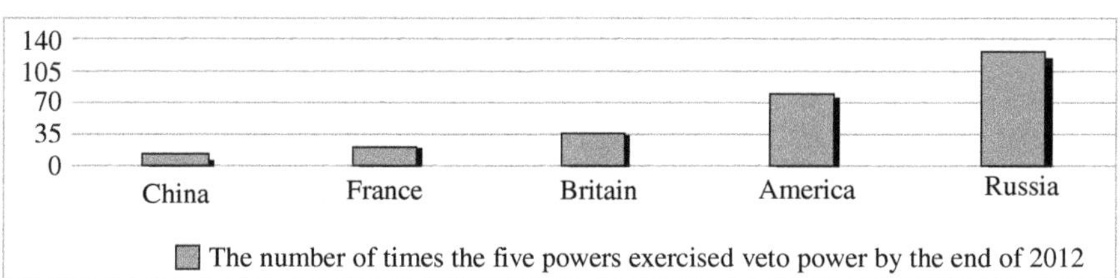

Figure 8-2: An overview of the number of times the permanent member states exercised veto power by the end of 2012

own interests and goals.[43] China's low exercise of the veto power in the past reflects its willingness to respect and safeguard world peace. This shows that it not only upholds independence, autonomy, and responsibility as a world power but also adheres to international morality in international political exchanges. Nevertheless, with the peaceful rise of China, the number of vetoes it exercises has gradually increased, indicating that China's voice in establishing the world order is growing increasingly powerful and confident. The great quantity of peacekeepers it dispatches also shows that the country is making its best efforts to maintain world peace in accordance with the law.

II. *Choices in the Real World*

1. *From Following Behind to Running Alongside*

The spread of the Internet all over the world originated in the US. Naturally, the country brought hegemony into cyberspace and further strengthened it, which has mainly manifested by its denial of cyber sovereignty in the name of internet freedom. Its proposition, which is for the sole purpose of protecting its own interests as a superpower in cyberspace, does not hold water from a legal perspective.

In the history of human civilisation, great inventions have always been owned by all human beings. For example, in the agricultural technology revolution that safeguarded the survival of mankind, the developers of the technologies that enabled the widespread cultivation of various crops did not charge users a patent royalty. Moreover, James Watt, the inventor of the steam engine, a great invention originating from the thermodynamic revolution of smelting technology that ushered in the industrial revolution, brought about a dynamic improvement in productivity and led humanity into the age of industrial civilisation. The inventions in the electric power revolution brought mankind into the electrical

[43] Zhu, J. M. (1986). *A New Theory on International Organizations* (p. 345). Beijing: Zhengzhong Book Company.

age. The generation, transmission, and distribution of electricity engendered drastic changes in energy. Now, some patents covering photoelectric conversion, including that of electric lamps and optical fibres, are owned by Corning Inc. (which was established by their inventor Thomas Edison) and are under the legal protection for patented technologies. However, on the whole, more than seven billion people in the world still benefit from the marvellous results of the electric power revolution, free of patent fees.

2. *Sharing and Co-Governance*

The users of network technology comprise more than half of the world's population of over seven billion people. Therefore, the shared ownership of this invention is also the result of the joint efforts of all experts and netizens around the world. Another example is the four great inventions of ancient China, whose legal ownership can by no means be exclusive to China, for they have brought great convenience to the inheritance of human civilisation and the development of the world's marine technology.

The abovementioned inventions have all proven that they cannot be limited by ownership and intellectual property as defined by the legal system, nor can they be regarded as a permanent tool for hegemony in international politics. The promotion of every great invention brings inclusive value to the progress of human civilisation, which should not be monopolised by any hegemonic power.

Under the framework of the UN, which consists of 196 member states, countries in the modern international community can generously share their great inventions in technology. Confined to the jurisdiction of sovereignty, which comprises the three elements of land, people, and government as stipulated by the UN Charter, cyber sovereignty was born with these three characteristics in its basic connotation. Therefore, even if the freedom in cyberspace transcends national boundaries, it is still restrained by the consensus of all people, as stipulated in the International Bill of Human Rights and the International Covenant on Civil and Political Rights, and cannot go against the norms on modern international relations such as sovereign equality and self-defence in a peaceful way, as stipulated in Article 1 and Article 59 of the UN Charter.

It is clear that cyber sovereignty outweighs internet freedom. Countries need to negotiate their boundaries, cooperation, and co-governance in cyberspace. In this process full of frictions and compromises, emerging countries and the country that invented the Internet should be aware that users around the world will work together to gain benefits from and advance the development of the Internet, the newest achievement of human civilisation, under the cyber sovereignty of their own countries. Therefore, the themes of development involving orderliness, controllability, autonomy, and cooperation are far more valuable than the early network patterns by means of technology, including monopolies and monitoring. As a significant invention that brought about the Fourth Industrial Revolution, network technology is bound to benefit human beings to a larger extent under the protection of cyber sovereignty and the promotion of internet freedom, which has a legal basis in that freedom in cyberspace can by no means outweigh cyber sovereignty.

On the whole, the development of cyberspace order in human history fluctuates as a curve from the initial monopoly to the technical competition, and finally to the contemporary civilised sharing.

Chapter Nine

Network and Overall Planning Entropy

There is a simple understanding of physical quantity that the whole is equal to the sum of its parts. However, according to Karl Marx, the whole is greater than the sum of its parts,[1] for the whole includes the unphysical consciousnesses emerging in the processes of awakening, cognition, self-consciousness, and self-conducted action on top of the physical consciousness. Marx also noted that these awakened consciousnesses comprise class consciousness, revolution consciousness, and freedom consciousness. In contemporary sovereign nations, these manifest themselves as the consciousness of overall planning in national security, the top priority for all countries. The key to the science of overall planning consists of the research and interpretation of the additions after adding all the parts together.

Section One: The Ideological Origin of Overall Planning

The thought and practice of the Great Unity in ancient China more than 3,000 years ago mark the earliest overall planning on record:

[1] Lee, W. L. (2014). *On Marx* (p. 74) (W.Q. Chen, Trans.). Beijing: Zhonghua Book Company.

"King Wen of the Zhou Dynasty ordered to designate the first month of the lunar year to rule the country at God's will, thereby making himself the very start of everything in the world, which was therefore a symbol of the Great Unity." The word "great" manifests the importance of and reverence for the process of unification; and "unity" here refers to the situation that all feudal princes were ruled by the king, a manifestation of the feudal system in the Zhou dynasty. There is also another explanation: "The Great Unity means the harmonised customs on the land under heaven and the unification of the 'Nine Regions'." Rather than reunification on the basis of regional sovereignty or hegemony, the Great Unity refers to the well-designed balance of a country's overall order, covering politics, economy, people, society, and culture.

For half a century, academic thought on overall planning almost simultaneously sprouted and blossomed and was tested and developed in the East and West. In China, it was first propounded by Mao Zedong and Hua Luogeng and was applied to the key areas critical to China's independence and development. In the West, it originated in the United States' (US) military and industry. Its practice and development in the technology, military, and economy fields were boosted by the fast-growing computer industry and the issue of the National Security Act of 1947. In the current era of the Internet, both Chinese and Western academic circles have begun to consider developing the method of overall planning into a science and applying it to the construction, operation, management, and governance of cyberspace.

I. *Overall Planning and Overall Planning Methods*

In 1956, Mao Zedong put forth the fundamental principle of "overall consideration and everyone being properly placed"[2] in the socialist construction in his article "On the Ten Major

[2] Mao, Z. D. (1976). On the Ten Major Relationships. *People's Daily*; Mao, Z. D. (1999). *Collected Works of Mao Zedong* (Vol. 7). Beijing: People's Publishing House.

Relationships". In 1957, he proposed the method of "overall consideration and proper arrangement" in his article "On the Correct Handling of Contradictions among the People".[3]

1. *Connotations of Overall Planning*

Most Chinese documents in history preferred operations research to overall planning, but it is recorded in official documents that Mao Zedong mentioned overall planning more than 30 times on different occasions. The concept was also embodied in his philosophical works such as *On Practice*, *Where Do Correct Ideas Come From?*, and *On Contradiction*. In this connection, Mao may have been the first ideologist in Chinese history to appreciate and advocate overall planning.

(1) Policy Implications of Overall Planning

At the Third Plenary Session of the 16th Communist Party of China (CPC) Central Committee in October 2003, the Scientific Outlook on Development was put forth, advocating the promotion of a balanced growth between urban and rural areas, different regions, economic and social undertakings, man and nature, and domestic progress and opening-up to the world for comprehensive, coordinated, and sustainable development.[4]

The report delivered at the 17th National Party Congress in October 2007 stated, "We must persist in overall consideration. We must take into overall consideration the relationships between the central and local authorities, between personal and collective interests, between interests of the part and those of the whole, between immediate and long-term interests and between the domestic and international situations."[5]

---

[3] Mao, Z. D. (1977). *Selected Works of Mao Zedong* (Vol. 5) (pp. 387–402). Beijing: People's Publishing House.

[4] *The News of the Communist Party of China*. (2016). Retrieved from http://www.people.com.cn/GB/shizheng/1024/2133923.html.

[5] *Interpretation of the Report to the 17th CPC National Congress: The Fundamental Method of Scientific Outlook on Development is Overall Coordination*. (2016). Retrieved from http://www.gov.cn/jrzg/2007-11/14/content_805327.htm.

The report delivered at the 18th National Congress held in November 2012 stated, "The whole Party must more purposefully take the holistic approach as the fundamental way of thoroughly applying the Scientific Outlook on Development... We must take a holistic approach to our work relating to reform, development and stability, to domestic and foreign affairs as well as national defense, and to running the Party, the country and the military. We must coordinate urban and rural development, development between regions, economic and social development, relations between man and nature, and domestic development and opening to the outside world. We must balance the interests of all parties and keep them fully motivated so that all people do their best, find their proper places in society and live in harmony." As such, it is necessary to "make overall planning for bilateral, multilateral, regional and sub-regional opening up and cooperation", "promote coordinated development of the social security system in urban and rural areas", "place basic pensions under unified national planning", "ensure both economic development and development of defense capabilities", and "coordinate the training of all types of personnel".[6]

The Decision of the Central Committee of the Communist Party of China on Some Major Issues Concerning Comprehensively Deepening the Reform passed by the Third Plenary Session of the 18th Central Committee of the CPC in November 2013 specifies that it is necessary to "make holistic planning", "promote the reform of Party organs, government departments and mass organizations as a whole", "make overall plans for developing urban and rural infrastructure and communities, and for building a network of service facilities", and "make a balanced allocation of compulsory education resources between urban and rural areas". It also notes that "we will adhere to the basic old-age insurance system that combines social pools with individual accounts, place basic old-age pension under unified national planning, and expedite the balanced development of the minimum living allowance system in both urban and

[6] *The Report to the 18th CPC National Congress.* (2016). Retrieved from http://news.sina.com.cn/z/sbdbg/.

rural areas"; "we will proceed with a comprehensive reform in medical security, medical care, public health, and the medicine supply and regulatory system"; and "we will establish a joint interregional mechanism for comprehensive land and marine ecosystem protection, restoration and pollution prevention".[7]

(2) Intendment of the Law of Overall Planning

In the Chinese legal system, overall planning in accordance with the law is mainly composed of overall planning in territory (embodied in the Urban and Rural Planning Law of the People's Republic of China, the Land Administration Law of the People's Republic of China, the Law of the People's Republic of China on the Administration of Sea Areas, the Civil Aviation Law of the People's Republic of China, and the Waterway Law of the People's Republic of China), finance and taxation (embodied in the Budget Law of the People's Republic of China, the Social Insurance Law of the People's Republic of China, the Insurance Law of the People's Republic of China, and the Law of the People's Republic of China on Promotion of Cleaner Production), and population (stipulated in the Labor Law of the People's Republic of China, the Employment Promotion Law of the People's Republic of China, the Law of the People's Republic of China on the Promotion of Small and Medium-Sized Enterprises, and the Higher Education Law of the People's Republic of China).

In addition, centralising power in accordance with the law, i.e. dominating as a whole, is mainly reflected in the overall planning of sovereignty. This can be manifested in laws. For example, Article 5 of the National Security Law of the People's Republic of China stipulates that "the central leading body for national security shall be responsible for coordinating policies and deliberations on national security work, researching, developing, and guiding the implementation of national security strategies and relevant major guidelines and policies, and conducting overall coordination of

[7] *The Decision, Communique and Statement of the Third Plenary Session of the 18th CPC National Congress*. (2016). Retrieved from http://www.ce.cn/xwzx/gnsz/szyw/201311/18/t20131118_1767104.shtml.

significant national security affairs and important task". Moreover, Article 8 specifies, "In national security work, overall arrangements shall be made on internal security and external security; territorial security and citizen security; conventional security and unconventional security; and own security and common security." Moreover, Article 52 of the Legislation Law of the People's Republic of China states, "The Standing Committee of the National People's Congress shall strengthen the overall planning and arrangements on legislative work in multiple forms such as the comprehensive legislative plan and annual legislative plans." Article 43 of the Counter-Terrorism Law of the People's Republic of China also stipulates, "The national leading institution for counter-terrorism efforts establishes a national counter-terrorism intelligence center, implements cross-departmental intelligence information working mechanisms and overall planning on counter-terrorism intelligence information work."

(3) Academic Meaning of Overall Planning

The term "overall planning" is composed of two words. The word "overall" reflects the comprehensive collection, analysis, selection, and employment of information within the users' jurisdiction; "planning" refers to a though process involving assessment, decision-making, and implementation for the sake of achieving one's goals.[8]

2. *Research on the Overall Planning Method*

Embodying the ideas of statistical systems and operational research, the overall planning method is both a quantitative method and a mathematical method. Professor Liu Tianlu, a student of Hua Luogeng, recalled that in naming the method, Luogeng drew his inspiration from the principle of overall planning advanced by Mao Zedong.[9]

---

[8] Zhu, G. L. (2010). *Science of Overall Planning* (pp. 4–5). Beijing: Current Affairs Press.

[9] Liu, T. L. (2004). *An Introduction to the Science of Overall Planning* (p. 31). Beijing: China Commercial Publishing House.

Inspired by the emergence of network technology and network methods in the international community in the 1950s, Luogeng "keenly noticed the inherent connection between network technology and China's traditional thought on overall planning" and then proposed the overall planning method. He redefined the method of "overall consideration and proper arrangement" as "pursuing development through overall planning, data management, and system construction" and made great efforts to develop it into a science.[10]

To secure the national grid, Chinese experts in the power industry have also focused on overall planning method research. Professor Qi Jianxun and his team at the North China Electric Power University have long been engaged in this research; they introduced the concept of entropy and defined "resource entropy", which serves as a new method to solve problems in resource levelling in the conventional overall planning method.[11]

In the opinion of Professor Qi Jianxun, operations research has only achieved the principle of "high probability" of the success of decision-making optimisation, i.e. the adoption of measures for a high probability of success, which manifests as the secure development function of the grid. However, this is merely commonplace for common people. The Massachusetts Institute of Technology has developed a "don't do" principle, i.e. do not get involved in tasks that can be completed by anything other than hard work because something everyone can do is less innovative and the completion of outstanding and original tasks is an all-too-rare event. Considering these factors, Qi Jianxun proposed that in addition to obtaining overall consideration, overall planning research should also focus on the main contradictions, which can be manifested in the combination of the function of secure development and the pursuit of excellence. This differs from operations research, which only obtains the first function.[12]

---

[10] Liu, T. L. (2004). *An Introduction to the Science of Overall Planning* (p. 17). Beijing: China Commercial Publishing House.

[11] Qi, J. X. (2010). *The Development and Frontier Issues of Overall Planning Method* (pp. 190–200). Beijing: Science Press.

[12] Ibid., pp. 206–207.

II. *Overall Research Planning at Home and Abroad*

Based on the abundant ideas of overall planning in ancient times, China's overall research planning in politics was proposed by Mao Zedong. Its planning in mathematics was advanced by Hua Luogeng,[13] and that in engineering was further developed by Liu Tianlu and Qi Jianxun. Moreover, research planning in the military was studied in depth by scholars including Zhu Guolin.[14] Apropos of the rule of law, the legislative thought on the overall planning of sovereignty was developed by laws represented by the National Security Law of 2015.

1. *Evolution of Overall Planning in the US*

In the 1960s, both China and the US began to study the "optimisation method and overall planning method" and the "critical path method" (CPM, or the activity-on-node method, employed in the Apollo Program).[15] The US military's research on CPM constitutes the theoretical origin of its internet technology monopoly to a certain extent.

To understand the ontology and elements of cyberspace, even countries like the US have had to resort to a century's experience of

---

[13] Scientific and Technical Information Institute of China. (1965). *Compilation of Domestic Material on Overall Method*; Hua, L. G. (1973). *Overall Method Analysis*. Division of Applied Mathematics of Guangxi Normal Institute. (1976). *Optimization Method and Overall Planning Method*; Leading Group of Hunan Provincial Revolutionary Committee for Optimization Method Promotion. Science and Technology Department of Sichuan Provincial Postal Administration. (1981). *Preliminary Application of Overall Planning Method*. Beijing: Posts and Telecom Press.

[14] Zhu, G. L. (1999). *Science of Overall Military Planning*. Beijing: National Defense University Press; Zhu, G. L. (2004). *Science of Overall Military Planning*. Beijing: PLA Press.

[15] Wiest, J. D., & Levy, F. K. (1983). *A Management Guide to PERT/CPM* (pp. 3–8). Beijing: China Machine Press.

rule of law. In the process of cyberspace theory, the technology, rule of law, and thoughts all display different characteristics in diverse stages of development, which shows that the consideration of the ontology and elements of networks have not yet risen to the height of philosophy nor reached a level ushering in a stable and clear consensus.

Before the introduction of cyber sovereignty, all other countries manifested the following feature with regard to the ever-changing technology, thought, and rule of law in the process of network theory. Thereafter, discrepancies in the process with different standpoints emerged gradually in this megatrend.

Many theories have been put forth by cyberspace jurists and ideologists in the US, but all lack a holistic philosophical foundation, scientific theoretical basis, and corresponding solutions. They just target the problems at one stage. To refine these defective ideas and develop them into an epoch-making ideological system, it is imperative to research and consolidate the scientific foundation and philosophical foundation. An operation system of policy and rule of law seeking both temporary and permanent solutions can only be established after the achievement of a consensus based on scientific theory and the construction of an ideological system of science in cyberspace. Of course, this system cannot be separated from mathematical expression.

The United Nations (UN) itself has not produced a consensus on cyber cognition but requires countries to report and make their positions and views public. However, the US refuses to report its stance, and other countries have announced only their perceptions of one stage. At present, it is not easy for the technology-based ideological system based on the theory of cyberspace ontology in various countries to achieve overall planning because it an unclear, fragmented system that is confined to one stage and difficult to reach a consensus on. Therefore, it is crucial to find a way to put forth a holistic cyberspace theory and create a theoretical system for cyber governance.

2. *Refinement of the Science of Overall Planning in China*

After reviewing the three phases of the evolution of overall planning from a method to a study to a science, Professor Liu Tianlu, a student of Hua Luogeng, came to the conclusion that "almost all distinctive scientific researches of overall planning are concentrated in China", thus providing a foundation for the development of the science of overall planning with Chinese characteristics to differentiate from and compare with other countries' research in management, systems engineering, and operations.[16]

In overall planning research, it is imperative to determine the answer to the following question: Can a formula be employed to measure the condition of overall planning and underpin the construction of a new theory featuring the scientific research on overall planning? That is, can an overall planning theory be constructed based on the "three theories" of information theory, cybernetics, and system theory? Functioning as the mathematical and philosophical bases of the ideological systems involving cyberspace cognition and cyber sovereignty, this new theory will play an important role in strengthening the theoretical foundation of and establishing a consensus on the governance system of cyber sovereignty.

Section Two: The Application of the Mechanism of Overall Planning

In general, the development of human undertakings is inseparable from the implementation of overall planning. Human's wisdom on overall planning and optimisation has been widely and historically used in all aspects of social life and in each factor of national sovereignty. Apropos of the three factors of territory (space), people (society), and political power (regime), both their security maintenance and orderly development rely on the optimisation and application of the principle of overall planning.

[16] Liu, T. L. (2004). *An Introduction to the Science of Overall Planning* (p. 3). Beijing: China Commercial Publishing House.

1. *Overall Space Planning*

Overall space planning is a constant topic for human beings to delve into. In the field of urban planning and construction, there are complete records of urban construction covering the civilisations of ancient Egypt, ancient Babylon, ancient India, ancient Greece, ancient Rome, the Middle Ages, modern times, and the design of "future cities".[17] From the Shang and Zhou dynasties to the Qin and Han dynasties to modern times, the number and types of urban planning and construction have been constantly increasing, embodying the characteristics of Chinese civilisation.[18]

Urban planning is an outgrowth of the concentration of a country's population that, according to recent research, features hidden "ordered complexity". Disappointingly, as most are derived from superficial understandings, classic urban plans have so many deficiencies that it is hard for them to achieve an ideal effect. Considering this, some scholars abroad have started to attack the urban planning in the US after in-depth reflection. For example, through reconsidering the uses of sidewalk safety, association, and assimilation, Jane Jacobs reintroduced some new principles for overall planning after rethinking the necessary urban functions in old neighbourhoods and small blocks to prevent cities from declining into "helpless victims of danger".[19]

Chinese scholars have also recognised the necessity of regional overall planning and the historical limitations of traditional spatial planning. China developed "multiple plan integration" in the National New-Type Urbanization Plan in 2014 after undergoing the "Five-Year Plan" with Soviet characteristics ("the first plan"), a

---

[17] Shen, Y. L. (2008). *The History of Urban Construction Overseas*. Beijing: China Architecture and Building Press.

[18] Zhuang, L. D., & Zhang, J. X. (2002). *The History of Urban Development and Construction in China*. Nanjing: Southeast University Press; Dong, J. H. (2008). *The History of Urban Construction in China* (3rd ed.). Beijing: China Architecture and Building Press.

[19] Jacobs, J. (2005). *The Death and Life of Great American Cities* (pp. 29–122) (H. Sh. Jin, Trans.). Nanjing: Yilin Press.

combination of urban planning and land-use planning ("the second plan"), the coexistence of social and economic development planning, urban planning, and land use planning ("the third plan"), and the introduction of the plan of ecological civilisation construction and ecological development ("the fourth plan"). Professor Gu Chaolin of Tsinghua University opined that this marked the arrival of the era of "spatial planning with integrated multiple plans" aiming to comprehensively resolve the imbalances in regional development at the natural, economic, institutional, and market levels to enter the "new normal" of development.[20]

The proposal of the overall planning of land and sea in China signifies the introduction of a broader and newer concept of overall spatial planning. In essence, Chinese scholars do not agree with Alfred Mahan's "Sea Power Theory" (i.e. that maritime hegemony is superior to land hegemony) but prefer the spatial development layout of the "coordination and overall planning of land and sea". Some domestic scholars proposed "land-sea overall planning to enhance both land power and sea power" at the Academic Forum in Memory of the 600th Anniversary of Zheng He's Expeditions to the Western Ocean, which was hosted by Peking University in 2004 after the Third Plenary Session of the 16th CPC Central Committee. "Five types of overall planning" involving balanced growth between urban and rural areas, different regions, economic and social undertakings, man and nature, and domestic progress and opening-up to the world were brought forward. The sea area within the jurisdiction of China covers three million square kilometres, accounting for nearly one-third of its land area. Regarding the overall planning of land and sea, the Academy of Macroeconomic Research of the National Development and Reform Commission set up major topics in 2013 to conduct in-depth research in which concepts of space optimisation, including "leaning against land and embracing the sea", "land-sea coordination", "land-sea integration", "land-sea interaction", and "land-sea overall planning", were

[20] Gu, Ch. L. (2015). *Spatial Planning of Multi-Rule Integration* (pp. 2–61). Beijing: Tsinghua University Press.

proposed. Preliminary ideas for the overall spatial planning of the Bohai Sea, Yellow Sea, East China Sea, and South China Sea were also developed.[21]

2. *Overall Population Planning*

Security and order are the two ultimate goals of overall spatial planning, which can be accomplished through overall population planning. In the West, social engineering centred on human security is in the exploratory stage. It emphasises that as one element of knowledge production, "information is not knowledge",[22] not to mention wisdom. Attackers' methods of thinking and information collection are quite different from those of defenders or ordinary people. They may use methods including hacking, cyberstalking, and scamming to encroach on the safety of others. Therefore, the government should conduct overall planning in all aspects for its people's security.

Overall population planning plays an important role in sovereignty planning. Since the founding of the People's Republic of China, it has gone through three historical stages, i.e. opposing the Malthusian theory of population, implementing family planning, and encouraging families to have two children, all of which were regulated by the distinctive laws and policies of overall population planning.[23] Social security (or social construction in the eyes of some scholars) placing emphasis on human safety has become the new orientation of China's current overall population planning. The overall social security planning involves sub-topics[24] such as endowment insurance, medical

---

[21] Cao, Zh. X., & Gao, G. L. (2015). *A Study on the Overall Planning for the Development of the Land and Sea of China* (pp. 2–28, p. 256). Beijing: Economic Science Press.

[22] Hadnagy, C. (2010). *The Art of Human Hacking*. John Wiley & Sons, Inc.

[23] Zhang, W. Q. (2007). *Book on the Overall Solution to Population Problems*. Beijing: China Population Press.

[24] Fan, X. G., & Chen, W. (2009). *Public Policy: Overall Planning of Urban and Rural Social Security*. Beijing: Economy & Management Publishing House; Zheng, Z. H. (2012). *Social Security: Overall Planning, Coordination, and Sustainable Development*. Hangzhou: Zhejiang University Press.

insurance, labour employment, charity and welfare, income distribution, and a basic living allowance. These are aimed to achieve social justice as well as people's safety and harmony.

3. *Overall Planning of Governance*

The 5,000-year course of Chinese civilisation is, to a certain extent, the history of effectively coordinating the relationship between the central and local governments after the Great Unity. Since the pre-Qin Dynasty, each dynasty has been confronted with inevitable challenges, including centralisation and decentralisation, enfeoffment and civil strife, the establishment of vassal states and weakening of their powers, and separatist activities and rebellion suppression. If the relations between the central and local governments were well-coordinated, the dynasty was more likely to maintain internal security and repel foreign invasion; if not, the dynasty ran into numerous internal and external problems.

Overall planning for urban and rural areas is a political and economic proposition in the context of the coordination between the central and local governments. Some scholars choose to research the conducts of local governments contrary to the orders of higher authorities and the failures of the macro-control of the central governments;[25] some analyse the correspondence between China's urban-rural overall planning and the Western spatial and economic relations between urban and rural areas in urban planning.[26] In short, satisfactory overall planning for urban and rural areas is the key prerequisite for improving the overall order of the coordination between the central and local governments.

The transformation from chaos fraught with conflict to a well-organised and harmonious order depends on the scientific theories and practices guided by the science of overall planning. From

[25] Zhang, Y. (2015). *Overall Planning and Coordination*. Beijing: Intellectual Property Publishing House.
[26] Li, W. K. (2015). *Methods of Overall Planning for Urban and Rural Areas*. Beijing: China Architecture and Building Press.

either the angle of scientific and technological practices or social practices, the discovery and refinement of a feasible understanding of overall planning are major historic propositions to achieve the needs in reality.

Section Three: The Proposal of Overall Planning Entropy

The term "entropy" is derived from the Greek word "εντροπία", which means conversion and change (of energy). In 1824, when analysing thermodynamic efficiency, French physicist Sadi Carnot, the father of thermodynamics, found that an engine working in a reversible cycle is at least as efficient as any other engine working between the same temperature limits, with the efficiency of such an engine being a function of the two limiting temperatures and not dependent on its mechanical design or working substance. This discovery is called Carnot's Theorem.

I. *The Formula of Overall Planning Entropy*

In 1850, German physicist Rudolf Clausius noted that "heat will not flow spontaneously from an object at a lower temperature to an object at a higher temperature; it can flow spontaneously from a hot object to a cold object, gradually reducing the heat distribution; then the orderly distribution of thermal system will gradually become disordered; eventually, homogeneity of the system will be achieved". This is recognised as the second law of thermodynamics.

1. *The Inertia of Conduction and Principle of Increase of Entropy*

In 1865, Rudolf Clausius introduced entropy, a function of state and process, stating that "the total entropy of any isolated thermodynamic system tends to increase over time, approaching a maximum value". In other words, there is always an increase in entropy reflecting the activity, state, and process (of temperature) in an isolated system. This statement is usually called the principle of increase of entropy. There is also another method to prove the principle of increase of entropy in an isolated system: assuming that there is a temperature difference between the two ends of an isolated system, the heat at the high-temperature end flows to the low-temperature end spontaneously without energy exchange with external substances. Accordingly, the temperature difference between the two ends lowers to zero over time; then, the heat transfer stops, and equilibrium will be achieved in the system when the systematic arrangement of gas molecules is replaced by a more random and less orderly movement of molecules. Since heat cannot flow from the low-temperature end to the high-temperature end, the decrease of entropy is proven to be impossible in an isolated system.

There are three types of systems in thermodynamics: open, closed, and isolated. An open system can exchange both energy and matter with its surroundings. A closed system can only exchange energy with its surroundings, not matter. An isolated system can exchange neither energy nor matter with its surroundings. The principle of increase of entropy indicates that the entropy in an isolated system keeps increasing until it reaches the maximum, i.e. the system reaches maximum disorder.

2. *The Measurement of Entropy and Orderliness of Entropy Decrease*

From Ludwig Edward Boltzmann's discovery in 1877 that entropy can be used to study both microscopic molecular motion and macroscopic thermal distribution to its scientific definition developed by scholars including Max Planck in 1900, the concept of entropy has become a scientific measure of a system's stability. In a system composed of a large number of particles (e.g. molecules, atoms), entropy indicates the degree of disorder in the arrangement of particles. The more disordered the system, the higher the entropy; the more orderly the system, the lower the entropy.

Thereafter, the concept of entropy extended its meaning to the range of the philosophy of science and technology: entropy can represent energy or matter in a system. An increase of entropy means a process of depreciation, degradation, and deactivation of energy, i.e. an increase of useless energy and reduction of available energy, indicating a measure of the degree of disorder or of the unavailability of energy. It breaks the traditional theory that energy is just a quantitative concept and develops the mathematical expression of a system's performance in internal governance in an innovative manner.

Since the introduction of the measure theory of entropy, the research on entropy has continued to develop, and its application has been gradually expanded. According to incomplete statistics, there are currently at least 70 to 80 types of entropy applied to agriculture, resources, economy, lives, and other fields in society, e.g. information entropy, resource entropy, entropy in landscape evolution, entropy in biology, soil system entropy, and entropy in economics. As such, can the measure concept and theoretical mode of entropy be used to evaluate the order in cyberspace for the information society and network era? Can the mathematical method of the measure theory of entropy be employed to assess the effect of the overall planning of governance under cyber sovereignty?

The value of the concept of entropy in the philosophy of science and technology can be summarised as follows:

(1) Entropy is a Function that Indicates the Stability of the System

The entropy in a system can be added up. When a system is composed of several subsystems, its entropy is the sum of that of the subsystems, which provides a basis for the incorporation of all the elements of the network into the network system.

(2) Entropy Indicates the Degree of Stability of a System

An increase of entropy signifies disorder, chaos, and activeness; a decrease of entropy means order, stability, and quietness.

There are both reversible and irreversible processes in cyberspace. If a process is reversible, the entropy can be reduced, while if the process is irreversible, the entropy increases the whole time.

The more concentrated the activities (replacing the word "energy") of the cyber elements distributed in the space, the lower the entropy; the more uniform and dispersed the activities of the cyber elements distributed in the space, the higher the entropy.

The increase and decrease of entropy dialectically represent the dynamic equilibrium among the elements of the network system. When considering the cyber elements, the concept of entropy can be used to measure the degree of disorder (activeness) or orderliness (quietness) of the activities of spatially distributed cyber elements.

3. *Measurement of Overall Planning Entropy in Cyber Security*

The entropy measures the amount of unavailable energy or ineffective energy in the system. The higher the entropy, the lower the effective energy. In a network system, a higher entropy and lower effective energy represent a higher degree of stability, orderliness, security, and governance. However, from another perspective, long-standing risks may be hidden and can appear at any time. Upon studying the curve of past entropy, one can obtain historical experience in ensuring security or avoiding risks. Therefore, when the concept of entropy is introduced into cyberspace, it is necessary to set the following two objective conditions in greater detail:

(1) Variables must include all the elements of the network system instead of a single element of energy.
(2) The measure should be the working time in the electromagnetic space rather than the temperature.

4. *Original Proposal of the Formula of Overall Planning Entropy*

Here, based on the existing basic theories of thermal entropy, information entropy, entropy in mathematics, and resource entropy, the book first presents the concept and formula of overall planning entropy to seek a unique mathematical solution to measure the state of cyberspace, which undergoes a transition from disorder to orderliness after the quantification process to develop an objective measure for the construction of cyber security, surveillance of cyber threats, evaluation of cyber governance, and exercise of network supervision.

The formula of overall planning entropy proposed in this book covers elements such as the subject, object, platform, and activity of cyber sovereignty. In response to the super-linear and hyperplane three-dimensional spreading method in cyberspace, "element aggregate, cubic proportion, and time measurement" approaches are adopted to indicate and measure the dynamic equilibrium of multiple elements in the network system or within the scope of cyber sovereignty.

The formula of overall planning entropy measures not only the degree of disorder (activeness) of cyber elements in their distribution in cyberspace but also their degree of quietness (orderliness). When integrated with continuous dynamic measurements on a time axis, the formula comprehensively reflects the spatial concentration and degree of activeness of the "activity" element (considered energy) among all four cyber elements in various regional subsystems.

The proposed formula is expressed in mathematics as follows:

$$\text{统筹熵} = \frac{\text{活动}^3}{\text{主体}^3 + \text{客体}^3 + \text{终端（平台）}^3}$$

$$ENTROPY(DOMINATING\ AS\ A\ WHOLE) = \frac{ACTIVITIES^3}{SUBJECTS^3 + OBJECTS^3 + TERMINALS^3}$$

$$E = \frac{A^3}{S^3 + O^3 + T^3}$$

The formula gives priority to the "activity" element because the degree of the spatial distribution of this element or its overall degree of "activeness" is the core indicator for the overall judgement of cyberspace order and cyber security as well as a quantitative presentation of the results of cyber sovereignty governance. In the formula of overall planning entropy, when the entropy tends to decrease, this means that the "activity" element is equally distributed in space or inactive; on the contrary, when the entropy tends to increase, this means that the "activity" element is more concentrated or active on the whole.

II. *The Value of Overall Planning*

Overall planning is a method to achieve the goals of overall security and harmonious order by effectively guiding and controlling various categories and subsystems in an ontological object. Over 2,000 years ago, Aristotle described in his book *Categories*, one of the first books dedicated to the study of logistics, the eight "scopes, domains, or categories" of an object that our thinking contends with[27] to express quantity, quality, relation, place, time, state, action, and affection. These scopes, domains, or categories represent various aspects of the ontological object. Therefore, the behaviour of being able to unify all aspects of the ontological object and possess comprehensive understanding, plan, control, and deployment of it is called overall planning.

1. *Two Intendments of the Law on Overall Planning: "Planning in Accordance with the Law" and "Centralising Power in Accordance with the Law"*

Overall planning has two intendments of law: "planning in accordance with the law" and "centralising power in accordance with the law". The former means planning as a whole, which is used in a large number of specialised areas such as territory, population,

[27] Aristotle. (1959). *Categories, On Interpretation*. Beijing: The Commercial Press.

government finance, and taxation; the latter means dominating as a whole, which is generally adopted in areas related to the overall security of national sovereignty, such as the US National Security Act of 1947, the Federal Constitution of Russia of 1991, and the National Security Law of the People's Republic of China of 2015.

2. *Overall Planning: Information as the Basis, Control as the Method, and System as the Object*

From the perspective of modern information theory, overall planning involves the information of all objects; from the perspective of cybernetics, it involves the control over all internal levels, powers, behaviours, and directions of the entity. From the perspective of system theory, the object of overall planning is a certain system, and its process involves the entire structure and accompanies the entire operation of the system. Overall planning theory integrates the objects dealt with by information theory, cybernetics, and system theory respectively into a unit, with the aim of realising the progressiveness of the era in which the "existence, security, and justice of human society are integrated as a whole".[28] See Figure 9-1 for the status and relations of overall planning theory.

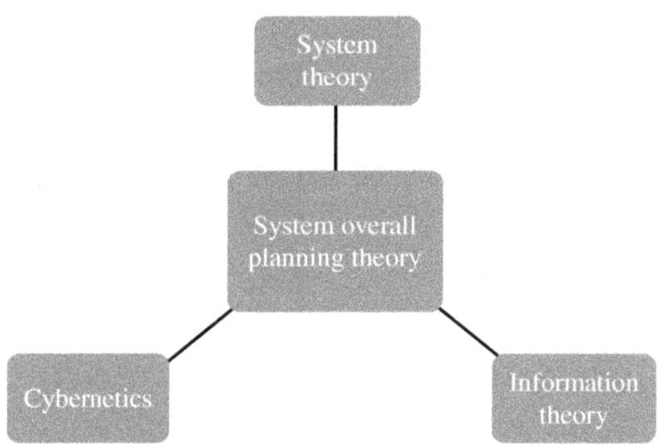

Figure 9-1: The relationship between overall planning theory, system theory, cybernetics, and information theory

[28] Zhao, H. R. (2015). *World Civilizations Aggregate Approach: China's Civilized Rise and Rule of Law in National Security*. Beijing: China Legal Publishing House.

If the information theory, cybernetics, and system theory are regarded as the points that birthed modern sciences and technologies, then we have every reason to believe that the three theories also provided tremendous materials for enriching and developing the Marxist philosophy and have laid a foundation, through modern natural science, for the further enrichment and development of dialectical materialism. Dialectical materialism is not static, as it changes with the development of natural science.[29] The formation of the three theories has created important conditions for activating qualitative change, realising overall planning, and achieving goals at critical moments.

3. *Overall Planning: Goal, Category, Tool, Elements, Philosophical System*

(1) Goal

The goal of overall planning theory is not confined to the information processing and information transmission studied in information theory, the signal communication and control laws studied in cybernetics, or the phenomena, relations, and characteristics of objective things studied in system theory. Rather, it is a new leap forward based on the abovementioned three theories to study an item or matter with judgment, examine qualitative changes, and control and regulate the related order. It implies comprehensive consideration, planning, coordination, command, control, and implementation at the levels of national sovereignty and safety, major life-or-death issues in international relations, and the ultimate destiny of humanity.

(2) Category

The category of overall planning theory is people-oriented and order-themed. Information theory is mainly used to study the common laws of information transmission in communication and control; cybernetics is mainly used to study the common laws of

[29] Wei, H. S. (1981). System Theory, Information Theory, and Cybernetics Give Rise to New Philosophical Issues. *Edition and Creation* (4), 16.

communication and control in biology, machines, and society. System theory is mainly applicable to the models, principles, and laws of all kinds of integrated systems or subsystems, such as the construction of a high building, railway, and the Three Gorges Project. Overall planning theory aims to establish corresponding positions based on a goal concerning the ultimate destiny of humanity and the survival of countries. For instance, national security is the fundamental issue of a country and involves its rise or fall. When considering the past, overall planning helps summarise the historical experience; regarding the present, it helps us think about how a country should survive contemporarily. In dealing with the future, it helps us make choices at a crossroad in national development. In a word, overall planning theory is regarded as a way to address the ultimate destiny of humanity.

(3) Tool
As a tool, overall planning theory is the tool of the ontological object, the tool of sovereignty, and the tool used to harness the "three theories". By borrowing the structural advantages of the three theories and using them as a tool, the overall planning theory is used to achieve systematic coordination in the "integration of existence, security, and justice" at the macro level. It aims to realise overall coordination by means of mutual restriction.

(4) Elements
The elements under overall planning are all the elements of the ontological object. Overall planning theory requires an awareness of serving overall interests. The systematic mechanism involved in system theory concerns only the object but not the subject. However, in overall planning theory, the subject included is required to be coordinated in aspects such as direction, awareness, action, and organisation.

(5) Object and Philosophical System
In terms of ontology, sovereignty is an ontological object capable of overall planning; in terms of epistemology, overall planning is the recognition and judgment of both internal and external

security situations, so cyberspace can be the object dealt with by epistemology. In terms of methodology, overall planning is used to address ultimate issues of human society such as summaries of the past, security in reality, and developmental directions in the future with tools like information theory, cybernetics, and system theory. Therefore, overall planning theory is a type of new philosophical system for science and technology in the information age.

4. *The History, Reality, and Future of Overall Planning Theory*

Overall planning has played an important role in history. Sima Qian wrote the first biographical general history book of China, in which a history of over 1,000 years was recorded in a coordinated manner. Under the personal leadership of Emperor Qianlong in the Qing Dynasty, the *Complete Library in the Four Branches of Literature*, comprising four traditional divisions of Chinese learning (classics, history, philosophy, and belles-lettres), was born as a whole. Guided under his concept of the "dialectical development of an absolute idea", G. W. F. Hegel systematically coordinated all his philosophical theories.

Overall planning is also of great significance in reality. For example, the National Security Law of the People's Republic of China was formulated via coordination in leadership, fields, arrangements, systems, and measures as well as the integration of "military, diplomacy, and intelligence" into "one thing as a whole". From the perspective of a nation's overall interests, the National Security Law of the People's Republic of China has established China's overall national security leadership system by means of legislation. The Belt and Road Initiative and the goal of the rejuvenation of the Chinese nation put forth by China in contemporary times are based on reality-based strategic planning.

As for the role of overall planning in the future, it is embodied in significant issues such as the direction of social development and the future of the humanity.

5. *The Value, Characteristic, and Role of Overall Planning Theory*

The characteristic of overall planning theory is that it aims to solve the ultimate fundamental issue and establish a top-level coordinated system. What overall planning theory coordinates is the top information in the information, the ultimate control in the control, the advanced system in the system, the superior law in the law, the unified understanding in thought, and the priority in action.

What is typical about the "as-a-whole" concept in overall planning theory is that information theory, system theory, and cybernetics are considered tools. This concept not only stresses mutual coordination and the use of each other's advantages but also the necessity of coordinating from the perspective of overall interests. This will advance the Marxist philosophy under new historical conditions and lay a theoretical foundation for the study of modern materialist theory, thus promoting and ultimately achieving progress in civilisation, which is reflected through the "integration of existence, security, and justice".

Regarding the historical need to solve ultimate fundamental issues and realise the rejuvenation of the Chinese nation, it is necessary to establish overall planning theory based on the aforementioned three theories in a scientific manner. Chinese scholars once considered merging information theory, cybernetics, and system theory into a whole unit. Qian Xuesen said, "I think control and information are incorporated in the concept of a system. Without the roles that control and information exchange play in the relations between various components of the system, the system cannot be what it is. Thus, the 'three theories' should be unified under system theory, not under either of the other two theories."[30] Therefore, in the era of rejuvenating the Chinese nation, the timing could not be better to establish overall planning theory in response to security threats from various traditional and non-traditional fields, like sea, land, air, space, and cyberspace.

---

[30] Qian, X. S. (2009). *Selected Letters of Qian Xuesen* (Vol. 1). Beijing: National Defense Industry Press.

Section Four: The Theory of Cyberspace's Overall Planning Entropy

Before the overall planning entropy formula was proposed, the traditional study of information communication focused on addressing issues such as the measurement, control, and transmission of network objects (information) but could not measure or describe the dynamic changes of all cyber elements as a whole. Traditional theories like this or the simple superposition and revision of these theories cannot meet and satisfy the requirements of the overall planning of cyber sovereignty.

I. *Overview of Cyber Elements*

Historically, although traditional theories based on system theory, cybernetics, and information theory have provided new ideas and methods for research on modern information science and have also been widely applied in biology, physics, psychology, and sociology, a question remains: when it comes to a larger extent than that of the "three theories", what kind of overall thought should be adopted to describe the movement rule of all embodied cyber elements? With regard to this fundamental question, no corresponding new formulas have been proposed previously, and no corresponding new theories have yet emerged.

1. *Origins of Information Theory, Cybernetics, and System Theory*

Information is one of the elements that enable humans to form a social network. A review of human theories of information in the modern world over the past century leads us to this finding: with the continuous progress in technology over human history, people's understanding of the definition of information has been deepening, with various new definitions coming into play, such as the theory of relationships between information and physics,[31] the theory of information transmission by electronic signal,[32] the theory of information identification,[33] the theory of internal and external exchange of information,[34] the theory of information data processing,[35] and the theory of transmission and application of information.[36] Among these theories, the concept of information theory was first put forth by American mathematician Claude Elwood Shannon. In his 1948 paper *A Mathematical Theory of Communication*, he proposed that information reduces random uncertainties, which became the origin of information theory.

In 1948, American mathematician Norbert Wiener believed that "information is a name for the content of what is exchanged with the outer world as we adjust to it, and make our adjustment felt upon it"; based on this, he developed cybernetics. Former East German philosopher Georg Klaus once praised this theory: "As for its revolutionary impact, it can be compared with the discoveries of Copernicus, Darwin and Marx."[37]

---

[31] This was mentioned in *Elementary Principles in Statistical Mechanics* by the American physicist J. W. Gibbs in 1889.

[32] American communications scientist Ralph Hartley proposed modern information theory, primarily electronic oscillation and electron transmission.

[33] This was put forth by American mathematician Claude Elwood Shannon.

[34] This was put forth by American applied mathematician and originator of cybernetics Norbert Wiener.

[35] In the book *Information Resources Management*, American management scholar F. W. Horton defined information as follows: "Information is data processed to meet the user's needs for making decisions." Simply put, information is processed data, or information is the result of data processing.

[36] Information as defined in Chinese textbooks often refers to news, messages, and the objects of transmission and processing of communication systems or everything that is spread around in human society. Information is defined as a form of universal connection. Through information, human beings distinguish between different things and understand and transform the world.

[37] Bertalanffy, L. V. (1987). *General System Theory: Foundations, Development, Applications* (p. 1) (K. Y. Lin *et al.*, Trans.). Beijing: Tsinghua University Press.

In ancient Greek, the word "system" in system theory refers to a complete organ consisting of components, i.e. an organic whole composed of various interconnected and interacting parts (elements) with certain functions. System theory was originally called "general system theory" and was first elaborated on by L.V. Bertalanffy, a biologist from Austria, in his book *General System Theory: Foundations, Development, Applications* in 1948. He defined systems as "complexes of elements standing in interaction". Simply put, the system contains several elements that are mutually connected and interact in different ways.

E. Rukov, a cybernetic philosopher of the Soviet Union, noted that cybernetics and system theory, following the theory of relativity and quantum mechanics, once again thoroughly changed the scientific landscape of the world and the way scientists think today.[38] From the perspective of mathematical aggregation (namely one of the original mathematical concepts of infinity, which generally refers to the aggregation of things combined with certain characteristics or rules), some scholars have described information theory, cybernetics, system theory, and aggregation theory collectively as system doctrines so that they can express system elements and the information relations between them.

2. *Differences Between Overall Planning Entropy and the "Three Theories"*

Differing from the traditional three theories in their single-purpose scientific description of information identification, information control, and information systems, overall planning entropy aims to describe the objective laws of ontological movement centred on human activities; thus, it plays a scientific and guiding role in response to the trends of the ontological movement.

To achieve overall planning and guidance, Engels once expressed, "Currently, not only can we point out the links between

---

[38] Wei, H. S. (1981). System Theory, Information Theory, and Cybernetics Give Rise to New Philosophical Issues. *Edition and Creation* (4), 12.

processes in various fields in nature, but, in general, we can also draw a vividly clear picture of their connections in a nearly systematic way."[39] Therefore, the formulation of the overall planning entropy formula is a new mathematical tool that explores internal connections to the extreme and provides us with a clear overview.

In an attempt to realise overall guidance, some scholars creatively developed the concept of "information entropy" to measure the degree of overall security of the national economy,[40] "management entropy" to evaluate the management performance of corporate knowledge systems,[41] and "game entropy" to quantify the degree of rationality in the balanced state of games.[42] These scholars consciously discovered the mathematical advantages of the "theory of entropy". As Albert Einstein said, "Entropy law is the premier law of all science." Arthur Eddington, a Nobel Prize winner, said in 1946, "The law that entropy always increases holds, I think, the supreme position among the laws of Nature." In 1994, Wang Bin attached the same high value to the theory of entropy as that of biological evolution.

However, there are some problems when the entropy formula in the three theories is applied in a simple manner. For instance, not all the elements in the system can be covered and summarised (one-sidedness in studying elements); it is impossible to understand the laws of movement of the system overall, which gives way to the theory of a "hypothesis based on a hypothesis" (hypothesis of theory); real dynamic data in the system cannot be found (revision

---

[39] Marx, K., & Engels, F. (2012). *Marx Engels Selected Works* (Vol. 4) (pp. 241–242). Beijing: People's Publishing House.

[40] Jiang, R., & Qian, H. P. (2015). *National Economy Security Risk Measurement and Early Warning Based on Information Entropy*. Beijing: Economy & Management Publishing House.

[41] Qiu, W. H. (2011). *The Science of Entropy of Management Decision and Its Application*. Beijing: China Electric Power Press; Xiong, X. B. (2011). *A Study on Comprehensive Evaluation of Organizational Knowledge Management Performance Based on Management Entropy Theory*. Chengdu: Sichuan University Press.

[42] Jiang, D. Y. (2008). *The Game Theory with Entropy and Its Applications*. Beijing: Science Press.

of mean value); and the proportion among system elements cannot be defined and the value of the data is set artificially (subjectivity of empowerment). These four problems in applying the formula share one thing in common: inexact, unscientific, inaccurate, and incomplete understanding of the ontological object of the target system. In other words, the formula often fails due to people's lack of ontology comprehension.

II. *Safeguarding Cyber Sovereignty*

With the development of the economy and society and the continuous progress achieved in ICTs (information and communication technology), human society is entering the cyberspace era.

1. *The Complexity of Cyber Activities*

People have to believe that although it is not easy to obtain a full picture of the Internet, like air and water, it is constantly affecting and changing people's lives. News media on the Internet are receiving increasing attention worldwide, and giving advice on policies online has also been figuratively described as an effective way for citizens to participate in national and social politics. The Internet, now the "fourth greatest media" after newspapers, radio, and television, has combined the advantages of newspapers, radio, and television; realised the integration of multiple information modes, such as text, pictures, audio, and videos, in a more refined way; and enabled its users to obtain information from every corner of the world. The emergence of the Internet represents a profound revolutionary transformation in the field of mass communication.

The rapid development and widespread application of the Internet are inseparable from its characteristics. It is fair to say that a network with a more open structure is the core idea of internet technology; various networks can be connected through a structure that features openness. This "borderlessness" advantage benefits from the open structure of the TCP/IP (Transmission Control Protocol/Internet Protocol) protocol it adopts. Each network can be designed and developed according to its specific environment and user characteristics and has its own separate interface to provide contents for its users; thus, it can be opened to a large extent.

The Internet has the characteristics of interactivity and uniqueness, which make it applicable in a wider scope. It combines network technology, multimedia technology, and hypertext technology, so it also has the function of releasing and communicating information. The Internet is not only an information and communication technology but also a social communication technology. With the help of the interconnection and penetration of information networks, the worship of innovation and individuality has become a value orientation among the public in modern times. Although advanced network technology has made copying and imitating information an easy job, it has also simultaneously highlighted the value of technological innovation. The most valuable information and most distinctive services on the Internet follow the rule that "excellence is everything".

The terminal memories connected to the Internet have mighty information resources that no information base can match. Their powerful information storage capacities can theoretically accommodate all information and knowledge and enable them to be shared by humans. People can already make full use of the latest scientific literature and data required in practical work from the Internet, and the information that can be shared online covers every field of daily life, including weather, traffic conditions, and tourism resources. The information online has been scientifically classified to make it easier for internet users to search for and retrieve information, which has shortened the cycle of information exchange, and promoted the development of society and the exchange of civilisations.[43]

2. *The Overall Planning of Cyber Sovereignty*

Due to the importance of network information for human development and technological transformation, new epoch-making

---

[43] Zhang, H. Y. (2013). Analysis and Research on the Characteristics and Development Trend of the Internet. *Modern Communication* (12), 32.

requirements are emerging with regard to cyber sovereignty to safeguard cyber security and order.

Research on the basic principles of the overall planning of cyber sovereignty and cyber security must be performed simultaneously in line with the network, information, and sovereignty theories. Cyber sovereignty is the guarantee for national security in the field of rule of law. Therefore, it is necessary to study how information technologies can be used digitally to rule and regulate the production, acquisition, handling, processing, circulation, and storage of network information, with the aim of safeguarding national sovereignty and national security in all aspects.

As for research on the basic principles of the overall planning of cyber sovereignty and cyber security, it is necessary to determine the new characteristics of cyber sovereignty and understand the nature cyberspace such as immediacy, borders, and orderliness from the perspectives of cyber sovereignty and security.

The immediacy of the overall planning of cyber sovereignty: Since the sending and receiving processes of information in a mathematical mode happen nearly synchronously, there is essentially no time lag compared to the traditional mode of information exchange. This means that while safeguarding cyber sovereignty, it is necessary to adopt the same review method used for the traditional information transfer process as well as to create a top-level security design to safeguard the national cyber "frontier", focusing on the four elements of the internet in the process.

The border of the overall planning of cyber sovereignty: Cyber information features not only an instantaneous state in time but also a virtual state in space. Due to the global interconnection of the Internet, it is difficult for a single country to draw a clear border of cyber sovereignty. A nation is only able to establish its range of rule of law in the autonomy of top-level logic, physical chips, information storage, and user management when the four elements of cyberspace and related technologies have been completely mastered. None of the four major technological capabilities mentioned above should be dispensable; otherwise, the border of cyber sovereignty will never be defined nor safeguarded.

The orderliness of the overall planning of cyber sovereignty: Based on the technical characteristics of the four elements gained through the understanding of cyberspace, it can be inferred that, in the overall governance of affairs under the sovereignty of the network, it is necessary to respect the order tradition and ethical law of the geographical population to avoid injustice, unfairness, and, thus, the escalation of disputes and conflicts between countries and bring the real benefits of the Fourth Industrial Revolution to humanity.

To realise overall planning in a grand system is to achieve harmony among the elements, a reinforced effect of orderliness, and a system upgrade. Research on the basic principles of the overall planning of cyber sovereignty and cyber security is essentially a macro study of the optimisation of system order. The purpose of finding the elements and clarifying the order is to achieve overall planning at a macro level. Parallel to existing scientific theories such as thermal entropy and information entropy, overall planning entropy indicates the quantitative effect of the overall planning of order and constructs the system and model of the overall planning theory based on the previously mentioned three theories.

Chapter Ten

The Overall Planning of Cyber Justice

Cyberspace is both a new tool and a new method. Through labour, humans created all civilisations in the world that have constituted the total wealth of civilisation on Earth. Studies have shown that the civilisation on Earth since the emergence of human beings has accumulated at least 1.15 trillion "man-years". At present, about 7 billion people live on the planet, with 140 million births and 57 million deaths each year. Everyone who ever existed contributed to the total amount of world civilisation just as we do today. Therefore, in the face of the future of the internet age, it is necessary to summarise the various relations between countries that were formed based on history from the perspective of the population through exchange and comparison and strive to discover, define, and clearly expound solutions to shed light on the direction and fairness pursued in international cyberspace governance that can facilitate and promote the development of civilisation.[1]

[1]Zhao, H. R. (2015). *World Civilizations Aggregate Approach: China's Civilized Rise and Rule of Law in National Security*. Beijing: China Legal Publishing House.

Section One: Historical Materialism

Population security, the most basic security of all countries in the world, is closely related to the development of a nation's society and economy and has formed the basis for other areas in the field of national security.

I. *Population Reproduction*

Appropriate management of population issues not only benefits the lives of people in a country or region as well as the coordination between the population and their environmental resources but also profoundly influences a country's national sovereignty, foreign policies, comprehensive national strength, and even prosperity and rise. Scholars such as Thomas Robert Malthus and John Maynard Keynes in the West and Ma Yinchu in China had studied the relationship between the control and management of populations and economic growth. Historically, however, no major country has ever become prosperous and strong because of a decreasing population.

The security and development of populations follow both the law of biological evolution and social and cultural inheritance. Charles Darwin noted in his book *On the Origin of Species* that "many more individuals of each species are born than can possibly survive".[2] This is the evolutionary principle of "natural selection and the survival of the fittest". Darwin's theory of the origin of species can be applied to human society; therefore, human society is divided into different groups due to diversified community cultures and language characteristics. Wu Wenzao believed that "community culture is a way of life that the residents in a certain community have taken... It can also be viewed as the aggregated achievement of a nation during the process of coping with the environment — the physical, symbolic, social and spiritual environment".[3]

[2] Darwin, C. (1983). *The Descent of Man, and Selection in Relation to Sex* (G. D. Pan *et al.*, Trans.). Beijing: The Commercial Press.

[3] Wu, W. Z. (1939). Civilization of Cultural Form. *Social Studies* (10).

By virtue of language, humans have realised the exchange of social information, accomplished the dissemination and identification of social status, and achieved the transmission and continuation of social cultures and rules.[4]

II. *Linguistic Diversity*

There are many diversified languages in the world today. The security and development of the world population can sometimes be attributed to language differences. According to *On the Origin of Species*, race comes after species, with groups, populations, and communities forming a differentiated interpersonal order. Among the current seven billion people in the world today, more than half of them are netizens. As the cyberspace subjects, netizens are distinguished according to their nationalities to some extent. China implemented the national governance structure of "unified script and specification of vehicle" more than 2,000 years ago, which made the then 1.4 billion people in China cyber subjects with a historical consensus.

There are currently more than 5,000 languages in the world, and each language usually has multiple dialects. Different languages or dialects represent different national and regional cultures on the one hand and give rise to possible misunderstandings and barriers between different language regions on the other hand. Thus, languages can influence cultural communication and ethnic policies.[5] Under the shell of communication, each language contains rich and unique humanistic knowledge. It records the profound humanistic features of a country in a full and comprehensive manner and is a key factor determining whether a country can stand long enough among the community of nations. Language is indispensable in people's daily lives. It is an important communication medium for

---

[4]Yue, T. M., & Gao, Y. J. (2008). Cultural Clash in Ethnic Communities and its Positive Significance. *Northwestern Journal of Ethnology* (2), 3–4.

[5]Chen, Zh. Y. (2013). *The Changes of Contemporary Chinese and the Development of Chinese Society — An Empirical Study Based on the Changes of Chinese* (PhD dissertation). Wuhan, Wuhan University Press.

people to exchange feelings, information, and other aspects of life. It is an important part of culture and an effective communicator and recorder of culture. It is also a symbol of a nation and an important criterion for measuring whether a nation is highly developed. The widespread use of language is viewed as an important embodiment of a country's soft power.

In Europe, for example, there are six founding members of the European Union (EU): France, Germany, Italy, the Netherlands, Belgium, and Luxembourg. As of 2014, the EU had 28 members with 24 official languages: English, French, German, Italian, Spanish, Portuguese, Dutch, Danish, Swedish, Finnish, Greek, Polish, Slovak, Maltese, Hungarian, Lithuanian, Latvian, Slovenian, Czech, Estonian, Irish, Bulgarian, Romanian, and Croatian. These languages share equal rights. All official documents, publications, important conferences, and official websites of the EU should be in these languages. Correspondence sent by member states to the EU can be in any official language; the EU's cost of translating multiple languages was about 11.23 billion euros in 2005, accounting for about 1% of its annual fiscal expenditure. This diversity of languages often increases the cost of translation through online communication and greatly reduces the efficiency of communication through the Internet in Europe. For example, the Eurozone International Finance Conference was held in Frankfurt, Germany in November 2013, with a total of more than 200 participants, including central bank governors, commercial bank leaders, and scholars from the 17 Eurozone member states. Under these circumstances, instead of using their own languages, all participants had to speak English only to communicate with each other (Britain did not attend because it is not a member state of the Eurozone). This means that all EU countries can only achieve direct political, economic, and cultural exchanges at the EU level through "translation" or a non-mother tongue. The diversity of EU languages has increased the cost of using the Internet in the internet era. Particularly after Brexit, whether English still retains its status as the EU's official language will be an outstanding issue. Therefore, the real situation of the populations and languages in Europe requires the establishment of a shared internet network platform in an active manner to strengthen the links among member states and with countries around the world as well as advocate the sharing and co-governance of cyberspace.

The United States (US) can be used as an example as well. The global hegemony of the US is not an accidental and isolated historical phenomenon. It is a part of the process in which English-speaking nations have spread from the British Isles to the world in modern times, and the cornerstone for its hegemony is the mighty expansion and strong discourse system of English-speaking nations worldwide. As the current reality shows, the Western media represented by the US has temporarily dominated the global "information game", while the people of non-Western countries have long been exposed to the "indoctrination" and invisible "ideological control" by Western media. Utilising the Internet and new media technologies, media from the West is spreading a variety of concepts and ideas under the guise of the seemingly righteous "universal value" to every corner of the world. From the Middle East to North Africa, Ukraine to Egypt, and Syria to Thailand, the recent political turmoil in many countries has been proven to be related to the interference of Western media, with the US media playing a leading role. Exposed to ceaseless blinded reports by US media, citizens of many sovereign countries have taken to the streets, plotted to instigate "colour revolutions", and then established various pro-American regimes after overthrowing their own existing governments. The global hegemony of the US in information is also embodied in the US' monitoring of information in countries across the world, with the Snowden incident as a case in point. This has facilitated the US in overthrowing the governments of other countries and undermining their stability. It is no exaggeration that no place in the world is out of the reach of the US as long as it wants to interfere. In recent years, many non-Western countries have seen the so-called "Nth Wave of Democratization", with domestic political confrontations, ethnic division, and civil wars cropping up, which indicates that it is easy for the US to create political incitement by virtue of its hegemony in information. If the propaganda department of the Soviet Union was viewed as a tool to carry out "ideological control" over its people, then the hegemony of the US in information today is tantamount to "political brainwashing" aimed at everyone. "The ideological and social systems of the US and the Soviet Union are completely opposite. They both have a sense of a sacred mission that they should spread their own social system to the whole world, as they believe their own social system is the best and most reasonable one for mankind." It is obvious that the US media has firmly held its global hegemony in information to conduct "ideological and political control" over people across the world, and its hegemony in information has constituted one of the major pillars for its dominance worldwide.[6]

There are about 400 million native English speakers in the world. From the perspective of the Internet and language, the "extent of language concentration", which reflects how widely the languages that most netizens use in the future, will decide to what extent online communication convenience will be created in the end. This is not a code-is-law matter but a matter of subject-object determinism, namely the historical trend that will be shown in the internet age under the influence of demographic and cultural determinism.

Section Two: Scientific and Technological Civilisation

The US' technological monopoly in cyberspace may not last long, and its cyber advantages may end soon. Currently, in the technological competition in cyberspace, it is not rare for other countries to achieve breakthroughs in the research and development of quantum communication, blockchain, trusted computing, high-performance computers, artificial intelligence, and other scientific technologies, which has broken the US' monopoly on technology.

[6] *The Historical Origin and Review of Contemporary American Global Hegemony*. Retrieved from http://bbs.tianya.cn/post-worldlook-1364157-1.shtml.

I. *Development of Civilisation*

The development of human civilisation is often marked by disruptive technological progress. In the face of the disruption coming from scientific and technological advancement and the breakdown of the existing order, it is of great significance to study, prevent, and defuse major cyber security risks. In 2015, academics, including Fang Binxing of the Chinese Academy of Engineering, conducted research on "cyber security strategy". By studying international cyber security strategies, sovereignty protection, element modules, the improvement of the rule of law, core technologies, disciplinary optimisation, administrative measures, review effectiveness, user authentication, and data protection, the cyberspace security subject, which focuses on countering cyber hegemony, is gradually developing. This discipline aims to overtake and surpass similar research in the US, where the Internet was invented, and formulate a comprehensive cyber security countermeasure system with Chinese characteristics. The overall structure of the system is to be composed of one centre and five modules to form a general research framework characterised by basic tandems, connotative connections, and clear goals, as shown in Figure 10-1:

To clarify the strategic position of cyber security in the field of global non-traditional security, we should scientifically assess the strategic planning of technologies, rules, and concepts in cyberspace; turn technical strength into propositions of law; implement the principle of "safeguarding national sovereignty in cyberspace" formulated in the National Security Law of the People's Republic of China; study the mechanism and system of countermeasures

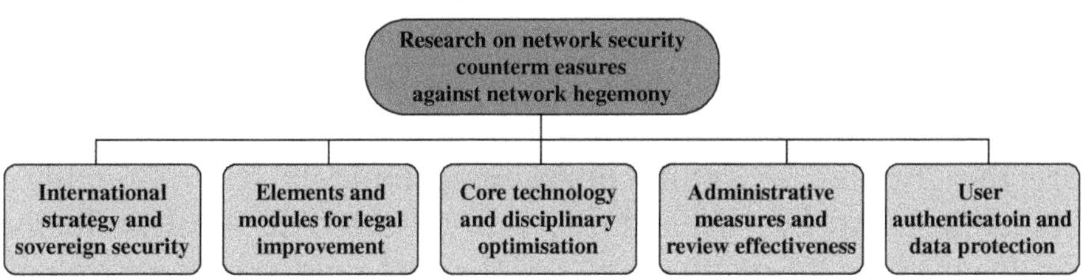

Figure 10-1: The overall framework of cyber security strategy

against cyber hegemony; actively promote the development of the new cyberspace security discipline in China; help promote forward-looking research and top-level designs that will lead China towards becoming a cyber power; strive to advance and enrich China's new innovative, coordinated, green, inclusive, and shared perception of development; and carry forward the research step by step to achieve related research results through a process involving the definition of cyber security elements, the study of cyber sovereignty boundaries, the optimisation of subject paradigms, the construction of countermeasure systems, and the promotion of cyberspace co-governance.

Pioneering and disruptive scientific and technological progress has, more often than not, become the "offensive move" and "active battle" to drive the leading development of human civilisation. On 16 March 2016, the research group of the Chinese Academy of Sciences (CAS) Key Laboratory of Quantum Information led by academician Guo Guangcan of the University of Science and Technology of China made an important achievement in the field of quantum chips: a new type of charge-encoded qubit with excellent quantum coherence, fast control speed, and sound controllability was successfully realised in a gallium arsenide (GaAs) semiconductor quantum chip. The research results were published in *Physical Review Letters*, an international authoritative journal of physics. According to the experimental results, this new type of qubit is similar to a charge qubit in terms of its ultra-fast control speed, but its quantum coherence is nearly 10 times higher than that of ordinary charge-encoded qubits. Meanwhile, the qubit encoding and regulation was realised through a new method of multi-electron orbital hybridisation that is of strong versatility, providing new ideas for research on the impacts of polar phonons and piezoelectric effects on quantum coherence in semiconductors.

Chips are the core of modern computers, and "quantum chips" are the "brains" of future quantum computers. Guo Guoping's research group has been devoted to researching semiconductor quantum chips for many years. For the first time, taking advantage of the asymmetry of semiconductor quantum-dot multi-electronic state orbits, the group successfully developed a new type of qubit of orbital hybridisation in the GaAs semiconductor system and integrated the ultra-fast speed of the charge qubit with the long-lived coherence of the spin qubit in such a way that both the desired results were obtained at the same time.[7]

II. *The Enlargement of Sovereignty*

At present, the scientific and technological advancement represented by artificial intelligence and 5G has become the focus of international competition on the one hand and enriched the connotation of the theory of sovereignty on the other hand. On 28 April 2012, Fang Binxing published an academic paper in *Guangming Daily* in which he stressed that cyber sovereignty is of extreme significance. He was the first scholar in China to systematically propose the study of cyber sovereignty. General Secretary Xi Jinping's speech in Wuzhen on 16 December 2015, Article 25 of the National Security Law of the People's Republic of China promulgated in 2015, and the Cyber Security Law of the People's Republic of China promulgated in 2016 are extensions of this academic opinion in the field of policy and legislation as well as processes from the advancement of academics by scholars to the implementation of policies by the government. In 2017, Lawrence Lessig conducted a study on the theory of cyber sovereignty conflict from the perspective of the US. He mentions in his book *Code Version 2.0: And Other Laws of Cyberspace* that France also opposed the erosion of English culture into French culture. In his book *Republic, Lost: The Corruption of Equality and the Steps to End,* he offers his latest views on cyber sovereignty. Upon comparison, these two scholars share something in common in the depth of their opinions, but there are differences wherein their opinions have been put into practice through policies.

---

[7] *Significant Progress Made in the Development of Semiconductor Quantum Chips*. Retrieved from http://www.cnstock.com/v_industry/sid_cyqb/201603/3737272.htm.

The US has extended its sovereignty to international cyberspace instead of considering it a "globally public area" that is shared by the whole world. There will always be conflicts and crimes in the global internet field that can only be resolved by governments. No country can play the role of world police to solve every problem in the global internet. These problems can only be addressed by the joint efforts of different countries through cyber sovereignty. In terms of cyber sovereignty, the US' law enforcement agencies, as authorised by the USA Patriot Act, have the right to require US internet companies to cooperate in intelligence, which is a specific method for the US government to perform its cyber sovereignty. Thus, it is obvious that countries rely on national sovereignty to combat cybercrimes.

The international consensus on cyber sovereignty refers to the issue of how sovereign states "view, make use of, and connect" the four elements of cyberspace. Traditional sovereign networks refer to telephone, telegraph, road, and power grid networks with a clear sovereign border and definite cross-border connection rules, which are determined by geographical and demographic factors and are part of the order of a peaceful world through the international rule of law. Non-traditional sovereign networks refer to the internet of things, social networks, and blockchains, which are derived from technologies like the Internet. This requires the deepening of technology, an evolutionary process that encompasses technological monopoly, technological competition, the game of strength, and extensive negotiation and governance, and will be interwoven with the hegemony-oriented and negotiation-oriented game in the global cyberspace order.

The international rule of law is often useless regarding cyber warfare and cybercrimes. In the face of hacker attacks, organised cybercrimes (e.g. money laundering, fraud, drug dealing, human trafficking, etc.), cyber terrorism, and cyber warfare in which states participate, there are no international treaties dedicated to cyberspace governance among the United Nations' (UN) international regulations, and global cyberspace governance is still limited to the level of domestic rule of law, plurilateralism, regional arrangements, and the attention of the UN.

Regarding actions taken by multiple countries, 30 countries, including member states of the Council of Europe and the US, Canada, Japan, and South Africa, reached an international convention in Budapest, i.e. the Budapest Convention on Cybercrime, in November 2001, which has been claimed to be the first and only regional international convention against cybercrime in the world. However, the convention is only applicable to legal cooperation and coordination between the countries for cybercrime issues and, thus, is not sufficient to cope with all or significant cyber threats. As far as some scholars are concerned, this convention is just a "chorus by Western countries" due to Russia's absence and China's role as an observer state.

Section Three: Counter-Hegemony

According to "The Internet is Undermining America's Power", an article published in *Time* on 22 February 2016, "China is developing new competing technologies. India, Europe, and other friends hold different visions of how to manage the Internet and protect privacy. The gap between the interests of American technology companies such as Google, Apple, Facebook and Amazon and Washington is growing. The global, open Internet, a wellspring of U.S. economic, political, and military power, is fragmenting as Beijing, Moscow, Tehran and many others are asserting cyber sovereignty."

As a "double-edged sword", the Internet creates a public space for free expression of opinions on the one hand and opens the door for the dissemination of bad information on the other hand. Cyberspace control and regulation have aroused the attention of governments and gradually become a shared challenge worldwide. However, countries differ in the specific practices that they adopt to control and regulate the Internet, and there are often discordant voices about internet control and regulation within the same country. This has led to disputes over the standards and limits of cyberspace control and regulation, particularly as to whether cyberspace control and regulation violate human rights and how to protect human rights. With the protection of "cyber human rights" as the standard for cyberspace control and regulation, the scope of cyberspace control and regulation can be reasonably limited, a dialogue platform for disputes over international cyberspace governance can be provided, and theoretical support for the guidance of China's cyberspace control and regulation can be offered. Meanwhile, it is necessary to be wary of the danger of copying Western standards of human rights and avoid falling into the trap of "cyber imperialism" based entirely on those types of standards. The cyber sovereignty practices of various countries are shown in Table 10-1.

Table 10-1: Cyber sovereignty practices in various countries

Cyber Sovereignty Practices	**Specific Measures of Various Countries**
Conflicts over cyber sovereignty	Attacks based on redirectors Fishing sites The loss of domain name data rights of CNNers.com by Chinese institutions Problems caused by big data Problems arising from disparity in principles of legality identification
Management of domain names through cyberspace sovereignty by countries	Control and regulation imposed by the US judicial system on domain name registrars located within its territory Anti-piracy by the US through confiscation of domain names via ICANN under the management of the government
Crack down on defamation online	The United Kingdom's (UK) crackdown on harmful rumours disseminated online Singapore's crackdown on harmful remarks disseminated online Germany's crackdown on terrorist remarks disseminated online
Crack down on personal attacks online	The German court adjudged that Google's activity violated the law The US imposed sanctions on personal attackers in accordance with the law

Table 10-1: (*Continued*)

Cyber Sovereignty Practices	**Specific Measures of Various Countries**
Crack down on the spreading of rumours online	South Korea has taken action to combat the spreading of rumours online
Supervision of websites	India controls and regulates network service platforms India blocks harmful websites
Prevent harmful information from spreading	The UK blocks infringing websites Germany has filtering requirements for the dissemination of illegal information online Russia blocks access to specific web pages France blocks terrorist websites Australia requires the installation of filters Japan blocks pornography websites from children South Korea has created a firewall to block the official website of North Korea The Department of Telecom of India asks internet service providers to block 39 websites
Crack down on false e-commerce	The UK's combat against illegal e-commerce The joint efforts of UK and the US to crack down on illegal e-commerce
Combat the spread of junk mail	Australia punishes spreading junk mail
Combat hacking	Australia combats online credit card theft The US' Cleanup Action Plan against botnets The Towa Plan against botnets through joint efforts in the international community
Combat fraud online	South Korea imposes criminal penalties on online fraudsters
Combat theft of privacy online	The US imposes legal sanctions on theft of personal privacy
Combat pornography online	The US' Operation Avalanche against online child pornography The UK's Operation Ore against online child pornography Canada's Operation Snowball against online child pornography Germany's combat against transnational online child pornography
Combat terrorist information online	The UK removes terrorist information online

(*Continued*)

Table 10-1: (*Continued*)

Cyber Sovereignty Practices	Specific Measures of Various Countries
Combat prejudice and discrimination, especially racial discrimination, online	France combats racist acts online The German court approved the arrest of a website leader making speeches supporting massacres
Crack down on piracy online	Operation Site Down is an international joint action against piracy online Sweden has taken action against film piracy
Combat gambling online	Israel combats gambling online
Combat fraud online	South Korea imposes criminal penalties on online fraudsters

Countering hegemony with human rights has become a world consensus. The subject of human rights concerns both individual natural persons and all human beings, and human rights must include freedom and equality. Human rights are the unity of due rights, actual rights, and statutory rights as well as the fundamental purpose for state power to realise; they are the fundamental value pursued by the rule of law and are protected by national law.[8] It is fair to summarise that cyber human rights are a raft of protectionist actions of basic human rights enjoyed by citizens in the process of using the Internet.[9]

Speaking of human rights, we must discuss their international legal basis, the Universal Declaration of Human Rights (UN General Assembly Resolution No. 217, A/RES/217). This is a declaration adopted by the UN General Assembly on 10 December 1948 to safeguard the basic rights of mankind. Though not a mandatory convention itself, the document paved the way for the establishment of two subsequent UN mandatory international conventions

[8] Zhang, X. L. (2006). *Basic Issues of Human Rights Theory* (p. 62). Beijing: Party School of the CPC Central Committee Press.

[9] Lin, Zh. (2006). *A Study of the Legal Institutions of Citizens' Fundamental Human Rights* (p. 12). Beijing: Peking University Press.

on human rights, namely the International Covenant on Civil and Political Rights and the International Covenant on Economic, Social and Cultural Rights. The International Covenant on Civil and Political Rights, adopted in 1966, represents an important part of the International Bill of Human Rights.[10] Since its entry into force, more than 160 countries have ratified or acceded to it, which has had a profound and extensive impact on the protection of international human rights. China signed the covenant in 1998. Determining how to coordinate a series of international standards of criminal proceedings established by the International Covenant on Civil and Political Rights with domestic legislative and judiciary standards in China and how to promote and improve the reform of China's criminal litigation system with reference to those standards have become issues of common concern for both the Chinese government and Chinese people. The International Covenant on Economic, Social, and Cultural Rights, another covenant on human rights, was adopted during the 21st session of the UN General Assembly on 16 December 1966 and entered into force on 3 January 1976. In this covenant, individual human rights in economy, society, and culture were, for the first time in history, confirmed by law. The covenant broke the limitations of traditional views of human rights, which gave sole priority to the rights of citizens and their political rights, and reflected the call of developing countries to give equal attention to the two categories of human rights. As a positive international human rights law, it has certainly brought benefits to people's lives. The three international covenants mentioned above and the rules of law and practices on cyber sovereignty in countries should become the basis of the consensus on taking action against hegemony, safeguarding sovereignty, and protecting human rights in the process of international cyberspace co-governance.

---

[10]The International Bill of Human Rights includes the International Covenant on Economic, Social and Cultural Rights; Universal Declaration of Human Rights; and International Covenant on Civil and Political Rights.

Section Four: Foresight for Justice

In the early end of the Cold War in 1993, Rand issued a report to warn, "Cyberwar is coming!"[11] The report classified cyber threats in the real world into five categories: network information theft, system paralysis, remote control, pre-war strikes, and composite strikes, which are non-traditional cyber security threats related to DNS (Domain Name System), software, hardware, and users.

I. *Justice Needs to Be Foreseen*

"Existence, security, and justice" are the eternal themes of the development of civilisation and the maintenance of sovereignty. Joseph S. Nye believes, "The world is only just beginning to see glimpses of cyber war. States have the greatest capabilities, but non-state actors are more likely to initiate a catastrophic attack. A 'cyber 9/11' may be more likely than the often-mentioned 'cyber Pearl Harbor'. It is time for states to sit down and discuss how to limit this threat to world peace."[12]

The reason the world's cyber security is under threat is that the world has not yet achieved a security order like "nuclear balance" and has not yet obtained a safe "balance point". Therefore, the international academic community needs to reach a theoretical consensus on the legal rights concerning "network users and network information" as soon as possible. As a fast-growing developing country among the three major economies of America, Europe, and Asia, China needs to adhere to its international stance of "safeguarding the rights of Internet users and safeguarding the security of information" and should take advantage of its total number of internet users and total amount of information to speak for justice in the game of international cyberspace.

---

[11] Arquilla, J., & Ronfeldt, D. F. (1993). Cyberwar is Coming! *Comparative Strategy* (12), 141–165.

[12] Nye, J. S. *E-Power to Rise up the Security Agenda*. Retrieved from http://www.nato.int/docu/review/2012/2012-security-predictions/e-Power-cybersecurity/EN/index.htm.

In terms of cyber sovereignty, there is also a different view: cyber sovereignty is the last thing we should have, as it hinders the free flow of information. This is a misconception given undue weight. In the EU and Schengen zones, there is no border control among countries, and people can move as freely as they like; however, this does not mean that only "EU sovereignty" exists and that there is no national sovereignty in those countries. When the US allows citizens of a certain country to enter its territory visa-free, this simply indicates that the US is exercising its power to stage customs clearances rather than lose its sovereignty. Likewise, when it comes to the free flow of information, the type of "order" that should be followed depends on public policies of the government, which is by no means an indication of whether national sovereignty is abandoned. In fact, cyber sovereignty is objective, beyond the will of humans. What matters is whether, when, how, and under what circumstances cyber sovereignty is exercised. British Prime Minister Teresa May once noted that in the five years after 2010, the British government removed 75,000 terrorism-related materials from the Internet, 70% of which were related to ISIS (Islamic State of Iraq and Syria), Syria, and Iraq. This is the "information order" established through the build-up of sovereign acts.

Cyber sovereignty is imposed within the network field, which still requires cyber sovereignty protection. There should be "cyber defence" in the territorial network similar to the existence of coastal defence in territorial waters, border defence in territorial land, and air defence in territorial airspace. This is not only the supporting point for cyber force to safeguard cyberspace as the first line of the defence of domestic cyber information infrastructure but also an important sign of the defence of national cyber sovereignty. Therefore, to maintain cyberspace sovereignty, cyber defence should be built.

General Secretary Xi Jinping has repeatedly expounded on the stance and proposals of China's governance of cyberspace on various international occasions. His keynote speech delivered at the second World Internet Conference, in particular, clearly put forth the goals of "promoting the transformation of the global Internet governance system" and "building a community of shared future in cyberspace".[13] China is a firm advocate and powerful defender of cyber sovereignty. It insists on handling the relationships between cyberspace freedom and order, security and development, and openness and autonomy through corrective measures and has found a way to govern cyberspace with Chinese characteristics. China will further promote the transformation of the global internet governance system, advance the formulation of international rules for cyberspace that reflect the will and interests of most countries on a more balanced basis, and jointly advance the sound development of the internet.

Cyber sovereignty is rooted in modern theories of law and is the extension of modern national sovereignty into the field of cyberspace. The formulation of laws, introduction of policies, government management, administrative enforcement of laws, judicial jurisdiction, dispute resolution, global governance, and international cooperation in the field of cyberspace are all methods of exercising cyber sovereignty. Domestically, the US has incorporated cyber security as part of the issues under its Homeland Security management and has successively unveiled a series of laws and regulations such as the Cybersecurity Information Sharing Act, which prominently reflects its sovereignty in cyberspace. Internationally, in 2013, the US government publicly announced that cyberattacks on the US will be treated as acts of war and fought against with force. Although the US considers cyberattacks against itself from the outside as a "launch of war", it calls its cyberattacks against and network monitoring of other countries "network freedom" and "information sharing". This is the point of view of the US on cyber sovereignty, which is hegemonic by nature. The international community has expressed strong indignation regarding this kind of hegemony, which is embodied by the US through giving

---

[13] Xi, J. P. (2015). *Remarks by H.E. Xi Jinping, President of the People's Republic of China, at the Opening Ceremony of the Second World Internet Conference.* Retrieved from http://www.xinhuanet.com/politics/2015-12/16/c_1117481089.htm.

priority to its own sovereignty while defying the sovereignty of other countries and stressing its own national security while ignoring the national security of others. Therefore, the international community has called for respect for cyber sovereignty and opposition to cyber hegemony in an attempt to advance the transformation of the global internet governance system and the construction of a new cyberspace order. This is an objective law and obligatory requirement in the development and governance of the global Internet.

Respect for cyber sovereignty is an inevitable trend in our fight against cyber hegemony. Since the establishment of the principle of national sovereignty by the Peace of Westphalia of 1648, upholding sovereignty and opposing hegemony have constituted important parts of the practice of the international system. Now, the world has changed from the time when several countries could join together to determine the direction of major events in the world. It is more likely that all issues should be settled through dialogues among nations. At present, certain behaviours that disregard other countries' cyber sovereignty are the embodiment and reflection of real-world hegemonism in cyberspace. They are a new variant of the Cold War mentality and have become the largest obstacle in the transformation of the global internet governance system. This transformation can only be promoted towards a more just and rational direction when we learn to respect cyber sovereignty and avoid cyber hegemony, interference in the internal affairs of other countries, and engagement in or support of cyber activities endangering the national security of other countries.

The principle of cyber sovereignty is the core pillar supporting the two network governance models: "multi-stakeholder" and "multilateral". Developed countries have long attempted to expand the role of the private sector in cyberspace governance based on the multi-stakeholder principle. To a greater extent, in fact, this can only meet the needs of developed countries, as most private ICT (information and communications technology) giants come from developed countries. Developing countries adhere to the principle of multilateralism and firmly support the leading role of the UN in the formulation of ICT policies because they face risks such as economic dependence on foreign resources, government disability and social disorder in their own cultures. From the colour revolutions, Ukrainian Crisis, Syrian Civil War, and rise of ISIS and the global spread of terrorism, we can see the hidden negative effects coming from cyber hegemony and ICTs. At present, developed countries have gradually started to accept the principle of cyber sovereignty. After the Occupy Wall Street Movement and the British riot in 2011 and the global spread of terrorism in 2015, Western countries have also realised the significance of controlling the Internet to ensure social stability and national security. China believes that sovereign states will still play a core role in cyberspace governance, but this does not mean that the role and use of the private sector must be weakened. The cyber sovereignty advocated by China is strategically based on the multi-stakeholder model and realised for its purpose of jointly promoting global cyberspace governance through international multilateral means. The cyber sovereignty advocated by China will not and cannot be as comprehensive and exclusive as traditional state sovereignty. In fact, although cyber sovereignty is legally derived from national sovereignty, the process of defining cyber sovereignty is more like a process of redistributing power and interests worldwide as well as an evolutionary process of dynamic development. Of course, two in-depth questions must be considered during this process. The first question is how to achieve balance among "safeguarding national security, ensuring human rights, driving innovation, and improving society" for the purpose of safeguarding traditional state sovereignty and benefiting global governance. The second question concerns how to implement cyber sovereignty, what kind of cyberspace capacity should be built by countries to guarantee their cyber sovereignty, and what principles should be followed to realise cyber sovereignty. Both aspects should be given great importance when it comes to key issues concerning internationally bilateral, plurilateral, or multilateral cyberspace diplomacy in the future under the framework of the principle of cyber sovereignty.[14]

---

[14] Wen, B. H. (2016). *Three Pillars of the Principle of Network Governance Sovereignty*. Retrieved from http://m.zaobao.com/story/598434.

The stakeholders model refers to the transition from hegemony to extensive negotiation and governance. "Stake" refers to the resources we have for negotiation, and "holders" refer to those involved. The US used the expression stakeholders in its policies twice in the 21st century. The term was first used when the US proposed to establish the G2 relationship with China (i.e. the co-governance relationship between China and the United States) and was later used in the transformation of the internet root servers and domain name system of ICANN (Internet Corporation for Assigned Names and Numbers). This type of expression is in line with the US' political "engagement" theory about China and differs from its political "containment" theory about Russia. However, historically, China, the US, and Russia have been allies on the side of justice, as in World War I (the Entente Powers) and World War II (the Allied Powers). This is a starting point for us to foresee the global order in the future.

Cyber sovereignty is a right as well as a responsibility. Only when countries reach a consensus on cyber sovereignty can they clarify their international responsibilities in cyberspace, promote the establishment of a fair global cyberspace order, and establish cyber justice. Cyber sovereignty is a concept of the rule of law. In other words, since there is no international convention on cyberspace, countries formulating their own laws about cyber sovereignty is an effective legal means to supplement the absence of international cyberspace conventions and will help translate the legal customs in the original traditional cyberspace into the non-traditional cyberspace. This will reinforce the interconnection of international networks and cooperation with the rule of law as well as eliminate areas beyond the rule of law. Laws on cyber sovereignty must be formulated with the principle of "ensuring both national security and public privacy" to achieve a good legal effect and sound governance. The most fundamental motive behind China's advocacy of the principle of cyber sovereignty is to provide a domestically legal basis for protecting its own national security interests. The US, however, regards cyberspace as a means to realise its own national interests. If left unchecked, its behaviours, including its global cyber monitoring projects against its allies as well as its irresponsible construction of offensive military cyber combat forces, will inevitably lead to the militarisation of cyberspace.

Meanwhile, the recognition of cyber sovereignty also means accepting corresponding international responsibilities, which will pave the way for cooperation among countries in cyberspace. On the basis of this principle, countries can unite to a greatest extent and better cope with global cyber threats. This is the legal logic of China's commitment to strengthen cyber cooperation with other countries and jointly fight against international cybercrimes.

II. *Cyberspace Governance Should Be Planned Overall*

Cyber governance, be it international or domestic, needs to be realised through overall planning. Regarding the issue of cyber sovereignty, we can come to the following conclusion by comparing domestic and foreign research and related cases concerning the rule of law. It will only be possible to construct a fair and reasonable global cyberspace order and national cyber security order when most countries break the shackles of existing theories about sovereignty, visions about the simple "study of cyber security", and the theoretical model of "cyberspace-over-sovereignty" advocated by the US and propose a new approach to overall planning. The introduction of the overall planning of cyberspace will provide theoretical guidance for the legal and social practices serving the governance of cyber sovereignty.

Relying on the overall planning of cyberspace governance is the theoretical interpretation of the principle of "comprehensively planning and coordinating cyber security efforts" stipulated in the Cyber Security Law of the People's Republic of China. The law specifically stipulates the leading role of overall coordination in cyber sovereignty. Under the guidance of the cyber sovereignty theory, it integrated the existing industrial informatisation with the legal governance of telecommunications, intellectual property rights with the legal governance of information, and the practices of civil and criminal laws with the legal governance of sovereignty to jointly establish the National Cyber Security Legal System. This reflects the theoretical value and legal justice of overall guidance, overall planning, and overall coordination in cyber sovereignty jurisdiction.

Overall governance is the "cure" for the problems of cyberspace legal governance. As a type of "new sovereignty" based on traditional "state sovereignty", cyber sovereignty is naturally aimed at network interconnection and can be governed comprehensively. Its objective basis lies in the fact that the ubiquitous integration of the "scientific features of cyberspace" and "social features of cyberspace" has universally deepened people's connections with each other. The jurisdictional effect of cyber sovereignty can be brought into play, and the safety of traditional state sovereignty can be secured in the network era when the four elements of cyberspace are identified and coordinated. To study and develop traditional theories of sovereignty and to extend and establish new theories of cyber sovereignty, approaches through overall planning must be employed to meet the practical demands arising from cyber security challenges. Without overall planning, it will be impossible to achieve comprehensive cyber security and cyberspace governance. Only with the help of overall planning can we suppress crime and secure justice. Controlling and managing cyberspace in line with laws through overall planning should be the new strategy for safeguarding national cyber security.

Governing cyberspace by means of overall planning embodies a nation's legitimate right regarding its sublime purpose of safeguarding national sovereignty. Three concepts — i.e. "cyberspace is within the scope of sovereign rights", "sovereignty has jurisdiction over cyberspace", and "the governance of cyberspace shall rely on overall planning" — should be integrated into a new theory in political philosophy, fresh progress in sovereignty law, and new step forward in international law. In contrast, cyber hegemony relies on technological monopoly to dominate cyberspace order. However, cyber sovereignty is proposed with the aim of governing cyberspace in line with laws through overall planning.

Due to the virtuality of cyberspace, its governance must be performed in compliance with laws in a coordinated manner. Territorial lands, seas, and airspace constitute the major parts of traditional areas of sovereignty. Cyberspace, as a new domain, can be neither seen nor touched, but it objectively exists in real life. There are naturally no boundaries in cyberspace. Thus, to maintain the international cyberspace order as well as the cyberspace security and national security of countries, methods of coordinated governance must be upheld to safeguard the cyberspace boundaries that are part of state sovereignty, protect cyber security, and promote international cooperation. The "overall planning entropy" formula was proposed in this book with the aim of measuring the degree of cyber security with the simplest mathematical formula of the total amount to provide a scientific basis for the rule of law of cyberspace sovereignty, seek a "sole solution" for cyberspace from chaos to order, detect cyber threats, assess cyberspace order, and improve the rule of law concerning cyberspace.

Establishing a cyberspace community with a shared destiny not only signifies progress in the theory of "relativity of sovereignty" in political philosophy and law but also a new goal of the overall planning and cooperation in cyber sovereignty. Cyberspace cannot exist independently without countries because the elements involved in the global information network, such as materials, domains, cyberspace boundaries, netizens, and social nature, exist objectively.

In terms of the research paradigm, this book adopted the approach of "all-inclusive connotation and denotation" to transform the cyberspace superstructure in the sense of science and technology into four philosophical cyberspace elements: the subject, object, platform, and activity. With this method, overall insight was achieved, and cyber sovereignty was expounded on and verified from the three perspectives of ontology, epistemology, and methodology. Through crossover studies involving international law, the philosophy of science and technology, international politics, cyber security, and information entropy mathematics, the author proposed a new concept of the science of overall planning and the "overall planning entropy" formula in an effort to determine the right scientific methodology for the use of cyber sovereignty through ontological and factor comprehension.

Appendix I

Report of the Group of Governmental Experts on Developments in the Field of Information and Telecommunications in the Context of International Security

[Document of the 70th Session of the United Nations (A/70/174)]

Summary

Information and communications technologies (ICTs) provide immense opportunities and continue to grow in importance for the international community. However, there are disturbing trends that create risks to international peace and security. Effective cooperation among States is essential to reduce those risks.

The 2015 Group of Governmental Experts on Developments in the Field of Information and Telecommunications in the Context of International Security examined existing and potential threats arising from the use of ICTs by States and considered actions to address them, including norms, rules, principles and confidence-building measures. In addition, the Group examined how international law applies to the use of ICTs by States. Building on the work of previous Groups, the present Group made important progress in those areas.

The present report significantly expands the discussion of norms. The Group recommended that States cooperate to prevent harmful ICT practices and should not knowingly allow their territory to be used for internationally wrongful acts using ICT. It called for the increased exchange of information and assistance to prosecute terrorist and criminal use of ICTs. In doing so, the Group emphasized that States should guarantee full respect for human rights, including privacy and freedom of expression.

One important recommendation was that a State should not conduct or knowingly support ICT activity that intentionally damages or otherwise impairs the use and operation of critical infrastructure. States should also take appropriate measures to protect their critical infrastructure from ICT threats. States should not harm the information systems of the authorized emergency response teams of another State or use those teams to engage in malicious international activity. States should encourage the responsible reporting of ICT vulnerabilities and take reasonable steps to ensure the integrity of the supply chain and prevent the proliferation of malicious ICT tools, techniques or harmful hidden functions.

Confidence-building measures increase cooperation and transparency and reduce the risk of conflict. The Group identified a number of voluntary confidence-building measures to increase transparency and suggested that States consider additional ones to strengthen cooperation. The Group called for regular dialogue with broad participation under the auspices of the United Nations and through bilateral, regional and multilateral forums. While States have a primary responsibility to maintain a secure and peaceful ICT environment, international cooperation would benefit from the appropriate participation of the private sector, academia and civil society.

Capacity-building is essential for cooperation and confidence-building. The 2013 report of the Group (see A/68/98) called for the international community to assist in improving the security of critical ICT infrastructure, help to develop technical skills and advise on appropriate legislation, strategies and regulation. The present Group reiterated those conclusions and emphasized that all States can learn from each other about threats and effective responses to them.

The Group emphasized the importance of international law, the Charter of the United Nations and the principle of sovereignty as the basis for increased security in the use of ICTs by States. While recognizing the need for further study, the Group noted the inherent right of States to take measures consistent with international law and as recognized in the Charter. The Group also noted the established international legal principles, including, where applicable, the principles of humanity, necessity, proportionality and distinction.

In its thinking on future work, the Group proposed that the General Assembly consider convening a new Group of Governmental Experts in 2016.

The Group asks Member States to actively consider their recommendations and assess how they might be taken up for further development and implementation.

Foreword by the Secretary-General

Few technologies have been as powerful as information and communications technologies (ICTs) in reshaping economies, societies and international relations. Cyberspace touches every aspect of our lives. The benefits are enormous, but these do not come without risk. Making cyberspace stable and secure can be achieved only through international cooperation, and the foundation of this cooperation must be international law and the principles of the Charter of the United Nations.

The present report contains recommendations developed by governmental experts from 20 States to address existing and emerging threats from uses of ICTs, by States and non-State actors alike, that may jeopardize international peace and security. The experts have built on consensus reports issued in 2010 and 2013, and offer ideas on norm-setting, confidence-building, capacity-building and the application of international law.

Among the complex issues that have emerged is the growing malicious use of ICTs by extremists, terrorists and organized criminal groups. The present report provides suggestions that can help to address this worrisome trend and contribute to the formulation of my forthcoming plan of action on preventing violent extremism.

All States have a stake in making cyberspace more secure. Our efforts in this realm must uphold the global commitment to foster an open, safe and peaceful Internet. In that spirit, I commend the present report to the General Assembly and to a wide global audience as a crucial contribution to the vital effort to secure the ICT environment.

I. *Introduction*

1. Pursuant to General Assembly resolution 68/243 on developments in the field of information and telecommunications in the context of international security, the Secretary-General, on the basis of equitable geographical distribution, established a group of governmental experts to continue to study, with a view to promoting common understandings, existing and potential threats in the sphere of information security and possible cooperative measures to address them, including norms, rules or principles of responsible behaviour of States and confidence-building measures, the issues of the use of information and communications technologies (ICTs) in conflicts and how international law applies to the use of ICTs by States, as well as relevant international concepts aimed at strengthening the security of global information and telecommunications systems.
2. An open, secure, stable, accessible and peaceful ICT environment is essential for all and requires effective cooperation among

States to reduce risks to international peace and security. The present report reflects the recommendations of the Group of Governmental Experts on Developments in the Field of Information and Telecommunications in the Context of International Security and builds upon the work of previous Groups (see A/65/201 and A/68/98). The Group examined relevant international concepts and possible cooperative measures pertinent to its mandate. It reaffirmed that it is in the interest of all States to promote the use of ICTs for peaceful purposes and to prevent conflict arising from their use.

II. *Existing and Emerging Threats*

3. ICTs provide immense opportunities for social and economic development and continue to grow in importance for the international community. There are, however, disturbing trends in the global ICT environment, including a dramatic increase in incidents involving the malicious use of ICTs by State and non-State actors. These trends create risks for all States, and the misuse of ICTs may harm international peace and security.
4. A number of States are developing ICT capabilities for military purposes. The use of ICTs in future conflicts between States is becoming more likely.
5. The most harmful attacks using ICTs include those targeted against the critical infrastructure and associated information systems of a State. The risk of harmful ICT attacks against critical infrastructure is both real and serious.
6. The use of ICTs for terrorist purposes, beyond recruitment, financing, training and incitement, including for terrorist attacks against ICTs or ICT-dependent infrastructure, is an increasing possibility that, if left unaddressed, may threaten international peace and security.
7. The diversity of malicious non-State actors, including criminal groups and terrorists, their differing motives, the speed at which malicious ICT actions can occur and the difficulty of attributing the source of an ICT incident all increase risk. States

are rightfully concerned about the danger of destabilizing misperceptions, the potential for conflict and the possibility of harm to their citizens, property and economy.

8. Different levels of capacity for ICT security among States can increase vulnerability in an interconnected world.

III. *Norms, Rules and Principles for the Responsible Behaviour of States*

9. The ICT environment offers both opportunities and challenges to the international community in determining how norms, rules and principles can apply to State conduct of ICT-related activities. One objective is to identify further voluntary, non-binding norms for responsible State behaviour and to strengthen common understandings to increase stability and security in the global ICT environment.
10. Voluntary, non-binding norms of responsible State behaviour can reduce risks to international peace, security and stability. Accordingly, norms do not seek to limit or prohibit action that is otherwise consistent with international law. Norms reflect the expectations of the international community, set standards for responsible State behaviour and allow the international community to assess the activities and intentions of States. Norms can help to prevent conflict in the ICT environment and contribute to its peaceful use to enable the full realization of ICTs to increase global social and economic development.
11. Previous reports of the Group reflected an emerging consensus on responsible State behaviour in the security and use of ICTs derived from existing international norms and commitments. The task before the present Group was to continue to study, with a view to promoting common understandings, norms of responsible State behaviour, determine where existing norms may be formulated for application to the ICT environment, encourage greater acceptance of norms and identify where additional norms that take into account the

complexity and unique attributes of ICTs may need to be developed.

12. The Group noted the proposal of China, Kazakhstan, Kyrgyzstan, the Russian Federation, Tajikistan and Uzbekistan for an international code of conduct for information security (see A/69/723).
13. Taking into account existing and emerging threats, risks and vulnerabilities, and building upon the assessments and recommendations contained in the 2010 and 2013 reports of the previous Groups, the present Group offers the following recommendations for consideration by States for voluntary, non-binding norms, rules or principles of responsible behaviour of States aimed at promoting an open, secure, stable, accessible and peaceful ICT environment:

    (a) Consistent with the purposes of the United Nations, including to maintain international peace and security, States should cooperate in developing and applying measures to increase stability and security in the use of ICTs and to prevent ICT practices that are acknowledged to be harmful or that may pose threats to international peace and security;
    (b) In case of ICT incidents, States should consider all relevant information, including the larger context of the event, the challenges of attribution in the ICT environment and the nature and extent of the consequences;
    (c) States should not knowingly allow their territory to be used for internationally wrongful acts using ICTs;
    (d) States should consider how best to cooperate to exchange information, assist each other, prosecute terrorist and criminal use of ICTs and implement other cooperative measures to address such threats. States may need to consider whether new measures need to be developed in this respect;
    (e) States, in ensuring the secure use of ICTs, should respect Human Rights Council resolutions 20/8 and 26/13 on the promotion, protection and enjoyment of human rights on

the Internet, as well as General Assembly resolutions 68/167 and 69/166 on the right to privacy in the digital age, to guarantee full respect for human rights, including the right to freedom of expression;

(f) A State should not conduct or knowingly support ICT activity contrary to its obligations under international law that intentionally damages critical infrastructure or otherwise impairs the use and operation of critical infrastructure to provide services to the public;

(g) States should take appropriate measures to protect their critical infrastructure from ICT threats, taking into account General Assembly resolution 58/199 on the creation of a global culture of cybersecurity and the protection of critical information infrastructures, and other relevant resolutions;

(h) States should respond to appropriate requests for assistance by another State whose critical infrastructure is subject to malicious ICT acts. States should also respond to appropriate requests to mitigate malicious ICT activity aimed at the critical infrastructure of another State emanating from their territory, taking into account due regard for sovereignty;

(i) States should take reasonable steps to ensure the integrity of the supply chain so that end users can have confidence in the security of ICT products. States should seek to prevent the proliferation of malicious ICT tools and techniques and the use of harmful hidden functions;

(j) States should encourage responsible reporting of ICT vulnerabilities and share associated information on available remedies to such vulnerabilities to limit and possibly eliminate potential threats to ICTs and ICT-dependent infrastructure;

(k) States should not conduct or knowingly support activity to harm the information systems of the authorized emergency response teams (sometimes known as computer emergency response teams or cybersecurity incident response teams) of another State. A State should not use authorized emergency response teams to engage in malicious international activity.

14. The Group observed that, while such measures may be essential to promote an open, secure, stable, accessible and peaceful ICT environment, their implementation may not immediately be possible, in particular for developing countries, until they acquire adequate capacity.
15. Given the unique attributes of ICTs, additional norms could be developed over time.

IV. *Confidence-building Measures*

16. Confidence-building measures strengthen international peace and security. They can increase interstate cooperation, transparency, predictability and stability. In their work to build confidence to ensure a peaceful ICT environment, States should take into consideration the Guidelines for Confidence-building Measures adopted by the Disarmament Commission in 1988 and endorsed by consensus by the General Assembly in resolution 43/78 (H). To enhance trust and cooperation and reduce the risk of conflict, the Group recommends that States consider the following voluntary confidence-building measures:
    (a) The identification of appropriate points of contact at the policy and technical levels to address serious ICT incidents and the creation of a directory of such contacts;
    (b) The development of and support for mechanisms and processes for bilateral, regional, subregional and multilateral consultations, as appropriate, to enhance inter-State confidence-building and to reduce the risk of misperception, escalation and conflict that may stem from ICT incidents;
    (c) Encouraging, on a voluntary basis, transparency at the bilateral, subregional, regional and multilateral levels, as appropriate, to increase confidence and inform future work. This could include the voluntary sharing of national views and information on various aspects of national and

transnational threats to and in the use of ICTs; vulnerabilities and identified harmful hidden functions in ICT products; best practices for ICT security; confidence-building measures developed in regional and multilateral forums; and national organizations, strategies, policies and programmes relevant to ICT security;

(d) The voluntary provision by States of their national views of categories of infrastructure that they consider critical and national efforts to protect them, including information on national laws and policies for the protection of data and ICT-enabled infrastructure. States should seek to facilitate cross-border cooperation to address critical infrastructure vulnerabilities that transcend national borders. These measures could include:

(i) A repository of national laws and policies for the protection of data and ICT-enabled infrastructure and the publication of materials deemed appropriate for distribution on these national laws and policies;
(ii) The development of mechanisms and processes for bilateral, subregional, regional and multilateral consultations on the protection of ICT-enabled critical infrastructure;
(iii) The development on a bilateral, subregional, regional and multilateral basis of technical, legal and diplomatic mechanisms to address ICT-related requests;
(iv) The adoption of voluntary national arrangements to classify ICT incidents in terms of the scale and seriousness of the incident, for the purpose of facilitating the exchange of information on incidents.

17. States should consider additional confidence-building measures that would strengthen cooperation on a bilateral, subregional, regional and multilateral basis. These could include voluntary agreements by States to:

(a) Strengthen cooperative mechanisms between relevant agencies to address ICT security incidents and develop additional technical, legal and diplomatic mechanisms to address ICT infrastructure-related requests, including the consideration of exchanges of personnel in areas such as incident response and law enforcement, as appropriate, and encouraging exchanges between research and academic institutions;

(b) Enhance cooperation, including the development of focal points for the exchange of information on malicious ICT use and the provision of assistance in investigations;

(c) Establish a national computer emergency response team and/or cybersecurity incident response team or officially designate an organization to fulfil this role. States may wish to consider such bodies within their definition of critical infrastructure. States should support and facilitate the functioning of and cooperation among such national response teams and other authorized bodies;

(d) Expand and support practices in computer emergency response team and cybersecurity incident response team cooperation, as appropriate, such as information exchange about vulnerabilities, attack patterns and best practices for mitigating attacks, including coordinating responses, organizing exercises, supporting the handling of ICT-related incidents and enhancing regional and sector-based cooperation;

(e) Cooperate, in a manner consistent with national and international law, with requests from other States in investigating ICT-related crime or the use of ICTs for terrorist purposes or to mitigate malicious ICT activity emanating from their territory.

18. The Group reiterates that, given the pace of ICT development and the scope of the threat, there is a need to enhance common understandings and intensify cooperation. In this regard, the Group recommends regular institutional dialogue with broad participation under the auspices of the United Nations, as well as regular dialogue through bilateral, regional and multilateral forums and other international organizations.

V. *International Cooperation and Assistance in ICT Security and Capacity-building*

19. States bear primary responsibility for national security and the safety of their citizens, including in the ICT environment, but some States may lack sufficient capacity to protect their ICT networks. A lack of capacity can make the citizens and critical infrastructure of a State vulnerable or make it an unwitting haven for malicious actors. International cooperation and assistance can play an essential role in enabling States to secure ICTs and ensure their peaceful use. Providing assistance to build capacity in the area of ICT security is also essential for international security, by improving the capacity of States for cooperation and collective action. The Group agreed that capacity-building measures should seek to promote the use of ICTs for peaceful purposes.
20. The Group endorsed the recommendations on capacity-building in the 2010 and 2013 reports. The 2010 report recommended that States identify measures to support capacity-building in less developed countries. The 2013 report called upon the international community to work together in providing assistance to: improve the security of critical ICT infrastructure; develop technical skills and appropriate legislation, strategies and regulatory frameworks to fulfil their responsibilities; and bridge the divide in the security of ICTs and their use. The present Group also emphasized that capacity-building involves more than a transfer of knowledge and skills from developed to developing States, as all States can learn from each other about the threats that they face and effective responses to those threats.
21. Continuing the work begun through previous United Nations resolutions and reports, including General Assembly resolution 64/211, entitled "Creation of a global culture of cybersecurity and taking stock of national efforts to protect critical information infrastructures", States should consider the following voluntary measures to provide technical and other

assistance to build capacity in securing ICTs in countries requiring and requesting assistance:

(a) Assist in strengthening cooperative mechanisms with national computer emergency response teams and other authorized bodies;
(b) Provide assistance and training to developing countries to improve security in the use of ICTs, including critical infrastructure, and exchange legal and administrative best practices;
(c) Assist in providing access to technologies deemed essential for ICT security;
(d) Create procedures for mutual assistance in responding to incidents and addressing short-term problems in securing networks, including procedures for expedited assistance;
(e) Facilitate cross-border cooperation to address critical infrastructure vulnerabilities that transcend national borders;
(f) Develop strategies for sustainability in ICT security capacity-building efforts;
(g) Prioritize ICT security awareness and capacity-building in national plans and budgets, and assign it appropriate weight in development and assistance planning. This could include ICT security awareness programmes designed to educate and inform institutions and individual citizens. Such programmes could be carried out in conjunction with efforts by international organizations, including the United Nations and its agencies, the private sector, academia and civil society organizations;
(h) Encourage further work in capacity-building, such as on forensics or on cooperative measures to address the criminal or terrorist use of ICTs.

22. The development of regional approaches to capacity-building would be beneficial, as they could take into account specific cultural, geographic, political, economic or social aspects and allow a tailored approach.

23. In the interest of ICT security capacity-building, States may consider forming bilateral and multilateral cooperation initiatives that would build on established partnership relations. Such initiatives would help to improve the environment for effective mutual assistance between States in their response to ICT incidents and could be further developed by competent international organizations, including the United Nations and its agencies, the private sector, academia and civil society organizations.

VI. *How International Law Applies to the Use of ICTs*

24. The 2013 report stated that international law, and in particular the Charter of the United Nations, is applicable and is essential to maintaining peace and stability and promoting an open, secure, stable, accessible and peaceful ICT environment. Pursuant to its mandate, the present Group considered how international law applies to the use of ICTs by States.
25. The adherence by States to international law, in particular their Charter obligations, is an essential framework for their actions in their use of ICTs and to promote an open, secure, stable, accessible and peaceful ICT environment. These obligations are central to the examination of the application of international law to the use of ICTs by States.
26. In considering the application of international law to State use of ICTs, the Group identified as of central importance the commitments of States to the following principles of the Charter and other international law: sovereign equality; the settlement of international disputes by peaceful means in such a manner that international peace and security and justice are not endangered; refraining in their international relations from the threat or use of force against the territorial integrity or political independence of any State, or in any other manner inconsistent with the purposes of the United Nations; respect for human

rights and fundamental freedoms; and non-intervention in the internal affairs of other States.

27. State sovereignty and international norms and principles that flow from sovereignty apply to the conduct by States of ICT-related activities and to their jurisdiction over ICT infrastructure within their territory.

28. Building on the work of the previous Groups, and guided by the Charter and the mandate contained in General Assembly resolution 68/243, the present Group offers the following non-exhaustive views on how international law applies to the use of ICTs by States:

    (a) States have jurisdiction over the ICT infrastructure located within their territory;
    (b) In their use of ICTs, States must observe, among other principles of international law, State sovereignty, sovereign equality, the settlement of disputes by peaceful means and non-intervention in the internal affairs of other States. Existing obligations under international law are applicable to State use of ICTs. States must comply with their obligations under international law to respect and protect human rights and fundamental freedoms;
    (c) Underscoring the aspirations of the international community to the peaceful use of ICTs for the common good of mankind, and recalling that the Charter applies in its entirety, the Group noted the inherent right of States to take measures consistent with international law and as recognized in the Charter. The Group recognized the need for further study on this matter;
    (d) The Group notes the established international legal principles, including, where applicable, the principles of humanity, necessity, proportionality and distinction;
    (e) States must not use proxies to commit internationally wrongful acts using ICTs, and should seek to ensure that their territory is not used by non-State actors to commit such acts;

(f) States must meet their international obligations regarding internationally wrongful acts attributable to them under international law. However, the indication that an ICT activity was launched or otherwise originates from the territory or the ICT infrastructure of a State may be insufficient in itself to attribute the activity to that State. The Group noted that the accusations of organizing and implementing wrongful acts brought against States should be substantiated.

29. The Group noted that common understandings on how international law applies to State use of ICTs are important for promoting an open, secure, stable, accessible and peaceful ICT environment.

VII. *Conclusions and Recommendations for Future Work*

30. There has been significant progress in recognizing the risks to international peace and security from the malicious use of ICTs. Recognizing that ICTs can be a driving force in accelerating progress towards development, and consistent with the need to preserve global connectivity and the free and secure flow of information, the Group considered it useful to identify possible measures for future work, which include, but are not limited to, the following:

(a) Further development by States collectively and individually of concepts for international peace and security in the use of ICTs at the legal, technical and policy levels;
(b) Increased cooperation at regional and multilateral levels to foster common understandings on the potential risks to international peace and security posed by the malicious use of ICTs and on the security of ICT-enabled critical infrastructure.

31. While States have a primary responsibility for maintaining a secure and peaceful ICT environment, effective international

cooperation would benefit from identifying mechanisms for the participation, as appropriate, of the private sector, academia and civil society organizations.

32. Areas where further research and study could be useful include concepts relevant to State use of ICTs. The United Nations Institute for Disarmament Research, which serves all Member States, is one such entity that could be requested to undertake relevant studies, as could other relevant think tanks and research organizations.
33. The United Nations should play a leading role in promoting dialogue on the security of ICTs in their use by States and developing common understandings on the application of international law and norms, rules and principles for responsible State behaviour. Further work could consider initiatives for international dialogue and exchange on ICT security issues. These efforts should not duplicate ongoing work by other international organizations and forums addressing issues such as criminal and terrorist use of ICTs, human rights and Internet governance.
34. The Group noted the importance of the consideration by the General Assembly of the convening of a new Group of Governmental Experts on Developments in the Field of Information and Telecommunications in the Context of International Security in 2016 to continue to study, with a view to promoting common understandings on existing and potential threats in the sphere of information security and possible cooperative measures to address them, as well as how international law applies to the use of ICTs by States, including norms, rules and principles of responsible behaviour of States, confidence-building measures and capacity-building.
35. The Group acknowledges the valuable efforts in ICT security made by international organizations and regional groups. Work among States on security in the use of ICTs should take these efforts into account, and Member States should, when appropriate, encourage the establishment of new bilateral, regional and multilateral platforms for dialogue, consultation and capacity -building.

36. The Group recommends that Member States give active consideration to the recommendations contained in the present report on how to help to build an open, secure, stable, accessible and peaceful ICT environment and assess how they might be taken up for further development and implementation.

Bibliography

I. *Political Philosophy*

1. A Draft of the International Monetary Institute of China Renmin University. (2015). *The Report of the Internationalization of RMB in 2015: The Monetary Strategy for the Belt and Road Initiative*. Beijing: China Renmin University Press.
2. Arendt, H. (2011). *On Revolution*. Nanjing: Yilin Press.
3. Arendt, H. (2014). *The Origins of Totalitarianism* (2nd ed.) (Zh. H. Lin, Trans.). Beijing: SDX Joint Publishing Company.
4. Aristotle. (1959). *The Athenian Constitution* (Z. C. Lin, & L. Ge, Trans.). Beijing: The Commercial Press.
5. Aristotle. (2003). *Politics* (Y. Yan, & D. H. Qin, Trans.). Beijing: China Renmin University Press.
6. Aristotle. (2008) *Politics: A Treatise on Government*. Book Jungle.
7. Bodin, J. (2008). *On Sovereignty* (W. H. Li *et al.*, Trans.). Beijing: Peking University Press.
8. Cai, C. H. (2015). *A Study of Political Development in the Internet Age*. Beijing: Current Affairs Press.
9. Cicero. (2013). *The Republic and the Laws* (S. P. Shen, & L. Su, Trans.). Beijing: The Commercial Press.
10. Dahl, R. (1987). *Modern Political Analysis* (H. N. Wang, Trans.). Shanghai: Shanghai Translation Publishing House.
11. Diamond, J. (2006). *Guns, Germs, and Steel: The Fates of Human Societies* (Y. G. Xie, Trans.). Shanghai: Shanghai Translation Press.
12. Fang, J. Zh. (2010). *The Constitutional Review Beyond Sovereignty Theory–A French-Centered Investigation*. Beijing: Law Press.

13. Feng, L. (2008). Theory of Creative Labor and Labor Value — Supplement to Marx's Labor Value Formula. *Journal of Henan Normal University (Edition of Philosophy and Social Sciences)* (5).
14. Fukuyama, F. (2015). *Political Order and Political Decay: From the Industrial Revolution to the Globalization of Democracy* (J. J. Mao, Trans.). Guilin: Guangxi Normal University Press.
15. Fukuyama, F. (2015). *The Great Disruption: Human Nature and the Reconstruction of Social Order* (L. Tang, Trans.). Guilin: Guangxi Normal University Press.
16. Grotius, H. (2013). *Rights of War and Peace* (Q. H. He *et al.*, Trans.). Shanghai: Shanghai People's Publishing House.
17. Hobbes, T. (1985). *Leviathan* (S. F. Li, & T. B. Li, Trans.). Beijing: The Commercial Press.
18. Hobhouse, L. (1996). *Liberalism* (Z. W. Zhu, Trans.). Beijing: The Commercial Press.
19. Houlgate, S. (2013). *An Introduction to Hegel: Freedom, Truth and History* (S. D. Ding, Trans.). Beijing: The Commercial Press.
20. Huang, R. W. & Liu, J. (2004). *A New Perspective of State Sovereignty*. Beijing: Current Affairs Press.
21. Huang, S. J., Yin, B. Ch., Wang, H. N. & Lin, Zh. H. (1987). *Contemporary Western Academic Thoughts*. Hangzhou: Zhejiang People's Publishing House.
22. Hume, D. (1980). *A Treatise of Human Nature* (W. Y. Guan, Trans.). Beijing: The Commercial Press.
23. Huo, W. D. (2015). *A Study on the Renminbi Bloc*. Beijing: People's Publishing House.
24. Jackson, J. H. (2009). *Sovereignty, WTO, and Changing Fundamentals of International Law* (L. Y. Zhao *et al.*, Trans.). Beijing: Social Sciences Academic Press (China).
25. Kahn, P. (2015). *Political Theology: Four New Chapters on the Concept of Sovereignty* (Q. Zheng, Trans.). Nanjing: Yilin Press.
26. Kant, I. (2005). *Perpetual Peace: A Philosophical Sketch* (Z. W. He, Trans.). Shanghai: Shanghai People's Publishing House.
27. Lachmann, R. (2013). *States and Power* (J. Li, & X. Zhang, Trans.). Shanghai: Shanghai Century Publishing Group.
28. Lasswell, H. D. & Kaplan, A. (2012). *Power and Society: A Framework for Political Inquiry* (F. Y. Wang, Trans.). Shanghai: Shanghai Century Publishing Group.
29. Li, Ch. (2014). *The Establishment of Super-Sovereign International Currency: The Reform of the International Monetary System*. Beijing: Beijing Normal University Publishing House.

30. Li, P. (2015). *The Belt and Road Initiative: Connectivity and Common Development — Energy Infrastructure Construction and the Integration of the Energy Market in the Asia-Pacific Region*. Beijing: China Social Sciences Press.
31. Li, R. (1998). *Political China: The Era to Make Choices About New Systems*. Beijing: China Today Publishing House.
32. Li, Y. N. (1992). *A Trans-Century Dialogue*. Chengdu: Sichuan People's Publishing House.
33. Liu, K. (2013). *A Study of Limited Transference of Self-Determination of State Sovereignty*. Beijing: China University of Political Science and Law Press.
34. Liu, Y. Q. (2012). Vertical and Horizontal Alliances Against Hegemony in the Ancient Time. *Xinkecheng* (Part I) (8).
35. Locke, J. (1964). *Two Treatises of Government* (Part 2) (J. N. Qu, & D. F. Ye, Trans.). Beijing: The Commercial Press.
36. Locke, J. (1982). *Two Treatises of Government* (Part 1) (J. N. Qu, & D. F. Ye, Trans.). Beijing: The Commercial Press.
37. Long, X. (2013). *Research on National Monetary Sovereignty*. Beijing: Law Press.
38. Ma, Ch. Y. (2015). *Collection of Papers on Collaborative Innovation of Territorial Sovereignty and Maritime Rights*. Beijing: China University of Political Science and Law Press.
39. Ma, Zh. Q. (2008). *Media and Sovereignty: The Global Information Revolution and its Challenges to State Power*. Beijing: Communication University of China Press.
40. Machiavelli, N. (2009). *The Prince* (H. D. Pan, Trans.). Beijing: The Commercial Press.
41. Maitland, F. (2015). *A General Survey of Events, Sources, Persons, and Movements in Continental Legal History* (W. S. Qu, Trans.). Shanghai: Shanghai People's Publishing House.
42. Mao, Z. D. (1976). On the Ten Major Relationships. *People's Daily*.
43. Marsh, D. *et al.* (2014). *The Future of Europe* (Z. Y. Xu, Trans.). Beijing: Economic Press China.
44. Montefiore, S. (2015). *Jerusalem: The Biography* (Q. H. Zhang, Trans.). Beijing: Democracy and Construction Press.
45. Montesquieu. (2011). *The Spirit of the Laws* (M. L. Xu, Trans.). Beijing: The Commercial Press.
46. More, T. (2008). *Utopia* (L. L. Dai, Trans.). Beijing: The Commercial Press.
47. Naim, M. (2013). *The End of Power: From Boardrooms to Battlefields and Churches to States, Why Being in Charge isn't What it Used to be* (J. M. Wang, Trans.). Beijing: CITIC Press.

48. Nietzsche, F. (2014). *Thus Spoke Zarathustra*. Beijing: SDX Joint Publishing Company.
49. Nozick, R. (2008). *Anarchy, State and Utopia* (D. Zh. Yao, Trans.). Beijing: China Social Sciences Press.
50. Panebianco, A. (2013). *Political Parties: Organization and Power* (J. Y. Zhou, Trans.). Shanghai: Shanghai Century Publishing Group.
51. Plato. (2003). *Complete Works of Plato* (Vol. 1–4) (X. C. Wang, Trans.). Beijing: People's Publishing House.
52. Quinn, M. (2016). *Ethics for the Information Age* (Y. M. Wang, Trans.). Beijing: Publishing House of Electronics Industry.
53. Ren, B. Q. (2007). *Globalization, State Sovereignty and Public Policy*. Beijing: Beihang University Press.
54. Ren, M. Sh. (2011). *International Communication and State Sovereignty: A Study of Communication Globalization*. Shanghai: Shanghai Jiao Tong University Press.
55. Rousseau, J.-J. (1982). *The Social Contract* (Z. W. He, Trans.). Beijing: The Commercial Press.
56. Russell, B. (2012). *Authority and the Individual* (Z. Y. Chu, Trans.). Beijing: The Commercial Press.
57. Russell, B. (2012). *Power* (Y. S. Wu, Trans.). Beijing: The Commercial Press.
58. Sandel, M. (2011). *Liberalism and the Limits of Justice* (J. R. Wan *et al.*, Trans.). Nanjing: Yilin Press.
59. Schopenhauer, A. (1982). *The World as Will and Representation*. Beijing: The Commercial Press.
60. Shaw, M. N. (2011). *International Law* (6th ed.) (G. M. Bai *et al.*, Trans.). Beijing: Peking University Press.
61. Shen, Q. L. (2008). *The State Sovereignty From the Perspective of WTO*. Beijing: Law Press.
62. Shinoda, H. (2015). *Re-examining Sovereignty* (Y. Qi, Trans.). Beijing: The Commercial Press.
63. Simpson, G. (2008). *Great Powers and Outlaw States: Unequal Sovereigns in the International Legal Order* (L. J. Zhu, Trans.). Beijing: Peking University Press.
64. Smith, A. (2015). *An Inquiry into the Nature and Causes of the Wealth of Nations* (Vol. 1). Beijing: The Commercial Press.
65. Smith, S. B. (2015). *Political Philosophy* (Q. Ch. He, Trans.). Beijing: Beijing United Publishing Company.
66. Tagore, R. (1982). *Nationalism* (R. X. Tan, Trans.). Beijing: The Commercial Press.
67. Tocqueville, A. D. (1992). *The Old Regime and the Revolution* (T. Feng, Trans.). Beijing: The Commercial Press.
68. Waltz, K. N. (2008). *Theory of International Politics* (Q. Xin, Trans.). Shanghai: Shanghai People's Publishing House.

69. Wang, F. (2015). *The "New Triffin Dilemma" and the Strategy of the Internationalization of RMB*. Beijing: China Renmin University Press.
70. Wang, H. N. & Feng, X. Zh. (2007). *Questions and Answers on the Amendment to the Party Constitution approved at the 17th CPC National Congress*. Beijing: Party Building Books Publishing House.
71. Wang, H. N. & Feng, X. Zh. (2007). *The Introduction to Mao Zedong Thought, Deng Xiaoping Theory and the Important Thought of Three Represents*. Beijing: Higher Education Press.
72. Wang, H. N. (1987). *Comparative Political Analysis*. Shanghai: Shanghai People's Publishing House.
73. Wang, H. N. (1987). *Introduction to the Science of Administrative*. Shanghai: Shanghai Readway Bookstore.
74. Wang, H. N. (1987). *National Sovereignty*. Beijing: People's Publishing House.
75. Wang, H. N. (1988). *Analysis of Contemporary Western Politics*. Chengdu: Sichuan People's Publishing House.
76. Wang, H. N. (1989). *Administrative Ecology Analysis*. Shanghai: Fudan University Press.
77. Wang, H. N. (1989). *Anti-Corruption–China's Experiment*. Haikou: Sanhuan Publishing House.
78. Wang, H. N. (1989). *Collected Works of Wang Huning: Comparison and Transcendence*. Harbin: Heilongjiang Education Publishing House.
79. Wang, H. N. (1990). *Corruption and Anti-Corruption–A Study of Corruption in Contemporary Foreign Countries*. Shanghai: Shanghai People's Publishing House.
80. Wang, H. N. (1990). *Democratic Politics*. Beijing: People's Publishing House.
81. Wang, H. N. (1990). *From "Utopia" to "Representative Government": An Interpretation of Western Politics Masterpieces*. Chengdu: Sichuan People's Publishing House.
82. Wang, H. N. (1991). *Family Village Culture in Contemporary China*. Shanghai: Shanghai People's Publishing House.
83. Wang, H. N. (1995). *Political Life*. Shanghai: Shanghai People's Publishing House.
84. Wang, H. N. (2008). *Introduction to the Fundamental Principles of Marxism*. Beijing: Higher Education Press.
85. Wang, H. N. (2008). *Outline of Modern Chinese History*. Beijing: Higher Education Press.
86. Wang, H. N. (2012). *The Logic of Politics: Principles of Marxist Politics*. Shanghai: Shanghai People's Publishing House.
87. Wang, H. N., Zheng, B. J. & Jin, Ch. J. (2006). *Ideological and Moral Cultivation and Legal Basis*. Beijing: Higher Education Press.
88. Weber, M. (2012). *The Protestant Ethic and the Spirit of Capitalism* (Q. Y. Ma *et al.*, Trans.). Beijing: Peking University Press.

89. Wheaton, H. (2003). *Elements of International Law* (W. L. Ding, Trans.). Beijing: China University of Political Science and Law Press.
90. Wigmore, J. H. (2004). *A Panorama of the World's Legal Systems* (Q. H. He *et al.*, Trans.). Shanghai: Shanghai People's Publishing House.
91. Xiao, J. L. (2003). *The Theory of State Sovereignty*. Beijing: Current Affairs Press.
92. Yi, H. (2009). *Cultural Sovereignty and National Cultural Soft Power*. Beijing: Social Sciences Academic Press (China).
93. Zhang, J. Ch. (2014). A Historical Verification of People's Democratic Dictatorship Theory and the Interpretation of its Contemporary Values. *Studies on Marxism* (9).
94. Zhang, Q. F. (2012). *State Sovereignty and Local Autonomy*. Beijing: China Democratic and Legal Publishing House.
95. Zhao, Y., Wang, W. G. *et al.* (2001). *Basic Issues of Marxism-Leninism*. Beijing: Party School of the CPC Central Committee Press.

II. *Scientific and Technological Philosophy*

1. Aristotle. (1959). *Categories. On Interpretation*. Beijing: The Commercial Press.
2. Aristotle. (1981). *Metaphysics*. Beijing: The Commercial Press.
3. Aristotle. (2014). *Interpretation of "Categories": With Commentaries in the Late Greek as a Clue* (L. Pu, Trans.). Shanghai: East China Normal University Press.
4. Aurelius, M. (2008). *Meditations* (H. H. He, Trans.).
5. Bergson, H. (1958). *Time and Free Will*. Beijing: The Commercial Press.
6. Bergson, H. (2014). *Creative Evolution* (Y. Xiao, Trans.). Nanjing: Yilin Press.
7. Bertalanffy, V. (1987). *General System Theory: Foundations, Development, Applications* (K. Y. Lin *et al.*, Trans.). Beijing: Tsinghua University Press.
8. Bruno, G. (2015). *On the Infinite, the Universe and the Worlds*. Beijing: The Commercial Press.
9. Bryson, B. (2005). *A Short History of Nearly Everything* (Y. Chen, Trans.). Nanning: Jieli Publishing House.
10. Buffon, C. D. (2013). *Natural History* (X. Q. Chen, Trans.). Nanjing: Yilin Press.
11. Burgin, M. (2015). *Theory of Information: Fundamentality, Diversity and Unification* (H. J. Wang *et al.*, Trans.). Beijing: Intellectual Property Publishing House.
12. Cajori, F. (2010). *A History of Physics* (D. N. Fan, & N. Z. Dai, Trans.). Beijing: China Renmin University Press.

13. Carus, T. L. (2014). *On the Nature of Things* (Sh. Ch. Fang, Trans.). Nanjing: Yilin Press.
14. Castiglioni, A. (2014). *A History of Medicine* (Vol. 1–3) (Zh. F. Cheng, & Ch. Zhen, Trans.). Nanjing: Yilin Press.
15. Cohen, H. F. (1994). *The Scientific Revolution: A Historiographical Inquiry*. Chicago: The University of Chicago Press.
16. Cox, B. & Forshaw, J. (2010). *Why Does $E=mc^2$* (Q. Li, Trans.). Wuhan: Changjiang Literature and Art Publishing House.
17. Dampier, W. C. (2010). *A History of Science* (H. Li, Tran.). Beijing: China Renmin University Press.
18. Darwin, C. (2005). *On the Origin of Species* (D. G. Shu *et al.*, Trans.). Beijing: Peking University Press.
19. Dent, H. (2014). *The Demographic Cliff*. Beijing: CITIC Press.
20. Descartes, R. (1986). *Meditation on First Philosophy: Refute and Answer* (J. R. Pang, Trans.). Beijing: The Commercial Press.
21. Descartes, R. (2000). *A Discourse on the Method of Rightly Conducting the Reason and Seeking Truth in the Sciences* (T. Q. Wang, Trans.). Beijing: The Commercial Press.
22. Diamond, J. (2012). *The Third Chimpanzee: The Evolution and Future of the Human Animal* (D. H. Wang, Trans.). Shanghai: Shanghai Translation Publishing House.
23. Einstein, A. (2006). *Relativity: The Special and the General Theory (A Popular Exposition)* (R. Y. Yang, Trans.). Beijing: Peking University Press.
24. Einstein, A. (2011). *Theory of Relativity* (New Revision) (H. B. Yi, & Zh. M. Li, Trans.). Nanjing: Jiangsu People's Publishing Ltd.
25. Engels, F. (2015). *Dialectics of Nature*. Beijing: People's Publishing House.
26. Fan, X. Sh. (2015). *Dialectics of Mathematics*. Beijing: Guangming Daily Press.
27. Fu, Z. Y. (2015). *The Information Theory: The Basic Theory and Application* (4th ed.). Beijing: Publishing House of Electronics Industry.
28. Fuller, S. (2000). *Thomas Kuhn: A Philosophical History for Our Time*. Chicago: The University of Chicago Press.
29. Fuller, S. (2004). *Kuhn vs. Popper: The Struggle for the Soul of Science*. New York: Columbia University Press.
30. Gamal, A. E. & Kim, Y. H. (2014). *Network Information Theory* (L. Zhang, Trans.). Beijing: Tsinghua University Press.
31. Gleick, J. (2013). *The Information: A History, a Theory, a Flood* (B. Gao, Trans.). Beijing: Posts and Telecom Press.
32. Gong, Y. Zh. (2012). *Dialectics of Nature in China*. Beijing: Peking University Press.
33. Guo, G. Ch. (2013). *A Brief Introduction to Dialectics of Nature*. Beijing: Higher Education Press.

34. Harari, Y. (2015). *Sapiens: A Brief History of Humankind* (J. H. Lin, Trans.). Beijing: CITIC Press.
35. Hawking, S. (2015). *A Brief History of Time* (M. X. Xu, & Zh. Ch. Wu, Trans.). Changsha: Hunan Science & Technology Press.
36. Hawking, S. (2015). *The Universe in a Nutshell* (Zh. Ch. Wu, Trans.). Changsha: Hunan Science & Technology Press.
37. Hawking, S. & Mlodinow, L. (2015). *The Grand Design* (Zh. Ch. Wu, Trans.). Changsha: Hunan Science & Technology Press.
38. Heidegger, M. (1996). *Introduction to Metaphysics* (W. Xiong *et al.*, Trans.). Beijing: The Commercial Press.
39. Heidegger, M. (2006). *Being and Time* (J. Y. Chen, *et al.*, Trans.). Beijing: SDX Joint Publishing Company.
40. Hu, Ch. F. (2016). *An Introduction to Dialectics of Nature*. Shanghai: Shanghai People's Publishing House.
41. Huxley, T. H. (2010). *Man's Place in Nature* (Ch. Y. Cai *et al.*, Trans.). Beijing: Peking University Press.
42. Journal of Dialectics of Nature. (2015). *Science Elite: People Deciphering the Mystery of Sphinx*. Beijing: World Publishing Corporation.
43. Kuhn, T. (1957). *Copernican Revolutions: Planetary Astronomy in the Development of Western Thought*. Cambridge: Mass Harvard University Press.
44. Kuhn, T. (2000). *The Road since Structure*. Chicago: The University of Chicago Press.
45. Kuhn, T. (2003). *The Copernican Revolution* (G. Sh. Wu *et al*, Trans.). Beijing: Peking University Press.
46. Kuhn, T. (2004). *The Essential Tension* (D. N. Fan, & Sh. L. Ji, Trans.). Beijing: Peking University Press.
47. Kuhn, T. (2012). *The Structure of Scientific Revolutions* (4th ed.) (W. L. Jin, & X. H. Hu, Trans.). Beijing: Peking University Press.
48. La Mettrie, J. O. d. (2011). *Man a Machine*. Beijing: The Commercial Press.
49. Lee, W. L. (2014). *On Marx* (W. Q. Chen, Trans.). Beijing: Zhonghua Book Company.
50. Leibniz. (1982). *An essay concerning human understanding* (X. Zh. Chen, Trans.). Beijing: The Commercial Press.
51. Li, M. X. (1996). Live Broadcast and Record Broadcasting. *Journalism Bimonthly* (2).
52. Li, Sh. Y. (2014). *Dialectics of Nature: Philosophical Basis of Science and Technology*. Beijing: Beijing Normal University Publishing House.
53. Livi Bacci, M. (2005). *A Concise History of World Population* (3rd ed.) (F. Guo, & J. Zhuang, Trans.). Beijing: Peking University Press.
54. Mach, E. (2014). *The Science of Mechanics: A Critical and Historical Exposition of its Principles* (X. M. Li, Trans.). Beijing: The Commercial Press.

55. Mach, E. (2015). *History and Root of the Principle of Conservation of Energy* (X. M. Li, Trans.). Beijing: The Commercial Press.
56. Mackenzie, D. (2015). *The Universe in Zero Words: The Story of Mathematics as Told Through Equations* (Y. X. Li, Trans.). Beijing: Beijing United Publishing Company.
57. Malthus, T. R. (2014). *An Essay on the Principle of Population* (Y. Zhu, Q. L. Hu, & H. Zh. Zhu, Trans.). Beijing: The Commercial Press.
58. Meadows, D., Randers, J., & Behrens, W. W. (2013). *Limits to Growth* (T. Li, & Zh. Y. Wang, Trans.). Beijing: China Machine Press.
59. Montague, W. P. (2012). *The Ways of Things* (Sh. D. Wu, Trans.). Beijing: The Commercial Press.
60. Morris, I. (2014). *The Measure of Civilization: How Social Development Decides the Fate of Nations* (Y. Li, Trans.). Beijing: CITIC Press.
61. National Institute of Standards and Technology. (2013). *NISTIR 7628: Guidelines for Smart Grid Cyber Security* (China Electric Power Research Institute, Trans.). Beijing: China Electric Power Press.
62. Needham, J. (2014). *Science and Civilisation in China* (Ronan, Adapt.). (The Staff of the Department of History of Science of Shanghai Jiao Tong University, Trans.). Shanghai: Shanghai People's Publishing House.
63. Newton, I. (2006). *Mathematical Principles of Natural Philosophy*. Beijing: The Commercial Press.
64. Nickels, T. (2003). *Thomas Kuhn*. Cambridge: Cambridge University Press.
65. Nietzsche, F. (2007). *Thus Spoke Zarathustra* (Ch. Q. Qian, Trans.). Beijing: SDX Joint Publishing Company.
66. Nozick, R. (2015). *Socratic Puzzles* (J. L. Guo *et al.*, Trans.). Beijing: The Commercial Press.
67. Partington, J. R. (2010). *A Brief History of Chemistry* (Z. X. Hu, Trans.). Beijing: China Renmin University Press.
68. Plato. (2012). *Sophist* (W. J. Zhan, Trans.). Beijing: The Commercial Press.
69. Phillips, D., Alcorne, B., & Chambers, C. (2010). *The Population of the World* (Z. X. Wang, Trans.). Shanghai: Shanghai Scientific and Technological Literature Press.
70. Reichenbach, H. (2015). *Philosophic Foundations of Quantum Mechanics*. Beijing: The Commercial Press.
71. Russell, B. (2012). *An Inquiry into Meaning and Truth* (K. Ch. Jia, Trans.). Beijing: The Commercial Press.
72. Sartre, J.-P. (2007). *Being and Nothingness* (Y. L. Chen *et al.*, Trans.). Beijing: SDX Joint Publishing Company.
73. Schrödinger, E. (2015). *What is Life? The Physical Aspect of the Living Cell*. Beijing: The Commercial Press.
74. Scott, J. F. (2010). *A History of Mathematics* (D. R. Hou, & L. Zhang, Trans.). Beijing: China Renmin University Press.

75. Vogurel, G. (2010). *A History of Astronomy* (Y. J. Luo, Trans.). Beijing: China Renmin University Press.
76. Wang, L. Zh., Zhang, W. (2012). *Maxims of Marxism: Dialectics of Nature.* Tianjin: Tianjin People's Publishing House.
77. Wang, G. P. (2015). *The Philosophy of Science and Technology: Anthology of Research Papers on Dialectics of Nature in Jiansu Over the Past 30 Years.* Nanjing: Jiangsu People's Publishing Ltd.
78. Weber, M. (2010). *Academic and Political* (Y. X. Qian *et al.*, Trans.). Guilin: Guangxi Normal University Press.
79. Weber, M. (2013). *The Methodology of the Social Sciences* (Sh. F. Han *et al.*, Trans.). Beijing: The Commercial Press.
80. Whitehead, A. N. (2011). *Process and Reality* (B. L. Li, Trans.). Beijing: The Commercial Press.
81. Whitehead, A. N. (2011). *The Concept of Nature* (G. Q. Zhang, Trans.). Nanjing: Yilin Press.
82. Wiener, N. (2009). *Cybernetics: Or Control and Communication in the Animal and the Machine)* (2nd ed.) (J. R. Hao, Trans.). Beijing: Science Press.
83. Wu, G. L, Xiao, F. & Tao, J. W. (2014). *An Introduction to Dialectics of Nature.* Beijing: Tsinghua University Press.
84. Yu, G. Y. (2013). *Philosophy of Science and Technology in China – Dialectics of Nature.* Beijing: Science Press.
85. Zhang, G. A. (2015). *An Introduction to Dialectics of Nature.* Guizhou: Guizhou University Press.

III. *Cyber Security*

1. Anderson, C. (2006). *The Long Tail* (J. T. Qiao, Trans.). Beijing: CITIC Press.
2. Barabási, A.-L. (2007). *Linked: The New Science of Networks.* (B. Xu, Trans.). Changsha: Hunan Science & Technology Press.
3. Barabási, A.-L. (2013). *Linked: How Everything is Connected to Everything Else and What it Means for Science, Business and Everyday Life* (10th anniversary ed.). Hangzhou: Zhejiang People's Publishing House.
4. Battelle, J. (2006). *The Search.* Beijing: CITIC Press.
5. Benkler, Y. (2006). *The Wealth of Networks: How Social Production Transforms Markets and Freedom.* New Haven: Yale University Press.
6. Benkler, Y. (2011). *Board and Advisory.* Board Sunlight Foundation.
7. Benkler, Y. (2013). *The Penguin and the Leviathan.* Hangzhou: Zhejiang People's Publishing House.
8. Benkler, Y. (2002). Coase's Penguin, or, Linux and the Nature of the Firm. *The Yale Law Journal* (429).

9. Benkler, Y. (2011). The Unselfish Gene. *Harvard Business Review* (89).
10. Bloomberg, M. (1998). *Bloomberg by Bloomberg* (J. Gu, Trans.). Beijing: China Industry and Commerce Press.
11. Bodenheimer, E. (2004). *Jurisprudence: The Philosophy and Method of the Law* (Zh. L. Deng, Trans.). Beijing: China University of Political Science and Law Press.
12. Bowen, C. D. (2013). *Miracle at Philadelphia: The Story of the Constitutional Convention, May to September 1787* (M. X. Zheng, Trans.). Beijing: New Star Press.
13. Boyle, J. (2008). *Public Domain: Enclosing the Commons of the Mind*. New Haven: Yale University Press.
14. Brown, J. S. & Duguid, P. (2003). *The Social Life of Information*. Beijing: The Commercial Press.
15. Cammons, D. (2012). *Network Centric Warfare Case Study II*. Beijing: Aviation Industry Press.
16. Cammons, D. (2012). *Network Centric Warfare Case Study III*. Beijing: Aviation Industry Press.
17. Canetti, E. (2003). *Crowds and Power*. Beijing: Central Compilation & Translation Press.
18. Chen, Sh. H. (2010). *Web.Com! The Recombination of New Order*. Beijing: China Machine Press.
19. Chen, Y. Q. *et al.* (2012). *Constructing Carrier-Grade IPv6 Network*. Beijing: Publishing House of Electronics Industry.
20. China Electronic Information Industry Development Institute. (2015). *Blue Book of the Cyber Security Development in China (2014–2015)*. Beijing: People's Publishing House.
21. Clarke, R. A. & Knake, R. K. (2012). *Cyber War: The Next Threat to National Security and What to Do About It* (X. X. Liu, Trans.). Beijing: National Defense Industry Press.
22. Cui, C. C. (2015). *Research on Japan's Electronic Records Obligation Law*. Beijing: Beijing University of Posts and Telecommunications Press.
23. Cui, C. C., Gong, Sh. Sh., Li, Y., Yang, X. B. & Wang, R. (2015). *Research on the Personal Information Protection Law*. Beijing: Beijing University of Posts and Telecommunications Press.
24. Cyberspace Administration of Beijing. (2014). *The Research on Internet Legislation in China and Abroad*. Beijing: China Social Sciences Press.
25. Cyberspace Administration of Beijing. (2014). *The Research on the Status of Internet Access Services and Related Management Strategies*. Beijing: China Social Sciences Press.
26. Davies, J. (2014). *Understanding IPv6* (3rd ed.) (H. L. Wang, Trans.). Beijing: Posts and Telecom Press.
27. Dong, N. (2012). *2020: World Cyberwar*. Changsha: Hunan People's Publishing House.

28. Duan, Y. Ch. (2014). *Ten Lectures on Internet Thought*. Beijing: The Commercial Press.
29. Dyzenhaus, D. (2013). *Legality and Legitimacy: Carl Schmitt, Hans Kelsen, and Hermann Heller in Weimar* (Y. Liu, Trans.). Beijing: The Commercial Press.
30. Fang, X. D & Hu, H. L. (2014). *Cyberpower: The Game Between China and the US in Cyberspace*. Beijing: Publishing House of Electronics Industry.
31. Fang, X. D. (2004). *IT History Part 1 (Chapters of Network Heroes, Software Heroes and Chinese Heroes)*. Beijing: CITIC Press.
32. Fang, X. D. (2004). *IT History Part 2 (Chapters of Entrepreneurship Pioneers and Technological Geniuses)*. Beijing: CITIC Press.
33. Fang, X. D. (2004). *IT History Part 3 (Chapters of Computer Heroes, Chip Heroes and Communications Heroes)*. Beijing: CITIC Press.
34. Fang, X. D. (2004). *IT History Part 4 (Chapters of Heroes in Thought and Science Elites)*. Beijing: CITIC Press.
35. Feinberg, J. (2013). *Harm to Others: The Moral Limits of the Criminal Law* (Vol. 1) (Q. Fang, Trans.). Beijing: The Commercial Press.
36. Feinberg, J. (2013). *Offense to Others: The Moral Limits of the Criminal Law* (Vol. 2) Beijing: The Commercial Press.
37. Gibbs, J. W. (1902). *Elementary Principles in Statistical Mechanics: Developed with Especial Reference to the Rational Foundation of Thermo Dynamics*. New York: Charles Scribner's Sons.
38. Hart, H. L. A. (2011). *The Concept of Law* (J. X. Xu, & G. Y. Li, Trans.). Beijing: Law Press.
39. Hobbes, T. (2010). *The Elements of Law, Natural and Politic* (Sh. Y. Zhang, Trans.). Beijing: China Legal Publishing House.
40. Holiday, R. (2013). *Trust Me, I'm Lying: Confessions of a Media Manipulator*. China: Lianpu Press.
41. Hu, Ch. P., Zou, X. & Yang, M. H. (2014). *Global Network Identity Management: Current Status and Development*. Beijing: Posts and Telecom Press.
42. Hu, Y. (2008). *The Rising Cacophony: Personal Expression and Public Discussion in the Internet Age*. Guilin: Guangxi Normal University Press.
43. Huang, A. W. (2011). *A Study of the US Post-War National Security Legal System*. Beijing: Law Press.
44. Jiang, P. & Yang, L. L. (2007). *Electronic Evidence*. Beijing: Tsinghua University Press.
45. Johnson, S. (2006). *Everything Bad is Good for You: How Today's Popular Culture is Actually Making Us Smarter*. Beijing: CITIC Press.
46. Kaufman, A. (2011). *Rechtsphilosophie* (2nd ed.) (X. Y. Liu, Trans.). Beijing: Law Press.

47. Kirkpatrick, D. (2010). *The Facebook Effect: The Inside Story of the Company That is Connecting the World* (L. Shen, Trans.). Beijing: Sino-Culture Press.
48. Lai, Y. X., Tian, G., Liu, J., Li, J. & Liu, D. N. (2015). *Cyber Security Protocol Analysis and Case Practice*. Beijing: Tsinghua University Press.
49. Lemley, M. A. (2014). *Software and Internet Law* (Vol. 1) (T. L. Zhang, Trans.). Beijing: The Commercial Press.
50. Lessig, L. (2015). *Republic, Lost: The Corruption of Equality and the Steps to End it*. Grand Central.
51. Levine, R., Locke, C., Searls, D., & Weinberger, D. (2002). *The Cluetrain Manifesto: The End of Business as Usual*. Beijing: CITIC Press.
52. Levinson, P. (2004). *Cellphone: The Story of the World's Most Mobile Medium and How it has Transformed Everything*. Beijing: China Renmin University Press.
53. Li, N. J. & Zorn, W. (2007). Review of China's Early Work on Internet Access. *Chinese Journal of Computer-Mediated Communication* (00).
54. Li, Z. F. *et al.* (2014). A study of the Evolution and Future Development Trends of World Maritime Networks. *Pacific Journal* (5).
55. Liao, G. W. (2015). *Research on Judicial Expertise of Authenticity of Electronic Data*. Beijing: Law Press.
56. Liu, H. Y., Li, J., Liu, X. Y. & Han, M. J. (2015). *Electronic Data Forensics*. Beijing: Tsinghua University Press.
57. Liu, J. (2011). Network Structure and Power Distribution: Explanation from the Perspective of Elementary Theory. *Sociological Studies* (2).
58. Lu, P. M. (2011). A Tentative Analysis of the Characteristics and Economic Effects of the Postal Network. *Studies on Posts* (2).
59. Lv, J. H. (2014). *A Study of U.S. Thought on Cyber Warfare*. Beijing: Military Science Publishing House.
60. Ma, M. H. & Guo, Y. (2013). *Study on Legal System of Network Monitoring*. Beijing: Law Press.
61. Ma, M. H. (2003). *Internet Security Law*. Xi'an: Xi'an Jiaotong University Press.
62. Ma, M. H. (2009). *EU Legal Framework of Information Security — Regulations, Directives, Resolutions and Conventions*. Beijing: Law Press.
63. Ma, M. H. (2013). *An Introduction to Law and Technical Standard of Network Monitoring*. Beijing: Law Press.
64. Marcella, A. J. & Guillossou, F. (2015). *Cyber Forensics: From Data to Digital Evidence* (H. T. Gao, Trans.). Beijing: China People's Public Security University Press.
65. Mayer, V. & Cukier, K. (2013). *Big data: A Revolution That Will Transform How We Live, Work, and Think*. Hangzhou: Zhejiang People's Publishing House.

66. McGonigal, J. (2012). *Reality is Broken: Why Games Make Us better and How They Can Change the World* (J. Lv, Trans.). Hangzhou: Zhejiang People's Publishing House.
67. Miller, P. (2010). *The Smart Swarm: How Understanding Flocks, Schools, and Colonies Can Make Us Better at Communicating, Decision Making, and Getting Things Done.* Taiwan: World Vision Publishing Co., Ltd.
68. Miwa, K. (2015). *Network Hardware Illustration* (R. Sheng, Trans.). Beijing: Posts and Telecom Press.
69. Morozov, E. (2014). *To Save Everything, Click Here.* Beijing: Publishing House of Electronics Industry.
70. Negroponte, N. (1995). *Being Digital* (Y. Hu, & H. Y. Fan, Trans.). Haikou: Hainan Publishing House.
71. Office of the Central Cyberspace Affairs Commission, Policy and Regulation Bureau of the Cyberspace Administration of China. (2015). *The Collection of Internet Regulations in China.* Beijing: China Legal Publishing House.
72. Office of the Central Cyberspace Affairs Commission, Policy and Regulation Bureau of the Cyberspace Administration of China. (2015). *The Selection of Internet Regulations Overseas* (Vol. 1). Beijing: China Legal Publishing House.
73. Patterson, D. A. & Hennessy, J. L. (2015). *Computer Organization and Design: The Hardware/Software Interface* (5th ed.) (D. H. Wang *et al.*, Trans.). Beijing: China Machine Press.
74. Pi, Y., Gao, M. X., Ma, K. Ch. & Chen, G. Zh. (2008). *The Original Theory of Cyber Security Law.* Beijing: China People's Public Security University Press.
75. Qi, A. M. (2004). *Study on the Theory of Personal Data Protection Law and Legal Issues of Transnational Circulation of Personal Data.* Wuhan: Wuhan University Press.
76. Qi, A. M. (2009). *Defending the Property in the Information Society: Theory of Information Property Law.* Beijing: Peking University Press.
77. Qi, A. M. (2009). *Saving the Personality from the Information Society: General Introduction to Personal Information Protection Law.* Beijing: Peking University Press.
78. Qi, A. M. (2015). *International Comparative Research on Personal Information Protection Law in the Big Data Era.* Beijing: Law Press.
79. Radbruch, G. (2013). *Rechtsphilosophie* (P. Wang, Trans.). Beijing: Law Press.
80. Raiser, T. (2014). *The Basics of the Sociology of Law* (Y. F. Wang, Trans.). Beijing: Law Press.
81. Ramachandran, U. & Leahy, W. D. (2015). *Computer Stems: An Integrated Approach to Architecture and Operating Systems* (W. Y. Chen *et al.*, Trans.). Beijing: China Machine Press.

82. Rao, A. & Scarruff, P. (2014). *A History of Silicon Valley: The Greatest Creation of Wealth in the History of the Planet*. Beijing: Posts and Telecom Press.
83. Reyes, A. (2015). *Cyber Crime Investigations: Bridging the Gaps Between Security Professionals, Law Enforcement, and Prosecutors* (N. Li, Trans.). Beijing: China People's Public Security University Press.
84. Rushkoff, D. (2013). *Present Shock: When Everything Happens Now*. Beijing: CITIC Press.
85. Russell, T. (2003). *Telecommunications Protocols* (Zh. Wang *et al.*, Trans.). Beijing: Tsinghua University Press.
86. Saylor, M. (2013). *The Mobile Wave: How Mobile Intelligence will Change Everything* (Zou, T., Trans.). Beijing: CITIC Press.
87. Schmitt, C. (2015). *Legality and Legitimacy* (K. L. Feng, Q. L. Li, & Y. B. Zhu, Trans.). Shanghai: Shanghai People's Publishing House.
88. Senn, U. (2014). *HTTP Illustration* (J. L. Yu, Trans.). Beijing: Posts and Telecom Press.
89. Shapiro, C. & Varian, H. (2000). *Information Rules: A Strategic Guide to the Network Economy*. Beijing: China Renmin University Press.
90. Shen, Y. (2013). *The US National Cybersecurity Strategy*. Beijing: Current Affairs Press.
91. Shen, Y. (2015). *Cyber Security and Cyberspace Order*. Shanghai: Shanghai People's Publishing House.
92. Shirky, C. (2011). *Cognitive Surplus: Creativity and Generosity in a Connected Age*. (Y. Hu *et al.*, Trans.). Beijing: China Renmin University Press.
93. Shou, B. & Cai, H. N. (2013). *Law Frontier of Information Network and High-Tech* (Vol. 6). Shanghai: Shanghai Jiao Tong University Press.
94. Singer, P. W., & Friedman, A. (2015). *Cybersecurity and Cyberwar: What Everyone Needs to Know* (China Academy of Information and Communications Technology, Trans.). Beijing: Publishing House of Electronics Industry.
95. Stallings, W. (2014). *Network Security Essentials: Applications and Standards* (5th ed.) (G. Q. Bai, Trans.). Beijing: Tsinghua University Press.
96. Stinson, D. R. (2016). *Cryptography: Theory and Practice* (3rd ed.) (D. G. Feng, Trans.). Beijing: Publishing House of Electronics Industry.
97. Sunstein, C. (2009). *Republic.com 2.0* (Huang, W. M., Trans.). Shanghai: Shanghai People's Publishing House.
98. Takashi, T., Kouhou, M., Toru, A. & Yukio, Y. (2013). *TCP/IP Illustration*, (Q. Wuniri, Trans.). Beijing: Posts and Telecom Press.
99. Tamanaha, B. Z. (2010). *On the Rule of Law: History, Politics, Theory* (G. L. Li, Trans.). Wuhan: Wuhan University Press.
100. Tanenbaum, A. & Wetherall, D. (2012). *Computer Networks* (5th ed.) (W. Yan, & A. M. Pan, Trans.). Beijing: Tsinghua University Press.

101. The Research Topic Group of the Development Research Center of the State Council. (2015). *2015 Research Series of the Development Research Center of the State Council: China — Informationization* (Vol. 1–2). Beijing: China Development Press.
102. Wang, D. Q. (1998). On the Jurisdiction Against Internet Cases. *Peking University Law Journal* (2).
103. Wei, L. & Wei, W. (2016). *Cyberspace Security*. Beijing: Publishing House of Electronics Industry.
104. Weinberger, D. (2003). *Small Pieces Loosely Joined*. Beijing: CITIC Press & Shenyang: Liaoning Education Press.
105. Weinberger, D. (2014). *Too Big to Know*. Taiyuan: Shanxi People's Publishing House.
106. Wu, T. (2011). *The Master Switch: The Rise and Fall of Information Empires*. Beijing: CITIC Press.
107. Xi'an Politics Institute of PLA. (2013). *Contemporary Studies on the Science of Military Law of China* (The Volume of 2012). Beijing: Law Press.
108. Xu, H. B. (2013). An Analysis of the Characteristics and Development Trend of Cable Transmission Technology. *Information and Communications* (7).
109. Yu, G. J. (2006). Complex Network Theory and its Application in Aviation Networks. *Complex Systems and Complexity Science* (1).
110. Yu, H. F., Sun, G., Di, H. & Liao, D. (2014). *Technologies of Virtual Network Mapping*. Beijing: Science Press.
111. Zheng, Y. N. (2014). *Technology Empowerment: The Internet, State, and Society in China* (Qiu, D. L., Trans.). Beijing: Oriental Press.
112. Zhong, Zh. Ch. (2014). *Internet Black Holes: Unprecedented Internet Apprehension*. Beijing: Publishing House of Electronics Industry.
113. Zhou, X. W. (2015). *Cyber Space and Security*. Beijing: National Defense Industry Press.
114. Zippelius, R. (2009). *Introduction to German Legal Methods* (Zh. B. Jin, Trans.). Beijing: Law Press.

IV. *Science of Entropy of Overall Planning*

1. Ba, Sh. S. (2015). International Financial Network and its Structural Features. *Hainan Finance* (9).
2. Bai, B. & Yu, C. (2012). *China Territory Knowledge: Safeguarding National Sovereignty and Territorial Integrity*. Beijing: Sinomap Press.
3. Bao, J. G., Xia, Sh. T. & Liu, X. J. (2013). *Information, Entropy, and Economics: The Road to Human Development*. Beijing: Economic Science Press.

4. Cao, Zh. X. & Gao, G. L. (2015). *A Study on the Overall Planning for the Development of the Land and Sea of China*. Beijing: Economic Science Press.
5. Chen, H. Y. (2016). *A Comparative Chronology of History Between China and Foreign Countries*. Beijing: Zhonghua Book Company.
6. Cheng, Q. (2015). An Analysis of Internet Corporation for Assigned Names and Numbers (ICANN) and the Future Trend of International Internet Governance. *International Forum* (1).
7. Hadnagy, C. J. (2010). *The Art of Human Hacking*. John Wiley & Sons, Inc.
8. Compilation Committee of National Territory Knowledge Reading Materials. (2015). *National Territory Knowledge Reading Materials*. Beijing: Sinomap Press.
9. Cui, C. C. (2014). Cyberspace Governance in the Post-PRISM Era. *Hebei Law Science* (7).
10. Division of Applied Mathematics of Guangxi Normal Institute. (1976). *Optimization Method and Overall Planning Method.*
11. Dong, J. H. (2008). *The History of Urban Construction in China* (3rd ed.). Beijing: China Architecture and Building Press.
12. Fan, X. G. & Chen, W. (2009). *Public Policy: Overall Planning of Urban and Rural Social Security*. Beijing: Economy & Management Publishing House.
13. Fei, X. T. & Fang, L. L. (2013). *Globalization and Cultural Consciousness: Selected Works of Fei Xiaotong in His Later Years*. Beijing: Foreign Language Teaching and Research Press.
14. Fei, X. T. (2003). *The Pattern of Diversity in Unity of the Chinese Nation* (Revised Ed.). Beijing: Minzu University of China Press.
15. Feng, D. & Feng, Sh. T. (2016). *The World of Entropy*. Beijing: Science Press.
16. Feng, X. Y. (1970). *From the Separated Planning to the Overall Planning of Urban and Rural Areas*. Beijing: China Agriculture Press.
17. Gu, Ch. L. (2015). *Spatial Planning of Multi-Rule Integration*. Beijing: Tsinghua University Press.
18. Hua, L. G. (1965). *An Analysis of Overall Planning Method and Supplement Materials*. Beijing: China Industrial Press.
19. Hua, L. G. (1973). *Overall Method Analysis*. Leading Group of Hunan Provincial Revolutionary Committee for Optimization Method Promotion.
20. Huang, G. R. (1997). On the Origin and Development of Maps in China. *Relics from South* (4).
21. Jacobs, J. (2005). *The Death and Life of Great American Cities* (Jin, H. Sh., Trans.). Nanjing: Yilin Press.

22. Jiang, D. Y. (2008). *The Game Theory with Entropy and its Applications*. Beijing: Science Press.
23. Jiang, R. & Qian, H. P. (2015). *National Economy Security Risk Measurement and Early Warning Based on Information Entropy*. Beijing: Economy & Management Publishing House.
24. Li, W. K. (2015). *Methods of Overall Planning for Urban and Rural Areas*. Beijing: China Architecture and Building Press.
25. Li, Y. F. (2014). *Chronology of World History*. Beijing: Zhonghua Book Company.
26. Liao, K. & Yu, C. (2008). *A History of Cartography in Modern China*. Jinan: Shandong Education Press.
27. Liu, T. L. (2004). *An Introduction to the Science of Overall Planning*. Beijing: China Commercial Publishing House.
28. Lu, Y. G. (2013). *Understanding Chinese History from Territory Maps*. Beijing: Sinomap Press.
29. Lu, Y. G. (2013). *Understanding U.S. History from Territory Maps*. Beijing: Sinomap Press.
30. Lu, Y. G. (2014). *Comparison in Historical Territories Between China and Empires in the World*. Beijing: Sinomap Press.
31. Lu, Y. G. (2014). *Understanding British History from Territory Maps*. Beijing: Sinomap Press.
32. Lu, Y. G. (2014). *Understanding Russian History from Territory Maps*. Beijing: Sinomap Press.
33. Niu, B. W. (2014). An Analysis of the Legal Definition of Information Sovereignty. *Journal of Beijing University of Posts and Telecommunications* (26).
34. Qi, J. X. (2010). *The Development and Frontier Issues of Overall Planning Method*. Beijing: Science Press.
35. Qiu, W. H. (2011). *The Science of Entropy of Management Decision and its Application*. Beijing: China Electric Power Press.
36. Rifkin, J. & Howard, T. (1987). *Entropy: A New World View*. Shanghai: Shanghai Translation Publishing House.
37. Sanford, J. C. (2010). *Genetic Entropy & the Mystery of the Genome* (X. Fan *et al.*, Trans.). Jinan: Shandong Friendship Publishing House.
38. Science and Technology Department of Sichuan Provincial Postal Administration. (1981). *Preliminary Application of Overall Planning Method*. Beijing: Posts and Telecom Press.
39. Shen, Y. L. (2008). *The History of Urban Construction Overseas*. Beijing: China Architecture and Building Press.
40. Shi, Y. (2002). Background Information and Latest Developments of ICANN. *Journalism Bimonthly* (4).

41. Sun, Zh. L. & Sun, T. Y. (2010). *Atlas of Chinese History*. Jilin Literature and History Press.
42. Tan, Q. Zh. (1982). *Atlas of Chinese History and Geography*. Beijing: Sinomap Press.
43. Tan, Q. Zh. (1991). *The Concise Atlas of Chinese History*. Beijing: Sinomap Press.
44. Tang, S. Y. (2008). Tackling a Century Mystery: Entropy. Hefei: University of Science and Technology of China Press.
45. The Academy of Chinese Learning, Tsinghua University. (2013). *Tsinghua Series of Chinese Learning: Collection of Wang Yong's Articles*. Nanjing: Jiangsu People's Publishing Ltd.
46. Thiel, P. & Masters, B. (2015). *Zero to One: Notes on Startups, or How to Build the Future* (Y. F. Gao, Trans.). Beijing: CITIC Press.
47. Wang, B. Y. (2009). A Comprehensive Analysis of Internet of Things Technology. *Journal of Electronic Measurement and Instrument* (12).
48. Wang, Y. (1959). *Outline of the History of Maps in China*. Beijing: The Commercial Press.
49. Wei, H. S. (1981). System Theory, Information Theory, and Cybernetics Give Rise to New Philosophical Issues. *Edition and Creation* (4).
50. Wiest, J. D. & Levy, F. K. (1983). *A Management Guide to PERT/CPM*. Beijing: China Machine Press.
51. Wu, Zh. Q. & Li, D. H. (2010). *Principles of Urban Planning* (4th ed.). Beijing: China Architecture and Building Press.
52. Xia, Sh. T., Bao, J. G. & Liu, X. J. (2015). *Entropy-Controlled Network — Information Theoretic Economics*. Beijing: Economic Science Press.
53. Xiao, D. F. (2009). *History of Publishing Pictures in China*. Guangzhou: Southern Daily Press of Guangdong.
54. Xiong, X. B. (2011). *A Study on Comprehensive Evaluation of Organizational Knowledge Management Performance Based on Management Entropy Theory*. Chengdu: Sichuan University Press.
55. Xu, H. (2014). *China: 2000 B.C.* Beijing: SDX Joint Publishing Company.
56. Yu, C. & Liao, K. (2010). *History of Chinese Cartography*. Beijing: Surveying and Mapping Press.
57. Yu, X. Q. (2007). Similarities, Differences and Correlation between OSI Reference Model and TCP/IP Model. *Science and Technology of West China* (27).
58. Zhang, H. Y. (2013). Analysis and Research on the Characteristics and Development Trend of the Internet. *Modern Communication* (12).
59. Zhang, J. G. & Singh, V. P. (2012). *Information Entropy — Theory and Application*. China Water & Power Press.
60. Zhang, W. Q. (2007). *Book on the Overall Solution to Population Problems*. Beijing: China Population Press.

61. Zhang, Y. (2015). *Overall Planning and Coordination*. Beijing: Intellectual Property Publishing House.
62. Zheng, Z. H. (2012). *Social Security: Overall Planning, Coordination, and Sustainable Development*. Hangzhou: Zhejiang University Press.
63. Zhu, G. L. (1999). *Science of Overall Military Planning*. Beijing: National Defense University Press.
64. Zhu, G. L. (2004). *Science of Overall Military Planning*. Beijing: PLA Press.
65. Zhu, G. L. (2010). *Science of Overall Planning*. Beijing: Current Affairs Press.
66. Zhuang, L. D. & Zhang, J. X. (2002). *The History of Urban Development and Construction in China*. Nanjing: Southeast University Press.

V. *International Relations*

1. Abdurakhmanov, Barishpolets, Manilov, Pirumov. *Basics of Russia's National Security*.
2. Aron, R. (2013). *Peace and War: A Theory of International Relations* (K. Y. Zhu, Trans.). Beijing: Central Compilation & Translation Press.
3. Arrighi, G. Hamashita, Takeshi, & Selden, M. (2006). *The Resurgence of East Asia: 500, 150 and 50 Year Perspectives*. Beijing: Social Sciences Academic Press.
4. Barnett, M. & Finnemore, M. (2009). *Rules for the World: International Organizations in Global Politics* (Y. Bo, Trans.). Shanghai: Shanghai People's Publishing House.
5. Baylis, J. (1989). Britain and the Formation of NATO. *International Politics Research Paper No. 7,* Department of International Politics, University College of Wales. Aberystwyth.
6. Brooke, J. L. (2014). *Climate Change and the Course of History: A Rough Journey* (X. R. Wang, Ed. & Trans.). Beijing: Gold Wall Press.
7. Brzezinski, Z. & Scowcroft, B. (2009). *America and the World: Conversations on the Future of American Foreign Policy* (Y. Zh. Yao, Trans.). Beijing: Xinhua Publishing House.
8. Brzezinski, Z. (2007). *The Grand Chessboard: American Primacy & its Geostrategic Imperatives*. Shanghai: Shanghai People's Publishing House.
9. Brzezinski, Z. (2012). *Strategic Vision: America and the Crisis of Global Power* (M. Hong *et al.*, Trans.). Beijing: Xinhua Publishing House.
10. Chen, J. G. (2012). *Crisis and Future: Francis Fukuyama's Speeches in China*. Beijing: Central Compilation and Translation Press.
11. Davis, D. E., & Trani, E. P. (2007). *The First Cold War: The Legacy of Woodrow Wilson in U.S.-Soviet Relations* (Y. H. Xu *et al.*, Trans.). Beijing: Peking University Press.

12. Douhet, G. (2014). *The Command of the Air* (Q. Sh. Liu, & Y. Y. Meng, Trans.). Beijing: Petroleum Industry Press.
13. Elov. *Security of Russia: Problems and Solutions* (Anthology/Ed Status 2006).
14. Finnemore, M. (2009). *The Purpose of Intervention: Changing Beliefs About the Use of Force* (Zh. Q. Yuan, & X. Li, Trans.). Shanghai: Shanghai People's Publishing House.
15. Finnemore, M. (2012). *National Interests in International Society* (Zh. Q. Yuan, Trans.). Shanghai: Shanghai People's Publishing House.
16. Fukuyama, F. (2014). *Blindside: How to Anticipate Forcing Events and Wild Cards in Global Politics* (P. Xin, Trans.). Beijing: China Social Sciences Press.
17. Fukuyama, F. (2014). *The End of History and the Last Man* (G. H. Chen, Trans.). Guilin: Guangxi Normal University Press.
18. Fukuyama, F. (2014). America in Decay: The Sources of Political Dysfunction. *Foreign Affairs Bimonthly* (September/October).
19. Galileo, G. (2015). *Dialogue Concerning the Two Chief World Systems — Ptolemaic and Copernican*. Beijing: Peking University Press.
20. Gao, Z. G. (2004). An Analysis of the Roots of American Hegemony. *Peace and Development* (4).
21. Gaudriault, C. & Fukuyama, F. (2014). *A Small Man in a Big World* (D. D. Li, & Zh. J. Liu, Trans.). Guilin: Guangxi Normal University Press.
22. Gilpin, R. (1981). *War and Change in World Politics*. Cambridge: Cambridge University Press.
23. Hamashita, Takeshi. (2009). *China, East Asia and the Global Economy: Regional and Historical Perspective* (Y. R. Wang, J. S. Zhao, & W. Zhang, Trans.). Beijing: Social Sciences Academic Press.
24. He, X. H. (2006). An Analysis of the View of the World in Ancient China. *Southeast Asian Studies* (1).
25. Huntington, S. P. (2008). *Political Order in Changing Societies* (G. H. Wang *et al.*, Trans.). Shanghai: Shanghai People's Publishing House.
26. Huntington, S. P. (2010). *The Clash of Civilizations and the Remaking of World Order* (Q. Zhou *et al.*, Trans.). Beijing: Xinhua Publishing House.
27. Huntington, S. P. (2010). *Who are We?: The Challenges to America's National Identity* (K. X. Cheng, Trans.). Beijing: Xinhua Publishing House.
28. Jacques, M. (2010). *When China Rules the World: The Rise of the Middle Kingdom and the End of the Western World* (L. Zhang, & Q. Liu, Trans.). Beijing: CITIC Press.
29. Johnston, A. I. (2013). How New and Assertive is China's New Assertiveness?. *International Security* (37).

30. Johnston, A. (2012). Stability and Instability in Sino-American Relations: A Response to Yan Xuetong's Superficial Friendship Theory. *Quarterly Journal of International Politics* (2).
31. Kaplan, R. D. (2015). *Hog Pilots, Blue Water Grunts* (Ch. Ch. Lu, Trans.). Chengdu: Sichuan People's Publishing House.
32. Katzanstein, P. J. & Keohane, R. (2012). *Anti-Americanisms in World Politics* (Sh. L. Zhu, & L. Q. Liu, Trans.). Beijing: China Renmin University Press.
33. Katzanstein, P. J. & Shiraishi, T. (2012). *Beyond Japan: the Dynamics of East Asian Regionalism* (X. Y. Wang, Trans.). Beijing: China Renmin University Press.
34. Katzanstein, P. J. (2007). *A World of Regions: Asia and Europe in the American Imperium* (Y. Q. Qin, & L. Wei, Trans.). Beijing: Peking University Press.
35. Katzanstein, P. J. (2009). *The Culture of National Security: Norms and Identity in World Politics* (W. Song, & T. W. Liu, Trans.). Beijing: Peking University Press.
36. Katzanstein, P. J. (2011). *Civilizations in World Politics: Plural and Pluralist Perspectives* (Y. Q. Qin, L. Wei, W. H. Liu, & Zh. L. Wang, Trans.). Shanghai: Shanghai People's Publishing House.
37. Katzanstein, P. J., Keohane, R., & Krasner, S. (2006). *Exploration and Contestation in the Study of World Politics* (Y. Q. Qin, Ch. H. Su, H. H. Men, & L. Wei, Trans.). Shanghai: Shanghai People's Publishing House.
38. Kaufman, D. J. (1992). *U.S. National Security Strategy for the 1990s* Washington: Johns Hopkins University Press.
39. Kaufman, W. (1956). *The Requirements of Deterrence in Military Policy and National Security*. Princeton: Princeton University Press.
40. Keohane, R. & Nye, J. (2012). *Power and Interdependence* (4th ed.) (H. H. Men, Trans.). Beijing: Peking University Press.
41. Keohane, R. (1999). *After Hegemony* (Ch. H. Su *et al.*, Trans.). Shanghai: Shanghai People's Publishing House.
42. Kingdleberger, C. P. (1973) *The World in Depression: 1929–1931*. Berkeley: University of California Press.
43. Kissinger, H. (2012). *On China*. Beijing: CITIC Press.
44. Kissinger, H. (2015). *World Order*. Beijing: CITIC Press.
45. Kissinger, H. *et al.* (2015). *China Misunderstood* (D. Gu, & R. B. Xie, Ed.). Beijing: Sino-Culture Press.
46. Kong, X. H. (2010). An Analysis of the Connotation and Main Theories of Geopolitics and its Approaches to Influence National Security Strategies. *World Regional Studies* (2).
47. Krauthammer, C. (2007). The Putin Doctrine II. *The Washington Post*.

48. Kubalkova, V., Onuf, N., & Kowert, P. (2006). *International Relations in a Constructed World* (F. Xiao, Trans.). Beijing: Peking University Press.
49. Larson, D. (1985). *Origins of Containment: A Psychological Explanation*. Princeton: Princeton University Press.
50. Lee, K. Y. (Oral Account). (2013). *Lee Kuan Yew: The Grand Master's Insights on China, the United States, and the World* (Allison, G. *et al.*, Ed.). Beijing: CITIC Press.
51. Li, D. K., Kissinger, H., Ferguson, H., & Zakaria, F. (2012). *Does the 21st Century belong to China?: The Munk Debate on China* (Z. Q. Jiang, Trans.). Beijing: CITIC Press.
52. Li, H. Q. (2013). *Introduction to the Communist Manifesto*. Beijing: Party School of the CPC Central Committee Press.
53. Li, J. Y., Li, Y. X., & Mearsheimer, J. *Mearsheimer: China's Long Journey for its Rise*. Retrieved from http://www.21ccom.net/articles/qqsw/zlwj/article_2012061161605.html.
54. Li, Y. Ch. (2007). *Myths of Hegemony: A Study on Mearsheimer's Offensive Realism*. Beijing: World Knowledge Press.
55. Liang, Sh. Y. (1997). On the National Territorial Sovereignty. *Journal of Law Application* (5).
56. Liao, Zh. K. (1919). The Relations between the Chinese People and Territories in the Construction of the New Country. *Construction Magazine*.
57. Liu, C. D. & Li, M. (2010). Lenin's Thought of Balanced "Two Systems" and the Deliberation and Innovation on the Traditional Equilibrium of Power in Europe. *Contemporary World and Socialism* (6).
58. Ma, Y. (2015). France's Another Lost: Anti-Terrorism War in Europe is Far from Over. *World Vision* (23).
59. Mackinder, H. (1984). *The Geographical Pivot of History*. Beijing: The Commercial Press.
60. Mackinder, H. (2014). *Democratic Ideal and Reality* (J. Ouyang, Trans.). Beijing: Petroleum Industry Press.
61. Mahan, A. T. (2012). *Naval Strategy*. Beijing: The Commercial Press.
62. Mahan, A. T. (2012). *The Influence of Sea Power Upon History* (B. Yi, Trans.). Beijing: Tongxin Press.
63. Mahan, A. T. (2013). *Sea Power in its Relations to the War of 1812* (Full Translation) (Sh. Y. Li, D. Ch. Jiang, *et al.*, Trans.). Beijing: China Ocean Press.
64. Mahan, A. T. (2013). *The Influence of Sea Power Upon the French Revolution and Empire, 1793–1812* (Full Translation) (Sh. Y. Li, H. Xiao *et al.*, Trans.). Beijing: China Ocean Press.
65. Mangold, P. (1990). *National Security and International Relations*. Routledge.

66. Mayers, D. (1988). *George Kennanand the Dilemmas of U.S. Foreign Policy*. Oxford: Oxford University Press.
67. Mearsheimer, J. (2008). *The Tragedy of Great Power Politics* (Revised Edition) (Y. W. Wang, & X. S. Tang, Trans.). Shanghai: Shanghai People's Publishing House.
68. Mearsheimer, J. (2014). America Unhinged. *The National Interest* (129).
69. Mearsheimer, J. (2014). Taiwan's Dire Straits. *The National Interest* (130).
70. Men, H. H. (2006). America's Hegemony and International Order. *International Review* (1).
71. Meng, H. Y. (2014). *On Primitive Belief and Shaman Culture*. Beijing: China Social Sciences Press.
72. Montbrial, T. (2007). *Action and Reaction in the World System* (Ch. Y. Zhuang, Trans.). Beijing: Peking University Press.
73. Morgan, F. E. (2012). *Deterrence and First-Strike Stability in Space: A Preliminary Assessment* (K. Bai *et al.*, Trans.). Beijing: Aviation Industry Press.
74. Morgenthau, H. (1964). *Politics in the Twentieth Century*. Chicago: University of Chicago Press.
75. Morgenthau, H., Thompson, K. & Clinton, D. (2006). *Politics Among Nations: The Struggle for Power and Peace* (7th ed.) (X. Xu, W. Hao, & B. P. Li, Trans.). Beijing: Peking University Press.
76. Naisbitt, J. & Naisbitt, D. (2011). *China's Megatrends: The 8 Pillars of a New Society* (Expanded and Upgraded Version) (P. Wei, Trans.). Beijing: All-China Federation of Industry and Commerce Press.
77. Naisbitt, J. & Naisbitt, D. (2015). *Global Game Change: How the Global Southern Belt will Reshape our World* (Y. Zhang, J. F. Liang, & Zh. J. Chi, Trans.). Beijing: All-China Federation of Industry and Commerce Press.
78. Nye, J. S. *E-power to Rise Up the Security Agenda*. Retrieved from http://www.nato.int/docu/review/2012/2012-security-predictions/e-Power-cybersecurity/EN/index.htm.
79. Nye, Jr. & Welch, D. (2012). *Understanding Global Conflict and Cooperation: An Introduction to Theory & History* (9th ed.) (X. M. Zhang, Trans.). Shanghai: Shanghai People's Publishing House.
80. Obama, B. (2015). *National Security Strategy of the United States of America*. Retrieved from https://obamawhitehouse.archives.gov/sites/default/files/docs/2015_national_security_strategy_2.pdf.
81. Pagden, A. (2013). *Peoples and Empires: Europeans and the Rest of the World, From Antiquity to the Present* (P. B. Xu, Trans.). Hefei: Anhui Renmin Press.
82. Parker, G. (1992). *Western Geopolitical Thought in the Twentieth Century* (Y. M. Li *et al.*, Trans.). Beijing: PLA Press.

83. Penna, A. N. (2013). *The Human Footprint: A Global Environmental History* (X. Zhang, & Zh. R. Wang, Trans.). Beijing: Publishing House of Electronics Industry.
84. Pomeranz, K. (2010). *The Great Divergence: China, Europe, and the Making of the Modern World Economy* (J. Y. Shi, Trans.). Nanjing: Jiangsu People's Publishing Ltd.
85. Project Manager Savelyev AG. (2007). *The Military, Political and Economic Problems of Russia's National Security in the Modern World.* IMEMO.
86. Qiao, L. (2014). *Transfinite War* (15th Anniversary Ed.). Wuhan: Changjiang Literature and Art Publishing House.
87. Qiao, L. (2016). *The Arc of the Empires: America and China at Each End of the Parabola.* Wuhan: Changjiang Literature and Art Publishing House.
88. Qin, Y. Q. (2008). Progress and Weakness in Theoretical Studies of China's International Relations. *World Economics and Politics* (11).
89. Rawls, J. (1988). *A Theory of Justice* (H. H. He, B. G. He, & S. B. Liao, Trans.). Beijing: China Social Sciences Press.
90. Rothkopf, D. (2013). *Running the World: The Inside Story of the National Security Council and the Architects of American Power* (Ch. H. Sun, & Y. Zh. Zhao, Trans.). Beijing: The Commercial Press.
91. Schmidt, H. (1975). *The Balance of Power: Germany's Peace Policy and the Super Powers.* Shanghai: Shanghai People's Publishing House.
92. Shi, Zh. (2002). The Security Council's Veto Power — Image of "Power Politics". *Europe* (6).
93. Sills, D. (1968). *International of the Social Science* (Vol. 11). Macmillan.
94. Spengler, O. (2014). *The Decline of the West* (Full Translation) (Q. Wu, Trans.). Shanghai: Shanghai Readway Bookstore.
95. Spykman, N. J. (2014). *The Geography of the Peace* (Sh. Zh. Lin, Trans.). Beijing: Petroleum Industry Press.
96. State Council Information Office of the People's Republic of China. (2011). *China's Peaceful Development.* Beijing: People's Publishing House.
97. State Council Information Office of the People's Republic of China. (2013). *The Diversified Employment of China's Armed Forces.* Beijing: People's Publishing House.
98. Strange, S. (2005). *The Retreat of the State: The Diffusion of Power in the World Economy* (H. Y. Xiao, & X. F. Geng, Trans.). Beijing: Peking University Press.
99. Subramanian, A. (2012). *Eclipse: Living in the Shadow of China's Economic Dominance* (Y. Ni, & B. Cao, Trans.). Beijing: CITIC Press.
100. Tang, J. (2007). *The Rise of Great Powers: An Interpretation of the History of the Rise of 9 World Powers Since the 15th Century.* Beijing: People's Publishing House.

101. *The Constitution of the Russian Federation* (Amendment) (Adopted on 12 December 1993, Moscow).
102. Toynbee, A. J. (2005.). *A Study of History* (Illustrated Ed.) (B. Ch. Liu, & X. L., Guo, Trans.). Shanghai: Shanghai People's Publishing House.
103. Toynbee, A. J. (2010). *A Study of History* (Vol. 1–2) (Somerville, D. C., Ed.). (X. L. Guo, & T. G. Du *et al.*, Trans.). Shanghai: Shanghai People's Publishing House.
104. Toynbee, A. J. (2012). *Mankind and Mother Earth* (Vol. 1–2) (B. Xu *et al.*, Trans.). Shanghai: Shanghai People's Publishing House.
105. Toynbee, A. J. (2012). *The Discourse of History: Translations of Modern Western Historical Philosophy* (W. J. Zhang, Ed.). Beijing: China Renmin University Press.
106. Toynbee, A. J. (2014). *A Historian's Approach to Religion.* Shanghai: Shanghai People's Publishing House.
107. Tsygankov, A. P. (2008). *Contemporary Russian International Relations* (Y. J. Feng, & X. M. Xu, Trans.). Beijing: Peking University Press.
108. Tsygankov, A. (2006). *Russia's Foreign Policy: Change and Continuity in National Identity.* Oxford: Rowman and Littlefield Publishers.
109. Walt, S. (2007). *The Origins of Alliances* (P. Q. Zhou, Trans.). Beijing: Peking University Press.
110. Walter, A. (1991). *World Power and World Money: The Role of Hegemony and International Monetary Order.* New York: St. Martin's Press.
111. Waltz, K. (2012). *Realism and International Politics* (R. Zh. Zhang, & F. Liu, Trans.). Beijing: Peking University Press.
112. Waltz, K. N. (2008). *Theory of International Politics* (Q. Xin, Trans.). Shanghai: Shanghai People's Publishing House.
113. Wang, G. B. (2010). *China Transformed: Historical Change and the Llimits of European Experience* (B. Ch. Li, & L. L. Lian, Trans.). Nanjing: Jiangsu People's Publishing Ltd.
114. Wang, H. N. (1991). *America Against America.* Shanghai: Shanghai Literature and Art Press.
115. Wang, X. S. (2012). *Catch-Up and Containment: Historical Logic of the China-US Game.* Wuhan: Changjiang Literature and Art Publishing House.
116. Wang, X. S. (2014). *Exploring the Miracle: The Truth Behind China's Modernization.* Beijing: Party Building Books Publishing House.
117. Wang, Y. Zh. & Tan, X. Y. (2009). *Sixty Years of China's Foreign Affairs.* Beijing: China Social Sciences Press.
118. Wegener, A. (2006). *The Origin of Continents and Oceans* (X. D. Li, Trans.). Beijing: Peking University Press.
119. Wendt, A. (1992). *Anarchy is What States Make of It: The Social Construction of Power Politics.* International Organization.

120. Wendt, A. (2014). *Social Theory of International Politics* (Y. Q. Qin, Trans.). Shanghai: Shanghai People's Publishing House.
121. White, H. (2013). *The China Choice* (B. Fan, Trans.). Beijing: Knowledge Press.
122. Wu, B. Y. (2001). The Chinese Security Concept and its Historical Evolution. *Journal of Contemporary China* (10).
123. Xi, J. P. (2013). Better Coordinate the Domestic and International Situations and Lay a Solid Foundation for the Path of Peaceful Development. *People's Daily*.
124. Xia, L. P. (2013). *China's National Security and Geopolitics*. Beijing: China Social Sciences Press.
125. Xia, L. P. (2015). *U.S. Outer Space Strategy and China-US Space Game Playing*. Beijing: World Knowledge Press.
126. Yan, X. T. (2015). *Transfer of World Power: Political Leadership and Strategic Competition*. Beijing: Peking University Press.
127. Yao, Y. Zh. (1998). *Post-War American Deterrence Theories and Policies*. Beijing: National Defense University Press.
128. Yu, L. (2012). A Study on the Role of the Internet in International Politics. *CASS Journal of Political Science* (4).
129. Yu, M. C. (2003). Legal Issues in the Application of Self-Defense Right. *Jurists Review* (3).
130. Yuan, J. J. (2016). Hegemony, System and U.S. Global Strategic Choices After the Cold War. *Forum of World Economics & Politics* (1).
131. Zhang, C. R. (2008). Philosophy About Safety in Traditional Chinese Culture. *Shidai Wenxue* (5).
132. Zhang, H. M. & Hao, Ch. Y. (2013). An Analysis of the Development Trend of Geopolitical Theory from the Perspective of its History and Status Quo. *Contemporary International Relations* (2).
133. Zhang, J. (2014). *National Security Councils of the Major Countries*. Beijing: Current Affairs Press.
134. Zhang, J. Ch. (2014). A Historical Verification of People's Democratic Dictatorship Theory and the Interpretation of its Contemporary Values. *Studies on Marxism* (9).
135. Zhang, W. M. (2012). *An Analysis of China's National Security Interests in World Geopolitics*. Beijing: China Social Sciences Press.
136. Zhang, W. M. (2012). *National Strategic Capabilities and the Game of Powers*. Jinan: Shandong People's Publishing House.
137. Zhang, W. M. (2014). *On China's Mmaritime Power* (3rd Ed.). Beijing: China Ocean Press.
138. Zhang, W. M. (2015). *India and the Indian Ocean: From the Perspective of China's Geopolitics*. Beijing: China Social Sciences Press.

139. Zhang, W. M. (2015). *The Impact of the Rise of Christianity and Buddhism to Eurasia Competitiveness*. Beijing: Tsinghua University Press.
140. Zhang, W. M. (2015). *Theory of China's Geopolitics*. Beijing: China Ocean Press.
141. Zheng, B. J. (2003). The New Path for China's Peaceful Rise and the Future of Asia. *Study Times*.
142. Zheng, B. J., Kissinger, H. *et al.* (2013). *In Search for a Path of Common Prosperity*. Beijing: CITIC Press.
143. Zhou, Sh. C. (2012). Vertical and Horizontal Alliances: A Brief Analysis of Military Diplomacy in the Middle Period of the Warring States Period. *Journal of Ningbo University (Liberal Arts Edition)* (6).
144. Zhu, Y. H. (2015). *A General Survey: China's Rise and the Reorganization of the Global Order*. Beijing: China Renmin University Press.

Lightning Source UK Ltd.
Milton Keynes UK
UKHW021242190122
397359UK00003B/255

9 789811 227783